SOCIAL CHRISTIANITY IN SCOTLAND AND BEYOND, 1800–2000

Scottish Religious Cultures *Historical Perspectives*
Series Editors: Scott R. Spurlock and Crawford Gribben

Religion has played a key formational role in the development of Scottish society shaping cultural norms, defining individual and corporate identities, and underpinning legal and political institutions. This series presents the very best scholarship on the role of religion as a formative and yet divisive force in Scottish society and highlights its positive and negative functions in the development of the nation's culture. The impact of the Scots diaspora on the wider world means that the subject has major significance far outwith Scotland.

Available titles

George Mackay Brown and the Scottish Catholic Imagination
Linden Bicket

Poor Relief and the Church in Scotland, 1560–1650
John McCallum

Jewish Orthodoxy in Scotland: Rabbi Dr Salis Daiches and Religious Leadership
Hannah Holtschneider

Modern Social Christianity in Scotland and Beyond: Essays in Honour of Stewart J. Brown
Edited by Andrew Kloes and Laura M. Mair

Scottish Presbyterianism: The Case of Dunblane and Stirling, 1690–1710
Andrew Muirhead

The Scots Afrikaners: Identity Politics and Intertwined Religious Cultures in Southern and Central Africa
Retief Müller

The Revival of Evangelicalism: Mission and Piety in the Victorian Church of Scotland
Andrew Michael Jones

Miracles of Healing: Psychotherapy and Religion in Twentieth-Century Scotland
Gavin Miller

George Strachan of the Mearns: Seventeenth-Century Orientalist
Tom McInally

Bantu Presbyterian Church of South Africa: A History of the Free Church of Scotland Mission
Graham A. Duncan

Dissent after Disruption: Church and State in Scotland, 1843–63
Ryan Mallon

Scottish Liturgical Traditions and Religious Politics: From Reformers to Jacobites, 1560–1764
Edited by Allan I. Macinnes, Patricia Barton and Kieran German

John Kennedy of Dingwall (1819–1884): Evangelicalism in the Scottish Highlands
Alasdair J. Macleod

Mission, Race and Colonialism in Malawi: Alexander Hetherwick of Blantyre
Kenneth R. Ross

Protestantism, Revolution and Scottish Political Thought: The European Context, 1637–1651
Karie Schultz

Civic Reformation and Religious Change in Sixteenth-Century Scottish Towns
Timothy Slonosky

Forthcoming titles

Emotions in Scottish Protestant Public Worship, 1560–1638
Nathan Hood

The Dynamics of Dissent: Politics, Religion and the Law in Restoration Scotland
Neil McIntyre

William Guild and Moderate Divinity in Early Modern Scotland
Russell Newton

edinburghuniversitypress.com/series/src

SOCIAL CHRISTIANITY IN SCOTLAND AND BEYOND, 1800–2000

Essays in Honour of Stewart J. Brown

Edited by ANDREW KLOES and LAURA M. MAIR

EDINBURGH
University Press

Edinburgh University Press is one of the leading university presses in the UK. We publish academic books and journals in our selected subject areas across the humanities and social sciences, combining cutting-edge scholarship with high editorial and production values to produce academic works of lasting importance. For more information visit our website: edinburghuniversitypress.com

© editorial matter and organisation Andrew Kloes and Laura M. Mair, 2024
© the chapters their several authors, 2024, 2025

Edinburgh University Press Ltd
13 Infirmary Street
Edinburgh EH1 1LT

Typeset in 10/12 ITC New Baskerville by
Cheshire Typesetting Ltd, Cuddington, Cheshire

A CIP record for this book is available from the British Library

ISBN 978 1 3995 1589 4 (hardback)
ISBN 978 1 3995 1590 0 (paperback)
ISBN 978 1 3995 1591 7 (webready PDF)
ISBN 978 1 3995 1592 4 (epub)

The right of Andrew Kloes and Laura M. Mair to be identified as editors of this work has been asserted in accordance with the Copyright, Designs and Patents Act 1988 and the Copyright and Related Rights Regulations 2003 (SI No. 2498).

Contents

List of Contributors	vii
Foreword by David Fergusson	xi
Introduction *Andrew Kloes and Laura M. Mair*	1
1 The Social Concerns of Brunswick Wesleyan Chapel, Leeds, in the Victorian Era *David Bebbington*	17
2 Navigating Cultural Pluralism: Christian Responses to Radical Unbelief in Early Nineteenth-century Scotland *Felicity Loughlin*	35
3 Wrestling with Dilemmas: Presbyterian Evangelism and Slavery in the American Ante-bellum South *Iain Whyte*	50
4 Awakened Protestants' Calls for 'Christian Socialism' and 'Christian Communism' in Germany, 1844–50 *Andrew Kloes*	66
5 James Baird and the Baird Trust: Industrial Philanthropy and Evangelical Activism in Victorian Scotland *Andrew Michael Jones*	85
6 In Person, Print and Prayer: The Shared Mission of Scottish and English Ragged Schools in the Nineteenth Century *Laura M. Mair*	99
7 Mary Magdalene and the 'Fallen' Sisters: The Social Gospel of the Magdalene Asylums in Scotland *Jowita A. Thor*	115
8 'Standing in the Gap': D. L. Moody and Evangelical Social Christianity in Chicago and Scotland, 1860–1900 *Thomas Breimaier*	133
9 'The Saving of the Body': Sport at Church in England since 1850 *Hugh McLeod*	150

10	Henry Scott Holland and Social Christianity in the English *Fin de siècle* Frances Knight	169
11	'Indignation would arise within you': Herman Bavinck on Racial Injustice in Europe and North America James Eglinton	187
12	'Woodbine Willie' and the Quest for a Social Christianity after the First World War Timothy Larsen	200
13	Billy Graham, the All Scotland Crusade of 1955 and the Social Gospel Kenneth S. Jeffrey	217
14	Social Christianity on the Mission Field: Shifting Patterns in British and American Protestant Globalism in the Nineteenth and Twentieth Centuries Brian Stanley	238

Bibliography of Stewart J. Brown   257
Index   271

Contributors

David Bebbington is Emeritus Professor of History at the University of Stirling. An undergraduate and postgraduate at Jesus College, Cambridge (1968–73), he subsequently became a research fellow of Fitzwilliam College, Cambridge (1973–6). He taught at the University of Stirling from 1976 to 2019 and he has also served several times as Visiting Distinguished Professor of History at Baylor University, Texas. He is a Fellow of the Royal Society of Edinburgh and his publications include *Evangelicalism in Modern Britain* (1989), *The Mind of Gladstone: Religion, Homer and Politics* (2004) and *The Evangelical Quadrilateral* (2 vols, 2021).

Thomas Breimaier is the Director for Learning and Training at Hope City Church in Edinburgh. He formerly lectured in church history and systematic theology at Spurgeon's College in London and continues to teach in a number of online venues. His most recent monograph, *Tethered to the Cross* (2020), explored the biblical hermeneutics of Charles Haddon Spurgeon.

James Eglinton is Meldrum Senior Lecturer in Reformed Theology at the University of Edinburgh, and was previously on faculty at the Theologische Universiteit Kampen. His most recent monograph, *Bavinck: A Critical Biography* (2020), won The Gospel Coalition Book of the Year for History and Biography (2020) and was a finalist in the ECPA Christian Book Awards (2021). He writes on religion and public life regularly for the *Times* newspaper.

David Fergusson is Regius Professor of Divinity at the University of Cambridge. From 2000 to 2021, he held the Chair of Divinity at the University of Edinburgh. He is a Fellow of the Royal Society of Edinburgh and a Fellow of the British Academy.

Kenneth S. Jeffrey is a senior lecturer in modern church history at the University of Aberdeen and a fellow of the Royal Historical Society. An undergraduate and a postgraduate student of Aberdeen and Stirling Universities, his interests lie in religious revivals. He has authored a number of articles in journals including the *Expository Times* and *Scottish Church History*, and is currently preparing a monograph on the All Scotland Crusade of 1955.

Andrew Michael Jones is an assistant professor of history at Reinhardt University near Atlanta, Georgia. His first book, *The Revival of Evangelicalism: Mission and Piety in the Victorian Church of Scotland*, was published in 2022 by Edinburgh University Press. His research focuses on religion, identity and race in modern Scotland and the Scottish diaspora.

Andrew Kloes is a historian in Washington, DC and a fellow of the Royal Historical Society. He is the author of *The German Awakening: Protestant Renewal after the Enlightenment, 1815–1848* (2019) and sixteen journal articles and book chapters on topics in the histories of Catholicism and Protestantism in modern England, Germany, the Netherlands, Poland and Ukraine.

Frances Knight is Professor Emeritus in the History of Christianity at the University of Nottingham, and also works as an independent academic consultant. Her latest book is *Ebenezer Howard: Inventor of the Garden City* (2023). She was President of the Ecclesiastical History Society in 2021–2, and a selection of that year's papers, edited with Charlotte Methuen and Andrew Spicer, has been published as *Studies in Church History* 59, *The Churches and Rites of Passage* (2023). She was elected a Fellow of the Learned Society of Wales in 2022.

Timothy Larsen is McManis Professor of Christian Thought at Wheaton College (Illinois). He received his DD from the University of Edinburgh and his PhD from Stirling University. He is an Honorary Fellow of the School of Divinity, University of Edinburgh, and an Honorary Research Fellow of the School of Theology, Religious Studies and Islamic Studies, University of Wales Trinity Saint David. He has been a Visiting Fellow at Trinity College, Cambridge; All Souls College, Oxford; and Christ Church, Oxford. He is the author or editor of twenty books including *Crisis of Doubt: Honest Faith in Nineteenth-Century England* (2007), *A People of One Book: The Bible and the Victorians* (2011), *The Slain God: Anthropologists and the Christian Faith* (2014) and *John Stuart Mill: A Secular Life* (2018).

Felicity Loughlin is a lecturer in the history of modern Christianity in the School of Divinity at the University of Edinburgh. She was previously an Early Career Fellow at Edinburgh and before that a Leverhulme-funded postdoctoral research fellow at the University of St Andrews, where she began research on belief and unbelief in modern Scotland. A revised version of her doctoral thesis on Enlightenment Scotland and global religions will be published as *The Scottish Enlightenment Confronts the Gods: Paganism and the Birth of Religion*.

Laura M. Mair is the Mary R. S. Creese Lecturer in Modern Scottish History at the University of Aberdeen and an Honorary Fellow of the University of

Edinburgh's School of Divinity. Her first book, *Religion and Relationships in Ragged Schools: An Intimate History of Educating the Poor*, was published in 2019. She has authored a number of articles in journals including *Church History*, *Family & Community*, *Scottish Church History* and the *Journal of Victorian Culture*.

Hugh McLeod is Emeritus Professor of Church History at the University of Birmingham. He was president between 2005 and 2010 of CIHEC, the international organisation of historians of Christianity. His books include *Piety and Poverty: Working Class Religion in Berlin, London and New York, 1870–1914* (1996); *Secularisation in Western Europe, 1848–1914* (2000); *The Religious Crisis of the 1960s* (2007); and *Religion and the Rise of Sport in England* (2022).

Brian Stanley is Professor Emeritus of World Christianity at the University of Edinburgh. He has published widely on the history of the Protestant missionary movement and the growth of Christianity as a world religion. His books include *Christianity in the Twentieth Century: A World History* (2018). His most recent major publication is an edited version of lectures given by the late Professor Andrew F. Walls, under the title *The Missionary Movement from the West: A Biography from Birth to Old Age* (2023).

Jowita A. Thor is a postdoctoral fellow funded by the Economic and Social Research Council at the Law School, University of Strathclyde. Her current research focuses on the socio-legal history of prostitution in nineteenth-century Scotland. Previously, she worked as a research assistant for a project on decarceration of Magdalene women in twentieth-century Ireland (Scottish Centre for Crime and Justice Research, Strathclyde), and as a Project Manager at the Centre of Theology and Public Issues (Edinburgh). She has published in *Studies in Church History* and *Scottish Church History*. She is currently preparing a monograph on Magdalene Asylums in Scotland.

Iain Whyte focused on the movement in Scotland to abolish the slave trade studied during his PhD at the University of Edinburgh, supervised by Professor Stewart J. Brown. His publications include *Scotland and the Abolition of Black Slavery* (Edinburgh University Press, 2005), *Zachary Macaulay: The Steadfast Scot in the British Anti-Slavery Movement* (2011) and *'Send Back the Money' – The Free Church of Scotland and American Slavery* (2012). As a student he was involved in the Civil Rights Movement in Mississippi and is an active member of Anti-Slavery International. He is a former President of the Scottish Church History Society.

FOREWORD

In Praise of Jay, Friend and Colleague

David Fergusson

I have often doubted whether it is possible for academics to excel in all three areas of their remit – administration, teaching and research. At most, there is sufficient time to do two of these well, while the other will suffer from neglect. But, if I have encountered a counter-example to this rule, then it is Jay Brown. His accomplishments reflect all three activities.

I first met Jay upon his arrival in Edinburgh in 1988. When he took up the Chair of Ecclesiastical History, I was a junior lecturer in systematic theology. Jay's appointment at a relatively early career stage had aroused some comment. The committee had overlooked the claims of two senior internal candidates, preferring instead a young red-haired American who had studied at New College a decade earlier as a Fulbright scholar. Would he manage to lead the department with so little experience and local knowledge? Might he soon return to a prestigious post in the USA, with Edinburgh a stepping stone to an Ivy League institution? His distinguished predecessor, Alec C. Cheyne, had no such fears. Knowing Jay from his Fulbright years, he regarded his scholarly work as of the highest order and trusted his commitment to New College. Jay vindicated his mentor by taking the chair to new heights during a long and distinguished tenure of thirty-four years.

His success can be attributed to an extraordinary capacity for sustained hard work allied to impressive intellectual and personal gifts. Exercising a leading role in the Faculty of Divinity, he served as Dean and Head of School from 2000 to 2004 and then again from 2010 to 2013. These heavy years of administrative labour were combined with his leadership of the team in ecclesiastical history and a continued commitment to teaching and supervision. Respected for his fairness, attention to detail and concern for the welfare of colleagues, he provided a steady hand on the tiller. His first spell as Dean coincided with the restructuring of the university. The Faculty emerged relatively unscathed, becoming a separate school in the newly founded College of Humanities and Social Sciences. Jay transitioned from being Dean to Head of School. These years were times of expansion in the student body, particularly in postgraduate numbers and in the Religious Studies programme. The School continued to perform well on all the metrics and several threats were averted, particularly the removal of the Special Collections of the New College Library to another location in the university. Such details soon recede in the memory; in retrospect, they appear as mere ripples in the life of the institution. Yet the leadership that has served New College so well over its history ensured that threats did not become crises and that the institution adapted successfully to sundry challenges and opportunities. Jay's own leadership stands alongside that of many distinguished predecessors.

He has long recognised that the work of the College and School cannot be separated from that of the wider university. Much of the success of New College has derived from its occupying an integral position in an institution that has grown significantly in terms of its size, finances and international significance. His involvement in university affairs – Senate, Court and numerous committees – could easily be overlooked, yet this too represented a major investment of time and energy. Mention should be made of the Gifford Lectures, which Jay oversaw for the best part of two decades after Stewart Sutherland, the University Principal, entrusted him with this responsibility. He undertook this with his characteristic wisdom and attention to detail, thus ensuring their continuing success as important public and intellectual occasions. A study of the forewords of the ensuing publications reveals the indebtedness of Gifford lecturers to the hospitality and organisational powers of the convener.

As a teacher, Jay has ranged across the history of modern Christianity from the eighteenth century to the present day. Though his grasp of intellectual history is formidable, he has not focused exclusively on the transmission of theological ideas. Due attention has been given to socio-economic and political factors and to the value of comparative study, often in conversation with the historians at George Square. In his involvement in collaborative projects and scholarly societies, he has commanded the respect of the wider guild. This has been much to the benefit of his work on modern Scottish church history of which he has become the preeminent exponent of his generation.

The scholarly rigour of his lectures and seminars has been consistently recognised by students. I recall an ordinand who had served as principal teacher of history in a local secondary school. When I asked her of her impressions in returning to university study, she remarked that she had immediately recognised in Professor Brown a historian of the highest standing. Doctoral students can testify to the diligence with which their work was scrutinised and directed. Some were surprised by the searching criticism they received at review boards from this seemingly gentle scholar, though they would testify afterwards that this had served them very well. They might have paraphrased Nietzsche – what doesn't kill you will make you stronger. And, unlike Alec Cheyne, who once said that he always liked to lecture in a room with an overhead projector so that he could make a point of not using it, Jay has sought to harness all the available technologies whether acetate slides, handouts or PowerPoint.

His teaching on the Enlightenment has provided vital training for postgraduates in history and theology; many have been spared from simple generalisations and lazy prejudices. Courses on social Christianity alerted students to the reforming energies of modern churches while also revealing the ethical and political ambiguities of much of this work. I vividly recall his inaugural lecture of 1988, which was one of the most significant in the recent history of New College. There he laid bare the extent to which the Church of Scotland had fomented anti-Catholic sentiment in the late 1920s and early 1930s by its denunciation of Irish immigration. This lamentable episode had somehow been ignored or forgotten; no mention had been made of it in the biography of John White. Yet the evidence was compelling and Jay's critical work would later lead to a public apology from the General Assembly.

His contribution to the teaching of New College has been firmly set within a team of church historians who deserve mention. Early colleagues and friends included Andrew Ross and David Wright, both members of the illustrious 'Cheyne gang'. Over the years, they were joined by Jane Dawson, Susan Hardman Moore, Sara Parvis, Brian Stanley and Simon Burton. Together they formed one of the strongest teams of historians of Christianity in the UK. As the established chair holder, Jay led them by example and encouragement.

* * *

In his published work, Jay has revealed a growing capacity to deal with broad themes in Scottish, British and European church history. Based on his doctoral thesis, his early work on Thomas Chalmers and the godly commonwealth revealed the extent to which Chalmers was animated by a classical Reformed vision of church and society united under the Word of God. It was more than a little ironic, therefore, that Chalmers should find himself leading a movement that eventually split the national church in 1843 and which, under a younger leadership, soon eschewed his principles. The tensions generated by the complexities of Chalmers's life and work are explored in a study that quickly became established as the leading work in the field. One reviewer simply remarked that 'as far as Chalmers himself is concerned, practically everything one would want to know is to be found right here'.[1] A landmark study, his book was awarded the Agnes Mure MacKenzie Prize by the Saltire Society.

Published in 2001, his major comparative volume on the national churches of England, Ireland and Scotland was the fruit of many years' painstaking research.[2] Amidst the attention to detail, a revealing overview emerges. Here we see how across the UK significant shifts took place whereby unitary state churches began to evolve into something more like free churches within a liberal polity, a shift that was itself welcomed in the churches. Described as 'a masterful work of synthesis founded on enormous erudition in both the contemporary and pamphlet periodical literature and the secondary scholarship', this book depicts the historical landscape that remains relevant to understanding the ambivalent status of our national and established churches on both sides of the Scottish border.³

Perhaps even more capacious, his 2014 study *Providence and Empire: Religion, Politics and Society in the United Kingdom, 1815–1914* surveys the extent to which religion was a salient force throughout the age of empire. Exploring in successive phases the overriding conviction that divine providence had ordained the empire for the spread of faith, his study reveals the vitality of religion as a social force throughout the nineteenth century. The extent to which multiple religious parties sanctioned and became involved in imperial and commercial ventures is narrated, but with a twist in the tale. Just as confidence in the capacity of the Christian faith to spread across the globe reached its height – at the end of the century around 40 per cent of all missionaries from the west came from the UK – the churches began to fall upon hard times at home. Following the trauma of the Great War, this decline would gather momentum through the twentieth century.

A recent addition to Jay's oeuvre has been his 2019 biography of W. T. Stead in the Oxford Spiritual Lives series. Now largely forgotten, Stead was widely read in his time as a popular journalist. A social reformer and non-conformist Christian, he sought to harness the power of the popular press in aid of his campaigns *inter alia* to end child prostitution, improve public health and support world peace. In later life, Stead developed a sympathy with spiritualism before he died when the Titanic went down in 1912. Jay's biography tells the story clearly, sympathetically, yet with critical balance. 'The great strength of Brown's biography is that he lets you make up your own mind.'⁴ This last comment captures both the measured judgements of his historical work but also the space in which he allows others to form their own assessment and to advance the subject. Though often magisterial, his scholarly work allows fellow scholars to enter the conversation and to make their own contribution. Alert to new questions and under-researched areas, he has encouraged a younger generation to make their mark.

This brief survey of four monographs scarcely captures the range of Jay's output. His career has been marked by a selfless contribution to his subject, guild and colleagues. Several Festschriften have been co-edited, collections of essays gathered, conference proceedings assembled and work undertaken for the prestigious Cambridge History of Christianity series. The list of edited works is formidable. In addition to those volumes in honour of Emmet Larkin (his *Doktorvater*), Alec Cheyne (predecessor and mentor) and Keith Robbins (friend and collaborator), further studies of key figures and movements in modern ecclesiastical history have been delivered. These have consolidated his reputation as the leading authority on the modern Scottish church while others demonstrate his broad range and comparative interests in British and European history.

With its excessive focus on single-authored research monographs, the UK higher education system has not always recognised the importance of editorial labour. Yet Jay has somehow maintained an admirable balance in producing his own work while enabling others to do likewise. Whether national or international, the various academic honours bestowed upon him have been richly deserved. These include a Fellowship of the Royal Society of Edinburgh and the honorary DD conferred by Debrecen University. To these we take much pleasure in now adding a Festschrift following the initiative of his appreciative students.

Benjamin Jowett features in several of Jay's courses. Jowett once remarked that the last ten years are the most important. As he embarks upon this next phase of his work, unencumbered by the rigours of teaching and administration, we can look forward to more significant work from Jay. There is much within the recent history of the Scottish churches that merits further study and we look to him to lead the way with his characteristic lucidity, thoroughness and collegiality.

As we thank him for his contributions over many years to New College, the University of Edinburgh and to his chosen field of study, we must also express our gratitude to Teri for her steadfast support and to Adam and Leandra, and to Lisa who have accompanied him along the way. They have made Edinburgh their home and contributed much to its life. Jay and Teri now deserve many more cruises to foreign parts, not to mention time with granddaughter Aurelia. He would not wish to be celebrated except in their company.

Notes

1. Richard B. Sher, '*Thomas Chalmers and the Godly Commonwealth* by Stewart J. Brown', *The Historian*, 48.1 (1985), pp. 100–1.
2. Stewart J. Brown, *The National Churches of England, Ireland and Scotland, 1801–1846* (Oxford: Oxford University Press, 2001).
3. John Wolffe, 'The National Churches of England, Ireland and Scotland, 1801–1846 by Stewart J. Brown', *Church History*, 72.2 (2003), pp. 410–11.
4. Peter Ackers, '*W. T. Stead: Nonconformist and Newspaper Prophet* by Stewart J. Brown', *The Journal of Ecclesiastical History*, 72.2 (2021), pp. 446–8.

Introduction
Andrew Kloes and Laura M. Mair

Stewart J. Brown and Christian Social Action

'My portrayal is that of a man, all too human, who burned with a rage against social injustice and human suffering—a man who, with a passionate religious faith, rose to greatness in his time.'[1] Stewart J. Brown penned these words in his introduction to *Thomas Chalmers and the Godly Commonwealth*, the first of many books and one which marked the commencement of an important and lengthy career as a historian of modern ecclesiastical history. While referencing a specific figure and a specific period, Brown's words are likewise applicable to the personalities, institutions, and movements explored across this volume. Christian social action – that is, the intertwining of faith and philanthropy made manifest in the myriad church responses to the challenges industrialisation and urbanisation posed – sits at the heart of this book. *Social Christianity in Scotland and Beyond, 1800–2000* aims to open a conversation on the multifarious initiatives known variously as 'social Christianity', 'Christian socialism' or the 'social gospel', that spanned countries, continents, decades and denominations. It explores the varying ways in which Christians have perceived and responded to the distinct social problems that emerged in Scotland and further afield in the nineteenth and twentieth centuries.

It did not take long to settle on an appropriate theme for a volume celebrating the career of Stewart J. Brown – one that speaks to Brown's prolific body of scholarship and his contribution to the discipline, while likewise giving space to the important new research from former colleagues and students whom Brown has influenced. One would be hard-pressed to consider the social outreach of the church in modern Britain or the emergence of a distinct social Christianity during the nineteenth and twentieth centuries without consulting something Brown has authored. While his imposing bibliography contributes to an array of subjects and testifies to his authority in matters including (but not limited to) the Enlightenment, the Oxford Movement and the Disruption, the matter of social justice and the emergence of a distinctively Christian social conscience has endured as a golden thread through much of Brown's research. It is a key focus of his *Godly Commonwealth* and emerges again as a notable theme in *Providence and Empire*, which gives space to both the paternalism of Young England

and the more radical Christian socialism.[2] Brown returned with vigour to the question of a godly commonwealth and the possibility of its inception in his biography of the controversial journalist and 'eclectic supporter of the social gospel', W. T. Stead.[3] Brown went back to his native Chicago through this research; it was in Chicago that Stead became acquainted with the Kingdom Movement, which sought to make manifest God's Kingdom on earth via social and political means.[4] Once again the medium of biography allowed Brown to trace a bigger sea-change, with Stead's concept of 'the "Church of the Future", the "Church of the New Era", or simply the "Civic Church"' reflecting the broadening of Christian thought in late nineteenth-century Britain.[5]

Brown's preoccupation with questions of social justice is not a solely intellectual one, but rather stems also from a keen social conscience that was shaped in his youth by the broader economic, political, and social ferment in America during the 1960s. In 1965, at the age of fourteen, Brown began to work in his father's lumberyard in Cicero, an inner suburb of Chicago, unloading railcars and loading trucks. It was during this period that he became keenly aware of the stark contrast between his own comfortable upbringing and the experiences of some of those alongside whom he worked. With the company's workforce largely comprised of African American men from Chicago's West Side, Brown engaged in breaktime conversations and formed friendships that would shape his perception of social inequalities and structural disadvantages. Such concerns led him to participate in both the civil rights movement and the anti-war movement. After commencing his doctoral studies at the University of Chicago, it was Chalmers's social action, as opposed to his theology, that Brown centred in his research, which included two years as a Fulbright Scholar at the University of Edinburgh.

For Brown, Chalmers's social conscience 'is all-important'; it is only through 'his struggle to realize an ideal Christian society – a "Godly commonwealth" – in response to the social dislocations of early nineteenth-century industrialization and urbanization' that we can come to understand the man himself.[6] The resulting book was simultaneously a frank biography of Chalmers and an immersive evaluation of the motivations, achievements and limitations of his 'Glasgow experiment' in territorial mission. In Brown's hands, Chalmers emerges from New College's extensive collection of manuscripts – consisting of upwards of 300 boxes – as 'something of an egomaniac – argumentative, self-centred, judgmental, unstable, and dogmatic', though we likewise see a man who was profoundly disturbed by the secularisation, suffering and social dislocation in urban-industrial Scotland.[7] The *Godly Commonwealth* not only reframed our understanding of Chalmers, it reimagined the meaning and significance of Christian social action in Victorian Scotland. This subject is not an insular one; rather, it speaks to the problems that continue to both perplex and provoke Christians in contemporary society. Evaluating the significance of Brown's biography of Chalmers, T. C. Smout noted that 'no one can read it without gaining new insight into the nineteenth-century mind'.[8] James Hasting Nichols's core critique was based on Brown's claim that, following Chalmers's death in 1847, 'his godly commonwealth vision faded rapidly from the public imagination'.[9] Nichols asked, 'Is this an unduly negative reading of the final phase of Christian social action based on an ecumenical and voluntary cooperation, as in the Evangelical Alliance and comparable agencies?'[10] This interpretation overlooks Brown's reference to Chalmers's notable legacy, not only as a model of Christian philanthropy more generally but as a forerunner of the social gospel movement in the United States. More particularly, Brown uncovers the tangible link between Chalmers's 'aggressive' pastoral ministry and the method employed by London's Charity Organisation Society later in the century.[11] The present book picks up this mantle, exploring how Christian social action adjusted and evolved over the nineteenth and twentieth centuries.

The State of Scholarship

Christian social action and the way that churches have responded to social needs have proven fertile ground for historians. The crucial role Christianity has played in inspiring philanthropic activity in modern Britain has been the focus of a book by Frank Prochaska.[12] Prochaska stresses the strong correlation between Christianity and philanthropy, writing,

> To most people in Britain today, the very idea of Christian social reform has a quaint, Victorian air about it. As we reject the pieties and social hierarchies of our ancestors, we tend to forget that benevolence and neighbourliness, self-help and helping others, were among the most urgent of Christian values.[13]

Of relevance here, Prochaska acknowledges the particularly close association between Protestantism and social action.[14] More precisely, for Prochaska in 'the movement for social reform, evangelicals provided a vanguard'.[15] Given that David Bebbington's oft-cited definition of Evangelicalism includes activism as a 'hallmark', it is unsurprising that social action has come to be associated with the Evangelical tradition.[16] Nonetheless, the emergence of Christian socialism in Britain in the 1840s, a movement often perceived to be grounded in liberalism, is similarly relevant and has been the focus of studies from Peter d'A. Jones, Edward Norman, Paul Thomson and David M. Thompson.[17] Contrary to scholarship from Jones, Thompson has argued that the 'sharp distinction' frequently made between evangelical and so-called 'Maurician' thought (a reference to the leading Christian socialist of the mid-nineteenth century, F. D. Maurice) may not have been recognised by contemporaries.[18] It is, Thompson suggests, an oversimplification that reflects the gulf between conservatives and liberals that grew increasingly prominent in the early twentieth century.[19]

While Shailer Mathews's entry in his 1921 *Dictionary of Religion and Ethics* has been described as 'one of the most cited' definitions of the term 'social gospel', the phase can be traced to the 1880s when it was used, explained and defined in England by figures such as Brooke Foss Westcott and John Clifford.[20] Again, the close association between Evangelicalism and the social gospel emerges as a common theme with Thompson identifying a 'line of continuity' between Clifford's thought and 'the great evangelical tradition rooted in the Anti-Slavery campaign of William Wilberforce and Fowell Buxton'.[21] Likewise, in his well-known study, Timothy L. Smith argued that revivalist preaching of repentance to personal holiness in the antebellum United States generated significant popular support for addressing social problems.

> Revival measures and perfectionist aspiration flourished increasingly between 1840 and 1865 in all the major denominations – particularly in the cities ... The quest of personal holiness became in some ways a kind of plain man's transcendentalism, which geared ancient creeds to the drive shaft of social reform. Far from disdaining earthly affairs, the evangelists played a key role in the widespread attack upon slavery, poverty, and greed. They thus helped prepare the way both in theory and in practice for what later became known as the social gospel.[22]

Perhaps the earliest use of the phrase 'social gospel' in America can be traced to 1889, when William Dwight Porter Bliss, the Episcopalian priest and Secretary of the American Christian Social Union, used the term on the cover of the Union's magazine, *The Dawn*, in 1889.[23]

The North American social gospel has received notable scholarly attention. Both Protestant social action and the later social gospel movement in the US were the focus of a book by Henry May, which argued that both were rooted in concern regarding urban conditions and a desire for the church to 'provide alternatives to socialism'.[24] Nonetheless, May identified a crucial distinction: 'The emphasis, however, was different. While their conservative colleagues were *chiefly* concerned to prove the rightness of existing institutions and to head off change, Social Gospel spokesmen were *primarily* concerned with the search for a better society.'[25] Christopher H. Evans's book on the subject opens with a definition of the social gospel in the American context that likewise foregrounds liberalism:

> The social gospel was an offshoot of theological liberalism that strove to apply a progressive theological vision to engage American social, political, and economic structures. Rooted in wider historical-theological developments in American Protestantism in the late nineteenth and early twentieth centuries, the social gospel integrated evangelical and liberal theological strands in ways that advocated for systemic, structural changes in American institutions.[26]

As suggested here, and in line with scholarship from Prochaska, the social gospel in the United States emerged from a longer history of Christian social action. Like Thompson, Evans recognises the movement's roots in both Evangelicalism and theological liberalism – a theme picked up in this volume by Brian Stanley.[27]

Scholars interested in the American context have identified the social gospel as a distinctive feature of the nation's ecclesiastical history. Writing in *The Rise of the Social Gospel in America*, Charles Hopkins endows the movement with the accolade of 'America's most unique contribution to the great ongoing stream of Christianity'.[28] A comparable conclusion emerges from Donald Gorrell's 'institutional history' of the social gospel, which considers how this theological concept came to be a distinctive and powerful force in American politics and society.[29] Biographies feature strongly in scholarship. Robert Handy's *The Social Gospel in America* considers how the movement did or did not change prior to the Second World War through detailed analyses of the lives and writings of Washington Gladden, Walter Rauschenbusch and Richard T. Ely.[30] Evans has likewise used biography to good effect and enriched understanding by including content on previously overlooked figures such as Georgia Harkness, Benjamin Mays, Frances Willard and Reverdy Ransom. Expanding beyond Protestantism, Evans considers how Catholic and Jewish communities engaged with and implemented social gospel ideals and argues that the movement exhibits a 'shared desire to fuse religion and progressive political action'.[31] Microhistory approaches have proven similarly insightful. Heath W. Carter's detailed study of Chicago 'recasts' understanding of social Christianity, adjusting the focus to the role working-class Americans played in shaping the movement – it was, he argues, 'union made'.[32]

Although frequently explored as a distinctively American movement, Mathews's definition referenced above cited England's Christian socialist movement of the mid-nineteenth century as an important influence. According to Matthews, the 'social message and power' prevalent in England (one might add Scotland also) had a significant reach that fed into later, more sociological ideas in the US.[33] Similarly, Handy cites the 'work and writings of such diverse British figures as Thomas Chalmers, Frederick Denison Maurice, Charles Kingsley, John R. Seeley, and Henry Scott Holland' as instrumental in giving 'rise to the Christian social movements in the United States'.[34] Paul T. Phillips has focused on both sides of the Atlantic, thereby granting important insights into the movement's cohesion, gravity and scope. The book's 'Gallery of social Christians', which showcases major American, Canadian and British figures, encapsulates Phillips's argument that social Christianity was 'a truly transatlantic phenomenon'.[35] Of particular relevance here, Phillips identifies Chalmers's territorial mission as an example of the way in which 'Americans duplicated the innovative methods applied by the British clergy to urban problems'.[36] In adopting an international perspective that extends beyond Britain and the US, this volume encourages a more comprehensive understanding of social Christianity as part of a multifaceted and fluid belief system that evolved and shifted according to context. Further, by utilising an expansive and inclusive definition of Christian social action, this book facilitates new insights into an economic, political, social and theological phenomenon that both was shaped by and helped to produce modern society. For conservative Evangelicals, 'Social Christians came to be identified with a lack of spirituality, as well as an abandonment of serious consideration of the "next life" and of a sense of personal responsibility for sin.'[37]

Outline

The essays in this volume explore different manifestations of social Christianity within a global context. The contributors consider how different individuals and churches sought to revive and reinterpret the idea of the Kingdom of God against the backdrops of class turmoil, economic crisis, mass deprivation, rising pluralism, racial and ethnic tensions, and global warfare. Given Scotland's important role as an exponent of Christian social thought – most notably in the figure of Chalmers, as Brown has identified – this book employs a comparative lens, considering sociological and theological developments in Scotland alongside comparable phenomena elsewhere in Britain, as well as on the Continent and across the Atlantic. The value of international perspectives, which allow global connections to be recognised, has recently been spotlighted by Brian Stanley in the history of Christianity in the twentieth century and is reflected in this volume's approach and contents.[38] The essays presented here are arranged in chronological order and analyse different facets of an international phenomenon that has yet to be fully understood.

In Chapter One, David Bebbington explores how British churches in the early and high Victorian years responded to the physical needs of impoverished members of their communities through a case study of Brunswick Chapel, a prominent Methodist congregation in Leeds. While the roles that many newly founded Christian voluntary associations played in responding to social needs during this period are well known, Bebbington challenges the view that local churches and chapels themselves neglected the social welfare of their neighbours. In his model microhistory, Bebbington demonstrates how male and female, affluent and modest members of Brunswick Chapel variously exhibited a keen social consciousness towards the destitute in their city by undertaking a range of initiatives on their behalf. Hereby, Bebbington argues that while the mid-nineteenth-century members of Brunswick Chapel did not expressly articulate a 'social gospel' message, as later generations of Methodists did explicitly, they nevertheless regarded offering material assistance as integral to their corporate Christian life.

Felicity Loughlin investigates how Scottish church leaders in the early decades of the nineteenth century became alarmed by the growth of irreligion and radical unbelief, especially in Scottish middle- and working-class communities, developments which some contemporaries attributed to the corrosive effects of industrialisation and urbanisation on individuals' and communities' spiritual lives. Loughlin charts how the advent of freethought introduced a new degree of religious pluralism in Scottish society. Scottish ministers and lay Christians responded with new efforts to re-engage with those who had become estranged from the churches, issuing rejoinders to published criticisms of Christianity, giving public lectures on recent scientific discoveries and theories from the perspective of Christian apologetics, and by offering material aid to the indigent. Loughlin's research shows how the rise of small numbers of convinced non-believers provided a powerful impetus to certain Scottish Christians to commit themselves to improving the living conditions of those whom they believed new economic pressures placed at risk from falling away from the faith.

Iain Whyte considers the influence that Scottish traditions of religious education had on slaveholding Presbyterians in the antebellum American South. Whyte examines Christianity's entanglement with slavery, focusing on three ministers, Charles Colcock Jones, Thomas Smyth, and James Henley Thornwell, who acquiesced to the practice of slavery while taking up evangelistic and catechetical work among enslaved men and women in Georgia and South Carolina. These ministers were motivated by paternalistic beliefs about the duties that Christian slaveholders possessed towards those whom they held in bondage. Whyte concludes that, despite the intentions of their teachers, through learning the Bible enslaved people acquired spiritual resources for resistance and self-liberation, especially after the outbreak of the Civil War.

Andrew Kloes assesses how the German Protestants associated with the early nineteenth-century religious Awakening movement responded to the rising economic inequality and concomitant immiseration of many in German society by urging their fellow believers to pursue what they called 'Christian socialism' and 'Christian communism' in the 1840s. Focusing on how two Hamburg social reformers, Johann Hinrich Wichern and Amalie Sieveking, developed these terms, Kloes analyses the social conscience of the Awakening movement and the beliefs that animated Protestants to found thousands of new institutions and voluntary societies throughout German-speaking Europe to pursue their philanthropic goals. Such Protestants have long been conceptualised as conservatives, orthodox, pietists, or traditionalists in religious matters and correspondingly opponents of revolutions and liberalism in the political realm. Kloes nuances this interpretation by examining how Sieveking and Wichern rebuked middle- and upper-class Christians for having corporately sinned against the working class and poor and argued that the former were thus collectively responsible to God for establishing better social conditions so that the latter might flourish physically and spiritually.

Andrew Michael Jones appraises the legacy of James Baird, a Scottish industrialist and Conservative MP for Falkirk Burghs, who endowed a trust in 1873 with £500,000 to support particular ministries of the Church of Scotland, of which he was a member. Baird mandated that these funds be used 'to assist in providing the means of meeting, or at least as far as possible promoting the mitigation of, spiritual destitution among the population of Scotland, through efforts for securing the godly upbringing of the young, establishing of Parochial Pastoral Work, and the stimulating of ministers and all agencies of the said Church of Scotland, to sustained devotedness in the work of carrying the Gospel to the homes and hearts of all'.[39] Through careful work in the archives of the Baird Trust, Jones lays out how these funds enabled Church of Scotland leaders to build new church buildings in urban areas, especially in the Presbytery of Glasgow, endow ministers' stipends, publish Christian evangelistic and educational literature, and finance the training of ministers. In all of these ways, Jones argues that the Baird Trust reflects a conservative vision of social Christianity in modern Scotland.

Laura M. Mair's analysis of 'ragged schools' in Victorian England and Scotland – evangelical institutions that provided a free education for poor children – draws attention to the crucial role Christians played in promoting schooling prior to the Education Acts of 1870 and 1872. Mair's chapter sheds light on the scale and significance of this movement as a prime example of paternalism. Through a detailed study of ragged school literature and newspaper reports, Mair highlights the cohesion and unity of purpose that was fostered through extensive print and patronage networks which spanned the border between the nations. In reconsidering the relationship between English and Scottish ragged schools, Mair's conclusions lead us to reconsider the weight and significance of this movement.

Jowita A. Thor evaluates an understudied expression of social Christianity in Scotland, the institutions that Protestant churches established to provide shelter and other support for those whom contemporaries referred to as sexually 'fallen' women and women who had previously worked as prostitutes, as well as other women who had struggles with alcohol or who were in financially difficult circumstances. Thor notes that beginning in 1797, at least 25 such institutions were established in Scotland and were known variously as Magdalene asylums, homes, houses of mercy, and refuges, two of which continued to operate into the 1950s. With attention to period pamphlet literature and the holdings of local archives, Thor analyses how these institutions were unique in preaching the gospel and providing social assistance to women who had become social outcasts, while interrogating nineteenth-century assumptions about gendered behavioural norms and standards of sexual purity as applied to men and women.

Thomas Breimaier concentrates on the transatlantic career of the American evangelist Dwight L. Moody between Chicago, Glasgow and Edinburgh, cities in which he participated in the founding of either urban social ministries or theological education institutions. Emphasising the impoverished circumstances in which Moody was reared – his father died when he was aged four, leaving his mother to bring up Moody and his eight siblings – Breimaier interprets Moody as a man who was intimately familiar with the profound personal challenges faced by the working-class people to whom he sought to spread the Christian message. Breimaier notes that while the institutions Moody established seriously attempted to ameliorate the living conditions of the poorest in society and facilitate their upward social mobility, Moody nevertheless prioritised individuals' religious conversion and spiritual reconciliation with God above advocacy for political and social reforms. In this manner, Breimaier understands Moody as a hinge between nineteenth-century evangelical revivalism and progressive social activism.

Hugh McLeod contributes a masterful overview of how Anglicans and, later, Nonconformist churches in England pioneered a range of new sporting initiatives between the 1850s and the 1920s, in their pursuit of various religious and social reform goals. McLeod observes that during the early decades of this period, clergy came to more and more regard providing sport and leisure opportunities to working-class men and youths in their communities as one means of discharging their pastoral duties. Particularly, they believed that such activities would foster social harmony between the more deprived and those from middle-class backgrounds, would encourage virtues, and would refute accusations that Christian men were 'effeminate'. Such positive attitudes towards sports constituted a stark departure from both historic Puritan and early nineteenth-century evangelical views that held sport in low regard as a distraction from the spiritual. Additionally, some clergy promoted sports and other clubs as a way of strengthening attachment to the church of the children of their members. Moreover, McLeod elucidates how proponents of sport among the English clergy articulated a holistic view of the human person that entailed care and respect for the body as God's creation.

Frances Knight provides an incisive reading to Henry Scott Holland's *fin de siècle* programme of social Christianity, with special attention to his discussion of social problems related to the lack of adequate housing and his proposals to address the issue. A third-generation Anglo-Catholic, Holland exercised prominent leadership positions within the Church of England that included a canonry at St Paul's Cathedral, London and the Regius Professorship of Divinity at the University of Oxford, while he also personally participated in the work of the Oxford House settlement in Bethnal Green, and the Maurice Hostel in Hoxton, two deprived communities in the East End of London. Knight traces the development of Holland's views on how Christians ought to be working for social justice in late Victorian and Edwardian England through the pages of *Commonwealth: A Social Magazine*, which he edited for 22 years. Knight observes how Holland ultimately concluded that, despite their best efforts, Christian voluntary societies alone were insufficient to the task and that the state too had to assume responsibilities for building the 'new Jerusalem' on earth.

James Eglinton furnishes readers with a case study of how a national church leader's eyes opened to racial injustice, one which he draws from the life of the neo-Calvinist university theologian and member of the Dutch parliament, Herman Bavinck. Eglinton explores how Bavinck's friendship with a fellow doctoral student at the University of Leiden, Christiaan Snouck Hurgronje, challenged his ignorance of antisemitism and thereby stimulated in Bavinck's theology an emphasis on the importance of different lived experiences, especially when considering differences in principles. After charting this intellectual growth in Bavinck through the letters he exchanged with Snouck Hurgronje, Eglinton argues that this attentiveness to lived experience subsequently catalysed Bavinck's avid interest in the writings of Booker T. Washington and W. E. B. Du Bois and shaped Bavinck's sharp critiques of racism in Jim Crow-era America.

Timothy Larsen takes as his subject Geoffrey Studdert Kennedy, a Church of England clergyman, who was better known by the affectionate nickname that the British troops whom he served as a military chaplain during the First World War bestowed upon him, 'Woodbine Willie'. During the war, in which he survived a gas attack, Studdert Kennedy gained widespread renown at the front for his personal bravery while providing pastoral care. At home his national reputation was based on his moving poetry and the popular style with which he delivered Christian messages to general audiences in unassuming language. Larsen concentrates on Studdert Kennedy's post-war advocacy for social Christianity, during which time he worked with the Industrial Christian Fellowship, before his unexpected death in 1929 at age 45.

> If we are to succeed in the re-evangelisation of England and of the world, we must definitely recognise that what is often called the social message of Jesus Christ is an essential part of the Gospel ... We must destroy within ourselves our present feeling that we descend to a lower level when we leave the song of the angels and the archangels and begin to study economic conditions, questions of wages, hours and housing.[40]

Larsen concludes that Studdert Kennedy reanimated the tradition of Anglican Christian Socialism in the aftermath of the national traumas of the First World War to address the much altered religious landscape of the interwar period.

Kenneth S. Jeffrey offers a retrospective on the social gospel in the sermons that the American evangelist Billy Graham preached in March and April 1955 during twenty-four revival meetings in Glasgow. After an illuminating discussion of how different Scottish churches wrestled with their previous responses to social questions and how they could do so more faithfully in the post-war period, Jeffrey introduces readers to the Church of

Scotland minister Tom Allan, who founded the Tell Scotland interdenominational evangelistic movement in 1953 and supported Graham's visit to Glasgow. Through a close reading of Graham's sermon manuscripts Jeffrey shows that Graham eschewed the idea of a social gospel, rather conceiving the scope of the gospel as limited to the good news that an individual could become spiritually reconciled to God through faith in Jesus Christ. Nevertheless, Graham remained adamant that the gospel necessarily had social implications and demanded social results, which he himself displayed in his public criticisms of segregation in the United States and apartheid in South Africa. Jeffrey further notes that some Scottish Christians separated from Graham on the sharp conceptual distinctions that he drew between 'evangelism' and 'witness', underscoring the subtle difference that some marked between the social gospel and social Christianity.

Brian Stanley closes the volume with an adroit interpretation of social Christianity within the history of Protestant global missions. Stanley begins by noting that while they prioritised religious conversions, nineteenth-century British missionaries also seriously attempted to improve the social and economic conditions of those to whom they preached the gospel, especially as they sought ways to discourage local participation in the African slave trade. Similarly, historically severe famines in China and India during the later decades of the nineteenth century prompted British and American missionaries to pioneer new initiatives to deliver emergency disaster relief alongside implementing longer-term, self-sustaining projects for local populations' social betterment. Stanley then considers how the dynamics of British and American Protestant missions changed after the First and Second World Wars, in whose wake the humanitarian needs of refugees were unparalleled. In response, many mainline Protestants focused their efforts more on philanthropic than on evangelistic goals, while after the 1974 Lausanne Congress on World Evangelization, Evangelical Protestants developed a new conception of missions that held economic and social development work as integral to the missionary enterprise.

Emerging Themes

Paternalism and socialism make uneasy bedfellows, yet social Christianity finds its roots in both. In adopting a chronological structure, this volume traces a gradual shift from conservative approaches to reform – as seen, for instance, in James Baird's philanthropic activities – to more liberal ones that strove to amend and Christianise social structures. It should be noted, however, that paternalistic thought is a recurring theme. Writing in the American context, May's evaluation that a 'large wing of the social movement was consistently conservative in its analysis and perceptions' is likewise applicable here.[41] May points towards the 'fear and horror' that the prospect of social unrest induced; while conservative figures sought to remedy the injustices and suffering associated with an industrialised society, the proposed solutions rarely challenged existing economic, political or social structures.[42] A comparable conclusion may be drawn here, with concerns about possible discontent and rebellion cited as primary incentives with regard to church sport initiatives, antislavery movements, as well as in Germany's religious Awakening. The inflexibility of class structures is likewise a theme that emerges from Thor's analysis of Scottish Magdalene asylums, which aspired to a familial setting not dissimilar to those in which domestic servants participated.

As found in Brown's depiction of Chalmers's 'warts and roughness', the figures who pioneered Christian social action were simultaneously faithful and flawed and their achievements all too often restricted by their broader social and political contexts.[43] The failings, inconsistencies and limitations of Christian social action are a recurring theme across this volume. For instance, in their chapters on Moody and Graham both Breimaier and Jeffrey highlight the prioritisation of individual conversion and 'general ambivalence toward political and social reforms'.[44] Both Loughlin and Knight comment on a lack of empathy, with Knight writing that a 'more self-conscious person . . . might have been more circumspect in revelling in the dirtiness of people'.[45] Though commonly upheld as the embodiment of Victorian philanthropy, Lord Shaftesbury emerges from Mair's chapter as an anxious and, at times, jealous man who was keen to receive appropriate credit for his work with the ragged schools.

While Larsen's chapter posits that any 'account of Anglican social Christianity in the first half of the twentieth century needs to reckon with the witness of Studdert Kennedy', he likewise cites the man's claim that wartime strikers 'ought to be shot'.[46] At the same time, however, Larsen astutely defends Studdert Kennedy from accusations that he was 'obstructing real reform by pretending to be engaging in it'. In response, Larsen writes simply, 'Studdert Kennedy had the insight to know what he did not know.'[47] Eglinton's survey of Herman Bavinck's theology is particularly key here; in exploring the process by which Bavinck's mature theology developed in conversation, Eglinton contextualises Bavinck's ignorance of antisemitism.

The sheer diversity of social action in which churches engaged is a consistent theme, with Bebbington's microhistory of Brunswick Chapel shedding light on the vast array of 'voluntary social work' that one church community performed.[48] Likewise, Jones's close analysis of the archives of the Baird Trust explores its efforts to advance social Christianity in Scotland, especially in Greater Glasgow. Visitations to the sick, poor or irreligious were widespread in the nineteenth century, as reflected in the chapters from Bebbington, Kloes, Loughlin and Thor. While sport as a vehicle for mission is the focus of McLeod's chapter, it is likewise touched upon in Breimaier's analysis of Moody. Mission to young people is a similarly recurring theme. In harmony with Brown's identification of education as one of Chalmers's core achievements, the crucial role that Christians have played in promoting schooling is demonstrated in the chapters from Bebbington, Kloes, McLeod and Whyte. Of especial relevance, Mair's analysis of the ragged schools highlights the vast scale of this movement to educate the children of the poor prior to later legislative intervention.

Although social action was in no way confined to explicitly religious causes, the chapters from Bebbington, Breimaier and McLeod all comment on the need for a religious justification. Interwoven with this, the chapters from Jeffrey, Larsen, McLeod and Stanley – all situated in the twentieth century – reference conservative reticence about social action on the grounds that it might lead to a loss of missional identity. This notion that social Christianity represented secularisation is tackled explicitly by Stanley, who explores the way in which mission came to be reorientated. The prioritisation of conversion over and above welfare would shift notably in the post-war period, with Stanley observing that by the 1974 Lausanne Congress on World Evangelization a multitude of factors – including the devastation caused by global conflict and the impact of photographic representations of suffering – 'combined to narrow, though never wholly eliminate, the gap between "conservative" church-centred mission and "liberal" social and economic development that had opened up in the wake of the two world wars'.[49]

The essays combined in this volume give insight into the international character of Christian social action that adds substantially to our understanding. While Scotland played a crucial role as an advocate of Christian social action, particularly through influential figures such as Chalmers, the global perspective taken here demonstrates the fluidity of ideas that spanned borders, countries and continents. Situated in the German context, Kloes's study touches on the broader European links that figures such as Johann Hinrich Wichern and Amalie Sieveking fostered. Similarly, though focused primarily upon the Dutch context, Eglinton's chapter demonstrates the important influences that both Germany and the US had upon Bavinck's thought. Likewise, Whyte, Breimaier, Jeffrey and Stanley trace the movement of people and ideas in both directions across the Atlantic, and around the world, as social visions of Christianity motivated philanthropy in Africa, Asia, Europe and North America. In bringing these diverse subjects together, this book opens up new understanding as to the breadth, scale and reach of this influential movement.

Notes

1. Stewart J. Brown, *Thomas Chalmers and the Godly Commonwealth in Scotland* (Oxford: Oxford University Press, 1983), p. xv.
2. Stewart J. Brown, *Providence and Empire: Religion, Politics and Society in the United Kingdom, 1815–1914* (Abingdon: Routledge, 2008).
3. Stewart J. Brown, 'W. T. Stead, the "New Journalism" and the "New Church" in Late Victorian and Edwardian Britain', in Brown et al., *Religion, Identity and*

Conflict in Britain: From the Restoration to the Twentieth Century: Essays in Honour of Keith Robbins (Routledge: London, 2016), pp. 213–32, p. 213.
4. Stewart J. Brown, *W. T. Stead: Nonconformist and Newspaper Prophet* (Oxford: Oxford University Press, 2019), p. 119.
5. Ibid., p. 115.
6. A. A. Maclaren, Review of *Thomas Chalmers and the Godly Commonwealth in Scotland* by Stewart J. Brown, *Journal of Modern History*, vol. 57 no. 3 (1985), pp. 555–6, p. 556; Brown, *Thomas Chalmers*, p. xv.
7. Richard B. Sher, 'Reviewed work: *Thomas Chalmers and the Godly Commonwealth* by Stewart J. Brown', *The Historian* vol. 48, no. 1. (1985), pp. 100–1, p. 101.
8. T. C. Smout, Review of *Thomas Chalmers and the Godly Commonwealth in Scotland* by Stewart J. Brown, *American Historical Review* vol. 89, no. 2 (1984), pp. 448–9, p. 448.
9. Brown, *Thomas Chalmers*, p. 378.
10. James Hastings Nichols, Review of *Thomas Chalmers and the Godly Commonwealth in Scotland* by Stewart J. Brown, *Church History* vol. 53, no. 3 (1984), pp. 407–8, p. 408.
11. Brown, *Thomas Chalmers*, p. 377.
12. Frank Prochaska, *Christianity and Social Service in Modern Britain: The Disinherited Spirit* (Oxford: Oxford University Press, 2008).
13. Ibid., p. 2.
14. Ibid., p. 5.
15. Ibid., p. 6. For further scholarship on the close association between Evangelicalism and social action see Ian Bradley, *The Call to Seriousness: The Evangelical Impact on the Victorians* (London: Jonathan Cape, 1976); Olive Checkland, *Philanthropy in Victorian Scotland: Social Welfare and the Voluntary Principle* (Edinburgh: John Donald, 1980); Kathleen Heasman, *Evangelicals in Action: An Appraisal of Their Social Work in the Victorian Era* (London: G. Bles, 1962).
16. David Bebbington, *The Evangelical Quadrilateral: Characterizing the British Gospel Movement* (Waco, TX: Baylor University Press, 2021), p. 39. See also, Bebbington, *Evangelicalism in Modern Britain: A History from the 1780s to the 1980s* (London: Routledge, 1993).
17. Peter d'Alroy Jones, *The Christian Socialist Revival, 1877–1914* (Princeton, NJ: Princeton University Press, 1968); Edward Norman, *The Victorian Christian Socialists* (Cambridge: Cambridge University Press, 1987); Paul Thomson, *Socialists, Liberals and Labour: The Struggle for London, 1885–1914* (London: Routledge and Kegan Paul, 1967); David M. Thompson, 'The Christian Socialist Revival in Britain: A Reappraisal', in J. Garnett (ed.), *Revival and Religion since 1700: Essays for John Walsh* (London: Hambledon Press, 1993), pp. 273–96.
18. Thompson, 'The Christian Socialist Revival', p. 275.
19. Ibid., p. 276.
20. *Dictionary of Religion and Ethics*, ed. by Shailer Mathews and Gerald Birney Smith (New York: Macmillan Company, 1921), pp. 416–17, p. 416. It is Christopher H. Evans who references Mathews's definition, though he critiques it as 'innocuous'. Christopher H. Evans, *The Social Gospel in American Religion: A History* (New York: New York University Press, 2017), p. 2. David M. Thompson, 'John Clifford's Social Gospel', *Baptist Quarterly*, 31.5 (January 1986), pp. 199–217, p. 207. See also Thompson, 'The Emergence of the Nonconformist Social

Gospel in England', in Keith Robbins (ed.), *Protestant Evangelicalism* (Oxford: Basil Blackwell, 1990), pp. 255–80.
21. Thompson, 'John Clifford's Social Gospel', p. 209.
22. Timothy L. Smith, *Revivalism and Social Reform: American Protestantism on the Eve of the Civil War* (Baltimore: The Johns Hopkins University Press, 1980), p. 8.
23. Thompson, 'John Clifford's Social Gospel', p. 207.
24. Henry F. May, *Protestant Churches and Industrial America* (New York: Harper & Row, 1967), p. 170.
25. Ibid., p. 170.
26. Christopher H. Evans, *The Social Gospel in American Religion: A History* (New York: New York University Press, 2017), p. 2.
27. Ibid., pp. 4–9.
28. Charles H. Hopkins, *The Rise of the Social Gospel in American Protestantism, 1865–1915* (New Haven, CT: Yale University Press, 1940), p. 3.
29. Donald Gorrell, *The Age of Social Responsibility: The Social Gospel in the Progressive Era, 1900–1920* (Macon, GA: Mercer University Press, 1988).
30. Robert T. Handy, *The Social Gospel in America, 1870–1920: Gladden, Ely and Rauschenbusch* (New York: Oxford University Press, 1966). The Baptist theologian and one of the leading lights of the American social gospel, Rauschenbusch in particular has been the subject of multiple biographies. See Christopher H. Evans, *The Kingdom Is Always but Coming: A Life of Walter Rauschenbusch* (Cambridge: Eerdmans, 2004); Paul M. Minus, *Walter Rauschenbusch: American Reformer* (New York: Macmillan Publishing Company, 1988); Donovan E. Smucker, *The Origins of Walter Rauschenbusch's Social Ethics* (Montreal: McGill–Queen's University Press, 1994). Notable works from Rauschenbusch include *Christianity and the Social Crisis* (New York: The Macmillan Company, 1907) and *A Theology for the Social Gospel* (New York: The Macmillan Company, 1917).
31. Evans, *The Social Gospel*, p. 11. See also Leliah Danielson et al. (eds), *The Religious Left in Modern America: Doorkeepers of a Radical Faith* (Cham: Palgrave Macmillan, 2018).
32. Heath W. Carter, *Union Made: Working People and the Rise of Social Christianity in Chicago* (New York: Oxford University Press, 2015), p. 4. See also Benjamin L. Hartley, *Evangelicals at a Crossroads: Revivalism and Social Reform in Boston, 1860–1910* (Durham, NH: New Hampshire Press, 2011).
33. *Dictionary of Religion and Ethics*, p. 416.
34. Handy, p. 4.
35. Paul T. Phillips, *A Kingdom on Earth: Anglo-American Social Christianity, 1880–1940* (Pennsylvania: Pennsylvania State University Press, 1996), p. xiv. Despite Phillips referencing the significance of Chalmers's 'Glasgow experiment', of the thirteen 'British' figures listed twelve are English and one Welsh.
36. Ibid., p. 58.
37. Ibid., p. xv.
38. Brian Stanley, *Christianity in the Twentieth Century: A World History* (Princeton, NJ: Princeton University Press, 2018).
39. James Baird, Esq., of Auchmedden, *'The Baird Trust.' Deed of Trust, Dated 24th July 1873* (Glasgow: Glasgow University Press, 1873), p. 5.
40. G. A. Studdert-Kennedy, 'Salvation', in Francis Underhill and Charles Scott Gillett (eds), *Report of the Anglo-Catholic Congress* (London: The Society of Saints Peter and Paul, 1923), pp. 148–9.

41. May, *Protestant Churches*, p. 163.
42. Ibid., p. 163.
43. Brown, *Thomas Chalmers*, p. xv.
44. Breimaier, p. 146.
45. Knight, p. 176.
46. Larsen, p. 208.
47. Larsen, p. 211.
48. Bebbington, p. 29.
49. Stanley, p. 252.

CHAPTER ONE

The Social Concerns of Brunswick Wesleyan Chapel, Leeds, in the Victorian Era

David Bebbington

The Methodists of the twentieth century were proud of their record of social concern. At the start of the century the Wesleyan Methodist Union for Social Service issued handbooks expounding the responsibility of Christians to engage with social questions.[1] In 1949 their governing Conference issued a 'Declaration of the Methodist Church on Christian Social and Political Responsibility'.[2] During the second half of the century Lord Soper, a Methodist minister, was the best-known figure in the land expounding Christian socialism.[3] There was a widespread consensus in the denomination that a Christian profession demanded social commitment. Methodists often appealed to their founder in the eighteenth century, John Wesley, as an exemplar of dedication to the cause of the poor. His pronouncements, they argued, 'make for social reconstruction'.[4] They were confident that their movement had begun with a robust sense of care for the welfare of society at large.

Methodists were less proud of how, as they supposed, 'the social tendencies of early Methodism' had been 'arrested in their development'.[5] It became the general view that after the death of Wesley in 1791 his followers had prospered and become careless of the needs of society, preaching an individualistic message of personal salvation that meshed with the interests of the wealthy.[6] In the middle years of the nineteenth century in particular Wesleyan Methodism had entered its 'mahogany age' with grand chapels displaying pulpits constructed out of that expensive wood and preachers who were to be found at 'the mahogany tables of wealthy laymen'.[7] Only towards the end of the century, it was held, had there been a stirring of social conscience. Hugh Price Hughes, the superintendent of the West London Methodist Mission from 1885 to 1902, had been a prophetic advocate of engagement with social issues. Hughes had expounded a social gospel in the pages of his newspaper the *Methodist Times* and on the platforms of the Forward Movement in Methodism. It was Hughes who had recaptured the passion of John Wesley for the welfare of the community.[8] In between the founder and Hughes, however, it was believed that there had been a dreary period of negligence when mahogany values had reigned. In that gap the Evangelical faith of the Wesleyans had been propagated at the expense of interest in relieving the physical circumstances of the mass of the population. This chapter is designed to explore that supposition. Other studies have explored the broader role of the nineteenth-century Free Churches in society at large.[9] This chapter, by contrast, is an exercise in microhistory. It takes a particular congregation, Brunswick Chapel, Leeds, as a case study of how far it is true that the practical needs of the poor were ignored by Wesleyan Methodists in the Victorian years. Was social Christianity in eclipse?

Leeds, the place where Brunswick Chapel was situated, was the largest of the industrial towns of Yorkshire. Woollen mills dominated the town, with spinning and dyeing common ways of earning a living. The mills required machinery and so engineering flourished. Metal-working and tanning were also strong manufacturing sectors.[10] The demand for labour meant that the population more than doubled between 1811 and 1841, to a figure of over 150,000.[11] The concentration of people made for poor living conditions. To a visitor in 1837 the town seemed 'the vilest of the vile'.[12] The streets were dirty and much of the housing cramped. In one yard near the town centre in 1839, 341 people lived in fifty-seven rooms.[13] Although some of the most overcrowded areas were cleared in subsequent years, back-to-back houses, homes with no access to the outside at the rear, a Leeds speciality, did not represent a huge improvement.[14] Impoverished Irish newcomers fleeing the famine in the 1840s and even more destitute Jews escaping the pogroms of eastern Europe from the 1870s added to the problems of the town.[15] Deprivation was real. Yet there was a widespread belief that individuals ought to be left to struggle with their circumstances. Samuel Smiles, a resident of Leeds, wrote in 1859 that 'so far from poverty being a misfortune, it may, by vigorous self-help, be converted even into a blessing'. The immensely popular book from which that quotation is taken, *Self-Help*, expressed the tone of high Victorian opinion: 'strenuous individual application', as Smiles put it, was the remedy for the ills of the growing industrial conurbations.[16] Did similar judgements make Brunswick Chapel neglect the problems around it?

Brunswick Chapel

The chapel, erected in 1825, was a large one, accommodating up to around 2,500 or 3,000 people. It was situated on the north-eastern edge of the growing town amid attractive Georgian terraces, though poorer streets were close by. It boasted a magnificent pulpit made of mahogany.[17] After the chapel's opening a majority of the trustees were eager to possess an organ suited to the dignity of the new building. They overrode the opposition by most of the local preachers to a 'popish' organ in a dispute that convulsed the denomination and led to the secession of over a thousand members in Leeds and more elsewhere.[18] Relatively few left Brunswick itself, where membership stood at 1,140 in September 1850, but it fell to 461 by December 1900. By that time, however, its branch nearby at Lincoln Fields, which shared many of its personnel with Brunswick, had reached a membership of 480.[19] The life of the chapel was dominated by the men who drove through the acquisition of the organ at the expense of popular support. They included, for instance, William Gilyard Scarth, a master dyer who was treasurer of the trustees and a Tory alderman of the town in the years 1835–8.[20] Scarth was a friend of Jabez Bunting, the minister who towered over the Wesleyan connexion during the second quarter of the nineteenth century, securing Bunting's support to engineer the introduction of the organ and sitting on three of the connexional committees that advised the Conference that governed the denomination.[21] By 1845 he had accumulated sufficient wealth to retire to Cheltenham.[22] Scarth's friend William Smith, a cloth merchant who was the prime instigator of the organ, also sat on connexional committees and was able to settle in Biarritz in the 1850s.[23] These successful businessmen probably acquired mahogany tables for their attractive homes on the outskirts of the town. Both men had been active in the creation of the Wesleyan Methodist Missionary Society at Leeds in 1813 and had subsequently supported it munificently.[24] Their bounty certainly promoted the cause of the gospel abroad, but the question arises of whether the chapel they supported extended its philanthropy to the industrial population of the town where they lived.

A third leading layman at Brunswick in the 1840s and 1850s, though he had previously been a member of the Old Chapel in the town centre and was later to move on to Roscoe Place Chapel close to his home, was Benjamin Randall Vickers, a prosperous oil merchant. He served as chapel steward for Brunswick in 1844–5 and 1851–4, the latter period a particularly trying time when many were leaving the chapel through resentment against the authoritarian policies of Bunting.[25] In 1830, having been in business for ten years, Vickers had written a private memorandum on his position in the world as a class leader, local preacher and trustee for three chapels and a Sunday school:

> I have, therefore, arrived at that Period of Life when I am called to be a Pillar in God's House and not only support it by consistant [sic] conduct and good character, but by pecuniary assistance. The Church of God has a claim upon me, the Poor have a claim upon me.[26]

Vickers saw responsibility for the poor as parallel to responsibility to the church. He was generous to the church, his family, for instance, giving a total of £58/16/- to the Centenary Fund raised by the Wesleyans in 1839.[27] He will also have been open-handed to the poor. There can be no guarantee that others saw financial obligations in the same way, but it seems likely that any 'Pillar in God's House' would think similarly.

Concern for Needy Members

The primary avenue by which the people of Brunswick gave to the needy of their own congregation was through the 'poor box'. This was brought out for contributions at two regular meetings, the Lord's Supper and the Lovefeast. The Lord's Supper normally took place quarterly at a Brunswick morning service. It was intended for members only, together with anybody obtaining a note from the superintendent, though sometimes others slipped in.[28] No regular attender at this communion service could escape the presumptive obligation to make a donation. Occasionally on Sacrament Sunday the evening congregation, which was normally larger, was asked to give too or on a given Sunday there might be a particular appeal for the poor fund.[29] The Lovefeast was a special service, at Brunswick usually in the afternoon, again quarterly, and again restricted to members, when bread and water were taken and spiritual testimonies were given.[30] Because it was an extra insertion in the standard sequence of services, attendance was smaller but the heightened spiritual atmosphere must have acted as an inducement to give. Two officials, the poor stewards, had the duty of planning for the Lord's Supper and the Lovefeast and of collecting the alms. They reported to the leaders' meeting, the body responsible for the spiritual welfare of the members.[31] Because the post of poor steward was normally held for two years before its occupant took up the most senior position in the congregation as a society steward, prominent individuals were willing to fill it and the job was performed efficiently. Although we do not possess figures for the collections, we know that in 1838 a sum of £5 – about half the annual income of an agricultural labourer – was given to a beneficiary because his son returned it twenty-nine years later.[32] We must conclude that significant sums were raised.

The distribution of the funds was in the hands of the ministers and the leaders' meeting. Names of the sick were to be submitted by the poor stewards to the ministers so that they could visit and provide relief.[33] Each of the four ministers of the circuit, the network that linked Brunswick with other chapels in the area, was entrusted with money so that he could dispense small sums at his discretion: ten shillings per quarter down to 1860; then £1 per quarter; and £2 per quarter for the superintendent minister from 1868 onwards. In 1875 it was agreed that £2 could be given away by each minister to people in the country places of the circuit, perhaps suggesting that by then there was less need in Leeds itself.[34] There was a standard procedure for approving cases for more substantial relief. The circumstances of individuals were considered by the leaders' meeting, with the leader of the class including a possible recipient required to be present to report on the individual's worthiness.[35] The rules governing the system were overhauled in 1893 so that afterwards the discussion of cases for possible relief became the main business of the leaders' meeting.[36] Before 1853 the policy had been to draw from the poor fund for Brunswick members only, but from then on it was settled that the resources of the chapel were also to be available for St Peter's, another of the town-centre Wesleyan chapels.[37] St Peter's was located in a much poorer spot closer to the old heart of the built-up area and so had more need. Frequently down to 1885, when a deputation from St Peter's to the Brunswick leaders' meeting was refused a grant, Brunswick subsidised its neighbour.[38] There was also help for Woodhouse Carr and Richmond Hill, both originally started from Brunswick.[39] Wesleyans in distress, even beyond the membership of the chapel, could count on support when they found themselves in financial difficulties.

There were also other ways in which Brunswick folk in need received benefits from their church. A basic method was by offering free seats. Like most nineteenth-century churches, Brunswick ensured a steady income for its upkeep by renting places in its pews. A proportion, however, was reserved for the poor without charge. Even on the grand occasion of the opening of the organ in 1828, when a silver collection was to be taken at the door, it was announced in advance that '[t]he Seats for the accommodation of the poor will be free as usual'.[40] Other means by which the less affluent members of the congregation could be helped were conceived. Each year at Christmas in the earlier part of the period it was customary to approach the well-to-do households for 'cast off Apparel & Articles of Clothing' so that they could be distributed to the poor.[41] There was also a plan in 1832 – though whether it was ever carried out is unknown – to form a Sick and Benefit Society for members of society in the two circuits that then comprised the Wesleyans of the town.[42] Another scheme, this time for assisting families of the Sunday school children, was mooted in 1846, though again it is unclear whether it became operational.[43] Each of these arrangements would have acted as a system of elementary insurance, paying for healthcare and funerals, and so would have required contributions, but they would have been kept to a minimum. Certainly a society of this kind was established in 1881 at the branch Sunday school at Lincoln Fields, situated in the less affluent streets to the east of Brunswick Chapel.[44] And a specialist scheme for local preachers, some of whom were at times in straitened circumstances, was established on a national basis in 1849 with support from Leeds in order to provide annuities as well as payments in sickness or on death. Moses Atkinson, a retired linen manufacturer, served as president of this Local Preachers' Mutual Aid Association in 1886 and long remained its stalwart supporter.[45] There was care for Methodists at times of hardship.

Chapel Visitors

The people of Brunswick did not merely hope that they would hear of cases of need but actively sought them out. Each year visitors of the poor were formally appointed by the leaders' meeting. In 1852 there were nine of them.[46] Their task was to identify and relieve those who were falling on evil days. One of the visitors of the poor was John Spink, a butcher who employed two youths in 1851.[47] He was a prominent person at Brunswick, acting in 1868 as a trustee – a position for men of means – and in 1873–4 as a society steward.[48] Spink, according to his obituary, was 'an ardent believer in the class-meeting', where religious experience was discussed on a weekly basis.[49] A class leader by 1850, he had as many as thirteen new members 'on trial' in his class nine years later, a sign that he was effective in evangelistic work.[50] He was a regular contributor to the Sunday night prayer meeting at Brunswick whose aim was the encouragement of conversions and active in outreach at the mission in Lincoln Fields.[51] 'He was a devout man', wrote his obituarist, 'and took counsel with God in all his undertakings.'[52] Here was a well-to-do individual whose priorities were spiritual. Yet he performed the duties of visiting the poor for twenty years, from 1852 to 1872.[53]

When Spink retired from the post he was replaced by John Bickers, a bachelor who was in business with his brother as a linen draper and who had acted as society steward, unusually for three years rather than two, in 1866–8.[54] Bickers was a trustee and treasurer of the savings bank at Lincoln Fields from 1861 into the 1890s, again a person of financial weight. He was active in the Sunday school at Lincoln Fields from 1844 for over half a century, serving as secretary from 1849.[55] Remarkably, he was a class leader from 1868 until 1893 even though he suffered from increasing deafness, compensating for his affliction by possessing a retentive memory.[56] Because of his disability Bickers might not have seemed the obvious choice for a visitor of the poor, but, having started this work in 1872, he continued in it until at least 1893.[57] 'According to his means', ran his obituary, 'he was a ready giver, his generous heart prompted him to help the poor, and his many acts of kindness to suffering humanity will be long and gratefully remembered.'[58] Like Spink, Bickers blended spiritual concern for the souls of his fellows with care for their physical welfare.

Men, however, were not as prominent as women in the work of visiting. In 1852 there were six female visitors of the poor at Brunswick and only three male visitors, a similar ratio to that in charitable societies generally around mid-century.[59] One a few years later was Sarah Kirkby, an unmarried Sunday school teacher at Lincoln Fields from 1879 to 1888.[60] Appointed a joint class leader in 1881, she admired qualities in her female class members such as living 'a simple beautiful life adorning the doctrine of Christ her Saviour in all things'.[61] She was a great recruiter, regularly having members on trial in her classes.[62] Her evangelistic endeavours were complemented, and no doubt reinforced, by her compassionate ministry. Kirkby was already a visitor by 1887 and remained one until at least 1891.[63]

Likewise Hannah Frost was a redoubtable visitor. Drawn into the outreach work at Lincoln Fields in 1863, she taught in its Sunday school until 1865 and again in 1874.[64] She was the leader of four classes at Lincoln Fields from 1867 and was still adding substantial numbers of members on trial in the late 1880s and 1890s, by which time Lincoln Fields had become a separate society from Brunswick.[65] Her main work, however, was the running of a mothers' meeting on a Monday afternoon from 1874 until her death in 1904. This agency, which fell under the auspices of the Leeds Ladies' Bible and Household Mission, provided weekly gatherings for around one hundred women, augmented by annual teas and railway trips.[66] Hannah Frost did not hold the formal post of visitor of the poor at Brunswick, but visitation of working-class homes, especially of those in her mothers' meeting, was her vocation. In the area round the Lincoln Fields chapel, according to a newspaper obituary, 'she was to be seen morning, noon, and night tramping, without regard to her own comfort or ease, from street to street, always on the same errands of mercy, charity, and practical benevolence'.[67] She was the only female speaker at the presentation of an illuminated address and thirteen books to John Bickers in 1894 to mark his half-century of service.[68] Hannah Frost and John Bickers were personalities with the same priority, identifying themselves with 'the philanthropic work of Leeds in the most hearty and thorough way'.[69]

The role of the official visitors from Brunswick changed gradually during the period. For one thing, their numbers decreased. The nine of 1852 had dwindled to two, one male and one female, by 1888.[70] For another, their work was differently understood. Although they were still sometimes called visitors of the poor, from 1872 the alternative title of visitors of the sick was being used.[71] With the improvement in the standard of living during the 1850s and 1860s, the most obvious recipients of care were now those who were ill, not those who were indigent. Most importantly, before the end of the century visitation had become one of the responsibilities of a paid member of staff. In 1896 Sister Edith was welcomed to the Brunswick leaders' meeting. With the aid of a group of 'lady helpers', she took charge of visitation.[72] Edith was a member of the Leeds Methodist Sisterhood, a uniformed company of women who in most cases lived together in a community house and served the Wesleyan congregations of the area. Classified as deaconesses, they acted as a reserve corps of personnel over and above the male ministers with a special vocation to reach 'the domestic life of the people'.[73] They were ranked as part of the Forward Movement, the new wave of socially committed Christianity that swept over much of Methodism in the last years of the nineteenth century, and were normally based at the central missions characteristic of the movement. Although seven of the thirteen Leeds sisters employed in 1901 were located at the chapels that had become units of the central mission, Edith was engaged by Brunswick, which stayed aloof from the mission. She was active in evangelism, reporting enthusiastically about a joint Free Church gospel venture in 1901, but her main role was to take domestic visitation out of the hands of the congregation.[74] The congregation of Brunswick no longer appointed its own members to mingle in the life of the deprived in the town. It could be argued that this phase of Wesleyan history represented an attenuation rather than an advance in commitment to the social application of the faith.

Concern for the Young

The young were also beneficiaries of care. The Sunday schools maintained by Brunswick were large and flourishing organisations. In spring 1853, when figures first become available, there was an average of 97 children in attendance in the morning and 164 in the afternoon at Brunswick itself together with 64 in the morning and 120 in the afternoon at the Lincoln Fields branch. There were also smaller branches at Little London and Woodhouse.[75] That was a low point for numbers, shortly after the mid-century disruption when hundreds deserted Wesleyanism for the reform movement that eventually generated the United Free Methodist Churches. By autumn 1869, however, there were 121 in the morning and 210 in the afternoon at Brunswick and 195 in the morning and 344, together with 205 infants, in the afternoon at Lincoln Fields.[76] The Sunday schools that catered for these large numbers could themselves be regarded as a form of social service. Originally formed in order to supply elementary education in reading and writing, they had contracted their scope in the 1820s in order to exclude the secular activity of writing from the curriculum on the sabbath. For a while the teachers kept up instruction in writing skills on weekday evenings instead. They abandoned it by 1844, though they seem to have revived it around 1857.[77] Certainly the ongoing Sunday school training in reading, and not just religious subjects, continued down to the 1870s, when the impact of the Education Act of 1870 made that provision redundant. Thereafter the Sunday schools concentrated on Bible knowledge, but in the middle years of the century the cultivation of literacy loomed large in their programme. The Sunday school library, a chief means of fostering reading skills, included, alongside works of popular devotion and lives of Christian worthies, fiction such as *Stories for Summer Days* and history such as a biography of William the Conqueror.[78] As a medium of secular instruction, the Sunday schools were an important dimension of the response of Brunswick to the needs of the community around the chapel.

The attitude of the Sunday school to measures of social assistance, however, did contain some ambiguity. When a savings bank was established in connection with the Brunswick and Lincoln Fields schools in 1857, it was explained that it 'encouraged habits of industry and provident economy on the part of the scholars'. Like classes on needlework and writing on weekday evenings, it gave the scholars skills that would assist them in later life. But the annual report of the schools went on to show some reserve about whether that was a proper aim:

> This attempt to connect secular advantages and aids with Sunday-schools, though not forming a part of the objects for which they were instituted, must be regarded in the light of a legitimate and powerful auxiliary to these objects; since parents are more likely to be convinced of the sincerity of our desires for the spiritual welfare of their children,

when they see us anxious to secure for them those temporal benefits which they can better understand and appreciate.[79]

Thus social benefits required a religious justification. The 'secular advantages and aids' were not intrinsically what a Sunday school should offer but were attractions for parents. In a similar way, the visitation of scholars to encourage regular attendance was primarily designed to ensure that they heard the message of the gospel, but the practice could have side-effects that promoted their welfare. Home visits to the scholars were supposed to be made by the teachers whenever the children were absent, though the Sunday school minutes frequently record that the teachers were failing in this duty.[80] From 1883 there were individuals who were commissioned to visit missing children when teachers were unable to call on them.[81] When visits were paid, as by the official church visitors, the children's ill health or other problems in the household might be discovered and addressed. Social gains flowed from spiritual motives. The Sunday schools aimed to create 'serious impressions' in the children that would result in 'religious decision', but, incidentally as it were, they became vehicles for personal care.[82] The evangelistic imperative that suffused Brunswick and its schools brought about this-worldly rewards.

The Bands of Hope that sprang from the Sunday schools were conceived as a way of addressing the social problems of the day. Strong drink was increasingly seen as the chief enemy of decent family life, wasting household resources and leading to street violence, child neglect and wife beating. One of the Methodist sisters who was employed in Leeds not at Brunswick but at Oxford Place put the case succinctly in 1901: 'The drink is our chief difficulty.'[83] A long-term remedy, education of the rising generation in teetotal principles, had been invented in Leeds in 1847. Jabez Tunnicliff, a General Baptist minister, set up meetings for children under fourteen called Bands of Hope and for older children 'The Cold Water Army'.[84] The former label stuck and a national movement took off. Children were encouraged to take the pledge not to drink alcohol, except for medicinal purposes, for their whole lives. Lincoln Fields established a Band of Hope in 1867 and Brunswick followed two years later.[85] Brunswick attained an average attendance of sixty by 1889 and Lincoln Fields, which threw itself more wholeheartedly into the venture, claimed as many as 500 members on its books by 1894.[86] Although there were nearly always talks on the evils of drink, there was also much poetry reading and choral singing. The meetings were lively and entertaining, and so the Brunswick Band of Hope was requested to provide recitations and songs at the annual Sunday school entertainment in December 1887.[87] Partly as a result of Band of Hope activity, temperance feeling grew markedly in the congregations as a whole so that by the 1890s total abstinence was normal. In that decade Brunswick backed political pressure on the temperance question, endorsing plans for demonstrations in favour of the Liberal government's Local

Veto Bill of 1893.[88] This solution to a social problem spilled over into the public arena.

The Spirit of Philanthropy

If the Bands of Hope were designed for the young, there was an institution associated with Brunswick that cared for the old. The church shared with St Peter's Chapel, which had formerly been in the same circuit, an almshouse at Richmond Hill, to the east of the town. Built in 1851 next to a new chapel, it consisted of a row of twenty houses called Wesley Terrace opening on to the street. It was a condition of entry that a person must have been a member of a Methodist society for at least twenty years and have been a member in Leeds for at least ten. It was run by a charitable trust that received legacies, and so was able to keep rent low, at only 4d or 6d per week.[89] Elderly members were recommended for a place by the leaders' meeting on the proposal of a class leader.[90] The vacancies were generally taken by those in particular need. In 1875, when Sarah Brown was suggested as a candidate for Richmond Hill, there was opposition from some members of the leaders' meeting on the grounds that she possessed the substantial sum of between £300 and £400. Nevertheless after a personal visit by a class leader her acceptance for a place was carried by nine votes to five, the only recorded instance of a vote on a candidate for admission.[91] The relative poverty of most occupants is also suggested by the provision of an annual Christmas 'dole' of ten shillings given to all those who had been recommended to the almshouse by Brunswick.[92] The rules were varied in 1892 so that admission was not restricted to society members, an opening to a wider clientele, but essentially the almshouse was designed for Methodists, not the public at large.[93]

Another distinctively Methodist institution, though in this case at a distance, that stirred the sympathies of Brunswick was the Children's Home in London. Founded by T. B. Stephenson, an inventive Methodist minister then stationed in Lambeth who was troubled by the neglected state of the children in the streets round his chapel, the home moved to Bethnal Green in 1871 and grew in scope over subsequent years.[94] From 1882 onwards a series of special fundraising events was held at Brunswick to support the venture. The Sunday school was the natural section of the chapel to sponsor the gatherings. The first was a concert, the second in 1883 a special service, the third in 1884 a quarterly missionary meeting.[95] Another was to be held at a harvest festival if one was to take place in 1885 and a further special meeting for the home replaced the harvest thanksgiving in 1887.[96] In 1891 a flower service was arranged with a collection for the home in honour of Stephenson's presidency of the Conference that year.[97] Twice, at the first and last of these occasions, the sum donated was augmented to the round sums of three and five guineas, a sign of the particular appeal of the home to the people of the chapel.[98] There were further collections at

Christmas for the home in 1896 and 1900.[99] Destitute children could touch the purse strings as well as the heart strings.

The philanthropic spirit displayed itself at Brunswick in other ways. The Leeds hospitals, still largely charitable institutions, attracted support. In 1876 the congregation participated in a united appeal for the local hospitals by taking a collection at one of its services.[100] The town public dispensary received the collections from the harvest thanksgiving services in 1882 and 1883, the children's ward of Leeds Infirmary and the workhouse hospital being given the fruit and flowers from the displays.[101] Appeals for calamities that appeared in the headlines also provoked generosity. When, during the American Civil War in the autumn of 1862, the lack of supplies of raw cotton threw the Lancashire mill workers into unemployment, Brunswick sent £5 to each of the leaders' meetings of Preston, Wigan and Stockport. The church despatched cast-off garments to Wesleyans in a succession of other Lancashire towns over the next few months.[102] Charitable aid could extend to others beyond the denomination. In 1847 during the Irish famine there were public collections for the relief of the distressed.[103] Five years later a dam collapsed at Holmfirth in the West Riding of Yorkshire, not too far from Leeds, flooding the valley, killing nearly a hundred people and making some 7,000 destitute.[104] Again collections were taken up at Brunswick's morning and evening services.[105] And in 1877 acute famine in India induced all the chapels of the circuit to make collections and pass the proceeds to the mayor of Leeds for forwarding to the Lord Mayor of London's appeal.[106] Social concern could at times have a wide scope, ignoring the religious allegiance of its recipients.

That was true of a society that drew significant support from Brunswick. It was one of the Strangers' Friend Societies set up by Methodists to assist newcomers to the growing urban centres of the United Kingdom. The first, founded in London in 1785, collected weekly contributions from members for distribution to non-Methodists and that undenominational policy was generally accepted in the societies that followed elsewhere.[107] The Leeds equivalent was established in 1789, appointing district visitors to relieve the deserving poor through visits to their homes. Although it gradually lost its distinctive Methodist identity and became a general relief agency, adopting the title of the Benevolent Society, it retained the support of prominent Wesleyans such as Charles Turkington, a Brunswick trustee, who joined its committee in 1829. It became part of the network of charitable organisations that arose to address the needs of Leeds in the first half of the nineteenth century.[108] In the desperate days of 1842, when trade depression was at its worst, an artisan in wool manufacturing, Robert Pounder, who was associated with Oxford Place Chapel, received a much appreciated donation of ten shillings from the society.[109] At the time the Benevolent Society was probably the chief organisation in Leeds providing relief outside the poor law.

The most stalwart member of the society during the second half of the century was James Walker, a committee member from 1841, vice-president from 1858, president from 1862 to 1889 and treasurer thereafter.[110] During three months in 1878 he attended meetings under its auspices every day in order to evaluate applications for relief. Walker was a corn merchant and maltster who must have been saved from the displeasure of his Wesleyan coreligionists at his abetting of the drink trade by his retiring from business on inheriting a fortune from a relative in the 1880s. An unusually wealthy man, he died with over £70,000.[111] Brought up an Anglican, he joined the Wesleyans on his marriage in 1841, becoming a class leader, society steward at Brunswick in 1848–50 and 1853–4, circuit steward in 1856–7 and secretary of the trust by 1880.[112] He was one of the first lay representatives to Conference when its restriction to ministers was first lifted.[113] As the long-term treasurer of the Sunday schools of the circuit, he provided a tea for 200 workers at the town schools in 1873 where he urged them to 'make the spiritual element more prominent than ever'.[114] The spiritual mattered to Walker. He held family worship night and morning and recorded in his diary feeling 'supremely happy in the Lord'.[115] Although he transferred to the Roscoe Place Chapel a few years before he died and in his later years often attended services in the Evangelical tradition of the Church of England, he had been an ornament of Brunswick for over half a century.[116]

Walker exemplified the commitment of his chapel to social engagement. The early death of his wife in 1876 meant that extra time was available for a multitude of good works.[117] Becoming a Justice of the Peace in 1880, he chaired the Discharged Prisoners' Aid Society, joined the Armley Gaol Visiting Committee and made a point of seeing condemned prisoners before their execution. Apart from his service in the Benevolent Society, Walker was on the committee of the Leeds Public Dispensary for thirty-five years and its chairman from 1880 to 1893. He supported the General Infirmary, introducing an ambulance to carry the injured to the hospital which was called 'Walker's Carriage'. He gave his backing to the Women and Children's Hospital, the Adel Reformatory School, the Watermen's Mission, the House of Recovery, the Shoeblacks' Brigade and the Tradesmen's Benevolent Institution.[118] He was a veritable Lord Shaftesbury of Leeds. Like Shaftesbury, he was an active Conservative, frequently appearing on party platforms, at a time when most leading Brunswickers were Liberal in their politics. Walker endorsed the Charity Organisation Society that encouraged discrimination between the deserving and the undeserving poor, but that policy seemed progressive in the later Victorian years. His heart was in charitable work, as he showed when cholera struck Leeds. As his obituarist recorded, 'he personally visited many of the sufferers in the slums, when visitors were few, carrying sympathy, comfort and practical assistance wherever he went'.[119] James Walker was devoted to the welfare of the people of his town.

Conclusion

This account of Brunswick Chapel suggests that the customary picture of Wesleyan policies on social issues requires modification. It has been common to regard Wesley's sympathy for the poor as having been eclipsed for much of the nineteenth century and resuscitated only with the advent of the Forward Movement, central missions and the social gospel at the century's end. On this understanding, the ministry of Hugh Price Hughes represented the opening of a new phase of social engagement that endured throughout the twentieth century. That view, however, exaggerates the novelty of the Forward Movement. For one thing, Hughes did not diverge from received Evangelical opinion, which was the foundation of his ministry and even of his social teaching.[120] For another, the central missions were not necessarily as groundbreaking in their policies on social work as has been believed. Oxford Place Chapel, a case in Leeds that was reopened by Hughes in 1898 as the core of a multi-site central mission, specialised in preaching, not care for the poor.[121] 'Our Social Work', according to the superintendent, Samuel Chadwick, 'is neither elaborate nor extensive.'[122] The social work at Oxford Place, in fact, was done 'almost entirely' by its Sister May.[123] No distinctive social gospel found a place on its platform. Chadwick was notable for his theological conservatism.[124] 'If we minister to people's bodily necessities', he wrote, 'it is that we may save their souls.'[125] That sentiment was very similar to the case for secular benefits as helps to the spiritual cause that Brunswick Sunday school had mounted in 1857.[126] Brunswick, in fact, hardly differed from the Leeds central mission in its approach to ministry at the opening of the twentieth century. By 1905, its minister reported that Brunswick was being run on Forward Movement lines, though still not a central mission and operating within a circuit.[127] Its activities embraced social work, but, as we have seen, that department was in the hands of its own member of the sisterhood. Oxford Place was not strikingly innovative; but insofar as it was, it hardly differed from Brunswick. In Leeds the Forward Movement did not represent a revolution in social concern.

That was partly because Brunswick already possessed a strong record of social commitment. Its members did not advocate state action to remedy particular social ills apart from alcohol abuse, let alone the universal benefits of a welfare state, but it could not be expected that mid-twentieth-century solutions would be advocated in the Victorian years. Instead they put into practice voluntary social work on a large scale. Evangelical theology did not inhibit them, but on the contrary effort to spread the gospel fostered concern for the poor. People such as Benjamin Vickers assumed that they had responsibilities towards the deprived around them. A poor fund gave assistance to members of the congregation and other chapels while other boons such as free seats and sick and benefit societies were arranged for the less well-off. Visitors, some male but increasingly female, were appointed to ensure that the needy were identified and received face-to-face attention. The Sunday schools and their offshoots the Bands of Hope, both drawing in a large clientele, supplied not just Bible knowledge but also secular skills and lively entertainments. An almshouse catered for the elderly of the town and the Children's Home in London helped the waifs and strays of the capital. The congregation supported local hospitals and supplied relief after disasters elsewhere. Individuals of means such as James Walker gave time and effort to a variety of agencies, supremely the Benevolent Society that was designed to benefit all. The attenders at this place of worship with a mahogany pulpit performed an enormous amount for the needy masses of the Victorian era. Brunswick was certainly not representative of the whole of Methodism, for many small rural chapels could not aspire to achieve so much. Nevertheless its record does illustrate what could be done by a large Wesleyan community in a major urban centre through chapel agencies, members' initiatives and associated voluntary societies. Brunswick Chapel championed not a social gospel but a different form of social Christianity.

Notes

1. Samuel E. Keeble (ed.), *The Citizen of To-morrow: A Handbook on Social Questions* (London: Robert Culley, 1906); Samuel E. Keeble (ed.), *The Social Teaching of the Bible* (London: Robert Culley, 1909).
2. *The Methodist Church: Declarations of Conference on Social Questions*, 2nd edn (London: Epworth Press, 1962), pp. 1–22.
3. Mark Peel, *The Last Wesleyan: A Life of Donald Soper* (Lancaster: Scotforth Books, 2008).
4. J. Ernest Rattenbury, 'John Wesley and Social Service', in Keeble (ed.), *Citizen of To-morrow*, p. 68.
5. Rattenbury, 'John Wesley and Social Service', p. 67.
6. E.g. Rupert E. Davies, *Methodism* (Harmondsworth: Penguin, 1963), pp. 132–57, spec. p. 151.
7. A. W. Harrison in A. W. Harrison et al., *The Methodist Church* (1932), p. 72, quoted by K. S. Inglis, *Churches and the Working Classes in Victorian England* (London: Routledge and Kegan Paul, 1963), p. 85.
8. Hugh Price Hughes, *Social Christianity* (London: Hodder and Stoughton, 1889); Hugh Price Hughes, *The Philanthropy of God* (London: Hodder and Stoughton, 1892); Hugh Price Hughes, *Ethical Christianity* (London: Sampson Low, Marston & Co., 1892). For a more judicious evaluation of Hughes, see Christopher Oldstone-Moore, *Hugh Price Hughes: Founder of a New Methodism, Conscience of a New Nonconformity* (Cardiff: University of Wales Press, 1999).
9. Lesley Husselbee and Paul Ballard (eds), *Free Churches and Society: The Nonconformist Contribution to Social Welfare, 1800–2010* (London: Continuum, 2012); Timothy Larsen and Michael Ledger-Lomas (eds), *The Oxford History of the Protestant Dissenting Traditions: Vol. 3: The Nineteenth Century* (Oxford: Oxford University Press, 2017).

10. E. J. Connell and M. Ward, 'Industrial Development, 1780–1914', in Derek Fraser (ed.), *A History of Modern Leeds* (Manchester: Manchester University Press, 1980), pp. 142–76.
11. C. J. Morgan, 'Demographic Change, 1771–1911', in Fraser (ed.), *A History of Modern Leeds*, p. 48.
12. Fraser (ed.), *A History of Modern Leeds*, p. xii.
13. Morgan, 'Demographic Change', p. 65.
14. Maurice Beresford, 'The Face of Leeds, 1780–1914', in Fraser (ed.), *A History of Modern Leeds*, p. 84.
15. Morgan, 'Demographic Change', pp. 61–2.
16. Samuel Smiles, *Self-Help with Illustrations of Conduct & Perseverance*, introd. Asa Briggs (London: John Murray, 1958), pp. 50–1.
17. *Centenary of Brunswick Wesleyan Methodist Chapel, Leeds* (n.p.: 1925).
18. D. Colin Dews, '"It cost a thousand pounds and a thousand members": The Brunswick Organ Controversy, Leeds: A Demand for Lay Rights?', *Wesley Historical Society (Yorkshire)*, 118 (Autumn 2020), pp. 1–19.
19. West Yorkshire Joint Services Leeds Archives, Leeds First Circuit Schedule Book, 1850–63 [hereafter SB, 1850–63], WYL 490/205; Leeds, Brunswick, Schedule Book, 1896–1907 [hereafter SB, 1896–1907], WYL 490/42. The schedule books for the intervening period are unfortunately missing.
20. D. Colin Dews, *The Church with a Mission: Oxford Place Methodist Chapel, Leeds, 1835 to 2010* (Leeds: Oxford Place Methodist Church and Centre, 2010), p. 18.
21. Margaret Batty, 'Stages in the Development and Control of Wesleyan Lay Leadership, 1791–1878' (PhD diss., University of London, 1988), p. 242.
22. West Yorkshire Joint Services Leeds Archives, Brunswick Chapel Trustees' Minute Book, 1826–79, WYL 490/72 [hereafter T], 5 January 1846.
23. John Rattenbury, 'The Late William Smith, Esq, of Gledhow', *Leeds and Yorkshire Biography*, vol. 3, pp. 605–6, Leeds Family and Local History Library.
24. W. D. Lawson, *Wesleyan Local Preachers: Biographical Illustrations of their Position in the Connexion, Utility in the Church and Influence in the World* (Newcastle-upon-Tyne: William D. Lawson, 1874), pp. 314–15; Rattenbury, 'The Late William Smith', p. 605. On the missionary support of Brunswick, see David Bebbington, 'The Missionary Concerns of Brunswick Wesleyan Methodist Chapel, Leeds, in the Victorian Era', in Alex Chow and Emma Wild-Wood (eds), *Ecumenism and Independency in World Christianity: Historical Studies in Honor of Brian Stanley* (Leiden: Brill, 2020), pp. 125–43.
25. T, 15 January 1844, 20 January 1845, 17 January 1851, 30 January 1852, 14 January 1853, 27 January 1854.
26. B. Randall Vickers, *This Family Business* (Leeds: Benjn. R. Vickers and Sons Ltd, 1954), p. 54.
27. 'List of Subscribers in the Leeds District', *General Report of the Wesleyan Centenary Fund* (Leeds: Anthony Pickard, 1844).
28. John C. Bowmer, *The Lord's Supper in Methodism, 1791–1960* (London: Epworth Press, 1961), p. 26.
29. West Yorkshire Joint Services Leeds Archives, Brunswick Leaders' Meeting Minutes, 1828–77, WYL 490/75 [hereafter L, 1828–77], 29 April 1868; Brunswick Leaders' Meeting Minutes, 1878–1911, WYL 490/81 [hereafter L, 1878–1911], 22 April 1898.

30. Frank Baker, *Methodism and the Love-Feast* (London: Epworth Press, 1957), pp. 16, 36.
31. *Directory for the Religious Services, Office Bearers, &c., of the Wesleyan Methodist Leeds Brunswick Circuit, No. 9, Jan. 16th, to Apr. 15th, 1876* (Leeds: H. W. Walker, 1876), p. 6.
32. L, 1828–77, 2 October 1867.
33. *Directory for the Religious Services, Office Bearers, &c.*, p. 6.
34. L, 1828–77, 11 January 1860, 18 January 1868, 6 January 1875.
35. L, 1878–1911, 11 May 1892.
36. L, 1878–1911, 14 June 1893.
37. L, 1828–77, 12 October 1853.
38. L, 1878–1911, 9 December 1885.
39. L, 1878–1911, 16 January 1878, 9 December 1885.
40. *Brunswick Chapel: The Large and Powerful Organ...* (flyer, 1828), Leeds Family and Local History Library.
41. L, 1828–77, 7 December 1836.
42. L, 1828–77, 7 March 1832.
43. West Yorkshire Joint Services Leeds Archives, Wesleyan Methodist Sunday School Minute Book Leeds First Society, 1842 to 1874, WYL 490/75 [hereafter S], 13 July, 10 August 1846.
44. James E. Ellison (ed.), *History of the Lincoln Fields Wesleyan Methodist Sunday School and Society (Brunswick Circuit, Leeds), 1830–1894* (Leeds: John Whitehead & Son, 1895), p. 42.
45. F. Harold Buss and R. G. Burnett, *A Goodly Fellowship: A History of the Hundred Years of the Methodist Local Preachers Mutual Aid Association, 1849–1949* (London: Epworth Press, 1949), pp. 65–6.
46. L, 1828–77, 28 January 1852.
47. England and Wales Census, 1851.
48. L, 1828–77, 5 March 1873, 14 January 1874.
49. West Yorkshire Joint Services Leeds Archives, Book of Obituaries, Brunswick Circuit, 1873–1917, WYL 490/32, entry for death on 29 December 1882.
50. SB, 1850–63, June 1859.
51. Ellison (ed.), *Lincoln Fields*, p. 112.
52. Book of Obituaries, 29 December 1882.
53. L, 1828–77, 28 January 1852, 10 January 1872.
54. L, 1828–77, 17 January 1866, 16 January 1867, 15 January 1868.
55. Ellison (ed.), *Lincoln Fields*, pp. 83, 69–70.
56. L, 1828–77, 3 June 1868; L, 1878–1911, 1 November 1893. Ellison (ed.), *Lincoln Fields*, p. 70.
57. L, 1878–1911, 22 November 1893.
58. Book of Obituaries, 2 January 1902.
59. L, 1828–77, 28 January 1852; F. K. Prochaska, *Women and Philanthropy in Nineteenth-Century England* (Oxford: Clarendon Press, 1980), p. 109.
60. Ellison (ed.), *Lincoln Fields*, p. 109.
61. L, 1878–1911, 24 August 1881; S. A. Kirkby, 'Mary Cordukes', Book of Obituaries, 14 September 1890.
62. SB, 1883–96.
63. L, 1878–1911, 19 January 1887, 25 February 1891.
64. Ellison (ed.), *Lincoln Fields*, p. 107.

65. SB, 1883–96.
66. Ellison (ed.), *Lincoln Fields*, pp. 74–5. *45th Report of the Leeds Ladies' Bible and Household Mission, 1904* (Leeds: J. Whitehead and Son, 1904), p. 5.
67. Book of Obituaries, 19/20 January 1904.
68. Ellison (ed.), *Lincoln Fields*, p. 70.
69. Book of Obituaries, 19/20 January 1904.
70. L, 1878–1911, 11 January 1888.
71. L, 1828–77, 10 January 1872.
72. L, 1878–1911, 16 December 1896, 7 April 1897.
73. *Leeds Methodist Sisterhood: 5th Annual Report, 1901* (n.p.: 1901), p. 11.
74. *Leeds Methodist Sisterhood, 1901*, pp. 10, 14.
75. S, 1842–74, 18 April 1853.
76. S, 1842–74, 10 January 1870.
77. S, 1842–74, 22 January 1828, 12 August 1844. *The Annual Report of the Wesleyan Methodist Sunday School Society, for the Leeds First Circuit, for the Year 1857* (Leeds: H. W. Walker, 1858), p. 6.
78. S, 1842–74, 14 April 1856.
79. *Annual Report of the Wesleyan Methodist Sunday School Society, 1857*, p. 6.
80. E.g. West Yorkshire Joint Services Leeds Archives, Leeds East Circuit Sunday School Minute Book, 1835–39, WRY 490/23, 26 January 1838.
81. West Yorkshire Joint Services Leeds Archives, Brunswick Sunday School Secretary's Minute Book, 1883–98 [hereafter SS, 1883–98], WYL 490/83, 24 January 1883.
82. *Annual Report of the Wesleyan Methodist Sunday School Society, 1857*, p. 5.
83. Sister May in *Leeds Methodist Sisterhood, 1901*, p. 17.
84. *A Century of Hope: The Official Centenary Handbook of the Yorkshire Band of Hope Union, 1865–1965* (n.p.: 1965), p. 8.
85. Ellison (ed.), *Lincoln Fields*, p. 28. S, 1842–74, 8 February 1869.
86. SS, 1883–98, 9 January 1890; Ellison (ed.), *Lincoln Fields*, pp. 75–6.
87. SS, 1883–98, 30 November 1887.
88. L, 1878–1911, 15 March 1893.
89. William M. Treen, *Methodism in East Leeds: Richmond Hill* (Leeds: Wildwood & Ward, 1947), pp. 30–1.
90. E.g. L, 1828–77, 26 January 1853.
91. L, 1828–77, 15 September 1875.
92. L, 1828–77, 7 January 1891.
93. L, 1828–77, 21 September 1892.
94. William Bradfield, *The Life of the Rev. Thomas Bowman Stephenson: Founder of the 'Children's Home' and the Wesley Deaconess Institute* (London: C. H. Kelly, 1913).
95. West Yorkshire Joint Services Leeds Archives, Brunswick Sunday School Secretary's Minute Book, 1865–82 [hereafter SS, 1865–82], WYL 490/79, 8 February 1882; SS, 24 January 1883, 25 March 1884.
96. SS, 1883–98, 8 April 1885, 7 September 1887.
97. SS, 1883–98, 24 July 1891.
98. Though on the second occasion the decision of whether to increase the sum was left to the discretion of the treasurer.
99. L, 1878–1911, 16 December 1896, 19 December 1900.
100. *Directory for the Religious Services, Office Bearers, &c.*, p. 5.

101. SS, 1865–82, 9 September 1882; *Methodist Recorder* cutting, 21 September 1883, following SS, 1883–98, 5 September 1883.
102. L, 1828–77, 24 September 1862, 26 November 1862, 3 December 1862, 10 December 1862, 25 February 1863.
103. L, 1828–77, 3 February 1847.
104. Joseph Irving, *The Annals of Our Time* (London: Macmillan and Co., 1875), pp. 346–7.
105. L, 1828–77, 25 February 1852.
106. West Yorkshire Joint Services Leeds Archives, Quarterly Minute Book Leeds First Circuit [hereafter Q], WYL 490/27, 24 September 1877.
107. John A. Vickers (ed.), *A Dictionary of Methodism in Britain and Ireland* (London: Epworth Press, 2000), pp. 339–40.
108. Robert J. Morris, *Class, Sect and Party: The Making of the British Middle Class: Leeds, 1820–1840* (Manchester: Manchester University Press, 1990), pp. 172, 208.
109. Robert Pounder, *The Notebooks of Robert Pounder*, Ann Alexander (ed.), *The Publications of the Thoresby Society*, 2nd series, vol. 25 (Leeds: The Thoresby Society, 2015), p. 49.
110. These and the following details about Walker, except where otherwise indicated, are taken from obituaries in the unidentified 'Y. D. O.' and *Yorkshire Post*, 10 June 1908, 'Leeds Obituary Notices', vol. 2, and *Leeds and its Suburbs*, 2:24 (September 1896), pp. 1–3, Leeds Family and Local History Library.
111. Probate for death, 9 June 1908.
112. Book of Obituaries, 9 June 1908. L, 1828–77, 19 July 1848, 9 January 1850, 5 January 1853, 11 January 1854. Q, 24 December 1855, 29 December 1856. West Yorkshire Joint Services Leeds Archives, Brunswick Chapel Trustees' Minute Book, 1880–1921, WYL 490/82, 30 January 1880.
113. Book of Obituaries, 9 June 1908.
114. Ellison (ed.), *Lincoln Fields*, 148.
115. Book of Obituaries, 9 June 1908.
116. Book of Obituaries, 9 June 1908.
117. Book of Obituaries, 9 June 1908.
118. Such Leeds voluntary societies are the subject of Morris, *Class, Sect and Party* (Manchester: Manchester University Press, 1990).
119. Book of Obituaries, 9 June 1908.
120. David W. Bebbington, 'The Evangelical Conscience: Hugh Price Hughes as Exemplar', *The Evangelical Quadrilateral: Vol. 2: The Denominational Mosaic of the British Gospel Movement* (Waco, TX: Baylor University Press, 2021), pp. 131–49.
121. D. Colin Dews, *Oxford Place Methodist Centre, 1835 to 1985* (Leeds: Oxford Place Methodist Centre, [1985]), p. 16.
122. *Leeds Wesleyan Mission: Oxford Place Chapel: Report, 1897*, p. 7.
123. *Leeds Wesleyan Mission: Oxford Place Chapel: Report, 1900*, p. 18.
124. Norman G. Dunning, *Samuel Chadwick* (London: Hodder and Stoughton, 1933).
125. *Leeds Wesleyan Mission: Oxford Place Chapel: Report, 1900*, p. 3.
126. See the above discussion of the Brunswick Sunday school at pp. 24–5.
127. John Elsworth, 'The Leeds Brunswick Circuit', *The Wesleyan Methodist Magazine* (1906), pp. 201–8 at p. 208.

CHAPTER TWO

Navigating Cultural Pluralism: Christian Responses to Radical Unbelief in Early Nineteenth-century Scotland

Felicity Loughlin

On the evening of 31 December 1869, Norman Macleod (1812–72), an influential minister of the Church of Scotland, picked up his journal and reflected on the dramatic social, intellectual and political transformations he had witnessed during his lifetime. 'In a few hours', he recorded, 'the century will have lived its threescore and ten years! I question if since time began, with the exception of three or four great eras . . . such an influential period has existed.'[1] Macleod's sense of bearing witness to an age of unprecedented social change was shared by his fellow clergymen across Scotland's churches. For many ministers and concerned lay Christians, the radical transformation of modern society raised urgent questions about its ramifications for the nation's spiritual and moral well-being. As the scholarship of Stewart J. Brown and Callum Brown has shown, a major concern was the apparent correlation between urbanisation, industrialisation and rising irreligion among the working classes.[2] Thomas Chalmers, Macleod's former teacher and one of the most influential Christian clergymen of the age, was particularly vocal in sounding the alarm. His ministry in Glasgow's deprived communities led him to rally his fellow Christians to remedy the 'mass of heathenism' in Scotland's large towns and cities through a wide-ranging programme of evangelisation.[3]

Chalmers's attempts to combat the perceived spiritual and moral decline of urban-industrial societies mainly focused on tackling religious indifference among the working classes. His activities therefore concentrated on reclaiming the 'still, sluggish, and stationary families' whose 'spiritual appetite is in a state of dormancy'.[4] Yet the first half of the nineteenth century also saw the emergence of new and alarming forms of radical unbelief among Scotland's working communities. From the 1820s, self-identifying 'freethinkers' or 'conscientious unbelievers' acquired unprecedented visibility and organisation in Scottish society, particularly though not exclusively in large towns and cities. Advocating scepticism, deism or atheism, they denied the divine inspiration of the scriptures and rejected Christian teachings and institutions, which they charged with perpetuating superstition, ignorance and social inequality. Unbelief of this kind attracted only a very small minority of Scotland's population, yet it deeply troubled many Christian observers and attracted a degree of attention that was vastly disproportionate to the small size of its supporters.

How did members of Scotland's churches explain the rise of radical unbelief among Scotland's middling and lower classes as a phenomenon of modern social change? How did they seek to remedy this perceived challenge to the nation's spiritual well-being? And how successful were their endeavours? By answering these questions, this chapter aims to expand our understanding of the challenges facing Scotland's churches in this period and to begin to reconstruct the process by which they navigated an increasingly pluralistic landscape of belief. In order to do so, it begins by introducing Scotland's radical freethinking communities.

The Challenge of Radical Freethought

The first organised communities of radical unbelievers emerged in Scotland amidst significant social and political unrest in the aftermath of the Napoleonic Wars.[5] Many were inspired by Richard Carlile, a revolutionary publisher in England, whose denunciations of kingcraft and priestcraft attracted sympathy across Britain after his imprisonment for blasphemy in 1819.[6] Like Carlile, Scottish freethinkers were attracted to the radical republicanism of the French revolutionaries, anti-Christian classics by French Enlightenment thinkers such as Voltaire and the Baron d'Holbach, and the writings of the deist Thomas Paine, whose influential *Age of Reason* (1793) launched a powerful attack on Christianity. By the 1820s, small numbers of freethinkers from Scottish towns and cities found a sense of community in the pages of British radical newspapers such as *The Republican* (1819–26).[7] This period also saw organised groups of radical unbelievers appear in Edinburgh (1820) and Glasgow (1824). Describing themselves as freethinking 'Zetetic' societies, they met weekly on Sundays to debate controversial theological and philosophical topics and they maintained a presence in Scottish society into the early 1840s. Gaining audiences of around three hundred at their peak, they particularly attracted male artisans, retailers, labourers and apprentices, though evidence suggests that some women and even children attended the Edinburgh Zetetic meetings in the early 1820s.[8]

Valuable glimpses into the beliefs and concerns of these radical communities are provided by their contributions to radical newspapers, their own published works and court records of blasphemy trials.[9] Theological opinions varied. Many leading freethinkers espoused a materialist atheism that denied all supernatural existences; others favoured deism, believing in a remote creator deity while denying the scriptures' God; while some remained sceptics and rejected the possibility of certain knowledge of a deity's existence and attributes. Freethinkers were united, however, in rejecting Christianity and in their conviction that all established beliefs needed to be supported by rational, empirical evidence. Many pointed to inconsistencies or immoral passages of the Bible, denied the soul's immortality and criticised harsher aspects of Calvinist theology such as double predestination and eternal punishment of the damned. They also shared a hostility towards the clergy, above all ministers of the established Church of Scotland, who were targeted for their perceived hypocrisy, social privilege and lack of Christian charity, humility and benevolence. Freethinkers were confident that the progress of science would overturn Christianity and they eagerly delved into geology, astronomy and early evolutionary theories. They hoped that rational enlightenment would eradicate the Christian establishment and its damaging social and political effects, including social inequality, ignorance and sectarianism.

As the late W. Hamish Fraser observed, freethinkers' concerns with advancing intellectual, material and social welfare and their hostility to religion fostered connections between the Zetetics and nascent socialist communities, which also began to gather momentum in Edinburgh and Glasgow from the early 1820s and attracted members of a similar social profile.[10] Attracted to the reformist ideas of the philanthropist Robert Owen, socialists aimed to replace individualistic capitalism with a new economic and moral system based on cooperation, community and universal charity.[11] Owen's vocal criticism of organised religion and fundamental Christian doctrines was attractive to radical freethinkers and many leading socialists were also prominent unbelievers. The connection between Owenite socialism and unbelief was heralded by the evangelical *Edinburgh Christian Instructor* throughout the 1820s; it declared in 1823 that socialist experiments aimed to promote a 'system of atheistical infidelity'.[12] Owen's denial of human responsibility was particularly controversial, based on his view that external social conditions exerted such a powerful influence on character formation that 'the will of man has no power whatever over his opinions'.[13] Such claims undermined the Christian emphasis on free will and thereby denied the rationale for divine judgement in the life to come. From the late 1830s, Owen's controversial writings on marriage also provoked alarm, particularly his assertion that married women became little more than serfs and his claim that the nuclear family was ill-suited to child-rearing.[14] Socialists were particularly active in Paisley and Glasgow, and they became increasingly organised from the mid-1830s, which saw the establishment of groups of the Owenite Rational Society across Britain.[15] By the early 1840s, socialist communities in Paisley and Glasgow, who shared the Zetetic Society's meeting hall in Nelson Street, were joined by new groups in Dundee, Edinburgh, Aberdeen, Arbroath and Kirkcaldy.

Although Scotland's freethinking and Owenite groups encountered intermittent repression from the civic authorities between the 1820s and 1840s, including periodic crackdowns on the circulation of their publications, they maintained a small but persistent presence in large Scottish towns and cities. Although the available evidence is limited as many unbelievers wished to maintain a low profile, we know that small groups of radical freethinkers also gathered in small towns such as Leven, and even in certain rural areas such as the farming village of Newmilns in Ayrshire.[16] Their strident criticisms of the Christian faith, clergy and institutions and their visions for radical social reform meant that despite their minority status they attracted a substantial response from the members of Scotland's churches, to which we now turn.

Explaining Popular Unbelief: Human Nature and Social Change

Numerous ministers and concerned members of the Church of Scotland drew attention to the unprecedented rise of radical popular unbelief in the nation's towns and cities. Several turned their attention to identifying the factors that had prompted its emergence. Their explanations frequently drew on the Calvinist theology that underpinned the majority of Scotland's Protestant communities, which stressed the fundamental weakness and depravity of fallen human nature. Such ideas strongly resonated with the formidable evangelical Andrew Thomson (1779–1831), minister of St George's parish in Edinburgh, who drew attention to the 'evil heart of unbelief' (Hebrews 3:12) in his popular *Sermons on Infidelity* (1821).[17] For Thomson, it was certain that 'by far the greatest number of unbelievers are so from the influence of Moral Depravity'.[18] Explanations of this kind were not restricted to the evangelical wing of the Church of Scotland. The weakness of fallen humanity was also stressed by John Inglis (1762–1834), a leading member of the Kirk's Moderate party. In an anti-deist apologetic published in 1830, Inglis argued that all human beings were prone to unbelief. As he explained, the corrupt human heart urges the mind to produce speculative arguments against Christ's divinity to fortify its rebellion against the Gospels' teachings.[19]

While these theological explanations remained influential, the 1820s and 1830s also saw the Church of Scotland pay increasing attention to the social and cultural conditions that fostered unbelief. In October 1836, an anonymous contributor to the *Church of Scotland Magazine* argued that an important factor in the apparent upsurge of 'vulgar infidelity' was the insufficient number of churches for the burgeoning population of large towns and cities.[20] A contemporary article in the *Church Review and Scottish Ecclesiastical Magazine* similarly argued that an inadequate supply of churches lay at the root of radical unbelief among the lower classes of Edinburgh.[21] These sociological explanations were not entirely disinterested. On the contrary, they took shape amidst heated debates with the dissenting churches, known as the 'Voluntaries', who were in the midst of a substantial campaign for the disestablishment of the Kirk. For defenders of the Church of Scotland, the rise of popular unbelief in areas with insufficient established churches proved the necessity of increasing the supply of state-funded religious provision and the error of disestablishment ideologies.[22] Such arguments diminished after 1843 with the Great Disruption of the Church of Scotland, when over a third of the established ministry left their positions and stipends to form the Free Church, in a principled protest against the perceived failure of existing church–state relations.

Throughout the period, other sociological explanations attracted greater consensus across the denominations. In particular, most agreed with the *Church of Scotland Magazine* that modern unbelief stemmed in large part from the 'near universal taste for reading' and the concomitant flourishing of cheap periodicals, newspapers and pamphlets.[23] This view even brought about a rare point of consensus between the Protestant and Catholic clergy. In 1845, William Wallace, a Catholic priest in the small Scottish Borders town of Innerleithen, emphasised the danger of freethinking publications, which were 'more read in parts of Scotland than the Bible'.[24] The civic authorities shared this view and the first half of the nineteenth century saw several radical booksellers in Edinburgh and Glasgow convicted for selling blasphemous pamphlets and newspapers.[25] The available evidence suggests that alarm over the circulation of cheap, radical literature among artisans and labourers extended in some instances to rural parishes. In 1839, for instance, Norman Macleod expressed his concern that there were 'infidel' parties among the weavers of his rural parish of Newmilns in Ayrshire where the works of Thomas Paine were read aloud.[26]

In addition to explicit anti-Christian newspapers and pamphlets, two categories of cheap publications were regarded as especially dangerous in fomenting unbelief among the people. Firstly, many were particularly troubled by cheap writings that advocated phrenology, a popular pseudo-science that claimed that the size and shape of the brain determined individual character traits and behaviour.[27] Developed in Germany by Johann Gaspar Spurzheim and Franz Josef Gall, it attracted widespread interest across Britain from the 1820s. Its leading advocate was the Edinburgh lawyer and deist George Combe, who established the Edinburgh Phrenological Society in 1820 and published a highly influential and controversial phrenological text-book, *The Constitution of Man* (1828).[28] Although phrenology did attract the support of some Christians, many felt that it struck a powerful blow at Christian orthodoxy, undermining belief in free will and the soul's immortality. The publication of cheap revised editions of the *Constitution of Man* in the mid-1830s consequently attracted widespread concern.[29] Secondly, numerous ministers across the denominations were anxious over the dissemination of socialist writings on moral, economic and political reform, including the British socialist newspaper *The New Moral World* (1834–45).

Finally, by the late 1830s some Christian observers increasingly explained the rise of popular unbelief as a result of the churches' perceived failure to provide adequate practical remedies for severe economic distress. In 1839, the lawyer and Methodist William Gillespie argued that 'extreme misery and wretchedness', particularly in manufacturing districts, had played an important role in paving the way for the popular interest in infidel socialism.[30] Many recognised that the socialists' radical vision of eradicating poverty and suffering through systematic economic reform allowed them to attract eager listeners. The *Glasgow Saturday Post* voiced such concerns in a review of Owen's lectures in the city's crowded Exchange Rooms in 1842, declaring that it was 'high time the ministers of all the different denominations were bestirring themselves and taking a more decided stand in defence of the suffering masses of the people'.[31] 'Would the people', the reporter enquired,

> if they were well provided for, and if when any Social evil required to be removed, their spiritual instructors were ever and at all times the first to step forward to do the work, be so ready to listen as they were on this occasion to the doctrines which were so openly propounded, and to the more than palpable insinuations of the non-existence of a supreme Being?

By 1847, many agreed with the view of Andrew Thomson (1814–1901), a former minister of the Church of Scotland who had recently joined the United Presbyterian Church, that the socialists' 'utopian' promises to provide a 'cure for all the ills of life' were highly significant in fostering popular unbelief.[32]

Remedying Unbelief

In addition to trying to explain the causes of popular unbelief, Scotland's churches developed numerous strategies to stem its spread and win unbelievers back to faith in Christ. The prime tactic was to answer the criticisms of radical freethinkers and defend Christianity through published pamphlets, treatises, religious periodicals and sermons. Andrew Thomson's *Sermons on Infidelity* (1821), for instance, offered guidance for Christians of various social groups, including 'those who fill the inferior stations of society'. Addressing the latter, he cautioned them to eschew those who would try to 'persuade you that Christianity is your foe' on the grounds that it keeps them in a supposed condition of 'depression and bondage'.[33] Such arguments, he asserted, were erroneous, for Christianity exalts the righteous, provides a moral guide necessary for 'worldly prosperity' and offers comfort in times of suffering. By contrast, John Inglis's *Vindication of Christian Faith* (1830) particularly addressed deists and sought to convert them to Christianity by engaging with their key objections to the veracity of the scriptures.[34] William Gillespie adopted a similarly targeted approach and contacted Zetetic communities in Edinburgh and Glasgow to alert them to his a priori demonstration of God's existence and attributes.[35] As Paul Baxter has shown, the 1830s and 1840s saw numerous ministers publish objections to radical claims that scientific developments had undermined fundamental Christian beliefs such as the creation of the world *ex nihilo*, divine providence and the nature of free will.[36] Most notably, phrenology was widely castigated as an erroneous science whose dangerous insinuations against orthodoxy must be vigorously opposed.[37] Numerous Scottish ministers were also swift to condemn the controversial *Vestiges of the Natural History of Creation* by the publisher Robert Chambers, printed anonymously in 1844, whose early evolutionary theories appeared to leave little room for God's role in creation.[38]

The churches also sought to reach out to unbelievers through personal encounters. This strategy included the domestic missions spearheaded by Thomas Chalmers, which divided large urban parishes into manageable districts and arranged 'aggressive' home visits by local agents. In 1832, for instance, the Edinburgh City Mission reported that they had met with at least eight 'professed infidels' in their visits through its wynds and closes.[39] The available evidence suggests that on some occasions these encounters served to deepen existing frictions rather than to promote valuable dialogue. This was certainly the experience of Thomas Finlay, a cabinet maker and member of the Edinburgh Zetetic Society who was prosecuted for circulating blasphemous books in 1844. At his trial, he described his frustration at the Home Missionary Society's 'many intrusive visits' to his family, in which he 'allowed them every facility, while they represented infidels and their opinions as anything but desirable'.[40] Other forms of outreach were more successful. In 1842, for example, Norman Macleod described how he was able to make headway with the freethinking weavers of Newmilns by offering them a series of lectures on geology. As he explained, the success of the lectures allowed him to dissuade them from viewing the established clergy as hostile to the intellectual improvement of the people and encouraged some of them to attend church.[41] Many preferred more combative tactics. In particular, from the late 1830s, numerous ministers and concerned Christians sought to engage socialists in public debates on religious topics.[42] In most cases, both sides tended to congratulate themselves on gaining the upper hand. Yet the Free Church did achieve at least one legitimate success in Aberdeen in 1847 following weeks of debate with local freethinkers. Organised by George Ogilvie, minister of Maryculter in Kincardineshire and William Martin, Professor of Moral Philosophy at Marischal College, the discussions prompted the conversion of a deist named David Wright, who had originally notified the radical press of the event.[43]

While events such as these tended to be arranged by individual ministers or lay believers, the 1840s also saw a burgeoning interest in developing more systematic efforts to combat popular unbelief. This approach was defended by an anonymous convert to Christianity from deism, who recounted his experiences in a striking contribution to the *Scottish Christian Herald* in December 1840.[44] An artisan who had lived in Aberdeen and Dundee, he revealed that he had lost his faith at the age of eighteen after his 'fellow-workmen in the shop' introduced him to the writings of Thomas Paine. He described how he remained a deist for twenty years until a concerned friend prompted him to read Joseph Butler's *Analogy of Natural and Revealed Religion* (1736), which in turn prompted him to read other apologetic works.[45] His experience led him to advise his fellow Christians to form a large society, 'whose object would be to print short and condensed views of the evidences of Christianity, to be distributed by the hand of one whose duty would be to seek out the unbeliever'.[46] Indicative perhaps of his own experience of hostile anti-infidel activities, he stressed that it was essential to adopt a gentle and temperate approach in encounters with unbelievers. 'Above all', he urged, 'whatever is done to insure [*sic*] success must be done mildly – scolding and hard words may alarm, more likely will irritate, but never can convince.'[47]

The deist convert was perhaps unaware that a small association, 'The Philalethean Society for Peaceably Repressing Infidelity', had already been formed by the lawyers William Gillespie and William Muir, a member of the Society of Solicitors of the Supreme Court for Scotland. Initially established in Edinburgh in 1839, it had expanded to a Glasgow office by 1841.[48] Despite the Society's chosen title, however, the Philalethean Society did not adopt an irenic or temperate approach. Setting its sights on 'socialist atheism', it issued a series of strident anti-infidel publications, including *Robert Owen in his True Colours* and *The Socialists: A Society of Beasts*, and concentrated more on exposing the folly of unbelief than demonstrating the truth of Christianity.[49] The combative tone of the Philalethean Society was mirrored in Gillespie's own dealings with freethinkers, whose 'fierce' and 'haughty' approach had been criticised by George Simpson, a member of the Glasgow Zetetic Society, in 1838. As Simpson declared, it seemed likely that Gillespie, 'in his zeal of God, does not conceive any great civility to be due to those who do not subscribe to his own creed'.[50] Such tactics do not appear to have attracted widespread support from the Scottish public as the society appears to have disbanded after 1844.[51]

Nevertheless, many Scottish Christians remained in favour of a systematic, collective approach to the problem of popular unbelief. In 1845, just two years after the seismic split of the established church, a multi-denominational society was established to unite Protestant efforts against the two great 'errors' of the age: Catholicism and unbelief. At its first public meeting, held in a hotel on Edinburgh's Princes Street in 1847, the 'Scottish Association for Opposing Prevalent Errors' drew a substantial number of supporters from the capital and beyond, including Paisley, Helensburgh, Dunfermline and Dundee.[52] Ministers and members of the Free Church and United Presbyterian Church were particularly well represented, and it also attracted a handful of representatives from the Church of Scotland and smaller communities such as the Congregationalists. It attracted lay believers as well as clergy, including James Douglas of Cavers, a laird from the Scottish borders, Sheriff officers and many of the great and good of Edinburgh, including the printer Thomas Constable, the artist George Harvey, the lawyer Allan Menzies and the physician and philanthropist William Beilby. In a circular of 1848, the Association cited the rise of radical unbelief among the 'handicraft multitudes' in large towns and manufacturing districts as a prime focus for its activities and issued a direct appeal for further support:

> Shall no attempt be made ... to watch the forms which scepticism assumes, and supply the antidote which is needed? In addition to the Ragged school, which throws its fostering care around the neglected *children* of our large towns, with a view to train them in the knowledge of divine truth and in the practice of virtuous habits, – should there not be an institution whose enterprise shall be to reclaim *young men* and *parents* who have become the dupes of a God-defying and Bible dishonouring creed?[53]

The complexity of the challenge, it stressed, demanded a concentrated and united Christian effort, which must be 'associated and catholic rather than denominational'.[54] In particular, it recommended tackling unbelief by issuing apologetic tracts and organising public lectures on the evidences of Christianity.[55] Its most notable publication was *Nature and Revelation Harmonious* (1846) by Charles J. Kennedy, a Congregationalist minister in Paisley, which adopted a strikingly moderate tone. Rather than denying the legitimacy of phrenology as a science, Kennedy focused on demonstrating that those theories which conflicted with Christian orthodoxy could not be supported by the available phrenological data. Although Combe, Britain's leading phrenologist, disagreed with much within Kennedy's pamphlet, he expressed his approval that Kennedy had eschewed 'vulgar vituperation and damnation' in his attempt to grapple with unbelief.[56] Ultimately, the Association hoped to establish a network of Christian agents who would reach out to unbelievers in all large Scottish towns. These missionaries would be 'men of intelligence and established Christian character' and 'well acquainted with the arguments for and against the Christian religion'.[57] They were to converse with 'working men whom they find to be sceptical in their views' and would visit the homes of the working classes, passing on 'a wholesome and general literature, as well as works intended to explain and defend the truths of Christianity'. Its ambitions were not restricted to Scotland and the society hoped it would develop affiliated branches in England and overseas.[58] This ambition was not to be realised and the association disappeared from view after 1849.

The decline of anti-infidel societies did not, however, signal a decline in the perceived necessity of combatting unbelief. On the contrary, the Free Church in particular adopted a particularly vehement stance over the presence of unbelief in Scottish society. Their commitment to tackling its arguments was enshrined in the lectures delivered to future ministers at the Free Church College established in 1843. Strikingly, its first two professors of Apologetic Theology chose to deliver their inaugural lectures on the problem of unbelief. The first incumbent, James Buchanan

(1804–70), urged his students of the urgent need to tackle the modern 'dissatisfaction with existing beliefs, which . . . reveals itself too clearly both in our philosophy speculations and our popular literature'.[59] His lectures concentrated on analysing the key types of unbelief, including phrenology, which had exerted a notable influence among 'the reading class of artisans and tradesmen', and on equipping his students with suitable apologetic defences of Christianity.[60] A similar approach was followed from 1849, when the Chair passed to James Bannerman (1807–68). Consciously adopting the rhetoric of warfare, Bannerman aimed to inspire young divinity students with the desire to do their bit to combat unbelief. He urged them to serve as 'watchmen' over the walls of the Church of Christ, to 'descry the form of the enemy through the gloom', and to be willing to 'mingle in the strife of the streets' by participating in the 'arena of controversy'.[61] For Bannerman, a holistic education was crucial in the task ahead, allowing ministers to mobilise science, philosophy, learning and solid argument against any unbelievers' critiques.

Finally, by mid-century some began to argue that the churches could not successfully combat popular unbelief through argument alone. Instead, they needed to take more active and robust steps to remedy the social suffering of urban-industrial communities. Thinking of this kind drew inspiration from Thomas Chalmers's post-Disruption efforts to foster cross-denominational social engagement. In particular, Chalmers's work in the deprived West Port of Edinburgh had emphasised the need to pay attention to the material as well as spiritual wants of those alienated from religion in Scotland's towns and cities.[62] In 1849, for instance, Andrew Thomson, a founding member of the Scottish Association for Opposing Prevalent Errors, addressed a meeting of the newly established Evangelical Alliance. In a lecture on the problem of popular unbelief, he urged his listeners to take a 'more lively interest in the temporal welfare of the people' if they wished to remedy radical freethought among the working classes.[63] A particularly ardent voice in the push to meet unbelief with more active social engagement was that of Norman Macleod. Speaking at a public meeting in Glasgow in 1852, he spoke against the 'common idea . . . that the whole function of the Church is to teach and preach the gospel; while it is left to other organizations, infidel ones they may be, to meet all the other varied wants of our suffering people'.[64] On the contrary, it was crucial that the churches meet the practical as well as spiritual needs of society. 'Let congregations', he urged, 'take cognizance of the whole man and his various earthly relationships . . . let them endeavour to meet all his wants as an active, social, intellectual, sentient, as well as spiritual being . . . I see no way of meeting Socialism but this.'[65]

Conclusion

The churches' response to the unprecedented visibility of radical freethought among the Scottish people was not monolithic, and despite the concerted activities of numerous individuals, attempts to rouse cross-denominational action ultimately fizzled out. Yet we have seen that many individual ministers and lay believers were deeply troubled by this new minority culture and felt compelled to explain its origins and to take remedial action. Although many continued to point to human depravity as a root cause of unbelief, the first half of the nineteenth century also saw Scottish Christians display increasing interest in identifying the wider social, cultural and intellectual factors that fuelled radical freethought. This was a small but significant shift that may have contributed to a long-term alteration in some Christian perceptions of freethinkers. This was certainly apparent in Macleod's New Year reflections on the cusp of 1870, which declared that it was increasingly apparent to him that 'no one but God can decide as to any man's character'. Indeed, he argued, 'many a so-called "infidel" is nearer the kingdom of God than many an "orthodox" minister'.[66]

This shift towards the broader causal factors underpinning popular unbelief also shaped the remedies proposed by concerned members of Scotland's churches. To combat the perceived influence of the popular press, many mobilised the power of print and public debate. They sought to respond directly to the criticisms and arguments of freethinkers, reviving Christian apologetics and mobilising new scientific discoveries. Here too there were small signs of an awareness that the spirit of hostile controversy was seldom successful, including the willingness to listen on occasion to converts to Christianity and attempts to adopt more moderate styles of debate. As the *Church Review* declared in an article opposing phrenology in 1836, 'intemperate abuse' tended only to strengthen freethinkers' objections to 'priestcraft' and the 'odium theologicum'.[67] Such approaches drastically contrasted with the more militaristic rhetoric deployed in the lecture halls of the Free Church, whose sense of embattled defensiveness is unlikely to have fostered cross-cultural dialogue. While individual approaches to debating with freethinkers continued to vary, the mid-century also saw new developments, as individuals began to stress that the churches could achieve more with unbelievers through active social engagement than through argument. The first half of the nineteenth century thus constituted a significant transitional era for Scotland's churches, in which differing approaches were developed for navigating an increasingly pluralistic cultural and intellectual landscape. These competing strategies for countering the modern phenomenon of popular unbelief not only conditioned the varying relations between freethinkers and Christians in Scotland's towns, cities and villages, they also served to underline the differences that separated different varieties of Scottish Christians.[68]

Notes

This chapter was supported by research funding from a Leverhulme Early Career Fellowship.

1. D. Macleod (ed.), *Memoir of Norman Macleod* (New York, 1877), 2 vols, ii, p. 314.
2. S. J. Brown, *Thomas Chalmers and the Godly Commonwealth in Scotland* (Oxford: Oxford University Press, 1982), pp. 91–151, C. G. Brown, *Religion and Society in Scotland since 1707* (Edinburgh: Edinburgh University Press, 1997), pp. 95–123.
3. T. Chalmers, *The Christian and Civic Economy of Large Towns*, 3 vols (Glasgow, 1821), i, p. 24. The classic study of Chalmers's life and works remains Stewart Brown's seminal biography, *Chalmers and the Godly Commonwealth*.
4. Chalmers, *Christian and Civic Economy*, i, p. 24 and p. 90.
5. Research on popular unbelief in nineteenth-century Scotland has received recent attention. See especially the pioneering study by Gordon Pentland, 'The Freethinkers' Zetetic Society: An Edinburgh Radical Underworld in the 1820s', *Historical Research*, 91 (2018), pp. 314–32. See also F. Loughlin, 'Scotland's Last Blasphemy Trials: Popular Unbelief and its Opponents, 1819–1844', *English Historical Review*, 137 (2022), pp. 794–822 and F. Loughlin, 'Scotland's Freethinking Societies: Debating Natural Theology, 1820–c.1843', in A. Fyfe and C. Kidd (eds), *Beyond the Enlightenment: Currents and Controversies in Scottish Intellectual Life, 1790–1914* (Edinburgh: Edinburgh University Press, 2023), pp. 89–106.
6. On British freethought, see E. Royle, *Victorian Infidels: The Origins of the British Secularist Movement, 1791–1866* (Manchester: Manchester University Press, 1974) and I. McCalman, 'Popular Radicalism and Freethought in Early Nineteenth Century England: A Study of Richard Carlile and his Followers, 1815–32' (Ph.D. thesis, Australian National University, 1975).
7. Correspondents to *The Republican* included individuals from Edinburgh, Glasgow, Paisley, Kirkcaldy, Falkirk, Dundee and Aberdeen.
8. Pentland, 'The Freethinkers' Zetetic Society', p. 322.
9. For a flavour of Scottish freethought, see, for example, *A Preliminary Address from the President of the Edinburgh Free-Thinkers' Zetetic Society to the Moderator of the Church of Scotland* (Edinburgh, 1823) and *Essay on the Question, Does our Experience in the Present World Warrant us to Expect a Future State of Conscious Existence: delivered in the Zetetic Hall, Nelson Street, by a Glasgow Operative* (Edinburgh, 1842).
10. W. H. Fraser, 'Owenite Socialism in Scotland', *Scottish Economic and Social History*, 16 (1996), pp. 60–91.
11. The fullest discussion remains J. F. C. Harrison, *Robert Owen and the Owenites in Britain and America: The Quest for the New Moral World* (London: Routledge and K. Paul, 1969).
12. Anon., 'The Presbytery of New Lanark – New Lanark Schools', *Edinburgh Christian Instructor* (October 1823), pp. 694–726.
13. R. Owen, *A New View of Society: Or, Essays on the Formation of the Human Character*, 3rd edn (London, 1817), pp. 107–8.
14. See especially R. Owen, *Lectures on the Marriages of the Priesthood of the Old Immoral World delivered in the year 1835, Before the Passing of the New Marriage Act* (Leeds, 1840).
15. Established in 1835 as the Association of All Classes of All Nations, the socialist group was renamed the Universal Community Society of Rational Religionists

in 1839, and became the Rational Society from 1842 until its dissolution in 1845.
16. See also the comments of a deist convert to Christianity who declared that unbelief was not only an issue for large towns and cities because 'villages and hamlets have individual unbelievers too', 'Narrative of Conversion', *Scottish Christian Herald* (19 December 1840), p. 815.
17. Originally published in 1821, a third edition of the *Sermons on Infidelity* was printed in New York in 1833.
18. A. Thomson, *Sermons on Infidelity*, 2nd edn (Edinburgh, 1824), pp. 1, 49–51.
19. J. Inglis, *A Vindication of Christian Faith: Addressed to those who, believing in God, yet refuse or hesitate to believe in Jesus Christ, whom he hath sent* (Edinburgh, 1830), p. vi.
20. Anon., 'Review: The Unscriptural Principles of Combe's Constitution of Man, by William Scott, Esq.', *Church of Scotland Magazine* (October 1836), p. 367.
21. 'Necessity of Church Extension in Edinburgh', *Church Review and Scottish Ecclesiastical Magazine* (October 1836), p. 422.
22. 'Voluntary Church Principles both of a Revolutionary and Infidel Nature' (October 1834), *Church of Scotland Magazine*, pp. 304–8; 'The Spirit of Voluntaryism – A New Argument for the Connection Between Church and State', *Church Review and Scottish Ecclesiastical Magazine* (February 1838), p. 823.
23. Anon., 'Unscriptural Principles', *Church of Scotland Magazine* (October 1836), p. 367.
24. W. Wallace, *The Owl and the Bats: Or, The Infidel and His Disciples* (Edinburgh, 1846).
25. On which, see Loughlin, 'Scotland's Last Blasphemy Trials', pp. 794–822.
26. Macleod, *Memoir of Norman Macleod*, p. 132.
27. On phrenology and popular radicalism, see especially R. Cooter, *The Cultural Meaning of Popular Science: Phrenology and the Organization of Consent in Nineteenth-Century Britain* (Cambridge: Cambridge University Press, 1984), pp. 201–23.
28. G. Combe, *The Constitution of Man: Considered in Relation to External Objects* (Edinburgh, 1828).
29. Concerned reviews of new editions appeared in *United Secession Magazine* (December 1835), pp. 566–70, the *Church Review and Ecclesiastical Magazine* (October 1836), pp. 385–97 and the *Church of Scotland Magazine* (October 1836), p. 368.
30. W. Gillespie, *An Examination of Anthitheos' Refutation of the Argument A Priori for the Being and Attributes of God* (Edinburgh and London, 1840), appended advert for the Philalethean Society, n.p. Glasgow University Library, Mu43-e.26.
31. Quoted in 'Paisley', *The New Moral World*, 26 Nov. 1842, p. 179.
32. A. Thomson in *Report of the Proceedings of the First Public Meeting of the Scottish Association for Opposing Prevalent Errors* (Edinburgh, 1847), p. 11.
33. Thomson, *Sermons on Infidelity*, pp. 272–3.
34. Inglis, *Vindication* (1830), pp. x–xiii.
35. Gillespie, *Examination*, pp. 11–12.
36. P. Baxter, 'Science and Belief in Scotland, 1805–1868: The Scottish Evangelicals' (PhD thesis, University of Edinburgh, 1985), pp. 158–317.
37. For a flavour of these arguments, see 'Phrenology and the Church', *Church Review and Scottish Ecclesiastical Magazine* (October 1836), p. 385. More unusually, individual Christian commentators sought to demonstrate the harmony

of phrenology and the scriptures, including the anonymous piece, *The Clergy Vindicated from the Charge of Hostility to the Diffusion of Science* (Edinburgh, 1836).
38. J. Secord, *Victorian Sensation: The Extraordinary Publication, Reception, and Secret Authorship of Vestiges of the Natural History of Creation* (Chicago: University of Chicago Press, 1994), pp. 261–90.
39. 'Necessity of Church Extension in Edinburgh', *Church Review and Scottish Ecclesiastical Magazine* (October 1836), pp. 422–4.
40. *The Trial of Thomas Paterson for Blasphemy before the High Court of Justiciary, Edinburgh, with the Whole of his Bold and Effective Defence. Also, the Trials of Thomas Finlay and Miss Matilda Roalfe* (London, 1844), pp. 64–5.
41. Macleod, *Memoir*, i, p. 167.
42. These meetings were frequently recorded. See *Report of the Discussion betwixt Mr. Troup . . . and Mr. L. Jones, . . . on the Propositions, I. That Socialism is Atheistical; and II. That Atheism is Incredible and Absurd* (Dundee, 1839). On the debates between the socialist Robert Cooper and divinity student John Macfarlane in Edinburgh in 1843, and socialist Henry Jeffrey and James Walker of the Free Church in Galashiels in 1845, see 'Glasgow, Jan. 16', *New Moral World* (28 January 1843), p. 251 and 'Galashiels, Feb. 10th', *New Moral World* (22 February 1845), p. 279.
43. See, 'Progress in Aberdeen', *The Reasoner* (24 February 1847), pp. 93–4, 'A Glance at the Recent Discussion in Aberdeen', *The Reasoner* (23 June 1847), p. 338–41, and 'Discussion in Aberdeen', pp. 618–23, *The Reasoner* (10 November 1847). A notice on Wright's conversion was listed in *The Reasoner* (7 April 1847), p. 37.
44. Anon., 'Narrative of the Conversion of an Unbeliever', *Scottish Christian Herald* (19 December 1840), pp. 814–16.
45. These included Charles Leslie's *Short and Easy Method with the Deists* (1697) and William Paley's *View of the Evidences of Christianity* (1794).
46. Anon, 'Narrative of Conversion', *Scottish Christian Herald*, p. 816.
47. Ibid., p. 816.
48. W. Gillespie (ed.), *The Philalethean Magazine and Gazette of the Society for Peaceably Repressing Infidelity* (Edinburgh, 1841), i, no. II, p. 60.
49. Ibid., i, no. II, p. 60; see appended 'Philalethean Magazine Advertiser', n.p.
50. Anon. [G. Simpson], *Refutation of the Argument A Priori for the Being and Attributes of God; Showing the Irrelevancy of that Argument, as well as the Fallacious Reasoning of Dr. Samuel Clarke and Others, Especially of Mr Gillespie, in Support of it* (Glasgow, 1838), p. iii.
51. A letter to a socialist newspaper claimed that the Society primarily comprised Protestant dissenters such as the Burgher Secession Church: 'Edinburgh – Signs of the Times', *The New Moral World* (27 July 1839), p. 634.
52. *Report of the Proceedings of the First Public Meeting of the Scottish Association for Opposing Prevalent Errors* (Edinburgh, 1847), p. 2.
53. *Scottish Association for Opposing Prevalent Errors* (Edinburgh, 1848), *National Library of Scotland*, Papers of George Combe (1788–1858), Combe.30(48), pp. 1–2.
54. Ibid., p. 2.
55. This included anti-socialist literature, such as *Socialism – What is its Tendency? No. II* (Edinburgh, 1847).

56. G. Combe, *Answer by G. Combe to the Attack on CM contained in 'Nature and Revelation Harmonious'* (Edinburgh, 1848), p. 4.
57. Ibid., pp. 2–3.
58. Ibid., p. 3.
59. J. Buchanan, *Faith in God and Modern Atheism Compared, in their Essential Nature, Theoretic Grounds, and Practical Influence* (Edinburgh, 1855), 2 vols, i, pp. vii–viii.
60. Ibid., ii, 264.
61. J. Bannerman, *The Prevalent Forms of Unbelief* (Edinburgh, 1849), pp. 25–6.
62. S. J. Brown, 'The Disruption and Urban Poverty: Thomas Chalmers and the West Port Operation in Edinburgh, 1844–47', *Scottish Church History*, 20 (1978), pp. 65–89. On Chalmers's wider influence, see S. J. Brown, 'The Christian Socialist Movement in Scotland, c.1850–1930', *Political Theology*, 1 (1999), pp. 59–84.
63. 'Infidelity among the Working Classes', *Free Church Magazine*, 6 (1849), p. 158.
64. Macleod, *Memoir*, ii, p. 7.
65. Ibid., ii, p. 8.
66. Ibid., ii, p. 315.
67. 'Phrenology and the Church', *Church Review and Scottish Ecclesiastical Magazine* (October 1836), p. 385.
68. I would like to take this opportunity to express my personal gratitude to my former teacher and doctoral supervisor, Jay Brown, whose scholarship, teaching and support has been a constant source of inspiration.

CHAPTER THREE

Wrestling with Dilemmas: Presbyterian Evangelism and Slavery in the American Ante-bellum South

Iain Whyte

The Legacy of the Scottish Reformation

The Scottish Reformation and its aftermath have often been parodied as the introduction into national life of a severe and austere Calvinism, one imposed by the Settlement of 1690, which guaranteed the permanent supremacy of Presbyterianism in national religious life.[1] Often other aspects have been ignored. The framework of a 'Godly Commonwealth', as attempted in Geneva by John Calvin, was the vision of prominent churchmen even in the nineteenth century. Moreover, so too was the passion for universal education from the earliest days, which made a significant mark on the nation in the centuries that followed.[2]

Scottish emigration in the centuries following the Settlement, mainly as a result of post-Union economic conditions or enforced removal from the land, saw numerous Scots settlements in the new world of America. With them they brought their culture, and not least their religious values, in which education and evangelism were deeply ingrained. This chapter will explore that theme, and its development for some of those of Presbyterian heritage in that nation. Although the United States achieved its freedom from the United Kingdom in the revolutionary war of 1775–83, many of its white citizens continued to hold millions of its black residents in permanent bondage.

The ecclesiastical compromises made by Presbyterians, in the cause of holding the church together in the face of slavery, are explored, alongside the efforts of three Southern church leaders to mitigate its effects. So too are the all too often ignored perceptions of enslaved people themselves, and the ways in which those in bondage used the tools of the Christian faith to further their liberation. Many scholars are convinced that this attempt to 'sanitise' enslavement was always a fruitless attempt to resolve the dilemma within the status quo, and that the inevitable Civil War was the only way to bring it to an end.[3]

The Curious Dilemma of the 'Peculiar Institution'

From the early days of the independent United States the proclamation of freedom and the rights of all men (less of women) sat uneasily alongside the entrenched enslavement of black people, whose families had been brought by force to the new nation.[4] Nowhere was this more evident than in what has been described as 'the boundaries of idealism', reflected in the practices of two Virginians who held office as the first and third presidents.[5]

George Washington and Thomas Jefferson both had strong words of condemnation of slavery at different times. In 1786 Washington wrote about his wish to see a plan adopted by the legislature by which 'slavery in this country' might be abolished 'by slow, sure and imperceptible degrees', and Jefferson spoke of the 'commerce' between master and slave as 'unremitting despotism on the one part and degrading submissions on the other'.[6] Yet both, when in office, failed to support proposals to effect emancipation, or even to limit the spread of slavery. It was a silence of pragmatism. They remained dependent for their wealth on hundreds of enslaved men and woman, although Washington in his will made conditional provision for a full emancipation of those 'owned' by him.[7]

The attitudes towards slavery were far from homogeneous throughout the eighteenth and nineteenth centuries, or uniform within the South's borders. An extensive study on the dilemmas over slavery and its continuance, indicated a distinction between the mood in the more northerly slave states, such as Virginia, Maryland and Delaware, and those in the lower South, such as Georgia, the Carolinas, Alabama and Mississippi.[8] Many whites in the upper states by the late eighteenth century saw slavery as a troublesome legacy from their economic past, as the importance of tobacco had diminished and the economy became less dependent on enslaved labour. A mixture of guilt at this obvious violation of republican ideals, fuelled by the spread of evangelical Christianity, and a genuine fear for white safety, led to ambivalence and discomfort over slavery.[9] By contrast, the lower South's dependence on cotton, which had expanded the numbers of the enslaved to 40 per cent of the population, meant that there was a tighter and more uncritical adherence to slavery in the thinking of whites.[10] This division was reflected in individual Presbyterian churchmen, as it was in the struggle of the Presbyterian Church in the United States to grapple with the dilemma.

Presbyterian Vacillation

In the early nineteenth century, the still united Presbyterian Church in the United States took a robust position on slavery. The church's General Assembly had wrestled with the question in its annual meetings between 1787 and 1795, opposing the practice of slavery while acknowledging that opinions within the church differed on the subject, and emphasising the importance of church unity.[11] The most comprehensive statement against slavery was made in 1818, and Southern churchmen were part of that gathering. The Assembly declared slavery to be 'utterly inconsistent with the law of God, and irreconcilable with the gospel of Christ'. It urged all Christians 'as speedily as possible, to obtain the complete abolition of slavery throughout Christendom, and if possible throughout the world', and it condemned any delay in 'extinguish[ing] the evil'.[12]

Most Southern ministers expressed unease about this, but the fact that there was no split in the church at that time between the Liberal (New School) party and the more Conservative and Calvinist (Old School) party masked increasingly conflicting attitudes to slavery.[13] The following year, the deliverances were watered down, with caution being urged over the speed towards emancipation, and it was fast becoming impossible for any who supported abolition, to have their ministry accepted in the South. The most robust position on slavery in the Calvinist family, came from one of the smallest denominations, the Reformed Presbyterian Church, whose roots were in seventeenth-century Covenanting immigrants from Scotland fleeing persecution.[14] In 1801 they deposed a minister for selling an enslaved man, and many of their members were active in the famed Underground Railroad, helping enslaved people on their way North and to Canada.[15]

Paternalism and its Obstacles

One compromise in the dilemma that was attractive to many in the South, not least to churchmen, was known in the early nineteenth century as 'paternalism', whose aim was to keep the existing order of bonded labour intact whilst 'humanising' it, offering salvation to enslaved people through evangelism, and providing opportunities for worship in their own tradition, but under white supervision.[16] Paternalism had four key elements. Whilst acknowledging their supposed 'inferiority' and 'limited potential', it recognised that enslaved people must be treated as human beings and not as beasts or objects. Secondly, the organising of an enslaved population should be modelled on the way in which male heads of families governed their own households – fair but firm, with a balance of affection and discipline. This, it was claimed, would lead to a more efficient labour force, and help to subdue any unrest. Thirdly, stewardship should be required from the master. Central to this was the obligation of Christian teaching and encouragement in the faith. And finally, beyond these responsibilities lay obligations for whites to work for a society that embraced these ideals and to influence neighbours to act accordingly.[17]

In his survey of the world of the enslaved, Eugene Genovese analysed it as representing 'an attempt to overcome the contradiction in slavery: the impossibility of the slave ever becoming the things they were supposed to be'. Paternalism for him defined 'the involuntary labour of the slaves as a legitimate return to their masters for protection and direction'.[18]

A number of white Southerners saw even this controlled paternalism as the thin end of an abolitionist wedge, and, judging by slave reminiscences, humanity on the plantations was frequently in short supply. So often when some of the most grotesque punishments were inflicted on those who were enslaved, later accounts indicated that these were inflicted by those who held a strong allegiance to religion and that they were accompanied by references to the Bible. Rev. James Pennington, who was once enslaved and later became a distinguished Presbyterian minister, recalled how his pious Episcopalian 'master' had brutally flogged an elderly man while the latter was praying.[19]

Two events in the early part of the century led to a strong reaction against any attempt to mitigate slavery. In July 1822 on Bastille Day, when the outbreak of the French Revolution was commemorated, the authorities in Charleston supposedly uncovered what would have been one of the largest rebellions in the United States. It was claimed that Denmark Vesey, a formerly enslaved man who had purchased his freedom, had called on enslaved and free blacks to kill their white oppressors and take control of the city. Vesey had been admitted to communion at Second Presbyterian Church in April 1817, but shortly afterwards he co-founded the African Methodist Episcopal Church in Charleston, where he held night classes and preached resistance to slavery.[20] He proclaimed that white ministers were fraudulent, and that they made 'a catechism different for the negroes' in whom 'much was hidden'.[21] His extensive study of the Old Testament led him to overturn the slaveowner's justification of slavery, and to use figures such as Joshua and Jeremiah as warrants for its violent destruction.[22]

Some historians believe that there is no concrete evidence of a plot, and the ruthless repression which followed, with sixty-seven men convicted and thirty-five hanged, including Vesey, simply underlined the growing fear of violent threats to slavery in the deep South.[23] That event and the uprising in Virginia nine years later, led by the enslaved Nat Turner, another Christian visionary, the authenticity of whose 'Confessions' have been similarly challenged, had a large bearing on the suspicion and public hostility that was then growing in response to the concerns of leading Presbyterian ministers to promote evangelism for enslaved and free blacks in their communities.[24] The continued refusal of Southern states to give legal sanction to marriages in enslavement, and the strict prohibition on literacy, were two major obstacles that three key Presbyterian pioneers of religious education in the lower South encountered in their work.

The Slaveowning Missionary

Charles Colcock Jones was a unique example of a plantation owner, missionary, preacher, scholar and teacher. Jones was born on the ironically named Liberty Hall plantation, and trained for the Presbyterian ministry in Andover Theological Seminary in Massachusetts and in Princeton Theological Seminary, New Jersey. Whilst there he agonised over the evils of slavery, but decided to return to the South, serving as minister of the First Presbyterian Church in Savannah, Georgia. At the same time he became master of three plantations through gifts from two uncles, and from his marriage in 1830. He reluctantly learned to accept slavery, and rationalised it by a decision to undertake itinerant missionary work amongst enslaved people on his plantations and beyond, alongside a campaign to persuade the Presbyterian Church in Georgia and South Carolina to extend this kind of evangelism.[25]

In 1831 Jones gathered together fellow planters in Liberty County, Georgia and persuaded some of them to join his Association for the Religious Instruction of Negroes. In the sermon addressed to them, he argued that far from such instruction leading to rebellion, it would in fact have the opposite result. 'We believe the duty of obedience will never be felt or performed to the extent that we desire it, unless we can bottom it on religious principle.'[26] For the seventeen years that the association existed, Jones worked for evangelism throughout the county, until he accepted a chair in 1848 at the new Presbyterian Columbia Theological Seminary in Georgia.[27]

In the autumn of 1831 Jones made a proposal to the local synod just two months after the Nat Turner rebellion. He questioned why the majority of white citizens who believed that slavery was sanctioned by the Bible, feared having 'the Bible, the whole Bible, and nothing but the Bible' being preached to their servants. He took it further. If, he argued, 'emancipation might come through the preaching of the Gospel', it would come peacefully and gently and 'thus may the Glory of the removal of an evil be laid at the foot of the cross'.[28] Although terming slavery an 'evil' hardly commended him to his fellow slaveowners, Jones had broken the ground on a wider front and his own missionary work enabled him to claim some victories by example. But always the plantation, with its strict discipline, and where the hunting down of any attempting to escape was a common policy at that time, provided a great contrast to the ideals of evangelising paternalism.

The document which best encapsulated Jones's philosophy was his *Catechism*, a collection of hymns, prayers, commandments and a table of questions and answers on the duties of husbands and wives, parents and children, and masters and servants.[29] The *Catechism* points to a clear Christian responsibility for the 'religious instruction of negroes'. Bending to contemporary prejudices, Jones wrote, 'their spiritual ignorance and their depravity are amazingly and awfully great. They cry out for instruction to the wise and good, in all the length and breadth of the land.'[30] In line with state law, the *Catechism* commended oral and not written instruction. Yet he recognised that this required far more than a few simple texts committed to memory. 'On the contrary', he wrote, 'we should aim to carry the people of our care through a regular and plain system of Scripture doctrine and practice, and thus put them in full possession of the plan of salvation.'[31]

Jones then addressed the 'duties of masters'. He quoted scripture against abuse, cruel punishment and overworking of servants, and laid the responsibility on masters to provide 'comfortable houses, comfortable clothing, wholesome and abundant food', laying himself open to investigation over whether Montevideo, Maybank and Arcadia, his own plantations, provided all of these things. Jones made it clear that the master was bound to 'instruct servants in a knowledge of the Holy Scriptures and to encourage them to seek their soul's salvation', and he reminded them that they would be shown no more favour by God than those who serve them, just because of their earthly position.[32]

The duties prescribed for the enslaved included, not surprisingly, a call to patient submission and, if necessary, patient suffering, in the hope of a later reward from God. St Paul's injunction 'slaves obey your masters' is featured strongly in the *Catechism* and they were urged to try to please even difficult and harsh masters. In a convenient passage for slaveowners, Jones strongly condemned lying, deception and stealing, some of the very tools of survival for many on the plantations.[33]

Charles Colcock Jones exemplified many Presbyterian values both in his farming and missionary work. He saw the running of the plantation as a Godly enterprise of good order and discipline. Angered by the excesses of many slaveowners, he nonetheless maintained strict discipline amongst enslaved people on his estates, and did not shirk from approving punishment that was inevitably harsh.[34] He took as his motto Calvin's insistence that 'rulers' (and such he was on his own lands) were 'ministers of God' who had the obligation to spread 'the true religion' amongst their dependents.[35]

The Moderate Irish Scholar

Rev. Thomas Smyth has been described as 'A Moderate Southerner'.[36] Born of an English father and Scottish mother and brought up originally in Belfast, for which city he retained a great affection, Smyth's family came to Charleston in 1830. He studied at Princeton, before becoming supply minister in the Second Presbyterian Church in Charleston. His whole ministry was with that church. Smyth was a shy and retiring man, given to long scholarly sermons and more at home with books than people.[37] He met Charles Colcock Jones at Princeton in 1835 and shared his enthusiasm for the religious education of the enslaved – the two collaborated on this within Presbyterian Church structures, often in the teeth of a great deal of civic opposition.[38]

Smyth also had severe reservations about slavery. Like Jones, he described it as an 'evil' which he claimed that 'God would remove in his own time', a position he held to throughout the turbulent decades of the mid-nineteenth century. In 1850 he published a book *The Unity of the Human Race*. The title was one that both excited and disturbed many. It was a scholarly look at anthropology, in which he was widely read. It challenged crude racial stereotyping, and thus came to different conclusions than those which defenders of slavery often used. Yet although common humanity was affirmed, Smyth did not in any way challenge the institution. But the book confirmed his cautious liberal views and led him to be under some suspicion in the increasingly entrenched circles of the South of the time. He was wrongly accused of being an abolitionist.[39]

Unlike Jones, Thomas Smyth owned no slaves and made it clear he had no wish to do so, although his wife Margaret Adger had inherited some. But his international contacts brought on him a wave of hostility, because of his perceived accommodation to the system. He befriended a delegation from the Free Church of Scotland which had split from the Church of Scotland in 1843, and in raising money in Charleston for them, he then became embroiled in a dispute which brought the anger both of American and Scottish abolitionists. As Smyth became more defensive of the Southern position on slavery, and came more under attack in Scotland and Ireland, he turned to his friend Thomas Chalmers, the first Moderator of the Free Church of Scotland and the best-known churchman in Scotland.[40] Both men shared a conservatism and regard for order in religion and in society where the values of the 'two realms' ruled. Chalmers appreciated the order of the old South and Smyth admired Chalmers's vision of the 'Godly Commonwealth' for Scotland. Chalmers assured Smyth that whilst all agreed that slavery was an evil that God would remove in time, there must be a distinction between the institution and the individual, and that there was no warrant to blame slaveowners who had inherited enslaved people, still less to deny them communion, communion, unless they treated their servants badly.[41]

The refusal of Smyth to support the excommunication from the church of any who were slaveowners alienated him from some old friends in the Presbyterian Church in Ireland, which took a much firmer line on slaveowning than the leadership of the Free Church in Scotland. Smyth was denied a seat at the Irish Assembly, at the instigation of Rev. Isaac Nelson, a leading Belfast abolitionist.[42]

Smyth went further than was perhaps safe for him when he addressed the Evangelical Alliance in London in 1846. The Alliance was fiercely debating the issue of whether it could include in its membership any church which had slaveowners in their congregations. Taking the same position as Chalmers, Smyth affirmed that they were all against slavery, but that the attitude to it should be left to individual consciences and should not be a matter of 'general obligation' to be pressed on the Alliance. It was, he maintained, a political matter and had no place in church courts. At the end of his speech he appealed to moral principles. 'The only hope', he said, 'for the removal of that system from America, was the Christian principle', and if left to gain strength without interference, it would finally remove 'that evil, not just from America, but the world.'[43] In this he echoed Chalmers's approach to social problems in ensuring sufficient religious and moral education in society.

Presbyterian Theologian of the South

The third leading Presbyterian, who strongly sought the cause of religious education for enslaved and free African Americans, was the minister, theologian, editor and Moderator of the General Assembly of the Presbyterian Church in the United States in 1847, James Henley Thornwell.

Thornwell founded the *Southern Presbyterian Review* and edited the *Southern Quarterly Review*. In both journals he discussed the issue of slavery extensively. Although he saw it as a 'curse' brought by sin in the world, he rejected any idea any idea of opposition to it as 'the misguided reason of man'. A conservative Calvinist, he believed strongly in accepting predestination, and his study of scripture led him to conclude that there was no divine condemnation of the institution any more than poverty, disease or death. It had to be accepted as a given from God.[44]

On the other hand he expressed deep concern about the 'abuses' and 'evils' of slavery, and in his strictures on the behaviour of masters, he went even further than Jones. The master, affirmed Thornwell, 'has no property in his slave as he has in the ox or the swine . . . his soul, his limbs, his heart lie in the slave'. All that the master had a right to was 'a claim to services'. He argued that the New Testament injunction in Colossians 4:1, 'masters give your servants that which is just and equal', made the enslaved 'a member of the family, although the lowest one'. The relationship should be compared to 'the vassals of the Middle Ages rather than the serfs of Russia'. Masters should seek for enslaved people 'the greatest amount of happiness that their condition will admit' and he agreed that masters who practised cruelty should be disciplined by the church.[45]

Although, in company with others, Thornwell saw the issue of slavery as a political and social one to be separated from the church's spiritual realm of authority, he was critical of the political powers in not giving protection in several areas. Marriage, he claimed, should be respected. Laws in Georgia and South Carolina, as in most of the South, did not then recognise slave marriages. Families could be split up by sale, and in most cases were.[46] The reframing of the law in South Carolina in 1834, preventing the teaching of reading to the enslaved, Thornwell described as 'disgraceful' and he and Charles Colcock Jones campaigned unsuccessfully to persuade the legislature to rescind it.[47]

This ban of course had severe consequences for the biblical education of the enslaved, and limited it to hearing teaching and preaching. Along with Smyth and Jones, Thornwell saw evangelism as the most crucial duty of masters, since that was the obligation of all Christians. He contended that baptising their slaves and their families was a prime duty, thus opening the way to salvation for them. Baptism was to be enforced by the master, and he insisted that it should not be neglected because of the supposed 'ignorance' of the enslaved in religious matters.[48]

But Thornwell also recognised that worship in white churches was often unacceptable to black people. There had been earlier attempts to establish black churches in Charleston, but the pioneering African Episcopal Methodist one, established in 1816, was constantly under harassment by white groups, and was burned down by vigilantes after the Nat Turner 'rebellion'. In 1850, nearly thirty years later, and in the teeth of much opposition, white Episcopalians and Presbyterians led by Jones, Smyth and Thornwell, completed the building of Zion Church in Charleston to house a black congregation.[49] Attitudes towards any relaxation of discriminatory legislation had hardened in the 1840s, not least because effective use of the postal service ensured considerable antislavery literature to enter the South. That year the Fugitive Slave Act had been passed as a result of Southern pressure on Congress.[50]

Black Church Control by Whites

Zion Church in Anson Street was only achieved by huge compromises. It was to be supervised by Smyth's Second Presbyterian Church, and white ministers were to be appointed to control it. Smyth's brother-in-law, Rev. John Adger, a former missionary in Armenia, was the first minister of the church, and the opening sermon was preached by Thornwell on the text 'masters give to your servants that which is just and equal, knowing that ye have a master in heaven'. The congregation at that service was entirely white.[51]

Thornwell spoke of the 'insane fury of the abolitionist philanthropy' that 'has aimed at stirring up insurrection in our midst' and 'threatens the utter ruin of this vast Republic'. Yet there was an admission that although in his view the South were unjustly calumniated for slavery, 'to say that we have run into no extravagancies in our defence of slavery is to say that we are not angels but men'. The remainder of the sermon, which lasted several hours, was a justification of slavery as 'regulated liberty' resisting 'the social anarchy of communism and the political anarchy of licentiousness'.[52] Thornwell stated clearly to the congregation that the plan of those who sought this new move was clear for him. 'Our design', he stated, 'in giving them the gospel, is not to civilise them, not to change their social condition – nor to exalt them into citizens of freemen – it is to save them.'[53]

Thornwell and his colleagues, who tried to remain loyal Southerners and yet hold a vision of humanity and a zeal for saving enslaved souls, were caught in an impossible trap. As the nation lurched closer and closer towards Civil War they were forced to take sides decisively and inevitably lost some of their earlier vision and humanity. Erskine Clarke summed up the significance of the founding of Zion Church in Charleston and its failure in these terms. 'Zion represented for these whites a moderate, middle way between the competing impulses of their Reformed tradition. They saw in it a model for the future, and when war came they were ready to envision a holy commonwealth, a new confederacy of regulated liberty, under white control.'[54]

When Charles Colcock Jones, despite preaching on the sacred bond of marriage to fellow planters, sent a family to the slave market in Savannah to clear some debts in 1857, it marked a watershed for him between earlier convictions about the evils of slavery and unwavering support for the South and the system of human bondage.[55] In the summer of 1862, as more and more sought freedom, Jones wrote to a friend about his hurt at one servant whom he always treated well, 'betraying' him by taking to the woods. He recommended turning over to the authorities, any who were caught trying to leave, as 'traitors' and 'spies' with the consequent brutal treatment.[56]

Several days before the guns at Fort Sumter rang out in April 1861, heralding the Civil War, Thomas Smyth received a letter from the Presbytery clerk, which commended him for a robust defence of slavery in an article in a scientific journal, and promising that it provided unanswerable ammunition to use against the abolitionists.[57] Smyth remained committed to the Union until the election of Lincoln, then his loyalty changed to the Confederacy and he fully embraced Secession.

Thornwell was the most publicly ardent conservative of the three, theologically and politically, but he too shared the dilemma in which more moderate Southern churchmen found themselves. He was increasingly torn between clinging to 'Southern values' and having to see the moral bankruptcy of its major social, economic and religious institution. In his 'Duties of Masters' he railed against 'the insane fury of philanthropy' (the abolitionist position) 'aimed at stirring up insurrection in our midst', while he confided secretly to a ministerial friend on the eve of the Civil War that he believed a gradual programme of emancipation should be started.[58]

Clarke saw Thornwell's vision as reflecting the 'self-interest of whites in the low country Reformed community'. 'It helped', he wrote, 'to legitimatise the present order – with whites in control – even as it called for a new order.' Not for nothing was Thornwell regarded by many of his contemporaries as the theological companion of that political champion of the South, Senator John C. Calhoun of South Carolina.[59]

Seeds of Liberation

Professor Bernard Powers, the African American historian of Charleston, was once asked whether religious education was more powerful as a tool of social control than one of liberation. 'On balance', he said, 'I am sure that it was the latter.' He expanded by observing that the biblical narrative opened up a new view of the world beyond their limited horizons for those who were enslaved.[60] It is an irony that despite the efforts of Jones, Smyth and Thornwell, alongside less prominent churchmen in the South, to advance paternalism and the saving of souls, in the end, they helped equip thousands of the enslaved to have the confidence and courage to liberate themselves. White attempts to control religious practice amongst enslaved people, and the growth and variety of black religion, were both components that encouraged self-liberation. Religious knowledge enabled, against all the odds, a sense of self-worth and dignity in enslavement. Through the stories of Moses, the parables of Jesus and much else, new hope for a better life in this world, as well as in heaven, was glimpsed.

In 1776 Samuel Hopkins, an early advocate of religious education for the enslaved, challenged the myth that most were made discontented with their lot by new ideas of freedom. 'They have', he wrote, 'a thousand times more discernment and sensitivity in this case than their masters or most others, and their aversion to slavery and desires of liberty are indistinguishable.'[61] Survival often depended in playing a role of acceptance, contentment and even gratitude to their 'owners', and other whites who offered ministry to them. For this to be effective, they had to know those who held them in bondage much better than their 'owners' knew them. The convenient myth of black lives as part of the white family seeped into the thinking of many white ministers and educators. And when during the Civil War enslaved people left even 'benevolent' plantations such as those owned by the Jones family, the feelings of disappointment at what was perceived as disloyalty simply reflected the whites' disconnection from reality.[62]

Accounts of slavery by many elderly men and women who had experienced it in the nineteenth century were recorded in the 1930s. There is a constant critique by the formerly enslaved of the selective biblical teaching and preaching by white ministers when the latter were permitted on the plantations, and the careful avoidance of the teaching of Jesus (but not of Paul) and the exclusion of the Exodus narrative in the Old Testament. Some accounts parody the attempts of ministers and faith leaders to offer threats of divine judgement in the face of any questioning, let alone rebellion, against the system. And other reminiscences witness to the eagerness to attend the often forbidden outside gatherings, in order to let their feelings be heard, and to worship in their own way, which they did at great risk.[63]

Breaking the Chains through Spirituals

The religious tradition of what became termed 'negro spirituals' were often seen, if not always encouraged, by some whites as necessary safety valve on a Sunday or at other times, and expressions over salvation in the hereafter were seen to distract from thoughts of earthly liberation.

It was naïve. There was certainly much eschatology and longing for a peaceful and joyful life for believers beyond the grave where no hellish enslavement could reach. But there was another vital aspect in the cause of earthly freedom. Songs such as 'Steal away to Jesus' became coded messages to indicate that the coast was clear to leave the plantation.[64] 'Let us break bread together on our knees with our face to the rising sun' looked to the promised land of Canada, part of the British Empire, where slavery had been abolished since 1834. Frederick Douglass wrote of his time in bondage, 'A keen observer might have detected in our repeated singing of "O Canaan, sweet Canaan, I am bound for the land of Canaan," something more than a hope of reaching heaven. We meant to reach the North, the North was our Canaan.'[65]

One of the most remarkable examples of the use of biblical song was by the formerly enslaved Harriet Tubman, who guided hundreds to freedom from the South and was termed 'Moses' by black and white abolitionists. As she wandered through the back roads (between different places) she sang. For many whites that passed she played the role of a pious old woman singing hymns to herself, but there were hidden messages in those choruses. 'Go down Moses . . . to the promised land' and 'Wade in the water . . . Gods gonna trouble the Water', were two frequent ones. The latter was indeed a reference to angelic divine healing through the movement of the water in Bethesda in Palestine in John's Gospel, but it was also a code to warn those escaping that they should go into the water to drive the plantation's bloodhounds off their scent.[66]

There is no doubt that the Christian message produced in all kinds of different ways a kind of 'liberation theology' in the nineteenth century. Denmark Vesey, Nat Turner and others drew deeply on a reinterpretation of the Bible, as did so many of the thousands, who, at great risk, sought their physical and psychological freedom. Isabella Baumfree ('Sojourner Truth'), the visionary antislavery and feminist activist who had to free herself from the version of faith, learned whilst in bondage from Dutch Calvinists, discovered a Pentecostal version that fired her decades-long campaigning.[67]

No Compromise with Evil

Dr Andrew Thomson, Minister of St George's Church in Edinburgh and the leader of the Popular Party in Scotland, in two speeches and a sermon, respectively, in 1829 and 1830, altered the nature of the movement for the abolition of slavery in Britain from a 'gradualist' to an 'immediate' position.[68] Thomson was a Calvinist, not least in his adherence to a separation of authority between church and state. But unlike his successor, Thomas Chalmers, he did not shrink from a theological analysis of the need for urgent and comprehensive action on such a fundamental issue.

Thomson refused to debate biblical passages that justified slavery. He simply claimed that he could never reconcile the spirit of Jesus with the bondage of 'those for whom he died'.[69] In response to those who claimed that there were good slaveholders, he argued that original sin meant that no mortal human could be entrusted with such power over others. To delay for a second the destruction of an evil such as slavery by means of 'mitigation' was, for him, to scorn God's obligation to destroy evil. He compared slavery to a poisonous Upas tree 'under whose shade all intellect languishes and all virtue dies'. To get rid of what he called 'the foul sepulchre' and 'the cup of oppression' he declared,

> The pestiferous tree must be cut down and eradicated; it must, root and branch of it, be cast into the consuming fire and its ashes scattered to the four winds of heaven. It is thus that you must deal with slavery. You must annihilate it – annihilate it now – and annihilate it for ever.[70]

Thomson's words found as eager acceptance amongst American abolitionists as it drew a furious reaction in the Jamaican Assembly that year.[71] He demonstrated the impossibility of holding together a middle ground on which the efforts of the Presbyterian white educators in the American South attempted to stand. It was ground on which deeply religious African Americans such as Harriet Tubman, 'Sojourner Truth' and James Pennington never stood, as they sought the total destruction of slavery, long before they all worked for the Union cause when war broke out in 1865. It was ground which was in the end totally inadequate to solve the dilemma in the face of one of the greatest crimes against humanity in human history, whose effects are all too evident, and unresolved, in contemporary America.

Notes

1. After King James VII (James II of England) was defeated by William of Orange in the battle of the Boyne in 1690, the new king agreed to acknowledge the Church of Scotland (Presbyterian) as the National Church and to defend its rights. The oath to uphold this was taken by King Charles III on his accession in 2022.
2. Graham Duncan, 'John Knox and Education', *HTS Theological Studies*, 73.3 (2017). Published online: https://hts.org.za/index.php/hts/article/view/4346/9639.
3. Erskine Clark, *Our Southern Zion: A History of Calvinism in the South Carolina Low Country 1690–1990* (Tuscaloosa: University of Alabama Press, 1996).
4. Kenneth Stampp, *The Peculiar Institution* (New York: Alfred Knopf, 1956).
5. David Brion Davis, *The Problem of Slavery in the Age of Revolution 1770–1823* (Cornell, NY: Cornell University Press, 1975), pp. 164–212.
6. 'George Washington to John Francis Mercer 9 Sept 1786', in Worthington Chauncey Ford (ed.), *The Writings of George Washington*, vol. 11 (New York: G. P. Putnam's Sons, 1891), pp. 62–3; Thomas Jefferson, *Notes on the State of Virginia* (Philadelphia: Pritchard and Hall, 1788), p. 172.

7. Henry Wiencek, *An Imperfect God: George Washington, His Slaves and the Creation of America* (New York: Farrar, Straus, and Giroux, 2003), pp. 40–1, 162–3, 222–4, 275–8, 358–9; Davis, *The Problem of Slavery*, pp. 164–85. Davis argued that Jefferson's reputation as an antislavery supporter is misplaced.
8. Lacy K. Ford, *Deliver Us from Evil: The Slavery Question in the Old South* (Oxford: Oxford University Press, 2009), pp. 19–48.
9. Ibid., pp. 23–30.
10. Ibid., pp. 94–103.
11. *Minutes of the General Assembly of the Presbyterian Church in The United States 1789–1820* (Philadelphia: Presbyterian Board, 1847), pp. 103–5.
12. *Minutes of the General Assembly of the Presbyterian Church in The United States 1789–1820* (Philadelphia: Presbyterian Board, 1847), pp. 692–3.
13. Although riven by tensions over theology and slavery the Presbyterian Church in the United States did not divide into Northern and Southern churches until 1861.
14. The Church of Scotland signed a Solemn League and Covenant in 1643 with the English Parliament to restore the Presbyterian supremacy in the land. Subsequent monarchs (Charles II and James VII/James II) attempted to reimpose Episcopal church orders and many resisters met secretly in the open air for Calvinist worship. They were ruthlessly hunted down in 'the killing times' of the late seventeenth century and many went into exile.
15. William Roulston, 'The Reformed Presbyterian Church and Anti-Slavery in Nineteenth-Century America', in Peter C. Messer and William Harrison (eds), *Faith and Slavery in the Presbyterian Diaspora* (Bethlehem, PA: Lehigh University Press, 2016), p. 155. The minister was the Rev. William Martin.
16. Erskine Clarke, *Wrestling Jacob: A Portrait of Religion in the Old South* (Atlanta: John Knox Press, 1979), pp. 105–7.
17. Ford, *Deliver us from Evil*, p. 145.
18. Eugene N. Genovese, *Roll, Jordan, Roll: The World the Slaves Made* (New York: Pantheon, 1972), p. 5.
19. J. W. C. Pennington, *The Fugitive Blacksmith or Events in the I History of James W.C. Pennington, Pastor of a Presbyterian Church, New York, Formerly a Slave in the State of Maryland United States* (London: Charles Gilpin, 1849), pp. 16–17. A number of written personal accounts of slavery were published in the mid-nineteenth century either in the North or abroad.
20. Clarke, *Our Southern Zion*, pp. 123–4.
21. Douglas R. Egerton, '"Why they did not preach up this thing": Denmark Vesey and Revolutionary Theology', *South Carolina Historical Magazine*, 100.4 (1999), pp. 299–317.
22. Thomas Wentworth Higginson, 'The Story of Denmark Vesey', *Atlantic Monthly* (June 1861), p. 730. Available online: https://www.theatlantic.com/magazine/archive/1861/06/denmark-vesey/396239/.
23. Ford, *Deliver Us from Evil*, pp. 213–34.
24. Kenneth Greenberg (ed.), *The Confessions of Nat Turner and Related Documents* (Boston: Bedford, 1996), pp. 16–17.
25. Erskine Clarke, *Dwelling Place: A Plantation Epic* (New Haven, CT: Yale University Press, 2005), pp. 82–96.
26. Clarke, *Wrestling Jacob*, p. 26
27. Ford, *Deliver Us from Evil*, p. 465.

28. Ibid., pp. 465–66.
29. Charles C. Jones, *A Catechism, of Scripture Doctrine and Practice, for Families and Sabbath Schools. Designed also for the Oral Instruction of Colored Persons* (Savannah, 1845).
30. Jones, *Catechism*, p. 4.
31. Ibid., p. 5.
32. Ibid., pp. 127–8.
33. Ibid., pp. 129–31. The term 'servant' was used frequently in the South, especially in religious circles, to soften the idea of slavery.
34. Clarke, *Dwelling Place*, pp. 271, 324–5, 328.
35. See John Calvin, *Institutes of the Christian Religion*, book IV, chapter 20.
36. Erskine Clarke, 'Thomas Smyth, Moderate of the Old South' (ThD diss., Union Seminary, Richmond, Virginia, 1970).
37. Thomas Smyth, *Autobiographical Notes, Letters and Reflections*, ed. Louisa Cheves Stoney (Charleston: Walker, Evans, and Coghill, 1914), pp. 15–19, 56–64, 214. Some of these comments on his character were made by Smyth himself, others were by his granddaughter Louisa Cheves Stoney.
38. Clarke, *Dwelling Place*, p. 107; Ford, *Deliver Us from Evil*, pp. 467–72.
39. Smyth, *Autobiographical Notes*, pp. 175, 215; Clarke, *Dwelling Place*, p. 167.
40. Iain Whyte, *'Send Back the Money': The Free Church and American Slavery* (Cambridge: James Clarke, 2012), pp. 43–56; Stewart J. Brown, *Thomas Chalmers and the Godly Commonwealth* (Oxford: Oxford University Press, 1982).
41. George Shepperson, 'Thomas Chalmers, the Free Church of Scotland, and the South', *Journal of Southern History*, 17 (1951), pp. 517–37.
42. Whyte, *'Send Back the Money'*, pp. 110–19; J. F. Maclear, 'Thomas Smyth, Federick Douglass, and the Belfast Anti-Slavery Campaign', *South Carolina Historical Magazine*, 80.4 (1979), pp. 286–97.
43. Evangelical Alliance, *Report of the Proceedings of the Conference held at Freemasons Hall, London from August 19th to September 2nd, 1846* (London: Partridge and Oakley, 1847), pp. 304–9.
44. Marilyn Westerkamp, 'James Henley Thornwell, Pro-Slavery Spokesman within a Calvinist Faith', *South Carolina Historical Magazine*, 87.1 (1986), pp. 49–57; James Oscar Farmer, *The Metaphysical Confederacy: James Henley Thornwell and the Synthesis of Southern Values* (Macon, GA: Mercer University Press, 1986), pp. 218–19.
45. J. H. Thornwell, 'Duties of masters', *Southern Presbyterian Review*, January 1850, p. 286; July 1850, p. 12, October 1854, pp. 270, 272.
46. Ibid., pp. 274–6.
47. Farmer, *The Metaphysical Confederacy*, p. 219.
48. J. H. Thornwell, 'Baptism of servants', *Southern Presbyterian Review* (1847–8), pp. 63–102.
49. Clarke, *Our Southern Zion*, pp. 195–9.
50. The numbers of enslaved men and women who liberated themselves and came North had substantially increased in the 1840s. Southern pressure on a weak President Millard Fillmore led to the Fugitive Slave Act in September 1850. It provided heavy penalties for harbouring fugitives and laid on Northern states the obligation to arrest and return them. The Underground Railroad continued to provide strenuous resistance.
51. Clarke, *Our Southern Zion*, pp. 189–92.

52. J. H. Thornwell, *The Rights and Duties of Masters, A Sermon Preached at the Dedication of A Church Erected in Charleston S.C. for the Benefit and Instruction of the Coloured Population* (Charleston: Walker and James, 1850), pp. 4–6, 28–30.
53. Ibid., p. 50
54. Clarke, *Our Southern Zion*, pp. 198–9.
55. Clarke, *Dwelling Place*, pp. 345–60.
56. Ibid., p. 415.
57. South Carolina History Society, Second Presbyterian Church records, 1809–1981, Church Session Minute Book 1852–1867 (428.04.01).
58. Farmer, *The Metaphysical Confederacy*, p. 219.
59. Clarke, *Our Southern Zion*, p. 195.
60. Bernard Powers, in conversation with the author, 4 November 2013; Powers, *Black Charlestonians* (Fayetteville: University of Arkansas Press, 1994).
61. Samuel Hopkins, *A Dialogue Concerning the Slavery of Africans, Showing it to be the Duty and Interest of the American Colonies to Emancipate all the African Slaves* (New York, 1776).
62. Clarke, *Dwelling Place*, pp. 414–15.
63. Norman Yetman (ed.), *Voices from Slavery: 100 Authentic Slave Narratives* (Mineola: Dover Publications, 2000), pp. 36–7. During the 1930s an extensive recording projected captured the accounts of elderly people who had been enslaved. Many witnessed to the secrecy needed to worship in their own way and the risks of punishment.
64. New Jersey Historical Commission, '"Steal Away": A Guide to the Underground Railroad in New Jersey', accessed 9 May 2023, https://dspace.njstatelib.org/xmlui/bitstream/handle/10929/24563/h6732002.pdf.
65. Frederick Douglass, *My Bondage and my Freedom* (New York: Miller, Orton, and Milligan, 1855), p. 275. Douglass's lecture tours in Scotland in the late 1840s focused on the campaign against the Free Church position on slavery.
66. Catherine Clinton, *Harriet Tubman: The Road to Freedom* (New York: Little Brown and Co., 2004), pp. 79–97. The Bible passage is John 5:1–9.
67. Nell Painter, *Sojourner Truth, A Life, A Symbol* (New York: W.W. Norton, 1996), pp. 24–31, 261.
68. David Brion Davis, 'The Emergence of Immediatism in British and American Anti-Slavery Thought', *Mississippi Valley Historical Review*, 49.2 (1962), pp. 209–30, p. 221.
69. Iain Whyte, *Scotland and the Abolition of Black Slavery 1756–1838* (Edinburgh: Edinburgh University Press, 2005), pp. 196–7.
70. Andrew Thomson, *Slavery not Sanctioned but Condemned by Christianity* (Edinburgh, 1829); *Substance of the speech delivered sat the Meeting of the Edinburgh Society for the Abolition of Slavery* (Edinburgh, 1830).
71. Hope M. Waddell, *Twenty-Nine Years in the West Indies and Central Africa* (London: T. Nelson and Sons, 1863), p. 76.

CHAPTER FOUR

Awakened Protestants' Calls for 'Christian Socialism' and 'Christian Communism' in Germany, 1844–50

Andrew Kloes

Introduction: Perceptions of Social Crisis in 1840s Germany

During the early 1840s two neologisms entered popular discourse in German-speaking Europe – 'communism' and 'socialism' – as many observers grappled with the manifest social problems that accompanied capitalism, industrialisation and urbanisation.[1] One measure of these ideas' penetration into public consciousness, into wider circles of thought beyond those of philosophers and revolutionaries, are the articles on communism and socialism that appeared for the first time, between 1843 and 1847, in the ninth edition of the *General German Encyclopaedia for the Educated Classes* (*Allgemeine deutsche Real-Encyklopädie für die gebildeten Stände*). This widely read encyclopaedia was published in Leipzig by the brothers Friedrich Brockhaus and Heinrich Brockhaus, and its contents reflect the recent political and intellectual debates ongoing among members of Germany's middle and upper classes.[2] In the eighth edition, which appeared between 1833 and 1837, neither 'communism' nor 'socialism' is included among the over 70,000 terms in the index for the encyclopaedia's twelve volumes.

The unsigned entry for 'socialism' published in 1847 in the ninth edition succinctly summarised the growing concerns many shared regarding the socio-economic landscape of Germany. 'For some time now, severe accusations against the conditions in our society have been arising among the nations who stand at the pinnacle of modern culture, which push even purely political passions into the background ... We are prophesied an upheaval more terrible than any political revolution.' The author continued, 'To be sure, ill will and lack of understanding have their part in these accusations. However, even the prudent observer, who keeps an eye on the principles and history of modern civilisation, no longer denies that our society suffers from evils that were unknown to such an extent in former times.'[3]

The author identified one particularly salient social issue:

> What oppresses us first and foremost, what is the regarded as the source of all the other disparities, is the extremely unequal distribu-

tion of wealth, the sharp contrast between the rich and the poor, between those who suffer privations and those who enjoy all that life has to offer, and the fear that this contrast must become ever more pronounced.[4]

In the author's view, nascent capitalism in Germany was proving itself a malevolent force:

> The field of industry, the arena in which the riches of modern culture are won and parcelled out, gives us a complete view of the evil and of all the threatening consequences that spring from it. This arena, where only blessings should reign, resembles a battlefield, where, through competition, the great crush the small, where everyone fends only for himself, where the manoeuvres of one capitalist threatens the existence of thousands.[5]

The Brockhaus family were supporters of political liberalism in Germany, and their firm's publications had at times been censured by the Austrian and Prussian governments for promoting revolutionary ideas.[6] However, not only those who held their political perspective warned about transforming effects that rising economic inequality was having on German society. Some monarchists and political conservatives, such as Christian Karl Josias Bunsen, also issued warnings about how inequality, combined with middle- and upper-class indifference towards the sufferings of the working class and those in poverty, fuelled revolutionary movements that threatened the commonweal.

Born into an impoverished, middle-class family in Hesse, Bunsen had an extraordinary rise through the Prussian diplomatic service, ultimately receiving a royal appointment as the Hohenzollern's ambassador to the Court of St James in 1841.[7] While in London, Bunsen partnered with evangelical members of the Church of England in voluntary societies that aimed to redress spiritual and physical needs in the British capital. For example, in September 1846, Lord Ashley, the Earl of Shaftesbury, and Bunsen, respectively, became president and vice-president of the Foreigners' Evangelical Society, which strove 'to seek the spiritual welfare of the numerous foreigners residing or visiting this country', by organising meetings at which attendees could hear a gospel message and by distributing to them literature on Christian topics.[8] Eighteen months later, on 9 March 1848, at a gathering of members of the Prussian diplomatic corps, Members of Parliament, and 'gentlemen', who had come together to raise funds for a hospital that attended to the needs of 'sick and diseased natives of Germany' in London, Bunsen commented on the revolutionary upheavals that had begun the previous month in Paris.

Reflecting on such news reports, Bunsen began,

> The events of these days make a mighty appeal to the higher and wealthier classes of our social order. The attack is a social one, the

> remedy must be a social one also. Let the higher and wealthier classes show more and more that they feel superior intelligence, education, and wealth are given to them not for mere enjoyment, not for selfish purposes, but for the benefit of the whole community.⁹

Bunsen encouraged the wealthy to undertake self-sacrificial philanthropy to aid the poor and vulnerable to help redress the underlying causes of revolutions.

> The events of our days speak to the hearts of all who can give support to charitable institutions. They say to all of us, 'Give what you can; and give not only your shillings and pounds, give as much of your time as you can spare from other duties; give ears; give affection; live with the poor and sick, or least live for them. Show by your acts that the feeling of brotherhood which you profess is really in you.'¹⁰

Through such solidarity, Bunsen envisaged achieving social harmony. 'The national societies, in which such principles practically prevail, will be so firmly knitted together, that neither revolutions from within nor attacks from without can rend them asunder.'¹¹ Ironically, nine days later, on 18–19 March 1848, violent street protests broke out in Berlin, which killed 300 demonstrators and 100 military personnel.¹²

This chapter explores how one group of German Protestants – those associated with the religious 'Awakening movement' (*Erweckungsbewegung*) that began after the end of the Napoleonic Wars in 1815 – responded to these widely felt problems in German society, as various politically radical proposals to deal with them gained currency throughout Germany.¹³ While communism and socialism in Germany subsequently developed strong connotations of secularism and atheism throughout the latter nineteenth and twentieth centuries, this was not always the case. The earliest use of the term 'Christian socialism' in Germany comes from an 1844 essay published by a Protestant pastor in Berlin. After analysing this essay, this chapter discusses how two of the period's most prominent social reformers and proponents of the Protestant Awakening movement, Amalie Sieveking (1794–1859) and Johann Hinrich Wichern (1808–81), called for 'Christian communism' and 'Christian socialism' before and after the nationwide revolutionary movements of 1848–9.¹⁴

Sieveking and Wichern were arguably among the most significant religious leaders in nineteenth-century Germany. They belonged to the same circle of awakened Protestants who lived in Hamburg, although they worked independently of one another in their respective ministries to the poor in the city.¹⁵ Indeed, Sieveking, the daughter of a merchant and senator of Hamburg, who chose to remain unmarried her entire life, helped fund Wichern's studies in theology in universities in Göttingen and Berlin after the death of his father, a notary, had left him, at age 15, the eldest of six children to his surviving mother.¹⁶ Beginning with her work to aid those suffering from cholera in Hamburg, Sieveking became the first woman to organise and lead a Christian ministry in modern Germany.[17] Wichern is well known among German Protestant communities for his work in children's education and prisoner rehabilitation.[18] For example, in 2008, the national, Protestant Church in Germany (*Evangelische Kirche in Deutschland*) marked the bicentenary of his birth, proclaiming an eponymous 'Wichern Year' of commemorations and reflections upon his legacy as a pedagogue, social reformer, church leader and Prussian government official. The German Chancellor herself, Angela Merkel, gave a speech at the festivities on Wichern's enduring significance.[19] Nevertheless, neither Sieveking nor Wichern's life and work has attracted much attention from scholars in the English-speaking world.

The German Protestants who belonged to the Awakening movement have long been interpreted as either conservatives, orthodox, pietists or traditionalists in religious matters and, concomitantly, supporters of throne-and-altar political conservativism vis-à-vis the contemporary liberal and revolutionary movements of their day.[20] While such characterisations are generally correct, the analysis of Wichern's and Sieveking's notions of 'Christian socialism' and 'Christian communism' presented here nuances the political philosophy of awakened German Protestantism. Furthermore, this essay explores these two leaders' assessments of the social problems of industrialisation and urbanisation and examines how they exhorted members of Christian communities in Germany to assume social responsibilities towards the most vulnerable in society. In so doing, Sieveking and Wichern imagined German Protestant church members as the harbingers of a distinct type of socialism/communism.

Protestant Voluntary Societies as 'Christian Socialism'

Did the religious Awakening movement within the historic Protestant communities of German-speaking Europe during the early decades of the nineteenth century foster a distinctly Christian form of socialism? Such was the bold argument that one Berlin pastor, Dr Heinrich Alt, advanced in an 1844 essay, 'The Christian socialism of our times in its various manifestations and its importance for church and state'.[21] In this lengthy article, Alt, who for over forty years served as a preacher at Charité, the renowned royal military and civilian hospital in the Prussian capital, welcomed the unprecedented growth of voluntary societies, associations and new institutions that Protestants were founding to foster the spiritual lives and ameliorate the physical needs and living conditions of some of the most vulnerable men, women and children in German society.[22] As the historian Hartmut Lehmann has noted, between 1815 and 1830,

> pious German Protestants, who were mostly middle or lower middle class, laboured unceasingly for what they called the building of God's

kingdom. Within a few years, they founded more organizations and established more institutions than in the whole history of Protestantism from [Martin] Luther to the end of the eighteenth century. Their activities far exceeded those of Pietists like [Philipp Jakob] Spener, [August Hermann] Francke, and [Nikolaus Ludwig von] Zinzendorf, whom they adored.[23]

Alt conceptualised these new religiously motivated initiatives as various expressions of 'Christian socialism' and thereby introduced the term into German Protestant religious discourse.[24] Furthermore, Alt contended that 'Christian socialism' exemplified the emphasis in awakened Protestant spirituality on the life of faith as the active obedience to Jesus' commands to love one's neighbour through the power of the Holy Spirit, and traced this doctrine back through the writings of the aforementioned seventeenth- and eighteenth-century Pietists to Luther.[25]

It is difficult to determine precisely how many new religious organisations the Protestants of the Awakening movement had founded between 1815 – when peace returned to Europe after nearly five million soldiers and civilians across the continent had lost their lives during the French Revolutionary and Napoleonic Wars of the preceding twenty-three years – and 1845.[26] According to one count taken that year by Ernst Huth, a German pastor in Mecklenburg-Schwerin, at least 1,457 Protestant associations had been established in the various Germany states and in the German-speaking parts of Switzerland. Among the Protestant voluntary societies enumerated by Huth were 407 associations for discouraging alcohol misuse, 309 for distributing Bibles, 77 for distributing Christian literature to those living in poverty and 230 to support the work of missionaries outside of Europe. This number also included 164 schools to provide education to children and youth in impoverished circumstances in Germany, 46 societies founded to care for the sick and poor in various cities, 28 residential care facilities for orphans and children whose parents could not care for them, and 12 societies to aid formerly imprisoned men and women reintegrate into society. Still other religious voluntary societies ranged from groups that campaigned against cruelty to animals in Germany to those that supported education for women in India.[27] Similar local surveys of newly founded Protestant religious associations in Hamburg in 1844 and Berlin in 1846 reported the same types of groups founded for the same interrelated evangelistic and social reform purposes that Huth had noted, with twenty-five new associations in the Hanseatic merchant city at the mouth of the Elbe and thirty-two in the Hohenzollern capital on the Spree.[28]

Huth's report immediately caught the attention of Johann Hinrich Wichern, who had recently begun to edit a national, twice-monthly periodical that covered the activities of his and other Protestant social reform societies. Wichern wrote that he hoped his periodical would function as a clearinghouse of information for all the various efforts aimed at ameliorating the lives of 'the immiserated, the poor, the abandoned, the forgotten, the lost, the rejected, the despised', and would, thereby, 'unite the voluntary efforts to build the Kingdom of God within Christendom'.[29] According to Wichern's own calculations, Huth had grossly undercounted the new Protestant religious voluntary societies in Germany. Including all the affiliated, auxiliary societies that existed in less populous localities outside of major cities, Wichern believed that the number of new societies totalled between 6,000 and 7,000 across German-speaking Europe.[30] As Heinrich Alt surveyed all these burgeoning, religiously motivated activities, he concluded that 'the awakening Christian life can be called the starting point of Christian socialism'.[31]

Karl Marx radically disagreed with Alt's views regarding the positive impact of Christianity on modern German society. In a September 1847 newspaper article in Brussels in the *Deutsche-Brüsseler-Zeitung*, Marx, then aged 29, denounced the growing number of calls by Christian social reformers to their fellow believers to address the living conditions of the urban poor as hypocritical. Marx took particular aim at some of the ones that had been recently published in the *Rheinischer Beobachter*, a politically conservative, Protestant newspaper that the Prussian government had established in Cologne in 1844.[32] When an anonymous author, whom Marx assumed to be a senior church official, argued that 'If only those, who have the calling to develop the social principles of Christianity do so, then the communists will soon become silent', Marx thundered, 'The social principles of Christianity have now had eighteen hundred years to develop and need no further development from the counsellors of the Prussian consistory.' Marx continued:

> According to counsellors of the consistory, the social principles of Christianity place the recompense for all infamies in heaven, and thereby justify the continuation of these infamies on earth. The social principles of Christianity declare all the perfidies of the oppressors against the oppressed to be either righteous punishment for original sin and sundry other sins, or trials that the Lord, in his infinite wisdom, has decreed for the redeemed. The social principles of Christianity preach cowardice, self-contempt, degradation, submissiveness, meekness, in short, all the qualities of dogs, and the proletariat, who do not want to be treated as dogs, need their courage, sense of self-worth, pride, and independence, even more than their bread. The social principles of Christianity are hypocritical, and the proletariat are revolutionary. So much for the social principles of Christianity.[33]

Similarly, in a series of articles that he contributed to the March and April 1839 editions of the Hamburg-based *Telegraph für Deutschland*, an 18-year-old Friedrich Engels harshly criticised the religious beliefs, personal character, and even the physical appearances, of the 'Pietist' artisans, pastors and manufacturers in his home city of Barmen, the latter of whom included his father and paternal grandfather.[34] Engels's criticisms are somewhat ironic given that his own immediate forebears had built, and maintained at their own expense, a school for the children of their factory workers, and had also established other institutions for poor relief in their community.[35] Nevertheless, during his apprenticeship to a merchant in Bremen on the North Sea coast of Germany, the scion of the Engels family contended that the awakened Protestant religious tradition in which he had been reared had exercised manifold deleterious influences on social life in the Wupper Valley of his native Rheinland.[36]

Marx's and Engels's own views on the ineffectiveness of Christian socialism and the antithetical relationship between Christianity and communism notwithstanding, in 1847, Wichern began to use the term 'Christian socialism' (*christlicher Sozialismus*) to urge his fellow believers to practice the type of self-sacrificial love for the poor that he insisted the Christian faith demanded.[37] For Wichern, 'Christian socialism' was a way of enacting the 'inward mission' or the 'home mission' (*innere Mission*), another neologism that became part of the German Protestant lexicon in this era. The concept of the 'inward mission' originated with Friedrich Lücke, a professor of theology at the University of Göttingen. In a November 1842 address to the Göttingen Missionary Society, Lücke maintained that just as German Protestants were sending missionaries to preach the gospel to non-Christian people groups in countries outside of Europe, they simultaneously had to begin doing so within Germany itself.[38] Lücke observed that there were many people in Germany, especially the members of the working class and the poor, who were largely unattached or estranged from the churches, even though they had been born in a long-standing Christian country and were thus generally assumed to be Christians. Lücke urged the Protestants of the historic German churches to look to the Methodist movement that John Wesley had led within the eighteenth-century Church of England as a model for the type of missionary work that he hoped they would undertake among their countrymen and women.[39]

Wichern first used the term Christian socialism in 1847, in the context of organising assistance on behalf of German workers who had gone abroad to seek employment. Wichern argued that the needs of tens of thousands of Germans who had fallen into poverty in England, France, Russia and the Ottoman Empire had been forgotten about at home.

> Nothing is more patriotic than Christianity, because it contains the seed and the strength for the inner perfection of the nation, which it does not destroy, but rather transfigures. Despite all its diverse political forms, the nation realises a higher unity not merely through trade policy or scholarship, but also through Christian socialism. Christianity teaches to rediscover one's 'neighbour' not only in physical space, but in popular sympathy, and to act with the power of saving love.[40]

The outbreak of violent protests the following year increased Wichern's impetus to discuss his vision for Christian socialism.

In an 1848 essay entitled 'The Revolution and the Inward Mission', Wichern lamented that so few German Protestants had previously paid attention to the sufferings of the poor. 'Unheard of things have happened and perhaps even more unheard of things will yet take place, but who could and will be surprised by this, who was really even somewhat familiar with the troubling conditions in the life of our people[?]'[41] Wichern continued,

> The inward mission, with its hundred, isolated, and, at least in Germany, for the most part, still muted voices, has long pointed to the abyss that has now opened up. It called, pleaded, begged, warned, advised, and pointed to how to help before this happened ... This peaceful war for salvation was partly not wanted, as for it there was neither time nor courage. Thus has this wicked war of destruction broken out among the peoples, and who knows how to predict its end.[42]

Wichern, however, did not counsel despair but rather admonished his readers to recommit themselves to practically improving the lives of the destitute and to preaching the gospel to them. Referring to the Revolution of 1848 that had begun in Paris, Wichern wrote,

> The day of the greatest unfolding of the inward mission has now dawned. Now, or perhaps never, it has the occasion and the calling to rise in its strength to embrace all people ... There is a Christian socialism of which the French kind is only a caricature. In the already active Christian associations that are dedicated to all kinds of practical aims, Christian socialism has already begun its work, as we have announced all along.[43]

Wichern went into greater detail regarding the building of Christian socialism in a two-part essay published in 1848, 'Communism and Its Remedy' ('*Kommunismus und die Hilfe gegen ihn*'). Wichern distinguished communism from socialism, noting that the former was as different from the latter as 'destruction is from construction'.[44] Wichern explained that he strongly opposed communism because certain communists had called for the dissolution or abolition of the state, the church, the family and marriage relationships to bring about the total 'equalisation' (*Ausgleichung*) of all people in society.[45] Wichern insisted that all these institutions had been created by God and were essential for human flourishing. While severe in his criticisms of communism, Wichern called for Protestant pastors to exhort their mostly middle- and upper-class parishioners to repent of the sins that they had committed against the working class and the poor.

> The members of the church, those who take part in its worship services, are in overwhelming numbers, property owners, the 'bourgeoisie', against whom, primarily, the arms of the proletariat are currently

stirred up. It is exactly within this circle that the clergy must proclaim that of which they have become aware: the guilt of the church towards the proletariat. It must be made clear and palpable to all members of the congregation that this guilt is shared. All must at least learn to see how sin has been at work in creating this conflict and how justice – which is at once faith and love – has to create here the beginning of a new era. Love for the poor is the foundational theme that must encompass all others.[46]

Wichern encouraged his readers to become involved in religious voluntary societies that met to relieve the needs of the poor and to support the building of churches in working-class districts of cities so that those men, women and children who lived there could hear the gospel message and participate in Christian worship.[47] Among the many practical examples of how Christian socialism could be pursued, Wichern pointed to the work of the London City Mission, which had been founded in 1835 by David Naismith and to that of numerous Christian women's associations throughout Germany that were modelled after Amalie Sieveking's work in Hamburg.[48] Writing in 1849, Wichern characterised Sieveking's and other women's efforts as 'effective Christian socialism', a year before Sieveking issued her 1850 'Appeal to the Christian Women and Maidens of Germany' (*Aufruf an christlichen Frauen und Jungfrauen Deutschlands*), in which she used the phrase 'a Christian communism' (*einen christlichen Communismus*) to describe the type of self-sacrificial love for the poor that the Christian faith demanded from its adherents.[49]

Amalie Sieveking and 'Christian Communism'

In September 1831, in response to an outbreak of cholera in Hamburg, Amalie Sieveking, published a plea in a local newspaper, urging others to join her in nursing the 'members of the poorer classes of our father city' in one of the emergency hospitals established for this purpose. Sieveking continued,

> We now live in a world that lies in a pitiful condition, a veritable showplace of sufferings and sorrows. We are living in so-called Christendom, but we are surrounded by those to whom 'Christianity' is just an empty word, those who have not experienced the sanctifying and quickening power of the gospel in their own hearts.

Sieveking insisted that Christians must act on behalf of the needy as the epidemic gripped their city. 'Perhaps a few of the lost may be called to Christ through the witness of our words', she asserted, 'but the greater witness of a life that is delighted in God and active in works of love is a sacred duty that is incumbent upon all Christians together.'[50] While no volunteers answered her calls on this occasion, the following year, in 1832, Sieveking was joined by twelve other women as she founded the Women's Association for the Care of the Poor and the Sick (*Weiblicher Verein für Armen- und Krankenpflege*) in Hamburg, thereby becoming the first woman to organise and lead a public Christian ministry in modern Germany.

Sieveking and the growing numbers of other women who joined her association over the next quarter-century visited the homes of families who were facing poverty and distress because of the death, disability, illness or unemployment of a breadwinner or other family member. Members of the Women's Association assisted those in need by providing food, clothing, medicine, vouchers for fuel to heat the home and money to pay for visits to the doctor and children's school fees, among other necessities. Additionally, members of the association talked with those whom they visited about spiritual matters, encouraging them to read the Bible and other Christian literature, participate in church worship services and receive communion. By Sieveking's death in April 1859, a total of 193 women had joined the association and they had collectively visited 1,192 impoverished families in Hamburg.[51] Sieveking chronicled her association's work on behalf of the city's vulnerable men, women and children in her comprehensive annual reports, whose circulation helped to inspire women in twenty-six other European cities and towns – including Bern, Bonn, Bremen, Danzig, Frankfurt-am-Main, Hannover, London, Paris, Potsdam, Rotterdam, Stuttgart, Tallinn and Zürich – to form associations modelled after her own.[52] The annual reports of the Women's Association for the Care of the Sick and the Poor furnished Sieveking with a platform to discuss political, socio-economic and theological topics related to her work and to discuss her views on communism.

Sieveking's earliest mention of communism appeared in 1844 in her twelfth annual report, as part of her discussion of Hamburg's recovery after the great fire of May 1842. According to a contemporary report, this disaster had killed 51 residents and left 19,995 men, women and children homeless, approximately 11 per cent of the city's population.[53] Sieveking observed that the rapid rebuilding of the city had led some to conclude that wealth was abundant in Hamburg and to question whether philanthropic initiatives, such as her own, were even still needed.

> It is true, many are able to make a better living than they were previously, however, this is not true to the extent that some imagine it to be. One is certainly wrong, if he believes himself justified in asserting that any man only has to want to work, in order to be able to find work that pays well enough to maintain himself and his family.[54]

Sieveking stressed that those workers who had health problems, whose wives were sick, and who had to provide for 'five or six children', often struggled to make financial ends meet. Moreover, she argued that the arrival of younger, unmarried journeymen from other areas exposed local craftsmen to greater competition, which drove down their wages at the same time that housing rents were rising. Sieveking added that when shopkeepers faced diminished profit margins, they frequently balanced their books by reducing the wages of the women and girls who worked for them. Sieveking expressed her concern that some people's increased wealth was having a corrosive effect on their character, making them more self-absorbed as they pursued various pleasures. Thus, in equal but opposite ways, Sieveking insisted that the waxing inequality of Hamburg society had alienated both the rich and the poor from God and from each other.

> But where toil and indulgence are the only destinies, how should life not become more and more detached from that which is above? How should such a life, which has become entirely subsumed by earthly activities, not be the most fertile soil for receiving the haughty, proliferating weed of communism, the communism that in so many places is already raising its head more and more violently and threatens to tear all social relationships apart at their seams?[55]

Sieveking founded the Women's Association for the Care of the Sick and the Poor in part to address this situation. 'To unite in Christian faith and Christian love a bond of community between the higher and lower classes, and thereby prepare a blessing for those who are lower and higher, that is the task of our association.'[56] Sieveking averred that the reformation of society had to begin with a change in the conduct of the most wealthy and powerful. 'In my personal judgment, the ruin of the poor is also always a reproach upon the rich, and instead of breaking the rod over the poor in judgment, in most cases the wealthy probably ought to denounce themselves before the throne of God for their own sloth and wanting zeal in love.'[57] Such was the essence of Sieveking's idea of Christian communism. 'I feel compelled to express my fervent conviction that the evil of communism cannot be remedied in any other way than homoeopathically, namely, [that] the communism of the poor [has to be driven out] by the communism of the rich.'[58]

Two years later in her 1846 report she elaborated on these themes, deploring how through the course of her ministry she had witnessed numerous 'injustices': men who worked diligently for insufficient wages; women who had taken in piecework to earn additional money to buy food for their families, only to be haggled down by their wealthier customers after working through the night to complete a job; and children who died young as a result of poor nutrition and lack of adequate clothing.[59]

> Consider, then, the serious word that the apostle speaks concerning those who have withheld the wages of their workers, whose groanings are in the ears of the Lord of Hosts and shall not go unavenged (James 5:4). Let us not overlook the grave signs of the times! The principles of communism are being preached ever louder and in ever wider circles.[60]

Sieveking called on her fellow Protestants to reconcile the rich to the poor, by admonishing them to meet their needs.

> When the imperfections of our social conditions do not permit everyone who is able and willing to work to eat his own bread and set something aside for the days of illness and old age, then a wide field is opened here for Christian love that helps others. This love should equalise and mediate, fill the gulf between the rich and the poor, and, through the ties of benevolence, bind hearts with hearts, ones which, if not previously hostile, were at least cold and alien to each other.[61]

Given how negatively Sieveking viewed radical political movements, it is somewhat surprising that in her 1848 annual report, she opposed state censorship of ideas with which she fundamentally disagreed. She argued that

> The most unlimited freedom of the press and speech has now been introduced among us, and how it is exploited by the proclaimers of unbelief, of socialism and communism! This shamelessness is carried to the extreme, up to the publicly pronounced assertion, that the idea of God is only an invention of those in power, to subjugate the masses.[62]

While displeased by such developments, Sieveking maintained that it expressed a lack of faith in God for Christians to request state authorities to suppress those who criticised Christianity.

> I have always spoken out in favour of the most perfect freedom of conscience and religious liberty. Even if such excesses must fill us with the deepest regret, I do not see in them any authorisation to slap restrictive chains on the free human spirit. Moreover, it always seems to me to show a kind of distrust in the divine power of truth when one thinks that to protect it against lies, one must take up physical weapons and resort to external means of violence. No, the sanctuary of the spirit, the faith of the gospel, is defended, only with spiritual weapons, otherwise it would not be what it is: divine in it its origin, if they were not sufficient to give it victory. Let the teachings of atheism and deism be opposed only by the teachings of pure Christianity, and soon the former will be recognised by sincere, truth-seeking souls in their emptiness and barrenness. But the opportunity for comparison must be given them.[63]

Nevertheless, as part of reflections on Acts 4:12 – 'I still hold fast the old word of the apostle: "There is salvation in no other, neither is there any other name given to men, whereby we must be saved, but the name of Jesus Christ"' – Sieveking feared what would happen in Germany, if the state itself ever turned away from Christianity.[64] 'To build a state on any other foundation than that of religion must seem like madness to every thoughtful observer. Take away from a people all faith in higher things and you transform them into a troop of rapacious beasts, among whom only the bloody law of the strong rules.'[65] For this reason, in her 1850 *Appeal to the Christian Women and Maidens of Germany*, Sieveking exhorted those who read her reports to pursue a type of 'women's emancipation' (*Emancipation des Weibes*). By this Sieveking did not mean emancipation 'in the anti-Christian sense of the communists', but rather, citing the example of ancient Christian women recorded by the second- and third-century church father Tertullian of Carthage, she articulated a 'Christian conception' of female emancipation based on her idea of building Christian communism in German society.[66]

Sieveking argued that

> As long as anti-Christian communism has not yet gained full acceptance, from which may God, in his grace, preserve us, for at least as long, bourgeois women are certainly not called upon to actively involve themselves in the affairs of state. But to what are they called? I would say, her calling is to assert in her circles, and as far as her influence reaches, a Christian communism, in opposition to those anti-Christian ones.[67]

At the time that she wrote these words, Sieveking was in her nineteenth year of visiting the Hamburg poor in their homes to deliver them aid, while her association also worked to help them obtain better employment opportunities and housing. She acknowledged that the scope of the social problems that she was trying to redress was enormous.

> There is scarcely a lie that is not based on some truth. We must not overlook this in the case of the monstrous lie of anti-Christian communism. Let us not hide it from ourselves. There really are outrageous evils present in social conditions that demand immediate relief. In a thousand cases the condition of the working classes is so beaten down and in a thousand cases the help granted to the poor is not right, that is, it is not implemented to raise them morally, but rather exercises a demoralising influence.[68]

Sieveking commended to her readers the numerous Christian religious voluntary societies that had formed to spread the gospel and address particular social problems, and called them to become a member of one, in which they felt that they were most suited to use their talents and abilities. 'It is love born of faith alone that can bring about what I above described as Christian communism.'[69]

Conclusion

Wichern's and Sieveking's calls for Christian socialism and Christian communism reflected the best of the social conscience of the Protestant Awakening movement. Through their personal experiences in ministering to men, women and children in highly difficult personal circumstances they developed an understanding of the Christian faith as one that was inherently social and demanded its professors to meet the bodily and the spiritual needs of those around them. Unlike many others who shared their generally conservative theological and political perspectives, they acknowledged that those who did not share their faith, and who even sometimes sharply attacked the churches, had valid criticisms of the churches and true insights into their society's problems, from which Christians could learn. In particular, Wichern's notion that the church itself had sinned against the proletariat and needed to repent corporately, and Sieveking's endorsement of freedom of speech for atheists and revolutionaries, are notably progressive views. More research is necessary to determine how others who were calling for justice in nineteenth-German society viewed their proposals. For example, research conducted under the auspices of the International Marx–Engels Foundation has so far identified 10,205 individuals who are named across the pages of the Marx Engels Collected Works. However, neither Sieveking nor Wichern are included among them.[70] Likewise, it would be illuminating to bring Wichern's and Sieveking's nuanced evaluations of socialism and communism into conversation with other nineteenth-century Christian interpretations and responses to the same.

Sieveking and Wichern lived through a period of fundamental transformation in Germany during which a distinctly modern society of classes (*Klassengesellschaft*) decisively replaced a much older society of social orders (*Ständegesellschaft*).[71] Much of their own thinking, however, was informed by the social and religious norms of the latter. In its ideal form, the society of social orders was organised around relationships of reciprocal obligations throughout the social hierarchy, which Sieveking and Wichern either did not critically examine, or which they considered to be organic, natural and God-given. The most creative aspect of their Christian social visions was their argument that the onus for establishing socialism or communism lay upon Christians of the middle and upper classes, who had to answer to God for the living conditions that prevailed among those less fortunate than themselves, and to whom they were obligated to help. Thus their proposals for Christian socialism and Christian communism may be seen as sincere attempts to sanctify the already existing social order, alternatives to which they could not imagine or dismissed as dystopian.

Notes

1. On their respective historical development of both terms see Wolfgang Schieder, 'Kommunismus', in *Geschichtliche Grundbegriffe. Historisches Lexikon zur politisch-sozialen Sprache in Deutschland*, vol. 3, ed. Otto Brunner, Werner Conze and Reinhart Kosselleck (Stuttgart: Klett-Cotta, 1982), pp. 455–529; Wolfgang Schieder, 'Sozialismus', in *Geschichtliche Grundbegriffe. Historisches Lexikon zur politisch-sozialen Sprache in Deutschland*, vol. 5, ed. Otto Brunner, Werner Conze

and Reinhart Kosselleck (Stuttgart: Klett-Cotta, 1984), pp. 923–96. On the introduction of communist and socialist ideas from into Germany, see also Jacques Droz, 'Le socialism allemande du Vormärz', in *Histoire Générale du Socialisme*, vol. 1, ed. Jacques Droz (Paris: Presses Universitaires de France, 1972), pp. 407–54.
2. 'Communismus', in *Allgemeine deutsche Real-Encyklopädie für die gebildeten Stände. Conversations-Lexicon*, 9th edn (Leipzig: F. A. Brockhaus, 1843), pp. 580–6; 'Socialismus', in *Allgemeine deutsche Real-Encyklopädie für die gebildeten Stände. Conversations-Lexicon*, 9th edn (Leipzig: F. A. Brockhaus, 1847), pp. 393–7. On the encyclopaedia itself, see Jeff Loveland, *The European Encyclopedia: From 1650 to the Twenty-First Century* (New York: Cambridge University Press, 2019), pp. 36–48 and Anja zum Hingst, *Geschichte des Grossen Brockhaus. Vom Conversationslexikon zur Enzyklopädie* (Wiesbaden: Harrassowitz, 1995), pp. 129–35.
3. 'Socialismus', in *Allgemeine deutsche Real-Encyklopädie*, pp. 393–4.
4. 'Socialismus', in *Allgemeine deutsche Real-Encyklopädie*, p. 394.
5. 'Socialismus', in *Allgemeine deutsche Real-Encyklopädie*, p. 394.
6. Norbert Bachleitner, *Censorship of Literature in Austria, 1751–1848*, trans. Stephan Stockinger (Leiden: Brill, 2022), pp. 158–61; Bärbel Holtz, 'Staatlichkeit und Obstruktion – Preußens Zensurpraxis als politisches Kulturphänomen', in *Preußens Zensurpraxis von 1819 bis 1848 in Quellen*, ed. Bärbel Holtz (Berlin: Walter de Gruyter, 2015), p. 75; Heinrich Eduard Brockhaus, *Friedrich Arnold Brockhaus. Sein Leben und Wirken*, vol. 3 (Leipzig: F. A. Brockhaus, 1881), pp. 183–246.
7. Walter Bußmann, 'Christian Karl Josias Freiherr von Bunsen', *Neue Deutsche Biographie*, vol. 3, ed. Otto Graf zu Stolberg-Wernigerode et al. (Berlin: Duncker and Humblot, 1957), pp. 17–18.
8. 'Foreigners' Evangelical Society', *Evangelical Magazine and Missionary Chronicle*, 24 (1846), pp. 543–4.
9. 'German Hospital', *London Evening Standard*, 10 March 1848, p. 4.
10. Ibid., p. 4.
11. Ibid., p. 4.
12. Christopher Clark, *Iron Kingdom: The Rise and Downfall of Prussia, 1600–1947* (London: Penguin Books, 2007), p. 475.
13. For recent analyses of the Awakening movement, see Andrew Kloes, *The German Awakening: Protestant Renewal after the Enlightenment, 1815–1848* (New York: Oxford University Press, 2019) and Gustav Adolf Benrath, 'Die Erweckung innerhalb der deutschen Landeskirchen 1815–1888. Ein Überblick', in *Der Pietismus im neunzehnten und zwanzigsten Jahrhundert*, ed. Ulrich Gäbler, vol. 3 of *Geschichte des Pietismus*, ed. Martin Brecht, Klaus Deppermann, Ulrich Gäbler and Hartmut Lehmann (Göttingen: Vandenhoeck and Ruprecht, 2000), pp. 150–271.
14. For introductions to Sieveking and Wichern, see: Hans-Martin Gutmann, 'Der Schatten der Liebe. Johann Hinrich Wichern (1808–1881)', in *500 Jahre Theologie in Hamburg. Hamburg als Zentrum christlicher Theologie und Kultur zwischen Tradition und Zukunft*, ed. Johann Anselm Steiger (Berlin: De Gruyter, 2005), pp. 155–88 and Inge Mager, 'Weibliche Theologie im Horizont der Hamburger Erweckung. Amalie Sieveking (1794–1859)', in *500 Jahre Theologie in Hamburg*, pp. 189–224. In addition to numerous German regional and topical studies of the Revolutions of 1848–9, major national and international interpre-

tations published since their sesquicentenary include: Gareth Stedman Jones and Douglas Moggach (eds), *The 1848 Revolutions and European Political Thought* (New York: Cambridge University Press, 2018); Dieter Hein, *Die Revolution von 1848/49* (Munich: Verlag C. H. Beck, 2016); Frank Lorenz Müller, *Die Revolution von 1848/49* (Darmstadt: Wissenschaftliche Buchgesellschaft, 2012). Frank Engehausen, *Die Revolution von 1848/49* (Paderborn: Schöningh Verlag, 2007); Wolfram Siemann, *1848/49 in Deutschland und Europa: Ereignis–Bewältigung–Erinnerung* (Paderborn: Schöningh Verlag, 2006); Hans-Ulrich Wehler, *Von der Reformära bis zur industriellen und politischen 'Deutschen Doppelrevolution' 1815–1845/49*, vol. 2 of *Deutsche Gesellschaftsgeschichte* (Munich: C.H. Beck, 2005).

15. Georg Daur, *Von Predigern und Bürgern. Eine hamburgische Kirchengeschichte von der Reformation bis zur Gegenwart* (Hamburg: Agentur des Rauhen Hauses, 1970), pp. 191–9; Ingrid Lahrsen, *Zwischen Erweckung und Rationalismus. Hudtwalcker und sein Kreis* (Hamburg: Friedrich Wittig Verlag, 1959), pp. 109–17; Hans Georg Bergemann, *Staat und Kirche in Hamburg während des 19. Jahrhunderts* (Hamburg: Friedrich Wittig Verlag, 1958), pp. 41–2.

16. Martin Gerhardt, *Jugend und Aufstieg. 1808–1845*, vol. 1 of *Johan Hinrich Wichern. Ein Lebensbild* (Hamburg: Agentur des Rauhen Hauses, 1927), p. 44; Martin Gerhardt (ed.), *Der junge Wichern. Jugendtagebücher Johann Hinrich Wicherns* (Hamburg: Agentur des Rauhen Hauses, 1925), pp. 147, 151, 189.

17. Emma Poel, *Denkwurdigkeiten aus dem Leben von Amalie Sieveking in deren Auftrage von einer Freundin derselben verfajst* (Hamburg: Agentur des Rauhen Hauses, 1860). While there is no modern scholarly biography of Amalie Sieveking in German, her life and work have been the subject of the following journal articles and book chapters: Andrew Kloes, 'Caring for the Sick in Hamburg: Amalie Sieveking and the "Dormant Strength" of Christian Women', *Studies in Church History*, 58 (2022), pp. 217–40; Inge Grolle, 'Amalie Sieveking (1794–1859)', in *Frauen gestalten Diakonie*, vol. 2, ed. Adelheid M. von Hauff (Stuttgart: Kohlhammer Verlag, 2006), pp. 120–31; Jutta Schmidt, *Beruf: Schwester. Mutterhausdiakonie im 19. Jahrhundert* (Frankfurt: Campus Verlag, 1998), pp. 36–60; Theodor Kuessner, *Die Erweckungsbewegung in Hamburg im Spiegel der Briefe, Tagebücher und theologischen Schriften Amalie Sievekings* (Hamburg: Wittig Verlag, 1986); Rainer Postel, 'Amalie Sieveking', in *Die Neueste Zeit*, vol. 9, part 1 of *Gestalten der Kirchengeschichte*, ed. Martin Greschat (Stuttgart: Kohlhammer Verlag, 1985), pp. 233–42.

18. Recent studies on Wichern include: Volker Herrmann and Roland Anhorn (eds), *Johann Hinrich Wichern. Theologe–Sozialpädagoge–Reformer* (Heidelberg: Diakoniewissenschaftliches Institut, 2010); Sigrid Schambach, *Johann Hinrich Wichern* (Hamburg: Ellert & Richter, 2008); Dietrich Sattler, *Anwalt der Armen, Missionar der Kirche: Johann Hinrich Wichern, 1808 – 1881* (Hamburg: Agentur des Rauhen Hauses, 2007); Volker Herrmann, Jürgen Gohde and Heinz Schmidt (eds), *Johann Hinrich Wichern – Erbe und Auftrag. Stand und Perspektiven der Forschung* (Heidelberg: Universitätsverlag Winter, 2007); Martin Gerhardt, *Johann Hinrich Wichern und die Innere Mission. Studien zur Diakoniegeschichte*, ed. Volker Herrmann and Jürgen Gohde (Heidelberg: Universitätsverlag Winter, 2002); and Jürgen Albert, *Christentum und Handlungsform bei Johann Hinrich Wichern (1808–1881). Studien zum sozialen Protestantismus* (Heidelberg: Heidelberger Verlagsanstalt, 1997).

19. Angela Merkel, 'Wichern hat vieles angestoßen, was heute noch Gültigkeit hat', in *Wichernjahr 2008*, ed. Peter Bosse-Brekenfeld (Frankfurt-am-Main: Gemeinschaftswerk der Evangelischen Publizistik, 2008), pp. 8–12.
20. For example, see: Laura Claudia Achtelstetter, *Prussian Conservatism 1815–1856: Ecclesiastical Origins and Political Strategies* (Cham: Springer, 2021); David L. Ellis, *Politics and Piety: The Protestant Awakening in Prussia, 1816–1856* (Leiden: Brill, 2017); Reiner Strunk, *Politische Ekklesiologie im Zeitalter der Revolution* (Munich: Christian Kaiser Verlag, 1971).
21. Heinrich Alt, 'Der christliche Socialismus unserer Zeit in seinem verschiedenen Erscheinungsformen und seiner Bedeutung für Kirche und Staat', *Kirchliche Vierteljahres-Schrift*, 1.3 (1844), pp. 1–55.
22. On Heinrich Alt (1811–1893), see his death notice in 'Personalien', *Theologisches Literaturblatt*, 14 (1893), p. 614.
23. Hartmut Lehmann, 'The Germans as a Chosen People: Old Testament Themes in German Nationalism', *German Studies Review*, 14.2 (1991), pp. 263–4.
24. Jochen-Christoph Kaiser, 'Sozialismus II', in *Theologische Realenzyklopädie*, vol. 31, ed. Gerhard Müller (Berlin: Walter de Gruyter, 2000), p. 449.
25. Alt, 'Der christliche Socialismus unserer Zeit', pp. 8–12.
26. David A. Bell, *The First Total War: Napoleon's Europe and the Birth of Modern Warfare* (London: Bloomsbury, 2007), p. 7.
27. Ernst Huth, *Evangelischer Vereinskalender Deutschlands und der deutsch-protestantischen Schweiz für das Jahr 1845* (Ludwigslust: Hinstof'sche Buchhandlung, 1845).
28. Johann Hinrich Wichern, 'Die in den letzten 25 Jahren gestifteten christlichen Vereine und Anstalten zur Hebung leiblicher und geistlicher Not unter Wittwen, Waisen, Armen, Gefangenen in Hamburg', *Fliegende Blätter aus dem Rauhen Hause zu Horn bei Hamburg*, 1 (1844), p. 187; Friedrich Gustav Lisco, *Das wohlthätige Berlin. Geschichtlich-statistische Nachrichten über die Wohlthätigkeits-Uebung Berlin's* (Berlin: G. W. F. Müller's Verlag, 1846), pp. 1–50, 183–94, 423–6.
29. Johann Hinrich Wichern, 'Vorwort', *Fliegende Blätter aus dem Rauhen Hause zu Horn bei Hamburg*, 2 (1845), p. 1–2.
30. Johann Hinrich Wichern, 'Neue Zeitschriften und Bücher, welche sich auf das Gebiet der inner Mission beziehen. Evangelischer Vereinskalender Deutschlands und der protestantischen Schweiz für das Jahr 1845', *Fliegende Blätter aus dem Rauhen Hause zu Horn bei Hamburg*, 2 (1845), p. 124.
31. Alt, 'Der christliche Socialismus unserer Zeit', p. 8.
32. On the *Rheinischer Beobachter*, see Lothar Dittmer, *Beamtenkonservativismus und Modernisierung: Untersuchungen zur Vorgeschichte der Konservativen Partei in Preussen 1810–1848/49* (Stuttgart: Franz Steiner Verlag, 1992), pp. 204–14.
33. Karl Marx, 'Der Kommunismus des "Rheinischen Beobachters"', in *Karl Marx Friedrch Engels Werke*, vol. 4, ed. Institut für Marxismus-Leninismus beim Zentralkomitee der Sozialistischen Einheitspartei Deutschlands (Berlin: Dietz Verlag, 1977), p. 200. Regarding the development of Marx's hostile attitude towards Christianity, see Owen Chadwick, *The Secularization of the European Mind in the Nineteenth Century* (London: Cambridge University Press, 1975), pp. 48–66.
34. On the *Telegraph für Deutschland*, see Wolfgang Rasch (ed.), *Karl Gutzkow. Erinnerungen, Berichte und Urteile seiner Zeitgenossen. Eine Dokumentation* (Berlin: De Gruyter, 2011), pp. 93–168.

35. On Friedrich Engels's grandfather and father, see Hermann Bollnow, 'Johan Caspar Engels (1753–1821)', in *Neue Deutsche Biographie*, vol. 4, ed. Historische Kommission bei der bayerischen Akademie der Wissenschaften (Berlin: Duncker and Humblot, 1959), pp. 527–8, and Wolfgang Köllmann, 'Friedrich Engels (1796–1860)', in *NDB*, vol. 4, pp. 520–1.
36. Friedrich Engels, 'Briefe aus dem Wuppertal', in *Karl Marx Friedrich Engels Werke*, vol. 1, ed. Institut für Marxismus-Leninismus beim Zentralkomitee der Sozialistischen Einheitspartei Deutschlands (Berlin: Dietz Verlag, 1981), pp. 413–32. On Engels's upbringing see Karl Kupisch, *Vom Pietismus zum Kommunismus. Zur Jugendentwicklung von Friedrich Engels*, 2nd edn (Berlin: Lettner-Verlag, 1965).
37. Johann Hinrich Wichern, 'Der Patriotismus, gemessen an der Erfahrung der inner Mission; der Mangel der allgemeinen nationalen Basis bei den moisten derartigen Bestrebungen', in *Die Kirche und ihr soziales Handeln*, vol. 1 of *Johann Hinrich Wichern Sämtliche Werke*, ed. Peter Meinhold (Berlin: Lutherisches Verlagshaus, 1962), p. 91.
38. Friedrich Lücke, *Die zwiefache innere und äußere Mission der Evangelischen Kirche, ihrer gleiche Nothwendigkeit und nothwendige Verbindung. Eine Rede in der Missions-Versammlung zu Göttingen den 13. Nov. 1842* (Hamburg: Perthes-Besser, 1843).
39. Lücke, *Die zwiefache innere und äußere Mission*, p. 12.
40. Wichern, 'Der Patriotismus, gemessen an der Erfahrung der inner Mission', p. 91.
41. Johann Hinrich Wichern, 'Die Revolution und die innere Mission', in *Die Kirche und ihr soziales Handeln*, vol. 1 of *Johann Hinrich Wichern Sämtliche Werke*, ed. Peter Meinhold (Berlin: Lutherisches Verlagshaus, 1962), p. 129.
42. Wichern, 'Die Revolution und die innere Mission', p. 129.
43. Wichern, 'Die Revolution und die innere Mission', pp. 129–30.
44. Johann Hinrich Wichern, 'Kommunismus und die Hilfe gegen ihn', in *Die Kirche und ihr soziales Handeln*, vol. 1 of *Johann Hinrich Wichern Sämtliche Werke*, ed. Peter Meinhold (Berlin: Lutherisches Verlagshaus, 1962), p. 133.
45. Wichern, 'Kommunismus und die Hilfe gegen ihn', pp. 133–4.
46. Wichern, 'Kommunismus und die Hilfe gegen ihn', p. 146.
47. Wichern, 'Kommunismus und die Hilfe gegen ihn', pp. 142–6.
48. Wichern, 'Kommunismus und die Hilfe gegen ihn', p. 149.
49. Johann Hinrich Wichern, *Die innere Mission der deutschen evangelischen Kirche. Eine Denkschrift an die deutsche Nation im Auftrage des Centralausschusses für die innere Mission* (Hamburg: Agentur des Rauhen Hauses zu Horn, 1849), pp. 132–3. Sieveking's appeal appeared in the following annual report of the voluntary society that she founded. Amalie Sieveking, *Achtzehnter Bericht über die Leistungen des weiblichen Vereins für Armen- und Krankenpflege* (Hamburg, 1850), pp. 24–57.
50. Amalie Sieveking, 'Amalie Sievekings Aufruf an christlichen Seelen', in *Quellenbuch zur Geschichte der Inneren Mission*, ed. Martin Hennig (Hamburg, 1912), pp. 165–6.
51. Kloes, 'Caring for the Sick in Hamburg', p. 237.
52. The copies of Sieveking's annual reports cited in this chapter were consulted in the Carl von Ossietzky Hamburg State and University Library. https://katalogplus.sub.uni-hamburg.de/vufind/Record/799137340.
53. Heinrich Schleiden, *Versuch einer Geschichte des großen Brandes in Hamburg vom 5. bis 8. Mai 1842* (Hamburg, 1843), pp. 219–24.

54. Amalie Sieveking, *Zwölfter Bericht über die Leistungen des weiblichen Vereins für Armen- und Krankenpflege* (Hamburg, 1844), p. 14.
55. Sieveking, *Zwölfter Bericht*, p. 15.
56. Sieveking, *Zwölfter Bericht*, p. 15.
57. Sieveking, *Zwölfter Bericht*, p. 15.
58. Sieveking, *Zwölfter Bericht*, pp. 15–16.
59. Amalie Sieveking, *Vierzehnter Bericht über die Leistungen des weiblichen Vereins für Armen- und Krankenpflege* (Hamburg, 1846), pp. 17–20.
60. Sieveking, *Vierzehnter Bericht*, p. 18.
61. Sieveking, *Vierzehnter Bericht*, pp. 19–20.
62. Amalie Sieveking, *Sechszehnter Bericht über die Leistungen des weiblichen Vereins für Armen- und Krankenpflege* (Hamburg, 1848), p. 40.
63. Sieveking, *Sechszehnter Bericht*, pp. 40–1.
64. Sieveking, *Sechszehnter Bericht*, p. 42.
65. Sieveking, *Sechszehnter Bericht*, p. 42.
66. Sieveking, *Achtzehnter Bericht*, pp. 24, 33.
67. Sieveking, *Achtzehnter Bericht*, p. 44.
68. Sieveking, *Achtzehnter Bericht*, pp. 44–5.
69. Sieveking, *Achtzehnter Bericht*, pp. 44–5.
70. 'Register', MEGAdigital, Marx–Engels-Gesamtausgabe, Internationale Marx-Engels Stiftung, accessed 30 January 2023, https://megadigital.bbaw.de/register/index.xql.
71. Jürgen Kocka, 'Stand–Klasse–Organisation. Strukturen sozialer Ungleichheit in Deutschland vom späten 18. Bis zum frühen 20. Jahrhundert im Aufrisß', in *Klassen in der europäischen Sozialgeschichte*, ed. Hans-Ulrich Wehler (Göttingen: Vandenhoeck and Ruprecht, 1979), pp. 137–40.

CHAPTER FIVE

James Baird and the Baird Trust: Industrial Philanthropy and Evangelical Activism in Victorian Scotland

Andrew Michael Jones

In 1843, anxieties surrounding the future of the established Church of Scotland reached new levels following the Disruption, in which a third of the clergy and perhaps half the laity seceded with Thomas Chalmers to form the Free Church.[1] In that same year, roughly thirty-five miles to the west of Edinburgh, the hot-blast furnaces of the industrialists James and William Baird reached new and unheard-of levels of pig-iron production.[2] The extraordinary wealth of James Baird – when directed into philanthropic channels four decades later in the form of a £500,000 donation – would prove a great boon to the health and vitality of the national Church. The Baird Trust, established to administer the funds, played a critical role in supporting the continued efforts of church endowment, church extension and home missions for the remainder of the nineteenth century and well beyond. Yet despite his leading role in promoting a conservative vision of social Christianity in urban Scotland in the context of the national Church, neither James Baird nor the Trust established in his name in 1873 have received the scholarly attention that their influence merits. In order to provide a clearer picture, this chapter will consider the motivations (social, economic, religious) for James Baird's commitment to church extension and evangelical philanthropy and trace the development of the Baird Trust's work during the years prior to 1900, in terms of institutional effectiveness, geographical impact and ministerial provision.

The best framework through which to understand both the motivations and the operations of the Baird Trust is the original Deed of Trust, written by James Baird in 1873. Early on, Baird established that the 'grand object' informing both his donation and the future work of the Trust was

> to assist in providing the means of meeting, or at least as far as possible promoting the mitigation of, spiritual destitution among the population of Scotland, through efforts for securing the godly upbringing of the young, establishing of Parochial Pastoral Work, and the stimulating of ministers and all agencies of the said Church of Scotland, to

sustained devotedness in the work of carrying the Gospel to the homes and hearts of all.[3]

The specific methods of achieving such goals then follow. First, the Trust would provide an endowment for an annual Baird Lecture to be given by a Church of Scotland minister.[4] Second, in order to support 'the spreading and preaching of the Gospel in connection with the Church of Scotland', grants would be made to support church building and endowment, stipends for ministers and research to better inform the church's approach.[5] Third, funding would be provided for the 'production and dissemination of sound literature'.[6] Finally, trust money could be directed towards financial support for divinity students training for ministry in the Church of Scotland, promoting Christian education in the nation's schools, and supplementing the work of the Home Mission, Education and Endowment Schemes of the General Assembly.[7] In sum, James Baird directed the Trust to use his £500,000 gift in support of the ongoing work of the Church of Scotland to offer the benefits of an active parish ministry to the entire Scottish nation.

James Baird: Background and Motivating Forces

The deed goes some way towards explaining James Baird's motivations, but a fuller understanding requires a consideration of his life leading up to the donation amidst the national and ecclesiastical developments of nineteenth-century Scotland. The man behind the Trust was born in the family farmhouse near present-day Coatbridge on 5 December of 1802 to Alexander and Jean Moffatt Baird.[8] His father was an upwardly mobile tenant farmer and entrepreneur who helped set James and his nine siblings (seven brothers, two sisters) up for success later by encouraging them to work together and expand beyond agriculture into industry.[9] He was educated at local parish schools, but left at age twelve to begin farm work. Around that time, Alexander Baird began to lease coalfields and established a mining operation. With the expansion of the family's coal business, James Baird left the farm and began to manage the mines, working alongside his older brothers William and Alexander. Then, in 1828, the elder Alexander and his sons signed a lease for ironstone access near their Gartsherrie coalpits and began to construct furnaces. James Baird managed the construction and operations of the ironworks at Gartsherrie, and the first furnace was put in blast in 1830.[10]

The ironworks of William Baird & Company (established in 1830) were immensely successful. As of 1843, sixteen furnaces were producing 100,000 tons per year. By 1870, they were 'reputed to be the world's leading pig-iron producer with 42 furnaces and a capacity of 300,000 tons per annum, with the profit that year alone put at £1,000,000'.[11] With wealth came freedom to invest time and resources in other affairs. A cradle conservative, James

Baird was elected Tory MP for Falkirk Burghs and held office from 1851 to 1857. He purchased or inherited a number of landed estates in Ayrshire, Inverness-shire and Aberdeenshire between 1854 and 1866, including the estate of Cambusdoon in Ayrshire.[12] Although he married twice, James Baird had no children. When he died without direct heirs in 1876, his estate was valued at £1,190,000.[13]

One key aspect of James Baird's identity was his conservatism. The Baird family were anomalous as Tories amongst Scotland's typically Liberal industrial elite.[14] More to the point, they also remained ardent supporters of the established Church of Scotland after the 1840s, when many families of a similar background joined the Free Church or United Presbyterian Church.[15] His economic worldview and ways in which he interacted with his workers were also markedly conservative and paternalistic. For Baird, frugality, morality and hard work would lead to stability and respectability. Unionisation and collective bargaining were signs of contempt and laziness. He made these views clear in the 1870s when he reflected upon an unsuccessful strike at the company's coalmines in 1837.[16] Yet he did consider it his duty to participate in programmes of social and religious uplift. He helped address public sanitation as the Chairman of the Parochial Board during a cholera outbreak in Coatbridge during the late 1840s, and both he and his brothers took an active interest in providing schools for their workers' children.[17] It was, however, his concern for the religious provision of his and other workers that consumed his time, resources and energy.

What Baird and others like him considered the pressing issues of the day resulted in large part from the ongoing effects of the industrialisation, urbanisation and demographic shifts for which he and his family were partially responsible. The development of heavy industry in Scotland began around 1800, following the mechanisation of textiles in the last decades of the eighteenth century. Firms like William Baird & Co. were able to take advantage of key inventions and local resources in the coal and iron industries. Their native Lanarkshire was home to rich deposits of coal and ironstone and J. B. Neilson's hot-blast furnace catalysed Scottish iron production on a new scale after 1830.[18] With industry came the rapid growth of Scotland's urban populations. The population of Scotland more than doubled between 1755 (1.26 million) and 1841 (2.62 million), and then nearly doubled again by 1911.[19] Much of the growth was concentrated in the industrial heartland around Glasgow, which by the turn of the century was a global leader in heavy industry.[20]

The social and economic developments during the first half of the nineteenth century posed extraordinary challenges for the Church of Scotland. The parishes of urban Scotland were growing faster than the ability of the national Church to provide the necessary accommodation and resources to the surging population. The Church's response to these 'lapsed masses' of 'spiritually destitute' working-class poor was pioneered in part by Thomas Chalmers, the popular preacher, political economist and leader of the Evangelical party of the Church of Scotland.[21] For Chalmers and his Evangelical colleagues, one critical solution was church extension – the process of building new churches (officially chapels) to evangelise the poor and provide them with the social and educational benefits of a traditional parish ministry. While they succeeded in building 210 new chapels between 1835 and 1839, the British government refused to provide endowments that would enable the ministers to focus on underprivileged areas without relying on congregational support to sustain their ministry.[22] At the Disruption of 1843, Chalmers went into the Free Church but the chapels built during the church extension campaign remained in hands of the Church of Scotland.[23] While the gargantuan task of endowing all of the chapels remained, the legal process for endowment was provided through an Act of Parliament in 1846. By the terms of the legislation, if £3,000 was invested providing a ministerial salary of £120 per annum, a chapel could be raised to the status of parish *quoad sacra* ('in regard to spiritual things') with a kirk session and all other infrastructure necessary to conduct active ministry within the territory of the parish.[24] Rev. James Robertson of Ellon continued Chalmers's mission of church extension and endowment by appealing for private donations in order to endow the chapels. Through his vigorous work, the new General Assembly Endowment Scheme (established in 1846) raised over £400,000 and helped endow 150 new parish churches.[25] In this way, the Church of Scotland attempted to provide parochial ministry to the nation's growing populace.

James Baird was a committed member of the Church of Scotland and participated in much of the work just described. By his own accounts, his earliest exposure to religion involved memorising psalms and going through the Westminster Shorter Catechism with his mother. As an adult he was an elder in the kirk and sometime member of the General Assembly.[26] Moreover, he was a faithful supporter of church extension at both the local and national level.[27] In 1836, he and his brothers arranged for their workers to attend Church of Scotland services at an on-site facility and brought in 'clergymen of eminence' to preach. The following year they even decided to shut down the furnaces on Sundays to provide a more appropriate environment for worship.[28] After helping erect a chapel in Gartsherrie in 1839, Baird was also – according to his later recollections – convinced by Chalmers himself to subscribe an undisclosed amount 'for each of the hundred churches which he proposed should be built'.[29] Then came Disruption.

While the established Church of Scotland suffered an immediate loss of talent and numbers in 1843, over the next decades it recovered and would go on to become the pre-eminent Presbyterian denomination in late Victorian Scotland. This was due to a number of factors, including a renewed evangelical impulse and the success of James Robertson's Endowment Scheme.[30] As a committed churchman, James Baird continued to support church extension by partnering with Robertson and personally endowing several churches on his own. In 1858, he endowed the Gartsherrie chapel.[31] In 1871, he subscribed £10,000 to the Endowment Scheme to be disbursed between 100 chapels, in 1873 gave £7,500 for five churches in Aberdeen, and in the final years of his life he provided support for two churches in Glasgow.[32] Yet his crowning achievement, of course, was the £500,000 donation to establish the Baird Trust.

Considering James Baird's background and previous work, it is clear that his donation and the establishment of the Baird Trust were shaped by an interrelated web of social, economic and religious motivations. First, the donation was likely motivated in part by social status and certainly motivated by social commitments. In terms of social status, large munificent donations were in keeping with the expectations of the evangelical industrial elite.[33] Inasmuch as James Baird was conscious of his social advancement (landed estates etc.), this could not have been far from his mind.[34] He also had no heirs. Associating his name in perpetuity with a historic act of philanthropy ensured a noble legacy for generations to come. Yet his social commitments factored in more concretely. As a conservative, James Baird's vision for Scottish society necessitated a strong established church to maintain and improve the whole social order of the Scottish nation.

Second, James Baird's economic motivations included a desire to apply the pragmatism and entrepreneurship of the business world to ecclesiastical systems and were driven by ability and opportunity. The conditions outlined in the deed for churches to receive financial assistance from the Baird Trust gave the Baird trustees a level of control over the constitution of new churches and encouraged the formation of a more businesslike managerial model of congregational oversight.[35] This feature of the Trust was viewed by several contemporaries as setting a dangerous precedent of giving laymen more power than ministers and taking away from the traditional role of the kirk session.[36] Yet over time these protests became muted. Baird's ability to contribute his donation was also shaped by the market and timing. The price of Scottish pig-iron peaked between 1872 and 1873 – the year Baird made the donation.[37] Further, in 1871 his nephew Alexander Whitelaw began to encourage him to consider how the aging magnate might spend his vast fortune in his final years.[38]

However, the pre-eminent motivation behind the gift and the Trust was a genuine religious concern, driven by a conservative and evangelical desire to provide increased access for working-class Scots to the parish ministry of the Church of Scotland. In this, Baird was not especially unique. The prevalence and popularity of evangelicalism in Great Britain was a major factor in the 'prosperous mid-Victorian years' becoming, in Frank Prochaska's words, 'a philanthropic golden age'.[39] With specific reference to Scotland, Olive Checkland contended that 'Scottish Victorian philanthropy . . . drew its strength from the evangelical movement'.[40] Like other established church evangelicals, James Baird saw the ordained clergy as the primary agents of converting their parishioners to an active, vibrant faith in Jesus

Christ.⁴¹ He believed that the solution to 'spiritual destitution' was 'securing that ministers faithfully preach and teach the Gospel'.⁴² This conviction seems to have flowed naturally from Baird's personal faith.

According to A. H. Charteris – the most prominent evangelical minister in the late Victorian Church of Scotland – James Baird was 'a man of great gifts both of head and heart; and his highest ambition was to serve God'.⁴³ Another Church of Scotland minister from the era described him as a 'man of pure life and deep religious convictions' with 'an unwavering faith in our old and well tried evangelical principles'.⁴⁴ The establishment of the Trust should also be seen as an extension of his previous work funding and endowing Church of Scotland parishes near his workers – the institutionalisation of a more local, 'informal benevolence' as it developed prior to 1873.⁴⁵

For Baird, the notion of 'evangelical principles' extended to a desire to champion a Reformed theological conservatism, as well. Another explicit reason he established the Trust was for the 'exposure and refutation of error' in church teaching.⁴⁶ The antidote was encouraging ministers and churches committed to 'sound religious principles'.⁴⁷ His chief end was a Church of Scotland rooted in the scholastic Calvinism of the Westminster Confession of Faith, 'the Inspiration of the Scriptures . . . and their supreme authority as the unerring rule of faith and duty', the divinity of Christ, 'His vicarious death as a sacrifice or satisfaction for sin', the resurrection, 'justification by faith alone' and 'the renewing and sanctifying work of the Holy Spirit.'⁴⁸ The means by which the Baird Trust would promote this theology was its programme of church extension and endowment, ministerial stipends and the annual Baird Lecture.

The Work of the Baird Trust: 1873–1900

One could be reasonably excused for walking past the offices of the Baird Trust at 168 W. George St in Glasgow's city centre and not thinking much of it.⁴⁹ A handsome building, it nevertheless would likely have blended into the background of the bustling 'second city' of the British Empire. Yet what happened inside 168 W. George St had an extraordinary impact on the Church of Scotland during the last decades of the nineteenth century and beyond. To the historian's delight, the meeting minutes of the Baird Trust were assiduously kept from the very beginning.⁵⁰ These records detail the work of the Trust and provide the means by which to assess the following categories referred to in the introduction: institutional effectiveness, geographical impact and ministerial provision. In other words, they give an answer as to whether or not the trustees maintained the goals and values laid out by James Baird in the deed three years prior to his death in 1876. That answer is, for the most part, yes. During the years under examination (1873–1900), the Baird Trust helped to build, endow and enlarge hundreds of churches, worked both deeply within urban spaces and widely within every region of Scotland, and furnished the nation's established church clergy with both financial and ideological support.

The deed and the minutes also reveal the mechanics of the Trust, including the men behind the minutes and the men behind the scenes. In the Deed of Trust, James Baird empowered the trustees to make financial decisions and outlined what he required of them. They would meet in Glasgow, and the meetings would be announced by way of a circular in the post with at least four days' notice. At any given time there would be between nine and seven trustees, and each of them was to be a member of the Church of Scotland and 'in full communion therewith'.[51] However, only one member of the Trust at any given time was to be a minister in the church.[52] The original seven trustees were nearly all members of the Baird family and company: James Baird, nephew William Baird of Elie, his nephews and business partners Alexander Whitelaw and William Weir, his great-nephew and business partner David Wallace, Alexander Campbell of Stracathro, and Rev. Archibald Scott.[53] While one of the trustees would serve as clerk and treasurer during the meetings with a chairman appointed from their number, the work of the Trust soon necessitated the hiring of a full-time salaried agent. The first to serve in this post, from 1874 until his death in 1879, was a schoolmaster from Clackmannanshire named John Maclurk.[54] The agent from 1879 until 1900 was yet another former schoolmaster, John Fraser of Glasgow.[55]

The most noteworthy figure yet to be mentioned was without a doubt Archibald Scott. As per the deed, Scott was the only Church of Scotland minister chosen to serve as a Baird Trustee, and he continued in his post for the duration of the period in question. Like Baird, Scott was the son of a Lanarkshire farmer. He was educated at the University of Glasgow and at the formation of the Baird Trust was minister of Greenside Church, Edinburgh. He would later transfer to St Georges, Edinburgh in 1880.[56] Scott's role in the Trust caused immediate friction in certain ecclesiastical circles. Not only were some concerned with the more businesslike management mentioned previously, others also worried that the Trust would elevate conservative elements within the church at the expense of liturgical and theological progressives.[57] Nevertheless, Scott soon became a leading figure within the General Assembly, serving on numerous committees and as Moderator in 1896. It is certainly not coincidental to his appointment that Scott shared James Baird's overarching vision for the church. Like Baird, he was deeply shaped by 'the territorial ideal of Chalmers as developed and applied by Robertson' and sought to continue church extension on those principles into the future.[58] He was also a conservative. While other evangelical leaders like Charteris began to adapt new methods of mobilising the laity, Scott held fast to traditional approaches.[59] Those approaches, moreover, were of the sort supported by the Baird Trust.

In terms of institutional effectiveness, the Baird Trust was hugely successful. As for the Baird Lecture, some of the most imminent and distinguished ministers and scholars of the Church of Scotland were appointed to the post of lecturer during the period in question. Their topics ranged from academic to practical theology, as evidenced by Robert Flint's 1876 'Theism' and Rev. William Smith's 'Endowed Territorial Work' from the previous year.[60] The minutes record the appointments and payments of the lecturers with regularity.[61]

The practice of funding lectures in perpetuity was not uncommon during the era in question. Indeed, in terms of nineteenth-century Scottish philanthropy involving the endowment of lectures, the Gifford Lectures offer a helpful exercise in contemporary comparison. The benefactor of the Gifford Lectures (established in 1888) was Adam Gifford, Lord Gifford. A wealthy retired lawyer and former member of the Court of Session (Scotland's highest court), he had wide-ranging and somewhat esoteric intellectual tastes and left £80,000 in his will to fund an annual series of lectures on religion at Scotland's four ancient universities (Aberdeen, Edinburgh, Glasgow, St Andrews). Like the Baird Lectures, the Gifford Lectures were thus established by another wealthy and well-known Scottish man with specific regard to religious themes.[62] Yet here the similarities mostly cease. In keeping with his Reformed and evangelical convictions, Baird made explicit in his Deed of Trust that the lecturer must not only be a minister in the Church of Scotland, but also 'a man of piety, ability, and learning, and who is approved and reputed in all the essentials of Christian truth'.[63] In contrast, Lord Gifford was a self-described 'Theopanist' who denied the verbal inspiration of scripture.[64] He thus desired his lectures to address natural or philosophical theology – broadly defined – delivered by anyone capable, regardless of denomination, religion or belief/unbelief.[65] In the landscape of contemporary endowed lectures, then, the Baird Lectures trod more traditional, ecclesiastical ground.

Despite the popularity and enduring relevance of the lectures, the vast majority of the secretarial ink spilled at the Baird Trust meetings during the period in question focused on grants made to promote church extension. In October of 1873, the Deed of Trust was printed and two copies were sent to each of the 1,280 ministers of the Church of Scotland – one for the minister and a second for the kirk session. A further fifty copies were sent to Scottish newspapers for wider distribution.[66] By the end of the year, the secretary recorded, 'A great many cases for Church building and Church Endowments and Augmentations were considered and the principles of them discussed and forwarded a stage.'[67] After developing a system of obtaining information from those seeking assistance and processing the applications, the trustees began to grant funds. The first major disbursement was made toward the endowment of the church at Wallacetown, Ayr in March of 1874.[68] From this point forward, the minutes show a steady stream of grants made to support the Trust's goal of promoting church extension. Each grant included the specific purpose, which included endowment, church building, both (usually referred to as 'establishment of new church and parish'), church enlargement, church improvement, extinction of debt, restoration and construction of church halls and mission halls. Of the categories listed, endowment and church building were by far the most common. Indeed, extension was largely prioritised over subsidiary purposes like promoting education and supplementing other General Assembly Schemes – both of which barely appear in the minutes.

While a bank book kept more complete records of the financial situation, for much of the time between 1873 and 1900 the minutes themselves provide various indications as to the amounts provided, both individually and in total. Most grants toward church extension were between £250 and £1,000. In its first year of full operation, the trustees voted £26,528 towards grants.[69] By 1877 the total number was just over £88,000.[70] The minutes from 1877 shift from noting the total amount of grants voted to a more comprehensive category of 'expenditure', yet the majority of the expenditures went towards making grants. The total expenditures at the end of 1880 reached £150,081.[71] By the end of the following decade, that number would more than double.[72] For unprovided reasons, the trustees decided to cease noting income and expenditures in 1892. At last mention, the total expenditures to date by the Baird Trust equalled £388,130.[73] During most of this period the income of the Trust (from loans, investments etc.) equalled or superseded the expenditures. When it did operate at a debt, it was rarely more than a few thousand pounds. Overall, the Baird Trust accomplished what it set out to achieve – especially in terms of church extension. It provided generous grants for hundreds of churches, many of which went towards endowment so as to enable the model of territorial parish ministry pioneered by Thomas Chalmers and championed by James Baird and Archibald Scott.

As for geographical emphasis, the deed did not restrict the work of the Trust to any specific region of Scotland, but rather encouraged a focus on urban spaces. Baird wrote, 'As such spiritual destitution exists to the greatest extent in populous places it is my wish that the operation of this Trust be directed in the first instance chiefly to such populaces places', specifically including 'the Synod of Glasgow and Ayr.'[74] So on the one hand, between 1873 and 1900 the Baird Trust supported nation-wide church extension and ministerial support. Those noted as receiving aid included parishes in the Borders, Central Belt, Northeast, Highlands, Inner and Outer Hebrides, Orkney and Shetland – as well as a grant to one of the remotest kirks in all of Scotland, for church building on Fair Isle in 1891.[75] Yet on the other hand, most of the disbursements recorded in the minutes went towards endowment and building in Edinburgh, Aberdeen, Dundee and Glasgow.

As per Baird's wishes, the trustees took a unique interest in church extension in and around Glasgow. Hew Scott's *Fasti Ecclesiae Scoticanae* – updated between 1915 and 1928 – lists 116 churches and chapels within the Presbytery of Glasgow.[76] Between 1873 and 1900, at least forty-two churches or chapels in the presbytery received some form of financial assistance from the Baird Trust.[77] Many received endowment grants and soon became functioning *quoad sacra* parishes. These Glaswegian churches receiving aid were located in some of the most urbanised and impoverished areas in all of Scotland, like Govan and the Gorbals. Rarely do the Baird Trust minutes of the period depart from a typically sparse, data-driven style and engage in descriptions of specific cases. However, the church extension needs of Govan were an exception to the rule. In 1887, the trustees met with Rev. John MacLeod of Govan and agreed to grant £500 toward a mission hall £2,000 towards extinguishing debt.[78] MacLeod returned again in 1893 and shared his plans for erecting and endowing two new churches and building two mission halls, at an estimated total cost of over £33,000. In response, the trustees voted to make one of the largest grants yet recorded – £7,150.[79] In summary, the trustees tended to give geographical priority to greater Glasgow, then to the other major cities, and lastly to smaller town and rural parishes.

Finally, the Baird Trust supported the ministers of the Church of Scotland in a variety of ways beyond endowing, building and improving their churches. Indeed, the support for ministers can be seen as matter of lifelong vocational encouragement that included both financial and theological elements. First, the Baird Trust helped students preparing for ministry. The early minutes note grants made towards 'student encouragement' or 'student aid' associations, and in 1897 they provided £1,000 'towards [a] residence hall for Divinity Students in Edinburgh'.[80] Second, the Trust offered small grants to supplement individual ministers' salaries. These were the most common, by far, and included two types: grants in augmentation of stipend and smaller livings grants. Third, they voted grants towards 'aged and infirm ministers', funds for those late in life who required pecuniary assistance.

While theological issues were not highlighted, the grants made towards promoting 'sound literature' centred on traditional, evangelical and conservative topics. For example, the Trust granted £200 in 1880 to help Professor A. F. Mitchell publish his transcriptions of the Minutes of the Westminster Assembly.[81] In 1890, they 'agreed to make a grant of £25–9/ towards the expense of distributing Pierson's "Crisis of Missions" among Divinity Students'.[82] The Pierson in question was the American missionary statesman and leading evangelical Arthur T. Pierson.[83] Then, in 1896, 'the meeting agreed to present an honorarium of £25 to the Rev. Professor [William Purdie] Dickson, D.D. in recognition of his pamphlet The Newer Light'.[84] The pamphlet in question was a conservative response to the work of Rev. Alexander Robinson of Kilmun, Argyll. In 1895, Robinson wrote a book entitled *The Saviour in the Newer Light: A Present-Day Study of Jesus Christ*.[85] His representation of Jesus aroused concerns that Robinson rejected the full divinity of Christ. After refusing to move on the issue, he was deposed for heresy by the General Assembly of 1897.[86] Beyond the realm of theological literature, the Trust also funded several series of lectures on practical theology.[87] By supporting ministers from training through retirement and holding fast to a general theological conservatism, yet again the trustees realised a number of the goals established by James Baird in 1873.

Conclusion

The work of James Baird and the Baird Trust between 1873 and 1900 represents one of the most important – and one of the last – examples of the practical outworking of a conservative vision of social Christianity in modern Scotland. Unlike later, more progressive Church of Scotland figures like Donald MacLeod and John Marshall Lang, James Baird was less concerned with the social and economic structures that perpetuated poverty and more concerned with the issue of 'spiritual destitution'.[88] As mentioned previously, Baird was no friend to organised labour. Yet like Chalmers, Baird's classical economics were tempered by a genuine – if paternalistic – evangelical concern for the well-being of his workers and other members of the Scottish working classes. This concern focused on religion, mediated to the people through the active, territorial parish ministry of the Church of Scotland.

Yet the traditional, Chalmersian approach of Baird and his trustees did not hinder them from accomplishing remarkable feats of church extension that added significantly to the vitality and strength of the late Victorian Church of Scotland. Hundreds of churches were built and endowed in places like Govan, where traditional sources of parochial fundraising were untenable and impractical. A great many ministers received grants in augmentation of stipends to continue their work, including Rev. George Wilson in 1875, who would later go on to become a leading figure in the Church of Scotland's evangelical Mission Weeks movement.[89] Indeed, this work continued beyond 1900 and continues up to the present. According to the Baird Trust website, the value of the Trust in 2019 was £11,000,000, and around £300,000 is disbursed every year to support the twenty-first-century vision of the Church of Scotland.[90] Finally, the intervening twelve decades of the Baird Trust offer exciting opportunities for future research, especially considering the existence of such rich primary sources as the meeting minutes. A twentieth-century study of the Baird Trust, for example, could explore the degree to which the work of the Trust changed, in dialogue with the historiography of secularisation in Scottish society.

Notes

1. See, for example, Stewart J. Brown and Michael Fry (eds), *Scotland in the Age of Disruption* (Edinburgh: Edinburgh University Press, 1993).
2. Robert D. Corrins, 'The Scottish Business Elite in the Nineteenth Century – The Case of William Baird & Company', in A. J. G. Cummings and T. M. Devine

(eds), *Industry, Business and Society in Scotland since 1700: Essays Presented to Professor John Butt* (Edinburgh: John Donald, 1994), p. 61.
3. James Baird, Esq., of Auchmedden, *'The Baird Trust.' Deed of Trust, Dated 24th July 1873* (Glasgow: Glasgow University Press, 1873), p. 5.
4. Ibid., pp. 11–12.
5. Ibid., p. 6.
6. Ibid., pp. 9–10.
7. Ibid., p. 10.
8. Andrew MacGeorge, *The Bairds of Gartsherrie: Some Notices of Their Origin and History* (Glasgow: Glasgow University Press, 1875), p. 48. MacGeorge's book was uniquely influenced by James Baird, and should be considered both a primary and secondary source. In the preface, MacGeorge notes that he received the information on the family background and James Baird through 'information obtained principally from Mr. Baird himself'. The book also includes long sections 'best given in Mr. James Baird's own words', where Baird effectively takes over as author. See, for example, pages 55ff.
9. MacGeorge, *Bairds*, p. 33; Corrins, 'Business Elite', p. 59.
10. MacGeorge, *Bairds*, pp. 45–59.
11. Corrins, 'Business Elite', pp. 61–2.
12. MacGeorge, *Bairds*, pp. 73, 87–8, 105–6.
13. Corrins, 'Business Elite', p. 64.
14. Ibid., p. 61.
15. Corrins, 'Business Elite', p. 61; David J. Jeremy, 'Important Questions about Business and Religion in Modern Britain', in David J. Jeremy (ed.), *Business and Religion in Britain* (Aldershot: Gower Publishing Company Ltd, 1988), p. 13.
16. James Baird, quoted in MacGeorge, *Bairds*, pp. 67–9.
17. MacGeorge, *Bairds*, pp. 85–6, 93–4; Corrins, 'Business Elite', p. 77.
18. I. G. C. Hutchison, *Industry, Reform and Empire: Scotland, 1790–1880* (Edinburgh: Edinburgh University Press, 2020), pp. 37–43.
19. Ewen Cameron, *Impaled upon a Thistle: Scotland since 1880* (Edinburgh: Edinburgh University Press, 2010), pp. 9–11.
20. Cameron, *Impaled*, p. 11; Hutchison, *Industry*, pp. 43–5.
21. Stewart J. Brown, *Thomas Chalmers and the Godly Commonwealth in Scotland* (Oxford: Oxford University Press, 1982).
22. Andrew L. Drummond and James Bulloch, *The Church in Victorian Scotland, 1843–1874* (Edinburgh: Saint Andrew Press, 1975), p. 117; Olive Checkland, *Philanthropy in Victorian Scotland: Social Welfare and the Voluntary Principle* (Edinburgh: John Donald, 1980), pp. 32–7.
23. Stewart J. Brown, 'After the Disruption: The Recovery of the National Church of Scotland, 1843–1874', *Scottish Church History*, 48.2 (2019), p. 109.
24. Drummond and Bulloch, *1843–1874*, p. 120; Francis Lyall, '*Quoad Sacra*', in Nigel M. de S. Cameron (ed.), *Dictionary of Scottish Church History & Theology* (Downers Grove, IL: Intervarsity Press, 1993), p. 688.
25. Brown, 'After the Disruption', p. 110; Checkland, *Philanthropy*, p. 37.
26. MacGeorge, *Bairds*, pp. 35, 106.
27. Corrins, 'Business Elite', p. 77.
28. James Baird in MacGeorge, *Bairds*, pp. 70–1.
29. Ibid., pp. 71–2.
30. See Brown, 'After the Disruption', and Andrew Michael Jones, *The Revival of*

Evangelicalism: Mission and Piety in the Victorian Church of Scotland (Edinburgh: Edinburgh University Press, 2022).
31. Hew Scott, Fasti Ecclesiae Scoticanae: The Succession of Ministers in the Church of Scotland from the Reformation, vol. 3 (Edinburgh: Oliver and Boyd, 1920), p. 251.
32. MacGeorge, Bairds, pp. 107–8; Scott, Fasti, vol. 3, pp. 402, 406.
33. Checkland, Philanthropy, p. 5; Jeremy, 'Business and Religion', p. 5.
34. Corrins, 'Business Elite', pp. 63–4.
35. Baird, Deed, pp. 7–9.
36. J. R. Fleming, The Church of Scotland, 1843–1874 (Edinburgh: T. & T. Clark, 1927), p. 232; Sir Christopher N. Johnston (The Hon. Lord Sands, LL.D), Dr. Archibald Scott of St George's, Edinburgh and His Times (William Blackwood and Sons, Edinburgh: 1919), pp. 70–1.
37. Hutchison, Industry, pp. 57–8; MacGeorge, Bairds, p. 84.
38. Corrins, 'Business Elite', p. 66.
39. Frank Prochaska, The Voluntary Impulse: Philanthropy in Modern Britain (London: Faber and Faber, 1988), pp. 22, 41.
40. Checkland, Philanthropy, p. 30.
41. Jones, Revival, pp. 21–2, 197.
42. Baird, Deed, p. 6. Checkland is instructive regarding this dynamic, as well: 'The Scotland of Victoria's reign saw a remarkable phenomenon, namely the attempt by the Church of Scotland and other churches in Scotland to stay the tide of secularism and to recall the nation to God and to his worship.' Checkland, Philanthropy, p. 30.
43. A. H. Charteris quoted in Arthur Gordon, The Life of Archibald Hamilton Charteris, D.D. (London: Hodder and Stoughton, 1912), p. 112.
44. Peter Anton, Kilsyth: A Parish History (John Smith and Son: Glasgow, 1893), pp. 257–8.
45. Prochaska, Voluntary Impulse, p. 8.
46. Baird, Deed, p. 3.
47. Ibid., p. 5.
48. Baird, Deed, pp. 5–6.
49. The Trust remained at this address from 1873 until 1899, when it moved nearby to 175 Hope St.
50. I owe a debt of gratitude to Mr I. A. T. Mowat, CA of the Baird Trust for allowing access to the records, Dr Jamie Kelly for digitising them, and to Morehouse College for a generous faculty grant to support the digitisation project.
51. Baird, Deed, pp. 16–17. This was non-negotiable. Leaving the Church meant resigning from the Trust.
52. Ibid., p. 16.
53. Ibid., p. 4.
54. Baird Trust Meeting Minutes, 11 August 1874. Hereafter cited as BTMM (day/month/year).
55. BTMM, 7/10/1879.
56. D.M. Murray, 'Archibald Scott', in Nigel M. de S. Cameron (ed.), Dictionary of Scottish Church History & Theology (Downers Grove, IL: Intervarsity Press, 1993), p. 753.
57. Johnston, Scott, pp. 68–71.
58. Ibid., p. 88.
59. Ibid., pp. 71–2, 88.

60. See Robert Flint, *Theism, Being the Baird Lecture for 1876* (Edinburgh: William Blackwood and Sons, 1877) and William Smith, *Endowed Territorial Work: Its Supreme Importance to the Church and Country, Being the Baird Lecture for 1875* (Edinburgh: William Blackwood and Sons, 1875).
61. BTMM, 8/4/1875 and 27/3/1876.
62. See Stanley L. Jaki, *Lord Gifford and His Lectures: A Centenary Retrospect* (Edinburgh: Scottish Academic Press, 1986).
63. Baird, *Deed*, pp. 11–12.
64. This is according to John Gifford, Lord Gifford's brother, in 'Recollections of a Brother, and of His Homes', in Jaki, *Lord Gifford*, p. 98.
65. Adam Gifford, Lord Gifford, 'Lord Gifford's Will', in Jaki, *Lord Gifford*, pp. 71–6.
66. BTMM, 22/10/1873.
67. BTMM, 11/17/1873.
68. BTMM, 17/3/1874.
69. BTMM, 12/11/1874.
70. BTMM, 8/1/1877.
71. BTMM, 17/12/1880.
72. BTMM, 23/10/1890. The October 1890 total was £365,235.
73. BTMM, 5/11/1892.
74. Baird, *Deed*, 5.
75. BTMM, 13/10/1891.
76. Scott, *Fasti*, vol. 3, pp. 371ff.
77. While impressive, the real number is likely much higher. The number forty-two is based on the years in which I did complete transcriptions (rather than selective annotations) of the minute books: 1873–6, 1880, 1885, 1890, 1895 and 1900.
78. BTMM, 13/5/1887.
79. BTMM, 30/10/1893.
80. BTMM, 28/10/1874, 11/12/1874, 25/9/1876, 17/12/1880, 4/11/1897.
81. BTMM, 26/10/1880.
82. BTMM, 10/4/1890.
83. See Dana L. Robert, *Occupy until I Come: A. T. Pierson and the Evangelization of the World* (Grand Rapids, MI: Eerdmans, 2003).
84. BTMM, 23/6/1896.
85. Alexander Robinson, *The Saviour in the Newer Light: A Present-Day Study of Jesus Christ* (Edinburgh: William Blackwood and Sons, 1895).
86. Johnston, *Scott*, p. 100.
87. BTMM, 4/6/1895, 30/10/1895, 3/9/1898.
88. Cameron, *Impaled*, pp. 25–6.
89. BTMM, 13/3/1875; Jones, *Revival*, pp. 159–61.
90. 'About the Baird Trust', The Baird Trust, accessed 26 March 2022, https://bairdtrust.org.uk/about-the-baird-trust/.

CHAPTER SIX

In Person, Print and Prayer: The Shared Mission of Scottish and English Ragged Schools in the Nineteenth Century

Laura M. Mair

I never engaged in a cause, as a man and a Christian minister, that I believe on my deathbed I will look back on with more pleasure or gratitude to God that he ever led me to work in than this cause of the Ragged Schools.[1] – Rev. Dr Thomas Guthrie

If the ragged school system were to fail I should not die in the course of nature, I should die of a broken heart.[2] – The Seventh Earl of Shaftesbury

Introduction

On Saturday, 19 January 1861 the *Birmingham Gazette* reminded its readers that the city was due to host a conference for ragged school supporters the following Wednesday.[3] It would, according to the newspaper, be attended by 'numerous visitors from all parts of the kingdom'. An illustrious list of names followed, including aristocrats, clergymen, philanthropists and politicians.[4] Among those mentioned was the Rev. Thomas Guthrie, the founder and leader of Edinburgh's Original Ragged Schools (EORS) – a title that gives a nod to the schism that marked its early days.[5] Making the most of his visit to Birmingham, Guthrie would deliver a sermon in the city's Music Hall the evening before. A separate article warned 'those who may wish to hear Dr. Guthrie preach' that stall tickets were 'nearly all disposed of'. Interested parties were reassured that 'precautions [had] been taken to prevent crushing'.[6] Following the event, and with no reported injuries among the crowd, the *Gazette* relayed details of the sermon. Although present in his capacity as the founder of the EORS, his account of his own school's successes was intended to enable and inspire those present to achieve comparable results in their own institutions. The organisers had been correct to anticipate a full attendance; Guthrie's 'wide-spread fame as a pulpit orator' drew an 'overflowing audience'.[7] Guthrie's popularity was similarly patent at Wednesday's conference. At the close of the gathering, the Rev. Canon Miller instructed all in favour of Guthrie returning to 'say aye' – the response was 'a vociferous

"Aye", such . . . as is only now and then heard in our noble hall'.[8] Guthrie was, however, not the only 'Scotch delegate' present at the conference; Sheriff William Watson of Aberdeen was likewise present.[9]

Ragged schools, the subject at the heart of the Birmingham conference, are a firm fixture in histories of Evangelical social action in the nineteenth century.[10] A prime example of Christian paternalism, these institutions were underpinned by a desire to improve the poor's condition rather than to exact significant change upon the social hierarchy.[11] Part of the broader so-called 'child-saving' movement, ragged schools were founded upon the notion that a simple and Christian education would redeem and reform the children of the poor. Their name, which proved divisive even among supporters, reflected the unkempt appearance of the children for which they were intended. With London's Ragged School Union (LRSU) formed in 1844 and presided over by Lord Shaftesbury, the number of institutions in the metropolis grew exponentially – increasing from 26 schools with 2,600 children in 1846 to 49,290 children in 560 schools by 1860.[12] An article on the 1849 annual meeting, held in London's Exeter Hall – that great symbol of Victorian philanthropy – relayed that it had attracted such a crowd 'that thousands were unable to obtain admittance'.[13] When Guthrie stood on the stage in Birmingham's Music Hall, 400,000 children had passed through London's ragged schools alone.[14] Though beyond the remit of the LRSU, ragged schools existed in the majority of industrial towns and cities across Britain by the 1860s. These institutions filled a crucial gap during a period when urban populations far exceeded schooling provision. 'Ragged' or, in the wake of the 1854 Reformatory School Act, 'Ragged and Industrial', schools were found in key urban centres across Scotland, including Aberdeen, Dundee, Edinburgh, Glasgow, Greenock and Inverness, as well as in towns such as Helensburgh, Kelso, Leith, Paisley, Stranraer and Tain.

Historiography

The nature of the relationship between Scottish and English ragged schools is something of a divisive topic among scholars. Scotland's institutions are depicted in one of two conflicting ways: as the 'poor cousin' of those in England (or, more specifically, London), or as distinct and superior initiatives that are no relation to those south of the border. For scholars such as Kathleen Heasman and E. A. G. Clark, Scotland's schools comprise little more than a footnote. These accounts regard the great umbrella organisation of the LRSU as the movement's core, with schools outside the metropolis as largely peripheral. While Heasman included Guthrie in a list of well-known figures associated with the movement (alongside the likes of General Gordon and Quintin Hogg), her account nevertheless focuses on the LRSU.[15] Despite categorising both Watson's efforts in Aberdeen and Guthrie's Edinburgh institutions as 'ragged schools', Heasman nevertheless focuses on the differences, rather than the commonalities, that separated schools either side of the border. Clark takes a harder line, summarising his stance succinctly: 'the London and Scottish schools had little in common except their name'.[16]

Scholars interested in the Scottish context have taken a markedly different stance that underscores the distinctiveness and significance of the schools north of the border. Writing in *Philanthropy in Victorian Scotland*, Olive Checkland claims, 'Scotland produced two philanthropic leaders of the Ragged School movement, Sheriff Watson and the Rev. Thomas Guthrie of Edinburgh.'[17] Although Checkland references the parallel movement in London, writing that Scotland's ragged school advocates 'held the same sort of views as Lord Shaftesbury, who was much involved with the movement in England', she doesn't expand upon the nature of the relationship between the two nations.[18] While Andrew G. Ralston has gone some way to highlight the impact of Guthrie and Watson in England, he falls short of acknowledging the reciprocal nature of the relationship.[19] Finally, in his study of Edinburgh's institutions, Peter Mackie outright rejected the notion that the schools were part of a broader movement, writing that, while 'some of the Scottish industrial schools, Dr Guthrie's in particular, called themselves "ragged schools", they differed to a considerable extent from those of Shaftesbury's Ragged School Union in England'.[20]

It is undeniable that Scottish and English schools worked within different legal and political frameworks. Nonetheless, there has been a tendency among scholars to become preoccupied with points of difference. While historians (and contemporaries) have identified distinctions in practice, this does not necessarily denote that the two nations had their own separate ragged school campaigns. Historians of education have recently critiqued the segregation of Scottish schools from their broader context in a manner that's not always beneficial or warranted.[21] In particular, Jane McDermid has noted that it is only when considering Scottish schools in their broader context that it becomes evident that the nation in no way 'passively follow[ed]' England, though Scotland might have imitated its neighbour's practices occasionally.[22] With specific reference to the ragged schools, the failure to look at these institutions as a part of an Anglo-Scottish venture has led scholars to significantly underestimate the movement's breadth and gravity.

This chapter provides a corrective account to existing scholarship by exploring the shared discourse, vision and, for want of a better word, 'manpower' that undergirded the movement. The decision to reference a singular 'movement' here reflects the strength of shared vision that unified these institutions. The associations between schools that aligned themselves with the ragged school cause – regardless of geographical location – were altogether more complex and substantial than has been acknowledged to date. Building on Gareth Atkins's recent scholarship on the patronage networks that underpinned evangelical Anglicanism in this period, this chapter considers the role that leading figures such as Guthrie and

Shaftesbury played in fostering a common ragged school philosophy.[23] Finally, it uses newspaper accounts of public gatherings and ragged school promotional literature to consider the extent to which a shared philosophy and vision brought cohesion and unity to a movement often regarded as disparate.

Print and Purpose

It is the differences, rather than the commonalities, between Scottish and English institutions that have been continually underscored by historians of the ragged schools. An oft-cited distinguishing feature of Scotland's ragged schools is the provision of free meals; the intention to feed both the bodies and minds of poor children has been noted as a unique marker of Scottish institutions across the historiography. Heasman, for instance, describes how 'Sheriff Watson . . . realised at the outset that children must be fed if they were to benefit at all from their education.' Following Watson's lead, Scotland's ragged schools 'aimed at keeping the children all day, providing them with meals and sending them home at night'.[24] The provision of food was likewise a central tenet of the plan Guthrie outlined in his 1847 *Plea for Ragged Schools*:

> Remove the obstruction which stands between that poor child and the schoolmaster and the Bible, – roll away the stone that lies between the living and the dead; and since he cannot attend your school unless he starves, give him food; feed him, in order to educate him; let it be food of the plainest, cheapest kind; but by that food open his way to school; by that powerful magnet to a hungry child, draw him to it.[25]

It was at the Birmingham conference in 1861 that the Secretary to the EORS, Dr George Bell, shared 'some interesting details respecting the Scotch system, show[ing] the necessity of providing food for the children'.[26] Moreover, England's failure to provide food for ragged scholars was starkly criticised as 'altogether inadequate' by Watson.[27] As is often the case, however, the issue was not as clear cut as such accounts suggest. Those English schools in a position to provide meals often did; ragged schools in Liverpool, Manchester, York and Westminster followed the 'Scotch system'.[28]

The focus on difference that has dominated historiography overlooks the common discourse and philosophy that transcended the border. Greenock Ragged School's first annual report, published in 1850, related the case of one child, which is representative of countless others:

> A boy, thirteen years of age, who was notorious for theft, and frequently imprisoned was admitted into school on it being opened . . . [He was now] regular in attendance, attentive to his lessons, in which he is making great progress, and has great love in committing to

memory Psalms, Hymns and passages of Scripture. This is a fair specimen of what Ragged Schools are calculated to do, in training young pests, who in all probability would remain so.[29]

Separated by twenty years and 400 miles, the Beadle of Field Lane Ragged School in London described an encounter with seven-year-old Thomas Loughlin in his diary.[30] When 'patrolling' Long Acre at 11.30 p.m., he found Loughlin 'shoeless, hatless, and in rags . . . begrimed with dirt, and one of his feet in sores'. Echoing the words and sentiment of Greenock's committee, the Beadle observed tacitly that young Loughlin was 'a real specimen of the street arab'.[31] Both of these descriptions of real, physical children draw on a shared concept and vocabulary of poverty and youth.[32] In speaking of a 'fair' or 'real specimen' the authors make reference to the broader notion of the street-child, identifiable through markers such as rags and dirt, and circulated through a common print-culture. Qualified by their rags, it was for children such as these – the 'unwashed, untamed, and untaught' – that the schools existed.[33]

For Guthrie, it was the centrality of Scripture and the open door to society's most deprived children that defined a ragged school. Speaking to the supporters of the EORS in 1852, he explicitly situated his school within a greater, British ragged school network:

> I think it right the public should know that the peculiar principle in which we take most delight is, that the Bible is in our school. In one sense this can scarcely be called a peculiar principle, since it is common to every Ragged School from John O' Groat's to Land's End.[34]

The notion that Scotland's schools were distinct enough to comprise a wholly separate movement would have been anathema to Guthrie. While the ragged school movement was highly localised – as stressed in Derek Webster research on the Lancashire schools – they were nevertheless underpinned by a common philosophy, shared through a common print culture.[35]

Reflecting upon the way in which the nation's printing presses had enabled and enhanced the movement over the preceding forty years, the *Ragged School Union Quarterly Record* (*RSUQR*) noted that 'essays, pamphlets, reports, pleas, leading articles, and magazines disseminated information and attracted public attention'.[36] In addition to ragged school publications, local and national newspapers were likewise crucial in circulating ideas, news and prayers from institutions across Britain. The 'scissors and paste' approach that was prolific in the printing industry during this period meant that news of ragged school meetings might be relayed to readers on the opposite side of the country.[37] The complex picture fostered by such reports is well illustrated in the *Essex Standard*'s article regarding the Newcastle Ragged and Industrial School's 1857 annual meeting, at which Guthrie's recent words to the EORS (that had been relayed in the newspapers) were read.[38] This practice ensured that ragged schools, regardless of their associations, location or eminence, were attuned to developments and practices elsewhere.

Although produced by the LRSU, the *Ragged School Union Magazine* (*RSUM*; and its child-oriented counterpart, *Our Children Magazine*) promoted and supported schools and teachers beyond the boundaries of the metropolis from the movement's earliest days. First published in 1849, the *RSUM* achieved a circulation of 5,000 within its first year.[39] Its reach extended far beyond its city of origin, with readers as far north as John O'Groats. In 1850 the *John O' Groats Journal* promoted the magazine as 'ably conducted, nicely got up, and very cheap', with its unsectarian basis making it 'deserving of universal support'.[40] Two months later the same newspaper featured a second advertisement for the *RSUM*, where it was described as 'full of sound and practical papers, suited to every capacity and ... of much interest to the various christian [sic] denominations throughout the land'.[41] Similarly, the *Dundee Courier* pointedly advised its readers that the fact the *RSUM* reinvested its profits into the schools 'should induce many to patronise this little serial'.[42] In addition to circulating inspirational and encouraging news from ragged schools across Britain, the *RSUM* aimed to equip prospective teachers and speakers by offering rich content that could be drawn upon (as most clearly exemplified in its regular 'Teacher's column'). A brief reference in the *Stirling Observer* reveals that the magazine was used in this way at the Stirling Ragged School, where it formed the basis of a speech to the institution's supporters in 1850.[43]

The LRSU has been described as a 'guiding and authoritative body', with its publications proving 'critical in spreading the ragged school template further afield'.[44] More than this, however, its magazine pooled relevant stories and testimonies from beyond the metropolis and offered a platform to associated figures from across Britain. The publication was quick to form associations with influential Scottish figures, with the magazine's second and third issues featuring articles penned by Watson about his Aberdeen efforts.[45] As such, from the publication's commencement the 'ragged school template' it offered was not exclusive to schools in the metropolis. While news of London-based schools dominated the publication, its editors were increasingly alert to the importance of both representing the movement's breadth and strengthening its associations across Britain. In the same way that local newspapers regurgitated institutional reports from elsewhere, the *RSUM* provided accounts of ragged school gatherings thought to be of interest to its readers. It was on this basis that Guthrie's speech at the EORS's fifth annual meeting was recounted over four pages.[46]

Despite its earlier efforts to represent Scottish schools, in early 1855 the *RSUM*'s editors reported with concern that the publication remained unknown in some parts of Scotland. With a view to rectify this, Scottish content was increased notably over the year. In addition to publishing lectures or articles from Watson and Guthrie, the magazine featured a series of articles headed 'Scottish ragged schools'.[47] Alongside the more well-known institutions in Aberdeen, Edinburgh and Glasgow, the publication provided coverage on those in Ayr, Dumfries, Dundee, Greenock and Perth. Such subject matter, it was hoped, would ensure 'our friends in North Britain will now feel that their labours are not unappreciated in the south'.[48] The question of London or England's dominance in accounts of the ragged schools was explicitly tackled – and challenged – in an article, originally published in *Leisure Hour* (a British weekly periodical published by the Religious Tract Society) and reprinted in the *RSUM* in 1858:

> The modern movement, which has for its object the reclamation of outcast children by the institution of Ragged Schools, and which in London and elsewhere has been productive of extraordinary benefits, is usually supposed to be a peculiarly English enterprise ... We believe that, as far as the British islands are concerned, the movement was primarily commenced in Scotland; and the Scotch have hitherto rather prided themselves on being foremost in the work.[49]

The *RSUM*'s editors were at pains to stress that supporters 'in the south' should not regard Scottish ragged schools 'as extraneous or unimportant'. Rather, they deserved appropriate credit as 'fellow labourers ... for the glorious cause', with 'England ow[ing] much to Scottish zeal, enterprise, and piety, in helping forward the Ragged School movement'.[50]

Space in the pages of the *RSUM* was likewise sought out by Scottish institutions, with secretaries proactively sending reports and news items relating to schools in Ayr, Campbeltown and Paisley.[51] In doing so these institutions aligned themselves with the LRSU and both added to and participated within the broader dialogue on the movement across Britain. Published in Edinburgh in 1851 to support the city's institution, Alexander Maclagan's *Ragged School Rhymes* likewise testifies to Scotland's participation in a bigger, cross-border movement. Alongside inspirational rhymes (such as the 'Mental working song') and moralising verses (like 'The lost found'), the book included a series of poems praising leading figures. As well as 'A song shall flow to Guthrie!' and 'We'll sing a song to Bell' (a reference to the EORS's Secretary), Shaftesbury was recognised in 'We will sing a song to Ashley!'[52] Perhaps more significantly, in May 1852 the *RSUM* grants a brief snapshot of Scottish children's engagement with its content. When the publication announced the winners of its 'Bible questions' competition, Scotland was well represented. Euphemia Murray and James Johnston from the EORS (both aged 13) and Perth Ragged School's Jessie Robertson were among the winners. The editors drew attention to their participation, noting that 'our Scotch readers are now evidently quite alive to the importance of attending to these questions'.[53]

Personalities and Pride

With philanthropic activity both a marker of respectability and an appropriate outworking of Evangelicalism, it is not surprising that the great and good of Victorian society were visible and outspoken advocates of the ragged school movement.[54] Leading figures made full use of the growing rail network to pursue a comprehensive programme of visits to local schools, speaking at annual meetings or opening new institutions. In comparing reports of ragged school meetings in England and Scotland it is evident that they drew upon a common pool of aristocratic supporters, who were equally likely to attend gatherings in Edinburgh as in London.

The Eleventh Earl of Dalhousie, Fox Maule, supported Guthrie's proposal for a ragged school in Edinburgh from the outset. Speaking at a public meeting for the cause, he referenced his joy at seeing a project where 'controversy is banished'.[55] Two years later, Dalhousie was present at the LRSU's fifth annual meeting at which he 'rejoice[d] to think that the good example of London is followed in Edinburgh, in Dundee, Aberdeen, and other places'.[56] The Duke of Argyll, George Douglas Campbell – who would be the major architect of the Scottish Education Act in 1872 – was likewise present. Addressing those gathered, Argyll described the success of the EORS in halving juvenile crime in the city.[57] He went on to reference his Scottish heritage, saying, 'An eminent countryman of mine ... Dr. Chalmers, used to say, in his own very peculiar but expressive phraseology, "It is wonderful what you can do when you get alongside of a human being."' Applying this notion to the work of the schools, Argyll added, 'It is wonderful what you can do when you get alongside even those who are grown up; but it is still more wonderful what you can do, when you get alongside those who are young.' His words were seconded by none other than Dalhousie.[58]

Eight years later, in 1857, Argyll chaired the ninth annual meeting of the EORS. Foreshadowing his future role as the champion of the 1872 Act, he concluded 'that in the existence of Ragged Schools, supported and countenanced by men of all shades of religious opinion, they had one of the best arguments for a national system of education'.[59] A small insight into the challenges such figures faced in being present at meetings across the country is seen in a report of a meeting of Ann Street Ragged School in St Pancras in 1861. According to the *Morning Chronicle*, 'much interest was excited' due to the 'presence of his Duke of Argyll as chairman'. Notably, a letter of apology was read from 'Rev. Dr. Guthrie of Edinburgh'. Making reference to this letter, Argyll acknowledged 'how difficult it was for gentlemen, whose engagements were so numerous, to attend the meetings to which they were invited'.[60]

Historians have, quite rightly, pointed to Shaftesbury as the movement's figurehead. Published the year of the philanthropist's death, one biography claimed that from 'the time that Lord Ashley joined the movement, the

Ragged School Union grew in importance and usefulness, and for over forty years his love for, and zeal in the cause never knew abatement or change'.[61] Similarly, an obituary featured in the *RSUQR* noted how from the 'outset [Shaftesbury] not only identified with the movement but became the chief around whom the heroic pioneers could rally'.[62] Charles Montague, superintendent of King Edward Ragged School in London and a former ragged scholar himself, likened Shaftesbury to the recently deceased Queen, writing that the pair had been 'two great workers for the English nation'.[63] More recently, Hugh Cunningham has attributed the movement's notable public profile to the LRSU's president, who 'command[ed] national attention'.[64] Yet, the confusion around the nature of the relationship between Scottish and English schools has muddied the waters; for instance, Shurlee Swain and Margot Hillel mistakenly attribute the LRSU's establishment to Guthrie, writing that in '1844 Guthrie's English followers came together to form the Ragged School Union, with Shaftesbury as its chair'.[65]

Shaftesbury's biographer, Geoffrey Finlayson, has shed light on the figure's anxious disposition, which led him to question his reputation and accomplishments. Having been prescribed rest by his doctor – with his ill health attributed to 'over-toil, over-anxiety, over-sensitiveness' – Shaftesbury and his wife holidayed in Scotland. He nevertheless used his time north of the border as an opportunity to visit the nation's ragged schools.[66] It was during one such tour in September 1850 that Lord and Lady Shaftesbury found themselves 'greatly pleased' with what they saw during a visit Greenock's recently established institution.[67] Five weeks later the *Inverness Courier* described his 'busy time of it' in Scotland's capital, where he was received with 'great applause' at a meeting in aid of the EORS.[68] Shaftesbury made a succinct note of this engagement in his diary afterwards, writing, 'a glorious meeting in the Queen Street Hall for Ragged Schools . . . spoke for an hour & a half, they say'.[69] Chairing the meeting, Guthrie told those gathered that the LRSU's president would speak to them 'on the great and blessed cause of the ragged schools, that he might stir them up to a still more lively interest in the circumstances of the lost'. He was quick to add, however,

> Not, he made bold to say, that they stood very much in need of any extraordinary exertion; not that they were obliged to work at the moment against a backgoing tide; not that their funds were failing; not that their friends were diminishing; not that their hopes were less . . . He was happy to say that, not only were their funds in a flourishing condition – which was only an encouragement to them to give still more – but, he might say also, that their labours had not been unsuccessful.[70]

Whether Guthrie's comments here were strictly informative, or whether they were intended to mark his territory as a key leader of the movement, it is not possible to ascertain. It is clear, however, that these two prominent personalities each had strong – and at times conflicting – claims to the movement.

The Scot's oft-cited accolade, bestowed upon him in Samuel Smiles's *Self-Help*, as the movement's 'apostle' recognises the vast influence of his numerous pamphlets and articles on the schools. According to Montague, Guthrie's 'books were much read in England and ... were followed in sympathy by the [ragged school teachers] of London'.[71] As early as 1852 the name 'Guthrie' was a watchword for charisma. After stressing that it was cheaper and easier to prevent crime than to reform criminals, the *RSUM* noted that such truths were 'so obvious, that less than the eloquence of a Guthrie might enforce them'.[72] Guthrie's reputation as an authority was again evidenced the following year, in February 1853, when he was 'summoned to London to appear before the committee of the House of Commons on juvenile delinquency'.[73]

Like Shaftesbury, visiting ragged schools and speaking at associated gatherings – whether in Scotland or England – was a mainstay of Guthrie's routine. A skilled orator and widely respected figure, he was known to draw a crowd. Four years after Shaftesbury's visit to Greenock, Guthrie addressed their fifth annual meeting.[74] His connection with the Greenock Ragged School was likely strengthened by his association with Alexander Murray Dunlop, a 'most intimate friend' and MP for the town.[75] Something of Guthrie's popularity is seen in a report from Liverpool in 1858, where 'the eloquent and distinguished Edinburgh clergyman' was met with 'loud applause'. Held in Hope Hall, the room was 'filled in every part by a large and most respectable audience'.[76] When Guthrie took to the platform in London's Exeter Hall to speak to the Young Men's Christian Association about ragged schools, the occasion's chair told those gathered of the leading role 'the philanthropists of Scotland [had played] in the establishment and development of the Ragged School system, among whom Dr. Guthrie was one of the earliest and most prominent'.[77]

The esteem with which Guthrie was held outside of Scotland is further illustrated by the weight of *RSUM* articles relating the news of his imminent retirement due to ill health in 1864.[78] In a piece entitled 'Retirement of Dr Guthrie' the magazine lamented the loss of a passionate and talented leader and 'much-esteemed servant of the Redeemer', pre-empting the 'feelings of deep regret' that 'the friends of Ragged Schools throughout the country' would undoubtedly experience.[79] In May 1864, a committee was appointed to raise 'a capital sum' for Guthrie. Representing the great and good of Scottish and English society, the committee testifies to the esteem in which Guthrie was held by ragged school advocates either side of the border. Knights of both the Thistle (the Earl of Dalhousie and the Duke of Argyll) and the Garter (Lord Shaftesbury) feature.[80] Following Guthrie's death in 1873, the legacy the *RSUM* described was distinctly British. While his work was 'chiefly confined to Scotland ... his heart was too large to care only for the work in which he was personally engaged'.

Underscoring Guthrie's commitment to England's schools, the publication noted pointedly that his last public engagement had been a visit to Gray's Yard Ragged School.[81]

Given Finlayson's account of Shaftesbury as both 'a masterful and commanding presence' and 'a man of complex temperament, given to moments of extreme depression . . . and with a strong streak of paranoia', its perhaps unsurprising that Guthrie's activities in England were perceived with discomfort by Shaftesbury.[82] Shaftesbury's 1850 visit to the EORS was not the first time the two men had met. On 27 March 1847, Shaftesbury's diary contained a notable appointment: 'To Pye Street at 11 o'c to show Ragged School to Fox Maule and Mr Guthrie. Lord, how we ought to bless thee for this measure of success!'[83] The institution's visitor's book grants a fragmentary insight into the thoughts of the Scots, who wrote of their delight 'with the whole management and arrangements and efficiency of the system; and look upon it as one of the most truly noble and blessed institutions of this city'.[84]

Just two weeks later Shaftesbury's diary adopts a starkly different tone, with his entry on 12 April conveying his sense of personal betrayal:

> 'Ragged Schools' to be founded in Edinburgh! I see by the *Witness* on Saturday last that Mr Guthrie and Fox Maule spoke there, and mentioned a ragged school that had been shown to them in Westminster (I was the shower) but they said not a word of kindness about our Ragged Union![85]

Given that Guthrie's *Plea*, only recently published, was receiving notable attention when the men met at Pye Street, the establishment of a ragged school in Edinburgh cannot have been a surprise. It was the lack of appropriate credit, either to the LRSU or its president, that troubled Shaftesbury, perhaps suggesting that he felt threatened or undermined by Guthrie's success.

The difficulty with which Shaftesbury read laudatory accounts of Guthrie's activities is most evident following the publication of an article in *The Times* on 28 September 1860. Advertising Guthrie's latest pamphlet on the movement, *Seedtime and Harvest*, the piece was explicit in its praise:

> To him, above all others, appertains the right of speaking authoritatively about *the seedtime and harvest of Ragged Schools*. It is true that he did not originate the movement . . . But until Dr. Guthrie took it up and advocated its claims, it was a very small affair. He at once saw the importance of it, and resolved to imitate the good example . . . his first plea in [*sic*] behalf of Ragged Schools . . . made a great sensation, and not only in Edinburgh, but all over the country. Ragged Schools became the order of the day.[86]

After reading the above, Shaftesbury confided his feelings of self-doubt in his diary. Writing on 2 October, his melancholy mood is evident:

> Mortified, I cannot conceal it, to see how utterly all my labours, by day & by night, all that I have done, and all that I have said, in so many, & so various, departments, is utterly forgotten, or ascribed to others. Every one, but myself, seems to have a friend in the Press. Even the Ragged Schools, which I thought to be 'a specialty' with me, are traced, in *The Times* of Sep. 28, to Dr. Guthrie, a most eloquent, laborious and worthy, man; but who, with the exception of his own School in Edinburgh, had no more to do with Ragged Schools in London & elsewhere, than he had with the courses of the Planets.[87]

Shaftesbury's emphatic claim here that Guthrie had no more to do with England's ragged schools than 'with the courses of the Planets' overlooks both the influence of the Scot's publications and the time he invested in visiting institutions south of the border. Moreover, it sits at odds with his own telling exclamation – 'how shall we supply his loss?' – that he penned in his diary upon learning that Guthrie was gravely ill in 1848.[88] Such hyperbole on Shaftesbury's part is indicative of his sense of injustice; his diary entry reflects the narrative he wished to be dominant, that the schools were his 'specialty'. Given the time and energy he had dedicated to the movement – having been the face of the LRSU for sixteen years – his reaction to such perceived unfairness is perhaps understandable. According to Finlayson, Shaftesbury had been 'depressed' by *The Times*'s account. His worries about how the public perceived him would surface again five years later, when he wrote that 'every day gave him fresh evidence that his public career was nearing a close'.[89] Given that historians continue to misunderstand the roots of the ragged school movement and the complexity of the relationship between Scottish and English schools, Shaftesbury's concerns regarding the perception of Guthrie may have been well founded.

Conclusions

The ragged school system represents an early and innovative response to the problems associated with urbanisation. When its scope and significance are properly recognised, the movement provides a vast and influential example of Christian social action. This Evangelical mission to save and civilise the children of the poor was propelled across Scotland and England – with national borders posing no barrier – by a shared philosophy that engendered a strong sense of unity and purpose. In contrast with existing scholarship on the schools, this chapter has shed light on the common identity and purpose that print culture, Evangelical networks and influential personalities fostered. Publications such as the *RSUM* pooled ideas and news stories from within and beyond the metropolis and acted as a unifying medium. This common print culture promoted an exchange of ideas – facilitating conversations between schools in the south of England and the very north of Scotland. A sense of cohesion was further promoted through the activities of leading figures, which illustrate that their commitment to the movement was not limited by national borders. The interpersonal tensions highlighted in Shaftesbury's diaries testify to the competition that might arise, as strong personalities staked their claim upon this increasingly influential and noteworthy movement. In focusing on the connections across England and Scotland, this chapter highlights both the limits that national boundaries can impose upon understanding as well as the value brought by a more holistic analysis of Evangelical social action.

Notes

1. 'Conference on ragged schools – Rev. Dr Guthrie in Birmingham', *Caledonian Mercury*, 26 January 1861, p. 4.
2. G. Battiscombe, *Shaftesbury: A Biography of the Seventh Earl* (London: Constable, 1988), p. 196.
3. I would like to acknowledge the kind assistance of Professor David Brown at the University of Southampton, who passed on relevant details from Lord Shaftesbury's diaries that proved invaluable for this chapter.
4. 'Conference on ragged schools', *Birmingham Gazette*, 19 January 1861, p. 5.
5. For more information on the schism see Andrew G. Ralston, *Opening Schools and Closing Prisons: Caring for Destitute and Delinquent Children in Scotland, 1812–1872* (Abingdon: Routledge, 2018), pp. 75–90.
6. 'Dr. Guthrie in Birmingham', *Birmingham Gazette*, 19 January 1861, p. 5.
7. 'Dr. Guthrie in Birmingham', *Birmingham Gazette*, 26 January 1861, p. 3.
8. 'Conference on ragged schools – Rev. Dr Guthrie in Birmingham', *Caledonian Mercury*, 26 January 1861, p. 4.
9. Ibid., p. 4; 'Schools for ragged and destitute children', *Birmingham Gazette*, 26 January 1861, p. 6.
10. See David Bebbington, *Evangelicalism in Modern Britain: A History from the 1730s to the 1980s* (London: Routledge, 1989); Ian Bradley, *The Call to Seriousness: The Evangelical Impact on the Victorians* (London: Jonathan Cape, 1976); Kathleen Heasman, *Evangelicals in Action: An Appraisal of Their Social Work in the Victorian Era* (London: Geoffrey Bles, 1962).
11. Stewart. J. Brown, *Providence and Empire: Religion, Politics and Society in Britain 1815–1914* (Harlow: Pearson Longman, 2008), p. 163.
12. 'The Ragged School Union', *The Times*, 10 June 1846, p. 8; 'The Ragged School Union', *The Times*, 8 May 1860.
13. 'The May meetings', *John O'Groats Journal*, 1 June 1849.
14. 'Proceedings of the seventeenth anniversary of the Ragged School Union', *Ragged School Union Magazine* (*RSUM*), June 1861, p. 143.
15. Heasman, *Evangelicals in Action*, p. 73.
16. E. A. G. Clark, 'The Early Ragged Schools and the Foundation of the Ragged School Union', *Journal of Educational Administration and History*, 1.2 (1969), pp. 9–21, p. 9.
17. Olive Checkland, *Philanthropy in Victorian Scotland: Social Welfare and the Voluntary Principle* (Edinburgh: John Donald, 1980), p. 246.
18. Ibid., p. 246.
19. Ralston, *Opening Schools and Closing Prisons*, pp. 91–109.

20. Peter Mackie, 'Inter-denominational Education in the United Industrial School of Edinburgh, 1847–1900', *Innes Review*, 18.1 (1992), pp. 3–17, p. 3. Mackie's reference here to 'Shaftesbury's Ragged School Union in England' is likely a reference to the LRSU.
21. Robert Anderson et al. (eds), *Edinburgh History of Education in Scotland* (Edinburgh: Edinburgh University Press, 2015).
22. Jane McDermid, 'Education and Society in the Era of the School Boards', in R. Anderson et al. (eds), *Edinburgh History of Education in Scotland* (Edinburgh: Edinburgh University Press, 2015), pp. 190–207, p. 190.
23. Gareth Atkins, *Converting Britannia: Evangelicals and British Public Life, 1770–1840* (Suffolk: Boydell and Brewer, 2019).
24. Heasman, *Evangelicals in Action*, p. 74.
25. Thomas Guthrie, *A Plea for Ragged Schools; or, Prevention Better Than Cure* (Edinburgh: Elder, 1847), p. 13.
26. 'Schools for ragged and destitute children', *Birmingham Gazette*, 26 January 1861, p. 6.
27. William Watson, *Chapters on Ragged and Industrial Schools* (Edinburgh: Blackwood and Sons, 1872), p. 29.
28. The term 'Scotch system' was used by the LRSU's Honorary Secretary, William Locke, to describe the provision of meals. Ralston, *Opening Schools and Closing Prisons*, p. 94.
29. 'Scottish ragged schools', *RSUM* (January 1855), p. 226.
30. For an account of Field Lane Ragged School and its reputation see Laura M. Mair, *Religion and Relationships in Ragged Schools: An Intimate History of Educating the Poor* (Abingdon: Routledge, 2019), pp. 16, 41–2.
31. Field Lane Beadle's Journal, 5 April 1870, London Metropolitan Archives (LMA) 4060/E/01/002.
32. For a fuller discussion of the way such narratives homogenised accounts of poor children see Mair, *Religion and Relationships*, pp. 67–102.
33. George Hall, *Sought and Saved: A Prize Essay on Ragged Schools and Kindred Institutions* (London: Partridge and Oakley, 1855), p. 19.
34. 'Edinburgh Original Ragged School', *RSUM* (1852), p. 54.
35. Derek Webster, 'The Ragged School Movement and the Education of the Poor in the Nineteenth Century' (unpublished PhD diss., University of Leicester, 1973).
36. 'With the friendless boys – Wandsworth', *Ragged School Union Quarterly Record* (*RSUQR*) (October 1880), p. 124. The *RSUQR* replaced the *RSUM* in 1876; as the title suggests, this was a quarterly rather than a monthly publication.
37. 'Scissors and paste journalism' is the practice of reprinting articles featured in other newspapers. It has recently been interrogated as part of the project 'Scissors and Paste: The Georgian Reprints, 1800–1837'.
38. 'Ragged schools', *Essex Standard*, 16 January 1857, p. 4.
39. Shurlee Swain and Margot Hillel, *Child, Nation, Race and Empire: Child Rescue Discourse, England, Canada and Australia, 1850–1915* (Manchester: Manchester University Press, 2010), p. 8.
40. 'Literary notices', *John O'Groats Journal*, 13 December 1850, p. 4.
41. 'Literary notices', *John O'Groats Journal*, 14 February 1851, p. 4.
42. 'Literature', *Dundee Courier*, 24 August 1853, p. 1.
43. 'Examination of the children attending Stirling Ragged School', *Stirling Observer*, 28 March 1850, p. 3. For further discussion of the guidance given

to ragged school teachers see Mair, 'They "come for a lark": London Ragged School Union Teaching Advice in Practice', *Studies in Church History*, 55 (June 2019), pp. 324–46.
44. Mair, *Religion and Relationships*, p. 49.
45. 'Industrial schools for the destitute', *RSUM* (February 1849), pp. 21–4; 'Industrial schools for the destitute', *RSUM* (March 1849), pp. 41–4.
46. 'Edinburgh Original Ragged Schools', *RSUM* (March 1852), pp. 51–4.
47. 'Rev. Dr. Guthrie on ragged schools', *RSUM* (March 1855), pp. 52–6; 'Phonetic ragged schools, Aberdeen', *RSUM* (March 1855), pp. 58–60; 'Scottish ragged schools – No. I – Edinburgh schools', *RSUM* (April 1855), pp. 61–7; 'Scottish ragged schools – No. II – The Glasgow houses of refuge', *RSUM* (June 1855), pp. 101–6; 'Scottish ragged schools – No. III – Dumfries and Dundee schools', *RSUM* (August 1855), pp. 145–50; 'Scottish ragged schools – No. IV – Perth Boys' School of Industry', *RSUM* (October 1855), pp. 185–9; 'Scottish ragged schools – No. V. – Greenock Ragged School Association', *RSUM* (December 1855), pp. 225–30.
48. 'Scottish ragged schools', *RSUM* (January 1855), p. 225.
49. 'The original ragged school-master', *RSUM* (January 1858), p. 10.
50. 'Scottish ragged schools', *RSUM* (January 1855), p. 229.
51. Ibid., p. 229.
52. Alexander Maclagan, *Ragged School Rhymes* (Edinburgh: Johnstone and Hunter, 1851). Lord Shaftesbury was titled Lord Ashley until his father's death in 1851.
53. 'Plans and progress: Bible questions', *RSUM* (May 1852), p. 132.
54. For relevant scholarship on respectability and philanthropy see John Tosh, *A Man's Place: Masculinity and the Middle-Class Home in Victorian England* (London: Yale University Press, 2007). With regard to Evangelicalism, see Bebbington, *Evangelicalism in Modern Britain*.
55. 'Ragged or industrial schools', *Scotsman*, 10 April 1847.
56. 'Proceedings at the fifth annual meeting of the Ragged School Union', *RSUM* (June 1849), p. 112.
57. Ibid., p. 110. The 1872 Education (Scotland) Act made elementary education compulsory between the ages of 5 and 13 and sought to create a more coherent and systematic schooling system through the establishment of locally elected school boards.
58. Ibid., p. 110.
59. 'The Duke of Argyll on ragged schools', *Inverness Courier*, 22 January 1857, p. 3.
60. 'The Duke of Argyll on ragged schools', *Morning Chronicle*, 24 April 1861, p. 3.
61. Edwin Hodder, *The Life and Work of the Seventh Earl of Shaftesbury*, vol. II (London: Cassell & Company, 1886), p. 148.
62. G. Holden Pike, 'Our late president', *Ragged School Union Quarterly Record* (January 1887), p. 8.
63. Charles Montague, *Sixty Years in Waifdom or, The Ragged School Movement in English History* (London: Chas. Murray & Co., 1904), p. 6.
64. Hugh Cunningham, *Children of the Poor: Representations of Childhood since the Seventeenth Century* (Oxford: Blackwell, 1991), p. 120.
65. Shurlee Swain and Margot Hillel, *Child, Nation, Race and Empire*, p. 8.
66. Geoffrey Finlayson, *The Seventh Earl of Shaftesbury, 1801–1885* (London: Eyre Methuen, 1981), p. 322.
67. 'Lord Ashley', *Morning Post*, 27 September 1850, p. 3.

68. 'Lord Ashley in Edinburgh', *Inverness Courier*, 7 November 1850, p. 4.
69. Diaries of Anthony Ashley-Cooper, Seventh Earl of Shaftesbury. Broadlands Archive, University of Southampton, MS62/SHA/PD/6, 1850–5, 31 October 1850. Quotations are provided with kind permission of the University of Southampton.
70. 'Lord Ashley in Edinburgh', *Inverness Courier*, 7 November 1850, p. 4.
71. Montague, *Sixty Years in Waifdom*, p. 39.
72. 'Pauperism versus ragged schools', *RSUM* (February 1852), pp. 28–9.
73. 'Edinburgh', *Inverness Courier*, 17 February 1853, p. 2.
74. 'Dr Guthrie on reformatory schools', *Caledonian Mercury*, 23 October 1854, p. 4.
75. Ralston, *Opening Towns and Closing Prisons*, p. 78.
76. 'The Rev. Dr. Guthrie on ragged schools', *Morning Post*, 30 December 1858, p. 2.
77. 'Rev. Dr. Guthrie on ragged schools', *RSUM* (March 1855), p. 52.
78. 'Retirement of Dr. Guthrie', *RSUM* (July 1864), pp. 157–8; 'Testimonial to the Rev. Dr. Guthrie', *RSUM* (August 1864), p. 187; 'Presentation to the Rev. Dr. Guthrie', *RSUM* (March 1865), p. 72.
79. 'Retirement of Dr. Guthrie', *RSUM* (July 1864), p. 157.
80. 'Testimonial to the Rev. Dr. Guthrie', *RSUM* (August 1864), p. 1.
81. 'In memoriam', *RSUM* (April 1873), p. 82.
82. Geoffrey Finlayson, 'The Victorian Shaftesbury', *History Today*, 33.3 (March 1983), pp. 31–5, p. 31.
83. Diaries of Anthony Ashley-Cooper, MS62/SHA/PD/4, 27 March 1847.
84. Aberdeen University, Thomson 38/17, 'First annual report of the juvenile refuge and school of industry' (February 1848), p. 7.
85. Ibid., 12 April 1847.
86. 'Ragged schools', *The Times*, 28 September 1860, p. 4.
87. Diaries of Anthony Ashley-Cooper, MS62/SHA/PD/6, 2 October 1860.
88. Diaries of Anthony Ashley-Cooper, MS62/SHA/PD/5, 9 September 1848.
89. Geoffrey Finlayson, *The Seventh Earl of Shaftesbury, 1801–1885* (London: Eyre Methuen, 1981), p. 420.

CHAPTER SEVEN

Mary Magdalene and the 'Fallen' Sisters: The Social Gospel of the Magdalene Asylums in Scotland

Jowita A. Thor

The social gospel of the nineteenth century was a vital development, contributing to British society's conceptualisation of charity. Nineteenth-century Britain witnessed a significant change in charitable endeavours and debates about the sexual morals and purity. The debates about prostitution – often referred to as the Great Social Evil – were gaining strength during the mid-nineteenth century. Activists such as Josephine Butler and Ellice Hopkins drew a lot of scholarly attention. The former was a leading face of the campaign against the Contagious Diseases Acts – legislation imposing compulsory medical examination on women suspected of being prostitutes and registering them as such. It was infused by Christian rhetoric and Butler's strong belief in the faith-based mission of her campaign in support of the vulnerable. Hopkins's campaign for 'social purity' (i.e., sexual purity) included founding the 'White Cross Army', which promoted sexual restraint among men and thus challenged the sexual double standards applied to men and women.[1]

The underlying thought behind these and other forms of activism and philanthropy was the Magdalene theology and movement, which played a crucial part in nineteenth-century social work and challenged existing attitudes towards sexual ethics. The Magdalene movement was an area of middle-class philanthropy aimed at supporting in various ways mainly working-class 'fallen' women – women who were prostitutes, had extramarital sex or were sexually assaulted. The name saint of the cause, Mary Magdalene, is usually overlooked by historians. This is a missed opportunity for understanding the intentions and theological stance of the activists. Both the use of the saint's name and its avoidance are a striking indicator of the movement's changing intentions throughout the nineteenth century. The movement emphasised the possibility of reclamation of the 'fallen' instead of outright condemnation and refused to accept the Great Social Evil as an unavoidable part of the city life. Looking at the history of Mary Magdalene's symbolism and portrayal will help us to appreciate the reformers' motifs, and the implications that this name carries.

Magdalene activism included missions among prostitutes, visiting brothels, midnight meetings aiming to convert 'fallen' women and publication of tracts. This conviction led to founding private charities – Magdalene asylums. These were residential refuges where either women from many different paths of life lived usually for one or two years, or that served as half-way shelters in which 'fallen' women found respite and received assistance to reconnect with their family.[2] They started with supporting sexually 'fallen' women. However, in the later nineteenth century they gradually extended their support to women who experienced extreme poverty, suffered from alcohol addiction or had criminal records. In some circumstances they also took in preventative cases reflecting the more interventionist character of later nineteenth-century philanthropic work.[3] The first Magdalene asylum to be established in Britain and Ireland was London's Magdalene Hospital (1758), followed by Dublin (1767) and Edinburgh (1797).[4]

The debates and campaigns related to prostitution and the Magdalene cause had an impact on contemporary attitudes towards acceptable sexual behaviour, and women's role in the public sphere. They subverted existing gender and sexual norms and facilitated a mixing of religious and feminist causes. While maintaining dominant values of the period pertaining to gender roles, they questioned the sexual double standards applied to women and men and called for paternalistic compassion towards the 'fallen sisters' and outreach to them. They maintained the belief in women being domestic guardians of spirituality and morality and at the same time paved the way for women to be involved in public debates on these issues.[5]

When Rev. Dr William Wardlaw was asked to give public lectures on the unsavoury topic of prostitution in Glasgow in 1841, only men were allowed to attend. It was considered inappropriate for women to listen to his talks. Wardlaw was a Scottish minister, a lecturer at the Congregationalist, Glasgow Theological Academy, and a well-known Christian thinker of liberal persuasions. He supported the disestablishment of the Church of Scotland and opposed slavery.[6] Wardlaw was deemed knowledgeable and suitable to speak on the topic because he was involved in the Society for Encouragement of Penitents.[7] The lectures proved to be so successful that Wardlaw delivered them again in Edinburgh, and they were later published.[8]

By the 1870s, the Magdalene cause was an outlet for middle- and upper-class women to voice their views and become visible in the public and political sphere. Women entered the forefront of the debates. Josephine Butler became involved in British and international politics. Dr Elizabeth Blackwell, who was the first female doctor registered with the General Medical Council in the United Kingdom, wrote in support of the Scottish policing system of prostitution. Local women in Dundee founded a Magdalene asylum under the auspices of the 'Women's Mission to Women' and other female activists voiced their concerns about laws and the fate of 'fallen' women.[9]

The laws controlling prostitution and sexuality were one of the central issues occupying Magdalene activists. Both Butler and Hopkins played an important role in passing the 1885 Criminal Law Amendment Act, which raised the age of consent from 13 to 16. The English Campaign against the Anti-Contagious Diseases Acts is another prominent example from the 1870s and 1880s. The Contagious Diseases (CD) Acts introduced a system of regulation of prostitution in selected towns in England and Ireland. In those towns women suspected of being prostitutes could be arrested, forced to undergo a gynaecological examination and either be registered as prostitutes or be practically incarcerated in a Lock Hospital if they were infected with a venereal disease.[10] These were finally repealed in 1886. In Scotland the legal landscape was quite different. The CD Acts had never been introduced there. Currently, there is very limited research on legal history of prostitution in nineteenth-century Scotland, so the details of these laws and associated debates remain to be carefully examined. Linda Mahood has presented an insightful account, which combined elements of policing and abuse discourses models in the application of the Glasgow Police Acts in the 1870s and 1880s.[11] However, the history of regulation goes far earlier and is more complicated due to numerous local and nation-wide laws that affected each city in a different way.[12]

The major difference between the CD Acts and the local Scottish regulations is that the CD Acts were a public health policy; they enshrined in law cooperation between police and Lock Hospitals.[13] The Scottish laws were concerned with public nuisance. They can be viewed as a precursor of current laws that police prostitution. The Glasgow and Edinburgh Police Acts outlawed, *inter alia*, soliciting and harbouring prostitutes in one's premises and they instituted fines and prison sentences for those who did so. They never mentioned medical treatment or 'reformation' of prostitutes. The police had no legal means to force a woman to go to a Lock Hospital (if there was one in the town) or to enter a Magdalene reformatory. It is vital to remember, therefore, that the 'Glasgow System' that Linda Mahood discussed was incidental and was not enshrined in law.[14] More research is needed into this area of Scotland's socio-legal past. For now, however, there is also no evidence that this nexus of law and medical and philanthropic oppression was present in other Scottish cities. What united Magdalene activists who rejected the CD Acts was the belief that women involved in, or at risk of entering, prostitution should be given support to choose a different path. This was intermingled with Christian conceptions of sin, redemption and salvation. Therefore, the Magdalene activists largely rejected the beliefs represented by the CD Acts that framed prostitution as a 'necessary evil' and a public health issue that required forced medical examinations and treatments, and regulations that made women less likely to be able to leave the profession. Instead, they embraced philanthropic work and mission among the 'fallen sisters'. Josephine Butler supported homes that would offer help for the 'fallen', which was in line with her work against the stigmatisation and inhumane treatment imposed on women by the CD Acts.[15] Charles Dickens, the great author known for his concern for the poor and vulnerable, supported the Urania Cottage, a reformatory funded by Angela Burdett-Coutts. Both Dickens and Burdett-Coutts considered the women as spiritually equal and needing help, not condemnation.[16]

Magdalene Asylums

The Magdalene movement was connected with various forms of social work – it was far from being constrained to supporting 'fallen' women. It reached out to former prisoners, those suffering alcohol addiction, and women who were homeless and penniless. An excellent example of how studying the Magdalene asylums relates to other kinds of Christian social work is the Female Shelter in Edinburgh. It was founded by the Scottish Ladies' Society for Promoting the Reformation of the Most Destitute of their Own Sex in Prisons and other Institutions in 1841. The originator of the Society was Elizabeth Fry, an English prisoner reformer and a Quaker reformer.[17] Its aim was to give a second chance to former prisoners and other women who applied from the street.

Magdalene shelters were also run by religious communities. The Anglican sisterhoods founded Magdalene asylums across England and two houses in Scotland.[18] There were also many Catholic Magdalene asylums, most notably in Ireland, where they existed until 1996.[19] The Irish asylums earned notoriety during the last three decades due to many reported cases of abuse and forced incarceration, as recounted by testimonies given by former inmates.[20] In Scotland there were four Catholic institutions that were based in Glasgow and Edinburgh.[21]

However, most of the Scottish institutions were run by lay individuals, who were invested in the discussions on social purity, home mission and social gospel. The first such asylum to appear in Scotland opened its doors in 1797 in Edinburgh. It initially functioned as support for former prisoners, possibly of both sexes, before slightly changing its profile and renting a building in the West Bow, in one of the most impoverished areas of the city.[22] The organisation soon moved to the Canongate, adjacent to the City of Edinburgh at its eastern border. It existed well into the twentieth century, ultimately closing in 1950. The next major institution of this kind was the Glasgow Magdalene Asylum founded in 1815. Its longevity matched its Edinburgh counterpart – it closed in 1958 – however, its existence was not continuous. It changed its function in the 1840s when it temporarily merged with a House of Refuge. It was renamed the Glasgow Magdalene Institution when it returned to its original function in 1859.[23]

These were the two biggest Protestant Magdalene institutions in Scotland. However, Scotland was a home to around twenty-five Magdalene refuges spread across the Central Belt and eastern shore. There were around eleven Protestant Magdalene asylums in Edinburgh alone. Others were located in

Glasgow (at least three), two or three in Aberdeen, two in Dundee, and one each in Greenock, Paisley and Perth. All these houses were Christian at their core.

Mary Magdalene

Scholars of the Bible, theology or history of Christianity will know that the long tradition of perceiving Mary Magdalene as a prostitute began relatively late and is highly contested by modern interpreters. Occasionally, however, this is sometimes forgotten or overlooked by historians who are not necessarily familiar with theological debates and their past.[24] Mary Magdalene is not portrayed as a prostitute or a 'fallen' woman in the Bible. The confusion has arisen as some interpreters merge a few female characters who are mentioned in different Gospel texts, Mary Magdalene herself, Mary of Bethany, the sister of Lazarus and Martha, and the unnamed woman who anointed Jesus at the home of a Pharisee, assuming that they are all one and the same.[25] This interpretation was solidified in Western Christianity by Pope Gregory the Great's sermon from 591.[26] Bart D. Ehrman, a New Testament scholar and public educator, harshly commented on Gregory's sermon:

> ... it is striking that Mary's body is seen as a threat, something that can be used to seduce men and lead them away. The only redeeming feature of her body is when it turns from its dangerous acts (dangerous, that is, to the men concerned) and falls to the feet of the man Jesus in repentance and sorrow. It is the sorrowful penitent who is acceptable; that is the kind of woman these texts seek. One can't help but think that the men who relish this recollection of Mary the penitent sinner are those who are trying to inform their own world with their own vision of what sexual and gendered relationships ought to be, with women not enticing men with the dangers of sex but falling at their feet in humble submission and penitence.[27]

However, these attitudes have never been universal. Dieter Roth describes her role in Christian devotion as associated with hope, contemplation and the life to come.[28] Mary Magdalene has also been known as the 'apostle of the apostles'. The Eastern Church continues to honour her as such and has never adopted the narrative of Mary Magdalene's being a reformed prostitute.[29]

In his history of the Magdalen Hospital, H. F. B. Compston dedicated a whole chapter to defending the name of the institution and explaining the minor controversy associated with it. The Magdalen Hospital was founded in 1758 in London.[30] Compston began with presenting biblical passages and introducing the reader to Mary Magdalene's role in Jesus's ministry. He then relates a public exchange between Jonas Hanway, one of the founders of the hospital, and Nathaniel Lardner, a prominent English theologian, who wrote an anonymous letter to Hanway. What prompted this exchange was Jonas Hanway's writing in which he implied that Mary Magdalene had been a prostitute. This misconception upset Lardner so greatly that he wrote a letter in response in which he vindicated Mary Magdalene's reputation by providing a careful biblical analysis. Jonas Hanway stood corrected and adjusted his publications accordingly. Interestingly, Lardner also criticised the naming the institution because he considered it 'popish' and encouraging adoration of the saints. In this instance, Hanway was less conciliatory. He retorted, 'Be pleased to take notice that we have not canonised Mary Magdalane [sic]. – It is only plain Magdalane House.'[31]

In the light of this exchange, Compston felt a need to justify the name 'Magdalen(e)'. He addresses the anticipated criticism: if Mary Magdalene was not a 'harlot' why would an institution for 'fallen' women be called after her? He presented two arguments. The first one is that the patronage does not imply the patron's character. Calling a 'lunatic' hospital Saint Luke's Hospital, he claimed, does not cast doubts about Luke's sanity.[32] The second argument was based on the inspirational value of Mary Magdalene's character. He concluded that if the 'saint's traditional story' inspires 'Magdalenes' and is 'an encouragement for their own upward striving' there should be no objections to the name. There is an obvious flaw in the argument. The hospital was not called 'St Mary Magdalene's Hospital' but 'Magdalen Hospital'. This implies not a patronage of a saint but association between her and a specific kind of 'sin' and a charitable cause which reinforces the image of Mary Magdalene as a sexually 'fallen' women. Compston's comments about inmates making the connection only strengthens this objection. All these connotations with Mary Magdalene are important for the movement and the institutions. The reference set the tone – Ehrman is right that there is a lot of negativity towards female body implied here and idealisation of submission and patriarchal structures. This, as Linda Mahood argues, was transferred unto Magdalene asylums that were part of the social system of controlling sexual norms.

Simultaneously, there was also a positive aspect of referencing Mary Magdalene. She symbolised forgiveness and hope, something that contemporary society was reluctant to grant to the 'fallen' women. In her 'Making of the Magdalen', Katherine Ludwig Jansen describes the different usages and narrations between Mary Magdalene, the Virgin Mary and Eve. Although she describes Roman Catholic theology in the later Middle Ages, the study is helpful at grasping the potency of Mary Magdalene imagery. One dichotomy used in the twelfth century was that of Virgin Mary and Mary Magdalene. Peter Comestor, a Parisian theologian and scholar, argued that since 'there are many more in the Church who have corrected their faults than there are those who never knew sin', most people followed the Magdalen path of justification and repentance.[33] Another, more startling contrast was provided by the Virgin Mary and Eve – the pure and the sinful.[34] Jansen suggests that the best way of understanding how the medieval thinkers understood this trio is to see them as 'three beams emanating from one source': Mary, mother of Jesus, was the brightest one. Mary Magdalene was less bright, and inspired penance *via media* or *via penitentiae* (middle way, way of penance). Eve was the *via perditionis* (the way of perdition), the dark and ineffective beam.[35] These three female roles are more visible in Catholic Magdalene asylums than in the Protestant ones, which is not surprising. The Catholic institutions were mainly run by nuns or sisters and encouraged inmates to stay in the asylum for life, were still able to cultivate the triple path of holiness (religious women), repentance (inmates) and perdition (unrepentant 'fallen' women). The Protestant theology in nineteenth-century Scotland did not include such veneration of Virgin Mary and presented a different understanding of the path to salvation.

Although the Protestant asylums in Scotland wanted to achieve inmates' conversion in a lay environment, the traditional story of Mary Magdalene still offered a powerful source of hope. It gave language and conceptualisation to justify the pursuit of charity and kindness towards 'fallen' women instead of social ostracism. The imagery of Mary Magdalene is certainly problematic due to its patriarchal implications. There is, however, positive value to it as well. Michael Mason goes as far as to conclude that religion played a key role in shifting attitudes towards this class of women in the nineteenth century. The religious discourse of social gospel offered support towards 'sinners'.[36] Religious sexual ethics played a key role in condemning these women in the first place. However, the Magdalene discourse tried to alleviate the consequences of that. Reaching out to 'fallen' women and offering them help was possibly the Magdalene movement's most important contribution to social work and charity for women.

Although the first British Magdalene institutions opened in England in the mid-eighteenth century, British society has never managed to fully eliminate judgmental attitudes towards female sexuality. Social ostracism towards 'fallen' women continued to be present throughout the nineteenth century. William Tait was a prominent Scottish voice and authority on the topic who was widely quoted by philanthropists and journalists. His *Magdalenism: An Inquiry into the Extent, Causes, and Consequences of Prostitution in Edinburgh* is an excellent example of this tension between compassion and judgement. He published the book first in 1840 and then again two years later. Like much of the Magdalene literature, the publication was full of contradictions and inconsistencies. While in one chapter Tait identifies the causes of prostitution as idleness and flaws of character, in other parts he offers a more mature commentary where he acknowledges the economic and societal hardships that drive women into prostitution. He also discusses men's seduction of women, a term that could mean various situations from rape to having sex after making a false promise of marriage, and acknowledged the hurt afflicted on the victims. Overall, his account probably sides on the compassionate side of the spectrum.[37]

The Magdalene movement of that period drew inspiration from those Christian teachings that focused on the ongoing possibility of salvation which aligned with the more compassionate attitudes towards social outcasts. In his sermon for the Edinburgh Philanthropic Society, which founded the Edinburgh Magdalene Asylum, Rev. James Black summarised the biblical quotation he had just read:

> Standing in this place to plead the cause of a poor and wretched class of fellow-creatures, who are in general considered as outcasts of society, I cannot conceive any subject better fitted to excite compassion, or to remove prejudices from our minds, then these memorable words of our blessed Lord, spoken in pity to those whose characters bear a strong resemblance to theirs.[38]

The Magdalene philanthropists went as far as questioning sexual double standards applied to men and women. They themselves problematised the existence of reformatories for women while recognising that there were no social repercussions for 'promiscuous' men and those men who had sexually assaulted women. James Miller, an Edinburgh medic who published a pamphlet on prostitution in Edinburgh in 1859 and supported the Magdalene cause wrote,

> Secondly, we desire elevation of the moral tone of general society as to the whoremonger. A woman falls but once, and society turns cold upon her so soon as her offence is known. A man falls many time, habitually, confessedly; yet society changes her countenance on him but little if at all.[39]

In 1886, one of the inmates in Paton's Lane Home in Dundee, Georgina Courtenay, had her poem published in one of the local newspapers. One stanza commented on the unjust treatment of women:

> Weel, maybe I am frae richt, but this indeed I ken –
> They ca' us fallen women – there's nae word o' fallen men;
> Yet they were those wha temptit us an' robbed us o' oor fame,
> An' helpit us to lead a life o' infamy and shame.[40]

The circumstances of this publication are unclear. We do not know to what extent the Magdalene home influenced the poem's content, but the home's managers must have approved it and submitted it to the journal. This means that they did not oppose the criticism of sexual double standards invoked by Courtenay. They might have even embraced it and considered it an important message to encourage 'sexual purity' among men in line with other Magdalene activists like Miller, Hopkins and Butler. What is important is that many Magdalene reformers were aware of the unfair treatment of women. They did not manage to question the status quo enough to change the attitudes towards 'fallen' men and women, but at least they reached out to the women and made that a legitimate concern.

Interestingly though, many institutions did not adopt the word 'Magdalene' in their name. In Scotland only three asylums shared that attributive.[41] Others chose more inconspicuous names such as house of refuge, shelter or home. This was probably because they wanted to avoid stigmatisation of the inmates for whom they later tried to find work. There was also another reason: many asylums distanced themselves from the idea of penance that was associated with Magdalene asylums. Directors clarified in their reports that the asylums were places of shelter and support but not punishment. One of the early Edinburgh Magdalene Asylum's reports reads,

> It must be recollected that the Edinburgh Magdalene Asylum is not a prison, but a *house of refuge* . . . The only prerequisite necessary to entitle the object to shelter is, that she is sincerely sorry for her past delinquencies, and desirous of being reformed.[42]

The asylums encouraged spiritual repentance but simultaneously they often acknowledged that inmates were victims of their circumstances. John Downie Bryce is an excellent example of a Magdalene reformer who strongly opposed the idea of a 'penitentiary' and advocated a different organisational style. J. D. Bryce closely worked with the Glasgow Magdalene Asylum (later renamed 'Glasgow Magdalene Institution') as one of its directors.[43] In 1859 he wrote a pamphlet recalling the history of the asylum and outlining his recommendations for its running and for the broader Magdalene cause. He complained that when the Glasgow Magdalene asylums merged with Glasgow's House of Refuge for young females charged with or convicted of crime, this gave the institution a 'penal aspect quite opposed to its real character'.[44] He rejected the practice of adopting uniforms or imposing silence on inmates during work:

> The uniformity is perhaps more pleasing to the eye than the ordinary mixture of attire, but neither this nor the unbroken silence of the work-room, are natural. Why should not every inmate retain her individuality, and speak and act with freedom enjoyed in a well-regulated family?[45]

Some Magdalene asylums periodically struggled with the distinction and even went as far as introducing abusive measures to discipline and test their inmates. Edinburgh Magdalene Asylum, for example, went through a period of shaving women's hair upon entrance to the institution. They hoped that this would 'help' a woman's resolution to stay in the institution for the prescribed two years of reformation.[46] William Tait heavily criticised that policy and indeed the asylum stopped the practice.[47] A snippet of evidence from Dundee indicates that the reformers there also struggled with striking the right balance between running a shelter and penitentiary, and their organisations swapped between these two patterns. Paton's Lane Home (founded in 1848) reported in 1873 that since the death of its foundress it shifted to being a penitentiary. This transition was clearly perceived as something undesirable because the article stated that they hoped the new matron would reverse that trend.[48] While many, if not most, reformers agreed that Magdalene asylums should be welcoming places without an unnecessarily disciplinarian atmosphere, it was much easier to follow this principle in smaller asylums of ten to twenty inmates than big institutions with around 100 or more residents.

Christian Mission

Much of the purity movement of the later nineteenth century had an interdenominational character.[49] This was reflected also among the Magdalene asylums that can be described as vaguely non-sectarian. There were a few Roman Catholic asylums in Edinburgh and Glasgow, and Episcopal ones in Edinburgh and Perth. The rest cultivated a Protestant ethos. Most asylums were not affiliated with any church in particular.

The surviving reports make explicit statements about non-sectarianism. St Andrew's Home and House of Mercy accepted women from various denominations. The Edinburgh Magdalene Asylum invited ministers from different Protestant churches to preach on Sundays.[50] Their committees consisted of people from various Protestant denominations. After the Great Disruption in 1843 those who joined the Free Church of Scotland continued to direct the asylum alongside those ministers who remained in the Established Church. In 1828, the Edinburgh Magdalene Asylum found itself in financial difficulties and applied to the town council to organise a general collection in local churches. They received such permission and in 1829 Catholic, Methodist, Presbyterian and Episcopalian churches held collections at their doors.[51] This possibly says more about the Catholic congregation than the asylum but nevertheless the Catholic Church must have believed both in the value of the cause and that Catholic women would be welcome at the institution.

Theoretically most asylums did not bar Catholics from entering. However, practically, denominational tensions were a common occurrence. Catholics were usually received upon the condition of accepting the Protestant worship and religious customs of the institution. The Greenock House of Refuge stated in its rules that no Roman Catholic priest was allowed to enter the premises. Catholic applicants were made aware of that upon entry.[52] The Dundee and District Female Rescue allegedly experienced difficulties with their Catholic inmates and decided, in very early stages, not to admit any more after just around a year after opening.[53] When reporting on the Edinburgh Magdalene Asylum, *The Scotsman* observed that it did not recognise Catholic customs (such as not eating meat on Friday) and noted that Catholics usually did not stay long.[54] There were clearly limits to the non-denominational characters of these institutions.

Magdalene asylums were social work centres, but a key role of their existence was also cultivating Christian life, mission and education. Most

Magdalene asylums waited for women to knock on their doors and apply for admission. Some asylums welcomed women who attended midnight meetings. These institutions were opened throughout the night in order to receive women who had a sudden religious conversion. It often happened that the newly received women changed their mind in the morning and left, but some stayed longer.[55] For instance, the establishment of the already mentioned Edinburgh's Rescue and Probationary Home for Fallen Women in 1861 was probably prompted by the religious revival in Scotland which led to many conversions and increased religious participation. Part of its function was to accommodate these new converts who otherwise had nowhere to go.[56] The Female Shelter in Edinburgh's Grassmarket (the one founded by Elizabeth Fry's Scottish Ladies' Society) similarly had its doors opened for midnight converts although it was not its prime function. Other women were encouraged to enter the institutions by city missionaries.[57] Episcopalian St Andrew's Home and House of Mercy was involved in an extensive city mission. The House was established in 1858 by a lay woman, Mrs Christina Garioch Mackenzie. The project was soon taken over by Sister Regina Grant, who was an important figure in Scotland's Episcopalian history. In 1865 she opened a ragged school whose children sometimes used the facilities of the House of Mercy. In the same year, she launched a city mission which involved Episcopalian clergy already connected with the House.[58] Two years later, Sister Regina founded Scotland's first Protestant religious community and thus became the first Episcopalian sister in Scotland.[59] These examples show how Magdalene asylums hold an important place in the history of Christianity in Scotland. They were part of the missionary efforts among the working-class women. In the case of St Andrew's community, the Magdalene cause was part of the history of Scottish Episcopalianism and the women religious.

Christian Household

All Magdalene asylums aimed to some extent to resemble a Christian household. This does not mean that they wanted to recreate relationships between family members. Their aim was twofold. Firstly, it was to socialise inmates into a domestic environment believed to be appropriate for women. Secondly, they wanted to create a community based on Protestant ideals and piety. The asylums thus often referred to themselves as homes and families.

Indeed, the life there resembled one of a community of domestic servants. Most institutions tried to provide single bedrooms for inmates to assure privacy, space for personal prayer and to prevent the potentially harmful influence of other inmates. They usually woke up between 5:30 and 8:00 a.m. The day was divided into prayer times (which usually took place twice a day), meals (three times per day) and work (around 9–11 hours per day), which usually consisted of doing laundry. The women also often received basic education in reading and writing and religious knowledge, and had leisure time to spend in the garden, if there was one.[60] Sometimes there were singing classes in the bigger institutions. On Sundays, inmates either had a worship service at the institution or went to one at a nearby church.[61] While this was an exhausting schedule, it was a sad reality of nineteenth-century, working-class women, including domestic servants.

The religious routine and indoctrination reflected the contemporary ideals promoted by Scottish Presbyterian Churches. 'Family religion' meant frequent acts of worship in the household, appropriate comportment and moral supervision of children and servants.[62] Magdalenes were supervised in a similar fashion to domestic servants. The Free Church recommended that servants should be treated as members of the family. This did not mean equality or familial affection. Instead, it meant that their spiritual 'well-being' should be of concern to their masters and mistresses. The Free Church recommended that servants should not be allowed to go out on Sunday evenings in accordance with their Sabbatarian beliefs.[63] Its General Assembly proclaimed in 1858 that servants 'should be instructed, watched over, guarded from temptation, directed, encouraged in duty'. They should be invested in the family's religious life.[64] William Tait, mentioned earlier, argued,

> Let all due liberty be given to servants during the week, and at such hours as they will have no chance of going astray. Leisure in the evenings is decidedly objectionable, as it is attended with the same bad consequences as liberty on the Sabbath. Nursery-maids ought on no account to be trusted out of sight with children, unless accompanied by some confidential person.[65]

This shows us that Magdalene asylums aspired to create the most optimal, according to contemporary views, environment for domestic servants. They trained a new generation of female workers. The asylums usually accepted women for one to two years and after that period gave them references and found suitable employment for them. They also supported them financially. An asylum might help women to get to their new place of employment, pay for a new set of clothes, pay into their newly created saving account, and assist them long-term with cash, or with in-kind donations, after leaving the asylum.[66] The reformers' goal was to assure that the Magdalenes could return to society and become independent and 'respectable' workers. Ideally, they were to go into domestic service in either the United Kingdom or abroad. However, many did not want to become servants and found other jobs. There were also some cases of some of the former Magdalenes being employed at the same or another Magdalene asylum.[67] Some women got married. A Magdalene asylum prepared them for a role as wife and mother as well. With the religious education received at the institution, and their assumed conversion experienced there, former Magdalenes were well-equipped to cultivate their families' faith and be angels of domestic hearth.

Conclusion

The Magdalene movement and thought constituted a vital part of the nineteenth-century social gospel. It has drawn a lot of criticism because the controversies surrounding the Magdalene laundries in twentieth-century Ireland, and the attention given to the 'Glasgow System', which needs to be further examined, but was an isolated and relatively short-lived situation. However, if one looks at the bigger picture, it is evident that the Magdalene discourse made it possible to shift the conceptualisation of 'fallen' and destitute women: from those who deserved condemnation and were a source of 'moral contamination' to those who needed support, and were victims of circumstances and male violence.

Undeniably the movement was full of tensions and contradictions. There was the tension between the desire to help and upholding sexual purity rhetoric. There was a contradiction between accepting that many women 'went astray' because of economic hardship or abuse, and the repeated claim that these women needed to be reformed because they had sinned and were not used to hard work. As Linda Mahood demonstrates, the Glasgow Magdalene Institution was involved in a heavy policing system. However, this was not an intrinsic characteristic or focus of the entire Magdalene movement. The movement's essential goal was to create opportunities for women to leave the life of poverty and prostitution. It does not mean that the movement and its philanthropists adopted the best possible approach. They certainly did not direct their activism enough at eliminating the causes of prostitution such as poverty, lack of social support and the ostracising of 'delinquent' women.

Paying attention to the symbolism of Mary Magdalene can help to understand these contradictions. On the one hand, the tradition of portraying Mary Magdalene as a prostitute and the consequent theology of redemption and ideals of femininity are highly problematic. Their emphasis on sexual purity and the submissive way of signalling one's regret and repentance creates space for sexual double standards and advocacy for the subordinate role of women in society. On the other hand, this tradition could be utilised to promote compassion, give hope and reduce social distance between the 'fallen' and the 'respectable' by using biblical imagery that promoted such approach rather than moralism and adherence to rules. The Magdalene movement should neither be vilified nor glorified. While remaining critical it is important that we appreciate its role within the nineteenth-century social gospel. Expanding our knowledge about the movement contributes significantly towards the historical understanding of Christian activism and theology, and the development of the attitudes towards prostitution in Britain.

Notes

1. See for example, Sue Morgan, *A Passion for Purity: Ellice Hopkins and the Politics of Gender in the Late-Victorian Church* (Bristol: Centre for Comparative Studies in Religion and Gender, University of Bristol, 1999); Judith R. Walkowitz, *Prostitution and Victorian Society: Women, Class, and the State* (Cambridge: Cambridge University Press, 1980); Stewart J. Brown, *Providence and Empire: Religion, Politics and Society in the United Kingdom, 1815–1914* (Harlow: Pearson/Longman, 2008), pp. 441–2.
2. I identified two asylums in Scotland that functioned mainly as half-way houses: the Rescue and Probationary Home for Fallen Women, and Rescue Home for Young Women, known as 'Springwell House'. *Rescue and Probationary Home for Fallen Women* (Edinburgh, 1862); *Rescue and Probationary Home for Fallen Women. Fourth Report* (Edinburgh, 1865); 'The Charities of Edinburgh.-No. X. Minor Magdalene Institutions', *The Scotsman*, 10 October 1864, p. 6.
3. See Helen J. Macdonald, 'Boarding-Out and the Scottish Poor Law, 1845–1914', *Scottish Historical Review*, 75.2 (1996), pp. 197–220, for a discussion on changing trends in social work in Scotland.
4. H. F. B. Compston, *The Magdalen Hospital: The Story of a Great Charity* (London: Society for Promoting Christian Knowledge, 1917), p. 15; María Isabel Romero Ruiz, *London Lock Hospital in the Nineteenth Century: Gender, Sexuality and Social Reform* (Bern: Peter Lang AG, 2014), p. 9; *Rules of the Philanthropic Society of Edinburgh, 1st August 1797* (Edinburgh, 1797); Maria Luddy, *Prostitution and Irish Society, 1800–1940* (Cambridge: Cambridge University Press, 2007), p. 78.
5. Sue Morgan, '"Knights of God" Ellice Hopkins and the White Cross Army, 1883–95', *Studies in Church History*, 34 (1998), p. 433.
6. Stewart J. Brown, 'Ralph Wardlaw (1779–1853), Congregational Minister and Theologian', in Henry Colin Gray Matthew and Brian Harrison (eds), *Oxford Dictionary of National Biography*, vol. 57 (Oxford: Oxford University Press, 2004), https://doi.org/10.1093/ref:odnb/28723.
7. Ian A. Muirhead, 'Churchmen and the Problem of Prostitution in Nineteenth-Century Scotland', *Records of the Scottish Church History Society*, 18 (1974), p. 226.
8. Ralph Wardlaw, *Lectures on Female Prostitution: its Nature, Extent, Effect, Guilt, Causes, and Remedy* (Glasgow, 1842), pp. vii, ix.
9. Elizabeth Blackwell, *Wrong and Right Methods of Dealing with Social Evil: as Shown by English Parliamentary Evidence* (New York, 1883); Minute Book, 24 October 1877–4 April 1879, Women's Mission to Women/Female Rescue Home, Milnbank/Dundee and Arbroath Rescue Home/Dundee and District Female Rescue Home/Girl's Training Home and Laundry, GD/X406/1/1, n.d., 2–3, Dundee City Archives; 'The Operation of the Edinburgh Police Act', *The Scotsman*, 17 March 1882, p. 4; Elizabeth Blackwell, 'Letters to the Editor: The Criminal Law Amendment Bill', *The Shield*, 19 July 1884, p. 126.
10. Contagious Diseases Act, 1866, 29 Vict. c. 35; Contagious Diseases Amendment Act, 1869, 32 & 33 Vict. c. 96. If an Act of parliament was passed in the 29th year of Queen Victoria's rule it will be described as '29 Vict.' Each Act of Parliament is assigned a chapter ('c.'). This is the number of the act for that particular year so it can be easily found. An act (or chapter) is usually further divided into sections and subsections. In the case of the 1866 CD Act, it was passed in

29th year of Queen Victoria's reign and was assigned number 35 in the volume containing the acts for this year.

11. Lucy Holmes, 'A Tale of Three Cities: Regulating Street Prostitution in Scotland', *Scottish Affairs*, 52.1 (First Series) (2005), pp. 72–88; Linda Mahood, *The Magdalenes: Prostitution in the Nineteenth Century* (London: Routledge, 1990).

12. Examples of relevant legislation: Burgh Police (Scotland) Act, 1892 – 55 & 56 Vict. c. 55; Edinburgh Police Act, 1848, 11 & 12 Vict. c. 113 (s. 154, 181); Edinburgh Municipal and Police Act, 1879, 42 & 43 Vict. c. 132; Edinburgh Municipal and Police Extension Act, 1882, 45 & 46 Vict. c. 161; Glasgow Police Act, 1843, 6 & 7 Vict. c. 99 s. 93; Glasgow Police Act, 1866, 20 & 30 Vict. c. 273 s. 142 & 144; Greenock Police Act, 1801, 41 Geo. III, c. 51; Greenock Police and Improvement Act, 1865, 28 & 29 Vict. c. 300. There are many more local and national acts that need to be compiled and carefully examined together with other relevant primary sources in order to understand the full impact of law on the life of working-class women and those women who were involved in prostitution.

13. Contagious Diseases Act, 1866, 29 Vict. c. 35; Contagious Diseases Amendment Act, 1869, 32 & 33 Vict. c. 96.

14. Elizabeth Blackwell also used the term 'Repressive System' to describe Glasgow's approach. She adopted this name in opposition to 'Female Regulation System' represented by the CD Acts and similar laws in Europe. She argued in support of the Repressive System because she valued the exit path from prostitution offered by Magdalene asylums and other charities. Blackwell, *Wrong and Right Methods of Dealing with Social Evil*, pp. 42–73.

15. Michael Mason, *The Making of Victorian Sexual Attitudes*, vol. 2 (Oxford: Oxford University Press, 1994), p. 102.

16. Mason, *Sexual Attitudes*, pp. 2, 88, 99, 108.

17. *Ninth Report of the Female Shelter in Connection with the Scottish Ladies' Society for Promoting the Reformation of the Most Destitute of their own Sex, in Prisons and Other Institutions* (Edinburgh, 1850), p. 3.

18. Valerie Bonham, *A Place in Life: The Clewer House of Mercy, 1849–83* (Windsor: privately printed, 1992); Rene Kollar, 'Magdalenes and Nuns: Convent Laundries in Late Victorian England', *Anglican and Episcopal History*, 73.3 (2004), pp. 309–34; Jowita A. Thor, 'Protestant Magdalene Asylums in Scotland, 1797–1914' (PhD diss., University of Edinburgh, 2022), pp. 84, 153–8.

19. There exists rich literature on the topic, for example: Luddy, *Prostitution*; Jacinta Prunty, *The Monasteries, Magdalen Asylums and Reformatory Schools of Our Lady of Charity in Ireland 1853–1973* (Dublin: The Columba Press, 2017); James M. Smith, *Ireland's Magdalen Laundries and the Nation's Architecture of Containment* (Manchester: Manchester University Press, 2008); Nathalie Sebbane, *Memorialising the Magdalene Laundries: From Story to History*, Reimagining Ireland 101 (Oxford: Peter Lang, 2021).

20. See for example: Claire McGettrick, Katherine O'Donnell and Maeve O'Rourke, *Ireland and the Magdalene Laundries: A Campaign for Justice* (London: I. B. Tauris, 2021). Department of Justice (Republic of Ireland), Report of the Interdepartmental Committee to Establish the Facts of State Involvement with the Magdalene Laundries (Deparment of Justice, 2013), accessed 20 February 2023, https://www.gov.ie/en/collection/a69a14-report-of-the-inter-departmental-committee-to-establish-the-facts-of/.

21. These were: Convent and House for Penitents in Mount Alvernia (Edinburgh), Sacred Heart Home for Penitents in Mount Vernon (Edinburgh), Magdalene Asylum in Woodfield in Colinton (Edinburgh), St Mary of Egypt's Home (Glasgow), Dalbeth Convent of Good Shepherd (Glasgow).
22. *Rules of the Philanthropic Society of Edinburgh Rules, 1797*, p. 3. David Black, *Christian Benevolence Recommended and Enforced by the Example of Christ. A Sermon preached before the Philanthropic Society* (Edinburgh: John Brown, 1798), pp. 39–40.
23. J. D. Bryce, *The Glasgow Magdalene Asylum, its Past and Present* (Glasgow, 1859), 4; William Wilson, *The Origin and Development of the Glasgow Magdalene Institution (Incorporated by Royal Charter)* (Glasgow, 1905), p. 4.
24. For example, Paula Bartley states that Mary Magdalene 'makes her first appearance in the Bible as a prostitute and ends it at Christ's feet when he lay dying on the Cross'. Paula Bartley, *Prostitution: Prevention and Reform in England, 1860–1914* (London: Routledge, 2000), p. 31. Similarly, James Smith associates the reinterpretation of Mary Magdalene's character to feminist theology, without including in his discussion the more complex and older discussions on the subject. See Smith, *Magdalen Laundries*, pp. 25, 212. Paying attention to the theological significance of Mary Magdalene in relationship to the purity movement would be an interesting project. It would contribute to the understanding of the movement's Christian beliefs.
25. These are just a few examples of the relevant passages. Bart D. Ehrman, *Peter, Paul, and Mary Magdalene: The Followers of Jesus in History and Legend* (Oxford: Oxford University Press, 2006), pp. 188–9; Dieter T. Roth, 'Other Friends of Jesus: Mary Magdalene, the Bethany Family, and the Beloved Disciple', in Chris Keith and Larry W. Hurtado (eds), *Jesus among Friends and Enemies: A Historical and Literary Introduction to Jesus in the Gospels* (Grand Rapids, MI: Baker Academic, 2011), p. 129.
26. Ehrman, *Peter, Paul, and Mary Magdalene*, pp. 190–1; Roth, 'Other Friends', pp. 129–30.
27. Ehrman, *Peter, Paul, and Mary Magdalene*, pp. 191–2.
28. Roth, 'Other Friends', pp. 137–8.
29. Roth, 'Other Friends', p. 130; Ann Graham Brock, 'Mary Magdalene', in Benjamin H. Dunning (ed.), *The Oxford Handbook of New Testament, Gender, and Sexuality* (New York: Oxford University Press, 2019), p. 443. See also: Katherine Ludwig Jansen, *The Making of the Magdalen: Preaching and Popular Devotion in the Later Middle Ages*, 1st edn (Princeton, NJ: Princeton University Press, 2001).
30. Compston, *Magdalen Hospital*, pp. 15, 55.
31. Compston, *Magdalen Hospital*, pp. 56–7.
32. Compston, *Magdalen Hospital*, p. 57.
33. Jansen, *Making of the Magdalen*, p. 239.
34. See Jansen, *Making of the Magdalen*, pp. 231–44, for a discussion on Mary Magdalene's being a symbol of hope.
35. Jansen, *Making of the Magdalen*, pp. 239–40.
36. Mason, *Sexual Attitudes*, pp. 2, 88.
37. William Tait, *Magdalenism: an Inquiry into the Extent, Causes, and Consequences of Prostitution in Edinburgh* (Edinburgh: P. Rickard, 1840), pp. 81–152.
38. Black, *Christian Benevolence Recommended*, p. 5.
39. James Miller, *Prostitution Considered in Relation to its Cause and Cure* (Edinburgh, 1859), p. 26.

40. Georgina Courtenay, Out of the Depths, 'Broadside', 1886, Lamb's Collection, 125/14, Dundee Central Library.
41. These were: Edinburgh Magdalene Asylum, Glasgow Magdalene Asylum/ Institution, Aberdeen Magdalene Asylum.
42. *Report from the Directors of the Edinburgh Magdalene Asylum for 1827, 1828, & 1829* (Edinburgh, 1830), p. 16. Emphasis found in the original.
43. Wilson, *The Origin and Development of the Glasgow Magdalene Institution (Incorporated by Royal Charter)*, pp. 4–5.
44. Bryce, *Glasgow Magdalene Asylum*, p. 5.
45. Bryce, *Glasgow Magdalene Asylum*, p. 10.
46. *Report Read at the Annual Meeting of the Society for the Support of the Edinburgh Magdalene Asylum . . . for 1833, 1834, & 1835* (Edinburgh, 1836), p. 6.
47. Tait, *Magdalenism*, p. 254.
48. The Home for Fallen Women, 1849 (?), Lamb's Collection, 53(3), Dundee Local History Centre. From a collection of cuttings found in Dundee Central Library numbered: 53(3). Newspaper article from October 1873.
49. Morgan, 'Knight of God', pp. 431–2.
50. For example, *Report of the Edinburgh Magdalene Asylum for 1827–9*, p. 12.
51. *Report of the Edinburgh Magdalene Asylum for 1827–9*, pp. 22–3.
52. *Rules of the Greenock House of Refuge with an Appendix. Instituted 1853* (Greenock, n.d.), p. 3.
53. DDFR Minute Book 1877–9: 17 November 1878. The Minutes mention both Scottish and Irish Roman Catholics.
54. 'The Charities of Edinburgh. No. IX. The Magdalene Asylum', *The Scotsman*, 1 October 1864, p. 3.
55. 'Minor Magdalene Institutions', p. 6.
56. Brown, *Providence and Empire: Religion, Politics and Society in the United Kingdom, 1815–1914*, pp. 219–21; 'Minor Magdalene Institutions', p. 6.
57. 'The Charities of Edinburgh', p. 3; 'Movement for the Reclamation of Fallen Women in Edinburgh', *The Scotsman*, 15 November 1860, p. 2.
58. Alexander Thomson Grant, *St. Andrew's Home and House of Mercy* (Edinburgh, 1868), pp. 2–8; David Gavine, *The Community of St Andrew of Scotland and Its Rescue Home* (Edinburgh: Scottish Episcopal Church, 2002), pp. 3, 42.
59. Peter F. Anson, *The Call of the Cloister: Religious Communities and Kindred Bodies in the Anglican Communion* (London: Society for Promoting Christian Knowledge, 1955), p. 413.
60. On education and training in Scottish Magdalene asylums see: Jowita Thor, 'Religious and Industrial Education in the Nineteenth-Century Magdalene Asylums in Scotland', *Studies in Church History*, 55 (2019), pp. 347–62. Further primary sources include: *Report of the Subcommittee of the Edinburgh Philanthropic Society*, Edinburgh Philanthropic Society (Edinburgh: John Brown, 1798), p. 42; 'The Charities of Edinburgh', p. 3; *Regulations of the Society for Support of the Magdalene Asylum* (Edinburgh: A. Balfour, 1814), pp. 12–13; Edinburgh Magdalene Asylum Directors and Subcommittee Minute Books, SL237/1/2, 1 June 1808, ECA; 'Minor Magdalene Institutions', 10 October 1864, p. 6; DDFR Minute Book 1877–9: 14 June 1878; GMA Reports for 1820 and GMI Report for 1868 as referenced in Mahood, *Magdalenes*, pp. 79–80. Unfortunately, the sources that Mahood references have by now been lost (GMI, *Annual Report 1868*, GMA, *Annual Report 1820*).

61. Thor, 'Magdalene Asylums', pp. 82–3.
62. Kenneth M. Boyd, *Scottish Church Attitudes to Sex, Marriage and the Family, 1850–1914* (Edinburgh: John Donald, 1980), p. 70.
63. Boyd, *Scottish Church Attitudes*, p. 86.
64. Boyd, *Scottish Church Attitudes*, p. 75.
65. Tait, *Magdalenism*, p. 212.
66. See for example, *Regulations EMA 1814*, p. 15.
67. See for example, Minute Book, 1879–89, GD/X406, Women's Mission to Women/Female Rescue Home, Milnbank/Dundee and Arbroath Rescue Home/Dundee and District Female Rescue Home/Girl's Training Home and Laundry, GD/X406/1/2, 26 January, 2 April 1880, Dundee City Archives; *The Rescue and Probationary Home. Fourth Report*, pp. 3–6.

CHAPTER EIGHT

'Standing in the Gap': D. L. Moody and Evangelical Social Christianity in Chicago and Scotland, 1860–1900

Thomas Breimaier

This chapter will explore the extent to which D. L. Moody typifies a nineteenth-century evangelical social Christianity in the ministries he established in Chicago and Scotland. It will note that Evangelical Protestants, such as Moody, were key players in a transatlantic effort to address the physical and spiritual needs of society, though their tactics to meet these needs often reflected a conservative approach, as opposed to more radical social gospel movements which followed.[1] Indeed, an article in *The Review of Reviews*, edited by the eminent journalist W. T. Stead, noted that Moody 'made a deeper mark upon many lives in Great Britain than any politician or literary man in the United States'.[2]

Raised in an impoverished household and having received minimal formal education, Moody understood the need for Christian individuals who could, in his terms, stand in the 'gap' between the educated, institutional clergy and those at the margins of society. His institutions purposefully sought to alleviate some of the worst effects of poverty in late nineteenth-century urban life. Though these ministries offered practical assistance for the impoverished, the key focus was on evangelism. Amid the positive examples of his activism, there is also space to critique Moody's exercise of social Christianity. While the ministries he established and supported largely accomplished the purposes they set out to achieve, it will be noted that much of the sponsorship Moody received came from wealthy Protestant business owners who had their own degree of responsibility for creating and sustaining the brutal conditions of working-class life. Through all these endeavours, however, Moody's social justice aims remained rooted in his desire to see the world transformed through the Christian gospel. As such, his ministries represent a fulcrum of sorts, a hinge between the pursuits of individual conversion and wider social activism.

Urban Social Work

While often remembered chiefly for his work as a celebrated revivalist preacher, Moody continually sought out opportunities to engage in and raise support for ministries of social transformation. These preceded his work as a revival preacher, and though in his later life he often acted simply as a fundraiser for various social ministries, they nevertheless remained a constant focus throughout his life. Moody's social conscience rose from his own lived experience. Raised in Northfield, a rural town in northern Massachusetts, Moody grew up in a nominally Unitarian household. His father, Edwin J. Moody, who died in 1841, and his mother, pregnant with twins at the time of her husband's death, struggled to raise their nine children. The family's poverty necessitated sending several of the children, including Dwight, to live in other households for months at a time. The interruptions of family life took their toll on the young man who received, 'at best', according to Gregg Quiggle, 'four years of education'.[3]

Thus, Moody's impetus for social engagement was not a political one. It came rather from the dual influences of his own lived experience and his theology. Experientially, Moody understood first-hand the plight of the impoverished in society. His theology, though never systematically articulated, was heavily influenced by the dispensationalism of John Nelson Darby and the Plymouth Brethren. Thus, Moody was convinced of a pessimistic outlook in which the world was rapidly moving toward its own destruction, which in turn led to his prioritising evangelistic engagement. Rising from a place of relative obscurity, initially dubbed 'Crazy Moody' by Chicago newspapers for his unconventional antics as a Sunday School teacher, by his fortieth birthday Moody had addressed an audience of several million in his London campaign alone. Though Moody was a man of comparatively limited financial resources, he nevertheless utilised his influence through both the printed press and relationships with wealthy Christians to stir the wider Protestant world toward a spirit of benevolent generosity. P. C. Simpson, the biographer of the Scottish academic Robert Rainy, noted that while Moody was 'in no sense a profound theologian', he nevertheless 'refreshed in Scotland the religious essentials of the Gospel – the love of God, the freeness of forgiveness, the power for holiness, and, it should be added, the Christian call to righteousness and even philanthropy'.[4] It was this final observation, Moody's mobilisation of philanthropy toward social ministries, that characterised much of his ministry outside of the revivals. While there are a number of case studies that might be considered, we will explore Moody's engagement via two case studies: the YMCA and the Carrubber's Close Mission.

The YMCA

Moody's engagement with social Christianity began early in his adult life. Moving to Boston at the age of seventeen to work in his uncle's shoe shop, the rural and under-educated young man quickly became aware of both the opportunities and temptations lurking in urban centres. It was precisely this context that brought him to a ministry which would remain close to him throughout the balance of his life in ministry.

The Young Men's Christian Association (hereafter YMCA) began in London in 1844. A draper named George Williams (1821–1905) sought to create a fellowship, in which young men who had moved to the city to work as apprentice drapers might avoid the temptation to sin in an environment where taverns, brothels and other enticing opportunities presented themselves. While the YMCA would become known perhaps principally for its athletic facilities, in the earliest days it was characterised primarily by prayer meetings and Bible studies.[5] In some ways it mirrored the Holy Club that had been established by the Wesley brothers a century earlier, in focusing primarily on in-depth study, the pursuit of personal holiness and promoting evangelistic activity. As William Baker notes, 'In search of familiar moorings among the fleshpots, religious young men from the boonies were attracted, not deterred, by strict YMCA standards.'[6] By the time of the Great Exhibition of 1851, there were twenty-one YMCA chapters in Britain, with seven working in different sections of London, and the group secured its first president, the Earl of Shaftesbury. The spectacle of the Great Exhibition introduced tourists in London to the YMCA's various activities, and it led to the first international exports of the movement. The Association in Montreal, Quebec was the first established in North America, with a Boston Association opening in the following month. The demand for such associations rapidly became evident, as by 1856 there were fifty-six North American associations listed in YMCA circulars, and by 1860 there were 205 in total.[7]

The YMCA offered a safe, familiar space to displaced young men, uneasy in their adjustment to urban life. Corresponding with his brothers in April of 1854, Moody wrote,

> I am going to join the Christian Association tomorrow night. Then I shall have a place to go when I want to go anywhere. And I can have all the books I want to read free from expense. Only have to pay one dollar a year. They have a large room and the smart men of Boston lecture to them for nothing and they get up and ask questions.[8]

The provision of library facilities and public lectures was a transformative one. Moody's son, in his biography of his father, notes that 'despite the discipline' of his Unitarian upbringing, which included attendance at Sunday School, as a young adult Moody was embarrassed at his lack of general biblical and theological knowledge. William Moody highlights a particular occasion where, in a Boston Bible class, 'on being asked to read a verse from Daniel, he was at a loss to know whether it was in the Old Testament or the New'.[9] Following his conversion, guided largely through the initiative of Edward Kimball, a Sunday School teacher associated with Mount Vernon Congregational Church, Moody leapt eagerly toward any opportunity to grow in his biblical and theological knowledge, and the Boston

Association gave him ample opportunities for further investigation. The YMCA also provided a model for generous evangelical catholicity, drawing in members from a range of Protestant denominations. This would be mirrored in Moody's revival work and training institutions, as an article in *Scribner's* magazine noted that Moody brought 'all the churches together upon common ground. The Presbyterian, the Baptist, the Methodist, the Episcopalian, sit on the same platform . . . They learn toleration for one another. More than this: they learn friendliness and love for one another. They light their torches at a common fire.'[10] Referring to his time in the Boston YMCA, Moody would later write, 'I believe in the Young Men's Christian Association with all my heart. It has, under God, done more in developing me for Christian work than any other agency.'[11]

When Moody relocated to Chicago in 1858, hoping to sell boots to the growing numbers of factory workers there, he quickly became a charter member of the Chicago Association. Within two years, he abandoned his sales business and worked as a full-time evangelist for the YMCA. This was a particularly decisive turn from a financial perspective. Sponsoring himself for the ministerial work, Moody quickly spent through his life savings, and slept in unused rooms in the Chicago Association hall.[12] His persistence eventually led him to become the President of the Chicago YMCA's board of directors. Under Moody's leadership, the Chicago YMCA prioritised evangelism, but it also addressed the particular material needs of the poorest in the city. An annual report from 1867 summarises the ethos, noting that 'Earnest working Christianity is apt to be comprehensive, and to care for both soul and body. No harm ordinarily comes from doing good in both simultaneously . . . It was the same Jesus who first preached the gospel all day to multitudes, that then fed them miraculously.'[13] The organisation put this ethos into practice with significant effect. In that same year, the YMCA distributed over $23,000 worth of bread, clothing and coal to needy families, the majority of whom were immigrants.[14]

Many of Moody's lifelong associations began through his work in the YMCA. It was in 1870, at an international YMCA convention in Indianapolis, Indiana that Moody first met a man named Ira D. Sankey, whose name would eventually become synonymous with Moody's as he provided the musical accompaniment to Moody's transatlantic revival ministry. In addition to fellow revival workers, the YMCA also afforded him connections with many influential men who would in turn become benefactors to his various ministries. These included the inventor and businessman Cyrus McCormick, the investment banker J. P. Morgan and the meat-packer Philip Danforth Armour, though perhaps his most important connection was with John V. Farwell, a wealthy merchant who took a particular interest in funding the YMCA. These wealthy Chicago barons did not all share Moody's evangelical fervour, but each recognised the potential economic benefit of converted industrial workers, specifically that newly converted evangelical Christians were less likely to seek revolutionary change in their respective industries.[15] Timothy Gloege suggests that for the elite industrialists, 'drawn by [Moody's] message of God's love restoring social harmony', problems related to worker unrest could be solved by evangelical conversions, whereby 'the working classes could be brought under the sway of churches and other traditional "civilizing" institutions'.[16] Moody was often bold in asking for support from these individuals, and occasionally invoked one benefactor when requesting support from another. In 1870, faced with the dilemma of a broken pipe organ in the YMCA hall, Moody wrote to Cyrus McCormick with a bold and optimistic request:

> Now Mr McCormick cant you give me $2000 – toard it if you can I think I can get the rest. Mr Farwell who has always helped me in all my work has spent $50,000 on the new Library-Building & he does not feel as if he could help me any on this organ – I am quite shure you would help me if you could see my congregation every Sabbath Evening I know that it would sturr your soul . . .[17]

While Moody undoubtedly viewed the YMCA with a great deal of fondness, he was nevertheless quick to critique developments which in his appraisal deviated from the Association's core identity. While he advocated for programmes which met the immediate physical needs of the poor, he was less than enthusiastic regarding some developments within the organisation. For instance, while the contemporary YMCA is almost synonymous with athletic programmes, Moody was initially resistant to any expansion of offerings beyond Bible classes. It was only toward the end of the 1870s that he began to recommend 'a gymnasium, classes, medical lectures, social receptions, music and all unobjectionable agencies' to expand the Association's offerings. Thus, Moody viewed the YMCA and its extant mission within the foci of conversionism and activism, but he was always careful to prioritise the former.

The Carrubber's Close Mission

While Moody's ministry was largely itinerant, he nevertheless became associated with a variety of ministries on both sides of the Atlantic. These ministries often reflected Moody's emphasis on both conversionism and activism. For instance, one group which arose following his revivals in Scotland, the Glasgow United Evangelistic Association, took seriously the need for both evangelistic fervour and social activism. Though Moody was not directly involved in the founding of the GUEA, it was one of several ministries which formed in Britain as a result of the wider influence of his revival meetings. One GUEA annual report noted that 'The Mission was the means of begetting throughout the Christian community a new sense of responsibility and deeper compassion in relation to the spiritual and temporal needs of the City's poor and its social outcasts.'[18] Hutchison notes that in addition to prayer meetings and evangelistic efforts, the Association also worked to provide free breakfasts for the homeless, and daily programmes for destitute children. Though Moody did not personally establish many ministries outside the United States, he often sought out Christian ministries and missions that were already in place, and utilised his entrepreneurial acumen and connections to raise financial support for them.

A good example of Moody's fundraising ability is the case of the Carrubber's Close Mission in Edinburgh.[19] Located adjacent to the High Street, in an area where opulence and poverty stood feet apart from one another, the mission sought to reach the impoverished of Scotland's capital. It came about largely through the influence of James Gall (1808–95), a Free Church of Scotland minister who was also an influential cartographer and astronomer.[20] Gall and his 'zealous coadjutors' identified a former chapel, which had housed a variety of religious groups, as an ideal base of operations for their work. The group took control of the building on 30 May 1858, though one author notes that upon securing the lease for the mission, and perhaps filled with an extra measure of evangelical fervour, they 'had to eject a club of Atheists' prior to taking residency.[21] Initially focusing on evangelism and a Sunday school programme for young people, the ministry expanded within the year to include 'Sabbath morning and evening schools, week-day classes for young men and women, a monthly mothers' meeting for prayer, a reading club for families, and an "Excelsior Institute, or Home College", for the improvement of young men'.[22]

Nevertheless, by 1872 James Gall lamented what he perceived to be the glacial pace at which the Scottish churches embraced new tactics for evangelistic work among the urban poor, critiquing church leaders' actions as 'bad generalship' and blaming the state of urban Christianity in Edinburgh on 'an unreflecting adherence to old forms of organisation, which were no longer suited to the altered circumstances and perilous times in which they lived'.[23] Whether or not Gall's assessment of the state of Scottish Evangelicalism is correct, the arrival of Moody and Sankey in 1873 heralded a new and transformative approach to evangelism. In the words of a *Saturday Review* editorial, 'old Formality has got his neck broken'.[24] Whilst the editorial castigated the 'eccentricities and buffooneries of the Yankee propaganda', and cast doubts on the duo's likelihood of success in their upcoming London mission, the meetings in Edinburgh, Dundee and Glasgow went on to draw unprecedented crowds.[25] Moody's campaign endorsements included the Free Churchmen W. G. Blaikie and Andrew Bonar, and from the Established Church he received the support of academics such as Archibald Charteris, who was a professor of biblical criticism at the University of Edinburgh, as well as a Moderator of the General Assembly of the Church of Scotland. Despite the impressive attendance at his meetings, there is some debate as to the extent of the Moody revival's influence on the urban poor. Though the campaign organised meetings in impoverished areas, such as the Corn Exchange, Mark Toone convincingly argues from reports circulating through the Scottish evangelical denominations that the mission saw its greatest impact in the 'revivifying of a large nominal segment within the church and this, particularly, among the middle classes'.[26]

While Moody's revival meetings in Scotland may have failed to directly appeal to the urban poor, his association with organisations such as the Carrubber's Close Mission would serve to widen the reach of his ministries. The Mission was closely aligned with Moody's general practice, as it offered a range of social projects but was primarily focused with evangelistic activity in and through these projects. It also fostered a spirit of evangelical catholicity, simply requiring its workers to be 'consistent members of some evangelical Church and be introduced to us by one of our number'.[27] Only a few decades following the Great Disruption of 1843, missions like Carrubber's often saw participation between both Free Church and Church of Scotland volunteers, working side by side to serve the city's impoverished citizens. The Scottish benefactors to the mission included the noted physician James Young Simpson, the pioneering figure behind the use of chloroform, who assisted in establishing a medical facility as well as a dispensary within the Carrubber's facility.[28]

Moody learned of the mission's work during his 1873–4 Scottish campaign, and paid it a visit during his time in Edinburgh. The mission had met in various locations since Gall's original meetings in Whitefield Chapel, including the Free Church Assembly Hall and the outdoor quad area of the New College. Moody raised £10,000 for the construction of a new, purpose-built facility for the mission, and laid its foundation stone in 1883. Situated on the Royal Mile, the mission had stepped from the obscurity of a hidden close to a place of prominence, located just a few steps from St. Giles' Cathedral. The following year, Moody presided over the building's formal opening, where Andrew Thomson, a United Free Church minister, attributed Moody's financial intervention to be 'a remarkable conjunction of providences'. Thomson continued, 'Just at the time when the Carrubber's Close old mission premises became too narrow and circumscribed, and their labours began to be arrested, their "beloved evangelist" . . . set himself to raise the sum for the erection of this previous building.'[29] Robert Rainy, Principal of New College, noted that the mission 'was an embodiment of the practical agreement of their evangelical Churches – not merely their agreement in truth, but their agreement in work and in the practical aims which out to command the continual exertion of all the Churches'.[30] Moody gave the final address of the session, offering his hopes that the mission would seek to provide a variety of different services throughout the day, making the best use of time. He saw the mission as 'a sort of half-way house between the outlying masses and the churches', and concluded his address to thunderous applause when he remarked that he saw in the audience 'no Established Church clergymen, no Free Church clergymen – only Christian brethren'.[31] The ministries associated with the mission grew rapidly in the following years, with one article celebrating that it featured a Sunday School, with over three hundred scholars; connected with it are no less than seven different Bible Classes, a Young Men's Christian Fellowship Association, a Children's Church, and an Evangelical Sabbath Meeting. There is a Penny Savings Bank, a Sabbath School Library, two Bands of Hope, with a choir and orchestra, a staff of Lady visitors, a Dorcas Society, a Mothers' Meeting, a Young Men's Literary Association, and a number of classes through the week conducted by members of the congregation for sewing, reading, writing, arithmetic, history, and other things, for all of which the building provides ample accommodation free.[32]

Thus, in his involvement with both the YMCA and the Carrubber's Close Mission, Moody embodied an evangelical form of social Christianity. He placed a high value on efforts to combat issues such as hunger, material need and addiction recovery amid communities who had little access to help. These principles and activities were derived from his Christian faith and his belief that it was every Christian's obligation to carry them out. These activities were also part of a wider evangelistic aim. For Moody, and indeed for many of his colleagues in ministry, both in Chicago and Scotland, while they sought to alleviate the temporal concerns of impoverished men and women, their ultimate aim was nothing less than evangelical conversion, which would provide an eternal hope.

Theological Training

Mentors and Models for Theological Instruction

A second area where Moody distinguished himself in the arena of social Christianity was in his approach to theological education.[33] As Morris has noted, 'Scotland, Ireland, England, and the United States are dotted with Young Men's Christian Association buildings and Bible Institutes of which he laid the foundations, metaphorically speaking, if not literally.'[34] For Moody, a wide access to theological education, combined with a robust commitment to evangelical conversionism, was a common theme in all of his educational endeavours. As with his other social Christianity projects, Moody's rationale for theological education was not particularly innovative in its approach. Rather, he identified models for the work that he viewed as positive examples to imitate, and crucially, to fund with the aid of wealthy benefactors. With regard to models for theological education, the clearest example is that of C. H. Spurgeon's Pastors' College in Newington Butts, London. Established in 1856 out of Spurgeon's conviction that theological education should be provided at an affordable cost to young men who were gifted preachers but lacking the usual financial and academic background of a typical university student, by the mid-1880s the College had trained the majority of new Baptist Union ministers and also invited students from other evangelical denominations to participate in the course.[35] Moody became personally acquainted with Spurgeon during his first tour of Britain in 1867, when he spent several days observing the noted English preacher. Moody himself noted that that Spurgeon 'sent me back to America a better man'.[36] When Moody set out to establish theological colleges, he embraced a similar aim, offering accessible training to students from a wide range of backgrounds at minimal cost.

The Chicago Bible Institute

The first of Moody's endeavours in theological education came about in Chicago, the city where his life in ministry began. Its roots lay primarily in the efforts of a woman named Emma Dryer, who established a 'school of "Bible work"' in the Chicago Avenue Church, which had itself grown from a mission Sunday school established by Moody in the late 1850s.[37] The programme of the school was focused on evangelism, 'including house to house visitation, women's prayer meetings, and tract distribution'.[38] It was Dryer, whose background included a time lecturing at the Illinois State Normal University, who pressed Moody to allocate resources toward the establishment of a robust, urban theological college in Chicago.[39]

In setting the curriculum for the institute, Moody valued practical subjects, focusing particularly on biblical studies and evangelism. Quiggle notes that Moody 'envisioned a typical day as mornings given to Bible lectures while the afternoon and evenings consisted of preaching and other evangelistic meetings throughout the city'.[40] Moody described the prospective students of the Chicago Bible Institute as 'gap-men', individuals who would bridge a gulf between the worlds of middle-class congregations with educated clergy and the experience of the poorest and vulnerable, particularly those in urban centres. Findlay suggests that Moody eschewed the 'intellectual frills' normally associated with seminaries. In Moody's mind, instructors at the Institute should 'Never mind the Greek and Hebrew . . . Give them plain English and good Scripture.'[41] Moody attempted to mirror the practice of Spurgeon's College in London, targeting a body of students who would have likely been turned away at the established universities and seminaries.[42] To this end, students were not charged tuition fees, nor were they subject to strict entrance examinations.

This ethos has led some to critique the intellectual rigour of the Bible Institute's curriculum, charging its founder with a spirit of anti-intellectualism. John Kent, referring to coverage of Moody's campaign in *The Spectator*, has critically suggested that Moody 'implied that ignorance and a lack of education were an advantage in matters of faith'.[43] Moody was indeed critical of institutions such as the liberal wing of German higher criticism, though the extent to which he understood their methods or conclusions is not immediately clear. This should not imply that Moody was inherently anti-intellectual, as he saw the value in sustained study of biblical and theological texts. Further, he maintained close associations with a number of conservative biblical and theological scholars. For instance, he held a long friendship with Archibald Charteris, a professor of biblical criticism at the University of Edinburgh. He invited R. A. Torrey, a graduate of Yale Divinity School, to lead the Chicago Bible Institute in its early days. Both men pursued doctoral studies in Germany and were conversant, though conservative, voices within wider theological scholarship. Thus, Moody's approach to theological education was not inherently anti-intellectual, but rather he sought partnership with informed lecturers who could facilitate training that was both practical and evangelical in its orientation.[44]

However noble Moody's aims to democratise American theological education might have been, there were inconsistencies between his theory and practice. Moody's social Christianity fits most neatly within the framework of *conservative* social Christianity, characterised by Henry F. May as fearful of 'current social unrest' and devoting 'a major part of their energies to pointing out the evils of socialism'.[45] Regarding the wider social Christianity implications of the Chicago Bible Institute, the traditional interpretation has been drawn largely from the work of the historian James Findlay, who argued that the institute was part of a larger scheme on the part of influential Chicago businessmen, intended to pacify unsettled industrial workers and suppress further revolts. Findlay rests his case largely on the events surrounding the Haymarket Riot of 1886, whereby workers at Cyrus McCormick's reaper plant staged a protest about their working conditions, requesting an eight-hour workday. A home-made bomb thrown at a gathering group of policemen resulted in a torrent of violence with eleven fatalities and dozens of others wounded. Findlay notes that 'Chicago's large immigrant population also included a nucleus of men nurtured on anarchism and Marxian dialectic', and suggests that against this backdrop 'Moody and his friends looked fearfully to the future, seeing in these protests a threat to law and order and their own favored position in society.'[46] Though Moody was never materially wealthy, particularly in comparison to the elite Chicago barons, Findlay suggests that he was nevertheless sympathetic to business owners. He makes reference to a March 1886 speech where Moody discussed the unconverted factory workers in Chicago, entreating that

> Either these people are to be evangelized or the leaven of communism and infidelity will assume such enormous proportions that it will break out in a reign of terror such as this country has never known. It don't [sic] take a prophet or a son of a prophet to see these things. You can hear the muttering of the coming convulsion even now, if you open your ears and eyes.[47]

Such comments, held alongside Moody's silence in the wake of the Haymarket Riot and the later violence associated with the Pullman Train

Strike in 1894, suggest that he was either in quiet agreement with the harsh business practices of his financial benefactors, namely Cyrus McCormick and George Pullman, or that he was afraid to critique them in public.[48] Lyle Dorsett, in his largely admiring biography, nevertheless observes that Moody's financial connections were 'always controversial, especially in times of economic depression, labor unrest, and confrontations between workers and owners of factories'.[49] As we will note in the next section, Moody's foray into establishing practical theological education in Scotland followed a similar path.

Glasgow Bible Training Institute

Moody's interest in formulating practical theological education was not limited to his work in the United States. As in Chicago, ministerial and financial connections established during his revival meetings in Scotland in the mid-1870s enabled him to explore a further educational endeavour nearly two decades later. In 1892, a small paragraph in *The Scotsman* noted that Moody had addressed the prayer meeting of the Glasgow United Evangelistic Association. The paper reported that he 'expressed a hope that the scheme for the establishment of a Bible Training Institute would be heartily supported. By means of such an Institute they hoped to raise a class of workers who would reach those who did not care for church.'[50] Unlike the Chicago Bible Institute, Moody acted largely as a facilitator for the Glasgow Bible Training Institute rather than a hands-on leader. He nevertheless suggested its first president, John Anderson, a shipping agent who established the Ayrshire Christian Union.[51] While there are limited resources available to track specific details, it is clear that the Bible Training Institute made a strong start toward its goal of practical training, graduating 625 students in its first fifteen years of operation.[52] Perhaps the most noteworthy student of this era was Joseph Kemp (1872–1933), the orphaned son of a policeman who pastored several Baptist churches in Scotland, including the Hawick Baptist Church and Charlotte Chapel, Edinburgh, before moving to New Zealand in 1920 where he established the New Zealand Bible Training Institute, now known as Laidlaw College.

In his Scottish campaign for theological education, as in his similar effort in Chicago, Moody accepted financial donations from business owners whose wealth was tied to unethical treatment of workers. Funding for the Glasgow Bible Training Institute came in large part from J. Campbell White, later Lord Overtoun, an elder in the United Presbyterian Church of Scotland, who had made a large fortune as a chemical manufacturer. Energised by the revivals in Moody's 1873–4 campaign in Scotland, he became the chairman of the Glasgow United Evangelistic Association and was a regular benefactor for evangelical causes throughout Scotland, including the YMCA and the Boy's Brigade. *The Scotsman* noted in June of 1893 that White's 'latest gift was one of £10,000 for the building of a Bible

Training Institute in Glasgow'.[53] White's association with evangelical causes were briefly scandalised when Keir Hardie, a founding Labour politician and noted Christian Socialist, published a series of scathing accounts of widespread unsafe conditions at White's chemical plants. Hardie, who had experienced unfair labour practices first-hand working as a child operating ventilation doors in the mining industry, criticised White for underpaying workers, forcing twelve-hour work days with no time off for meals and for not enforcing safety standards at the plant. The lax standards led to several employees developing so-called 'chrome holes', ulcerative lesions caused by prolonged exposure to cromate solutions, which cause persistent open wounds on workers' exposed skin. As serious as these conditions were, in the world of Victorian Scottish Presbyterianism, perhaps Hardie's most significant blow was to note that despite White's ardent Sabbatarianism, his factory was not closed on a Sunday, forcing his workers to break the Sabbath rest. Hardie's language in the article was both provocative and prophetic, particularly as he railed,

> Whilst Lord Overtoun conducts family worship at Overtoun House, or bends in lowly reverence before the altar of God's grace in church, or offers a grace of thankfulness before breakfast, dinner and tea, his white chrome-eaten victims toil and sweat in the malaria hold in Shawfield, adding to the wealth of their sainted master ... And he calls around him in conference holy men to decide on how to save Glasgow from sin whilst his works are violating, at his bidding, and for his selfish gain, one of the divine commandments: *Remember the Sabbath day to keep it holy*.[54]

These articles stirred considerable reaction among British readers, with one letter to the editor suggesting that 'Every gospel hall he has built is cemented with the blood of the workers, whose lives he has blasted and shortened and helped to destroy prematurely.'[55] Unable to deny the accuracy of the articles, White acknowledged that the charges were true, but attempted to shift the blame to his nephews, to whom he had transferred the day-to-day operations of the factory.[56]

These controversies, both in Chicago and Scotland, warrant some critical assessment of Moody's judgement in fundraising. Findlay, for instance, was quick to suggest that Moody's acceptance of funds was effectively aligning him to the priorities of his wealthy benefactors. He goes on to posit that Moody's education projects were primarily a necessary 'counterforce to radicalism and unrest among the laboring classes'.[57] While it is certainly true that Moody was unsettled by the growing gulf between the classes, particularly in the wider context of the American Gilded Age, Findlay's focus on the political dimension fails to recognise the extent to which Moody worked to disassociate himself from politics, focusing instead on the eternal implications for individual souls. In this respect, Moody was critical of the more radical end of the emerging social gospel movement, as evidenced by his comment to Henry Ward Beecher that 'There is no use attempting to make a deep and lasting effect on masses of people, but every effort should be put forth on the individual.'[58] His advice toward working men and women, particularly toward the end of his life, often seemed to indicate a lack of awareness of the working conditions of factory labourers. In a temperance meeting in Boston, Moody suggested that workers should

> Work faithfully for three dollars a week, it won't be long before you have six dollars and then you will get ten dollars, and then twelve dollars a week. You want to get these employers always under an obligation to you. You must be such true men and be so helpful to your employers that they cannot get along without you and then you will work up and your employer will increase your wages.[59]

While Moody made rather brash comments regarding the role of the working class in society, this did not come at the expense of equally strong critique of the wealthy, particularly later in his life. Moody castigated business owners who were guilty of 'sweating' their employees and paying 'starvation wages'.[60] Nevertheless, even in his critique of abuse among the upper classes, he still demonstrated a degree of naivete. In 1890, for instance, he wrote, 'We have too much wealth and too much poverty. Why don't some of the people who have made their fortunes stop and go out into the highways and byways and help the poor? That's my idea of socialism, and it's founded on the ideas of Christ.'[61] There is a strange tension between Moody's statements on the respective roles of workers and business owners. There are several potential explanations, including an over-reliance on Moody's part of his own personal experience whereby he secured relative financial comfort having been raised in extreme poverty. They may have been rooted in a refusal to believe that the Christian men who were financing his ministry were truly capable of carrying out exploitative business practices. It is also worth noting that Moody's speech in which he admonished the workers to be 'true men' was spoken in the context of a temperance address, and as such would have been aimed toward a more corrective tone than might appear in a sermon. Perhaps the most plausible explanation is the recognition that Moody's theological worldview, grounded in a pessimistic premillennial theology, believed that the eternal consequences of an unrepentant life were far more serious than the temporal matters of labour conditions. Bebbington is right to note that, for Moody, 'what human beings needed was not a patching up job but regeneration'.[62] As such, his sermons and indeed his life's work emphasised salvation over solidarity.

Conclusions

While Moody organised and supported a range of activist ministries throughout his life, his stalwart focus on individual conversion, combined with his general ambivalence toward political and social reforms, largely separated him from more radical figures in the wider movement of social Christianity. This tension was recognised in his own day. For instance, the *Review of Reviews* noted that

> despite his lack of sympathy with the ever-enlarging school of Christian thought represented by advocates like Tolstoi [*sic*], Kingsley, Ruskin, Herron, and Charles S. Sheldon, and those who put emphasis on the Gospel as a possible agent in redeeming society *en bloc*, as it were – despite all this, it remains true that Mr. Moody's value to the spiritual life of the time in which he lived transcends that of any other preacher of the Gospel.[63]

Moody's transatlantic ministry was focused first and foremost on the task of evangelism, but he recognised that a component of social transformation could and should be woven into that task. In carrying out this effort, he established a number of institutions which championed these goals, several of which still operate in the contemporary Christian landscape.

Notes

1. I am following Henry May's terminology with regard to the terms 'social gospel' and 'social Christianity'. For May's discussion on evangelical social Christianity in particular, see Henry F. May, *Protestant Churches and Industrial America* (New York: Harper & Row, 1967), pp. 163–9.
2. George Perry Morris, 'Character Sketch: Dwight L. Moody', *The Review of Reviews*, February 1900, p. 114.
3. Gregg William Quiggle, 'An Analysis of Dwight Moody's Urban Social Vision' (PhD diss., The Open University, 2009), p. 21.
4. Patrick Carnegie Simpson, *The Life of Principal Rainy*, vol. 1 (London: Hodder & Stoughton, 1909), pp. 408–9.
5. For a good overview of this debate, see William J. Baker, 'To Pray or to Play? The YMCA Question in the United Kingdom and the United States, 1850–1900', *The International Journal of the History of Sport*, 11.1 (April 1994), pp. 42–62.
6. Ibid., p. 44.
7. Charles Howard Hopkins, *History of the Y.M.C.A. in North America* (New York: Association Press, 1951), p. 23.
8. Letter from D. L. Moody to his brothers, 9 April 1854. Referenced in William R. Moody, *D. L. Moody* (New York: Macmillan, 1930), p. 30.
9. Ibid., p. 14.
10. 'Topics of the Time: Revivals and Evangelists', *Scribner's Monthly*, 11 (April 1876), p. 887. Referenced in Thomas E. Corts, 'D. L. Moody: Payment on Account', in Timothy George (ed.), *Mr. Moody and the Evangelical Tradition* (London: T. & T. Clark, 2005), p. 69.
11. Richard C. Morse, *The History of the North American Young Men's Christian Associations* (New York: Association Press, 1918), p. 122.
12. Quiggle, 'An Analysis of Dwight Moody's Urban Social Vision', pp. 82–3.
13. Referenced in ibid., p. 85.

14. Ibid., p. 85.
15. James Findlay, *Dwight L. Moody: American Evangelist* (Chicago: University of Chicago Press, 1969), pp. 326–31.
16. Timothy E. W. Gloege, *Guaranteed Pure: The Moody Bible Institute, Business, and the Making of Modern Evangelicalism* (Chapel Hill: University of North Carolina Press, 2015), p. 44.
17. Letter from D. L. Moody to Cyrus McCormick, 1 December 1870, D. L. Moody Family Papers, Northfield Mount Hermon School Archives. I have left Moody's original spelling intact.
18. Referenced in I. G. C. Hutchison, *A Political History of Scotland 1832–1924: Parties, Elections and Issues* (Edinburgh: John Donald, 1986), p. 137.
19. For an excellent overview of the Carrubber's Close Mission in wider context, see Christina Lumsden, 'Class, Gender and Christianity in Edinburgh 1850–1905: A Study in Denominationalism' (PhD diss., University of Edinburgh, 2012).
20. Gall originated what is now referred to as the 'Gall–Peters Projection', an influential means of representing the three-dimensional spherical earth on a two-dimensional map.
21. J. Barbour Johnstone, 'Carrubber's Close Mission, Edinburgh', in William Reid (ed.), *Authentic Records of Revival: Now in Progress in the United Kingdom* (London: James Nisbet, 1860), pp. 451–2.
22. Ibid., p. 452.
23. Referenced in Mark James Toone, 'Evangelicalism in Transition: A Comparative Analysis of the Work and Theology of D. L. Moody and His Proteges, Henry Drummond and R. A. Torrey' (PhD diss., University of St Andrews, 1988), p. 87.
24. 'The Comic Gospel', *The Saturday Review*, 18 April 1874, p. 496.
25. Ibid., p. 496.
26. Toone, 'Evangelicalism in Transition', p. 138.
27. Anonymous, *These Fifty Years: The Story of Carrubber's Close Mission Edinburgh 1858–1909* (Edinburgh: The Tract and Colportage Society of Scotland, 1909), p. 42.
28. Lumsden, 'Class, Gender and Christianity', p. 153.
29. 'The Carrubber's Close Mission', *The Scotsman*, 5 March 1884, p. 10.
30. Ibid., p. 10.
31. Ibid., p. 10.
32. W. J. Gordon, 'The Problem of the Poor', *The Sunday at Home: A Family Magazine for Sabbath Reading*, 13 October 1888, p. 654.
33. It should be noted that Moody also established two schools in Northfield, Massachusetts, the Northfield Seminary for Women and the Mount Hermon School for Boys, which more closely resembled other New England boarding schools. While these schools were far more traditional in their approach, they nevertheless embodied Moody's desire for accessible education, and thus issued scholarships for poor and disenfranchised students. For further discussion of these schools, see Quiggle, 'An Analysis of Dwight Moody's Urban Social Vision', pp. 224–34.
34. Morris, 'Character Sketch: Dwight L. Moody', p. 115.
35. See Mike Nicholls, 'Charles Haddon Spurgeon, Educationalist: Part 2 – The Principles and Practice of the Pastor's College', *Baptist Quarterly*, 32.2 (April

1987), pp. 73–94; Ian M. Randall, *A School of the Prophets: 150 Years of Spurgeon's College* (London: Spurgeon's College, 2005); Thomas Breimaier, *Tethered to the Cross: The Life and Preaching of C H Spurgeon* (Downers Grove, IL: IVP Academic, 2020).
36. C. H. Spurgeon, *C. H. Spurgeon's Autobiography, Compiled from His Diary, Letters, and Records, by His Wife and His Private Secretary, 1878–1892*, vol. 4 (Chicago, New York and Toronto: Fleming H. Revell, 1900), p. 247.
37. James Findlay, 'Moody, "Gapmen", and the Gospel: The Early Days of Moody Bible Institute', *Church History*, 31.3 (September 1962), p. 323.
38. Ibid., p. 323.
39. Material on Dryer is limited, but there is a useful introduction in Rima Lunin Schultz and Adele Hast (eds), *Women Building Chicago 1790–1990: A Biographical Dictionary* (Bloomington: Indiana University Press, 2001), pp. 230–1.
40. Quiggle, 'An Analysis of Dwight Moody's Urban Social Vision', p. 179.
41. Referenced in Findlay, 'Moody, "Gapmen", and the Gospel', p. 326.
42. Spurgeon, unlike Moody, acquired a rudimentary understanding of Greek and Hebrew, and encouraged students with linguistic ability to learn the biblical languages as well.
43. John Kent, *Holding the Fort: Studies in Victorian Revivalism* (London: Epworth Press, 1978), p. 131.
44. For further exploration on this topic, see Toone, 'Evangelicalism in Transition', pp. 117–19.
45. May, *Protestant Churches and Industrial America*, p. 163.
46. Findlay, 'Moody, "Gapmen", and the Gospel', p. 324.
47. Ibid., p. 324,
48. See Heath W. Carter, *Union Made: Working People and the Rise of Social Christianity in Chicago* (New York: Oxford University Press, 2015), pp. 81–2; Lyle W. Dorsett, *A Passion for Souls: The Life of D. L. Moody* (Chicago: Moody Press, 1997), pp. 407–9.
49. Dorsett, *A Passion for Souls*, p. 407.
50. 'Mr D. L. Moody', *The Scotsman*, 18 November 1892, p. 4.
51. Graham Cheeseman, 'Training for Service: An Examination of Change and Development in the Bible College Movement in the UK, 1873–2002' (PhD diss., The Queen's University of Belfast, 2004), p. 44.
52. Ibid., pp. 61–2.
53. 'The Queen's Birthday Honours', *The Scotsman*, 3 June 1893, p. 9.
54. Keir Hardie, 'Lord Overtoun', *Labour Leader*, 22 April 1899, p. 125.
55. 'Lord Overtoun's White Slaves', *Labour Leader*, 4 March 1899, p. 69.
56. Callum G. Brown, *Religion and Society in Scotland since 1707* (Edinburgh: Edinburgh University Press, 1997), p. 127.
57. Findlay, 'Moody, "Gapmen", and the Gospel', p. 332.
58. Charles R. Erdman, *D. L. Moody: His Message for Today* (Chicago: Fleming H. Revell, 1928), p. 58.
59. D. L. Moody, *'To All People': Comprising Sermons, Bible Readings, Temperance Addresses, and Prayer-Meeting Talks Delivered in the Boston Tabernacle* (New York: E. B. Treat, 1877), pp. 489–90.
60. D. L. Moody, 'When Jesus Comes Again', *The Christian Herald*, 21 December 1910, p. 1208.

61. 'Mr. Moody Speaks Out', *The New York Times*, 12 March 1890, p. 9.
62. D. W. Bebbington, *The Dominance of Evangelicalism: The Age of Spurgeon and Moody* (Leicester: Inter-Varsity Press, 2005), p. 45.
63. Morris, 'Character Sketch: Dwight L. Moody', p. 117.

CHAPTER NINE

'The Saving of the Body': Sport at Church in England since 1850

Hugh McLeod

In 2004 John Paul II marked the start of the Athens Olympics by adding a 'Church and Sport' section to the Pontifical Council for the Laity. The new section had a broad remit, ranging from 'acting as a reference point for national and international sports organisations', to 'sensitising local churches of the need to provide pastoral care in sports environments', to 'encouraging a sports culture which promotes sport as a way to develop the whole person and as an instrument at the service of peace and brotherhood between nations'.[1] Over the years John Paul II, who had been a footballer in his youth and remained a keen skier while Archbishop of Kraków, made numerous addresses to gatherings of athletes, in which he celebrated sport, 'when played and understood in the right way' as 'a shining expression of the highest vales of human life and social harmony'.[2] In fact, though John Paul was unique among popes both in the frequency of his pronouncements on sport and in the extent of his sporting practice, many of his predecessors, going back to Pius X in the early 1900s, have shown an interest in sport and have spoken publicly about its potential value.[3]

Several Archbishops of Canterbury have practised sports and watched sporting events. For example, Randall Davidson (Archbishop 1903–28) enjoyed fishing and shooting and George Carey (1989–2002) is an Arsenal fan. But they have until recently seen it as a private hobby. However, in 2019 the Bishop of Derby, Libby Lane, was appointed the church's Bishop for Sport. Then in February 2020, the church announced its 'National Sport and Wellbeing Project'. This had a more specific agenda than that of the Catholic 'Church and Sport' section, since it was attached to the church's 'Evangelism and Discipleship Team'. Quoting estimates of the proportion of English people engaged in some form of sport, its declared aim was 'to use sport as a conduit for evangelism and mission, connecting with nearly 50% of England's population, the vast majority of whom are not in church regularly'.[4]

I

In the nineteenth and early twentieth centuries, there were no top-down initiatives of this kind, but churches of most denominations and many different theological tendencies provided sporting facilities or sponsored teams, and sport also had a major role in most Christian youth movements. Often it was young men and, later, young women attached to the church who took the lead. But in other cases it was a clergyman or youth leader, motivated by concerns varying from a hope that it might divert the youth from less wholesome recreations, to a dogmatic faith in the moral and religious, as well as physical, benefits of sport – and sometimes simply a love of sport for its own sake. From small beginnings around the middle of the nineteenth century, the drive to provide sport at church developed rapidly in the later part of the century, reaching a high point in the 1920s and 1930s, before declining after World War II, at first slowly and then in the 1970s and 1980s more precipitously.[5]

These early initiatives differed in important ways from those in more recent times. The pioneers of the Victorian Christian sporting movement were Broad Church Anglicans and the early practitioners of Nonconformist sport often had a liberalising agenda, though they soon won support in all but the most conservative sections of their churches. Their reasons for promoting sport were often quite pragmatic and they tended to use a less exalted language than that favoured by the sporting Christians of today.

Most historians of sport make some mention of the role of churches in the Victorian sporting boom, but those who offer analysis have reached contradictory conclusions. For Peter Lupson, who has explored the part played by churches and chapels in the origins of a number of the elite football clubs of today, the alliance between Christianity and football was natural and beneficial to both.[6] On the other hand, Hugh Cunningham sees it as a sign of weakness on the part of the churches, whose natural instincts, he implies, would have been to keep their distance: 'By the end of the third quarter of the century, the churches were accommodating to society, rather than changing it, and this meant that they had come to accept secular leisure as a good.'[7] Similarly Peter Bailey, in his study of the 'rational recreation' movement, argues that churches' interest in recreation had limited impact. He concludes that

> Church patronage of sport was not yet convincing enough to dispel the image of the clergyman as killjoy, and the sporting churchman was always a minority in a profession which remained generally suspicious of popular sport as corrupter of morals, despite the new and respectable models.[8]

Bailey argues that religious reformers did for a time play an important role in the promotion of new forms of recreation, but that this phase was short-lived, as working-class 'customers' rejected the products provided by rational recreationists or rebelled against attempts by the clergy to control what happened in the facilities they provided. However, Douglas Reid in his study of leisure in nineteenth-century Birmingham challenges the implied assumption that religion and recreation are necessarily in tension.

He claims that the clergy were uniquely powerful shapers of opinion and that from the 1850s some influential preachers were presenting a more positive view of recreation.[9] Meanwhile, two historians of cricket, Dennis O'Keefe and Jack Williams, have shown that the prominent involvement of places of worship in recreational cricket, and indeed in many other sports, far from being a temporary phenomenon, continued at least into the 1930s. O'Keefe argues that this was because churches and chapels were accepted local institutions which took on a range of functions within the community.[10] The most thorough examination of these issues is by Dominic Erdozain, who has yet another perspective – partly arising from the fact that his book is a contribution primarily to religious and intellectual, rather than sports history. He sees the attention given to leisure provision by the churches and by other religious organisations, such as the YMCA, in the later Victorian period as a diversion from more important concerns and as marking an inner secularisation of the church.[11]

In this essay, I will trace the growing involvement by the churches in sport from the mid-nineteenth century up to the interwar years, offering my own explanations for this process.

In the 1840s and 1850s older forms of sporting involvement by the Anglican clergy continued, while new and very different forms were beginning. Some of the Anglican clergy had always participated in the recreations of their social equals, and since the growth of clerical incomes in the later eighteenth and early nineteenth centuries, these social equals often included members of the gentry. Most notoriously these recreations included hunting, though by the middle years of the century clerical participation in the hunt was strongly discouraged by many bishops and was in rapid decline. In the 1850s and 1860s a few bishops, including the High Church Samuel Wilberforce of Oxford and the Evangelical J. C. Wigram of Rochester, even discouraged their clergy and ordinands from playing cricket – though Diana McClatchey in her study of the clergy in the Oxford diocese notes that there were a number who failed to comply.[12] Indeed, newspaper reports from that time of matches by leading clubs frequently showed that clergymen were among the players.[13] The links between cricket and the church were more explicit in the 'Clergy v. Laity' matches reported by *Bell's Life in London*, the paper of the sporting gentry, in the 1850s. The social tone of the match at Canterbury in 1858, in which the clergy were victorious, was clear enough from the score card. The laity included a knight and three military officers, and the other players were all styled 'Esquire'. A similar match in a Suffolk village in 1856 was played over two days 'in the pretty grounds' of the Rev. A. Bond.[14]

However, from the 1840s and more especially from the 1850s a newer kind of involvement by the clergy in the world of leisure was beginning. This arose not so much from a wish to enjoy the privileges associated with their social status as from a sense of their public responsibilities. The 1850s saw the proliferation of 'institutes', many of them attached to

Anglican parishes.[15] Typically they provided non-alcoholic refreshments, opportunities for indoor games or music, and a library. Many of them also included opportunities for outdoor recreation, usually including cricket. Local papers in the 1850s and early 1860s reported cricket clubs attached to church institutes in Luton, Wakefield, Bolton and Preston.[16] In Birmingham at least four parishes had a Working Men's Association in the later 1850s.[17] The prototype was the historic parish church of St Martin's, where the influential rector, the Rev. John Cale Miller, established the Association in 1854, adding cricket to the programme in 1855.[18] Miller was an Evangelical and there is no reason to think that he was influenced by the anti-puritan agenda of some of his Broad Church or High Church contemporaries. His provision of leisure facilities was principally a response to the social crisis of the 1830s and 1840s. It was assumed that those most in need of such facilities were working-class men and youths, and that the lack of such facilities was one of the causes of working-class discontent. (It should be noted, however, that although its principal focus was on the needs of men and boys, membership of the Working Men's Association also included many women.) Furthermore, it was hoped that sport and other forms of recreation would provide an arena within which members of different social classes could meet on friendlier terms. Cricket, in particular, was seen as the magic ingredient in the quest for social harmony.

As Bailey argues, middle-class interest in working-class leisure began from a humane concern, but this was reinforced by a fear of working-class radicalism, and desire for more effective social control.[19] Bailey also suggests that these initiatives were motivated by the clergy's wish to increase the size of their congregations. But this was not necessarily so. The motives were as likely to be a combination of wishing to improve the quality of working-class lives and diverting the beneficiaries from what were seen as harmful alternatives. Thus, the Oxfordshire vicar who provided the youths of his village with bat, ball and stumps, insisting only that they refrain from playing during the hours of divine service, did not insist that the young men attend the service.[20]

By the 1860s the question of the Church of England's role in relation to popular recreation was one of the issues of the moment for the clergy. (Nonconformists and Catholic were not yet discussing what their role might be.) It was the theme of sessions at the Church Congress in 1866 and 1869. On both occasions the majority of speakers said that the church should play a positive role, though some still had reservations of various kinds. Those advocating a positive role made three main points. First, it was a duty of the clergy to promote healthy forms of recreation; second, that bad forms of recreation were prevalent; and third, that the puritanism of some clergy or lay cliques had had counter-productive effects.

The Rev. E. J. Randolph introducing the discussion in 1866 of 'Social Condition and Recreations of the Poorer Classes' began by stating that while some people think that 'religion and recreation can hardly co-exist', he saw the problem as being 'the divorce of religion and recreation'. Like some other speakers, though, he did not use the term, he harked back to the days of 'Merrie England', when holy days were 'days of joy': 'the spirit would be upraised to Godly exercises of a directly religious nature, and the body would be refreshed by amusements of a cheerful but not irreligious kind', and rich and poor would dance together on the village green. He also advocated cricket, football, quoits 'or other manly games', as well as music and lectures. 'The great remedy for our present social and spiritual ills is sympathy.' Randolph wanted no 'Puritanical moroseness', and the next speaker, the Hon. and Rev. Canon Lyttelton was more explicit. He decried the 'Manicheanism' of religious men in the early nineteenth century, 'from the effects of which we are still suffering'. He deplored a narrowly spiritualised version of Christianity, and wanted the clergy to actively support the recreations of their parishioners. He called for a shortening of working hours, so more time for leisure was available. Moving to the education provided in the Anglican National Schools, he condemned the narrow emphasis on the 3Rs. Education should be for 'human nature as a whole' – 'bodily, mental and spiritual'.[21] Evidently these speakers reflected the High Church and Broad Church critiques of the hitherto dominant Evangelicals, as well as the continuing impact of the social crisis of the 1830s and 1840s.

In 1869, when the theme was 'The Recreations of the People', most of the speakers wanted the parish church to be actively involved in providing and supporting recreation, and most of them felt that the church was not doing enough. Again, there were objections to any clear-cut separation of the 'spiritual' from the 'secular'. The Rev. J. C. Chambers claimed that 'All that tends to health of mind and body is handmaid to moral and religious culture.' Some drew upon the stereotype of the 'killjoy parson', noted by Bailey. Chambers referred to 'Parson Killjoy', while Archdeacon Emery of Ely condemned 'narrow-minded' clergy who opposed popular recreations, and he claimed that 'We go around with long faces making religion look miserable'. The Rev. T. Griffiths blamed a 'clique' of laypeople with 'gloomy views'. So clearly there was opposition, but those who felt sufficiently strongly about the question to participate in the debate were all in greater or lesser degree in favour of the church's involvement in sport or in other forms of amusement, such as concerts.[22]

Increasing depleted congregations was not a major theme in the debates, though one speaker added, on lines that would often be repeated in later years, that recreation could be an effective means of keeping teenage boys attached to the church after they had left Sunday School. By 1874 and 1877 none of the speakers at the Church Congress was prepared to condemn involvement in sport by the church – though some warned against *too much* sport. Again the main emphasis of the contributions was on the social obligations of the clergy, rather than on boosting congregations. The focus of the debate was now shifting to the theatre, which continued to be controversial. Some clergy and devout laymen were enthusiasts for the theatre but many others saw most of the plays currently performed as morally harmful.[23]

The 1870s were the key decade for the increasing sporting involvement of the churches. The growth, in particular, of cricket and the two forms of football, was now moving beyond the upper middle class to involve large numbers of men of the lower middle and working classes. A crucial factor here was the increasing practices of closing factories around the middle of the day on Saturdays and of early closing of shops on Wednesdays or Thursdays. Saturday afternoons and the afternoons and evenings of Wednesday or Thursday became the favoured times both for recreational sport and increasingly for spectator sports. Meanwhile, churchgoers were as interested in sport as anyone else. Many clergymen and Sunday School teachers, as well as being enthusiasts themselves, were anxious to harness this interest in sport. Young men were generally seen as the section of the population most likely to break away from the church. As early as 1857 a speaker at a conference of schoolteachers and clergy on 'the best means of retaining the elder scholars in connexion with the church and religion after leaving school' had suggested that the clergy should take the lead in forming cricket clubs.[24] Already at this time some churches or Sunday Schools were taking up the idea. For instance, in 1859 there was a cricket match between two Anglican Sunday Schools in Bradford. At this time cricket was already a normal part of Sunday School Anniversary celebrations. For example, at the anniversary celebrations of St Paul's Church School in Huddersfield in 1857, the boys played cricket as well as running races, while the girls played games 'of a more feminine character'.[25] By the 1870s and 1880s it had become widely accepted that Sunday Schools needed a more regular sporting programme, with cricket generally taking pride of place, though by that time football was also increasingly popular.

Anglicans were initially the leaders in the movement to provide sport at church, though the Nonconformists would eventually catch up, or even overtake the Church of England. In 1869 eight of the thirty cricket clubs in Bolton whose games were reported in a local paper were based in a church, all of these (with the possible exception of a Sunday School of unstated denomination) being Anglican. However, by the 1870s, Nonconformist chapels were joining in, even though some ministers and chapel-goers were still strongly opposed. In 1878, when games played by twenty-nine cricket clubs in Bolton were reported, eleven of these were based in a church or chapel, including two Congregationalist, two Wesleyan and one Baptist.[26] The many football or cricket clubs formed in churches, chapels or Sunday Schools at this time could come into being in different ways. Some were founded by a clergyman or Sunday School teacher. Others were formed by young men already attached to the church, who had imbibed the passion for sport which was taking hold of so many young men – and of some young women too – at this time.

To begin with the clergymen and Sunday School teachers: for some the promotion of sport was instrumental – they saw it as a means of strengthening the hold of the church or school on its younger members. For others, however, sport was encouraged for its own sake. Some clergymen could even be regarded as evangelists for sport, and I shall return to them later.

The instrumental view was frankly stated by the Unitarian Domestic Missionary in Birmingham, David Heap, who said that the Athletic and Amusement Clubs attached to the mission were 'a means to an end rather than an end in itself'. His successor in reviving the cricket and football clubs in 1888 explained, 'I look forward to this Club helping to keep the members of the class together. I think it may also be the means of binding the lads of classes I and A to the Schools and Church.'[27] Many churches provided a gymnasium or a football club with the proviso that those enjoying the sporting facilities should also attend church services or take part in other religious activities.

The mixture of religion and sport reached its fullest development in the Settlements and Missions established, especially in London but also in other major cities, between 1880 and 1914. The Settlements were predominantly Anglican, but included some that were Nonconformist or unconnected with a religious denomination. They focused especially on study of 'social questions' and involvement in local politics or reforming campaigns. But some also provided sport. For example, Oxford House, the High Church Settlement in east London, was renowned for boxing. The Missions, also predominantly Anglican, were often associated with Oxbridge colleges or public schools. They were staffed both by clergymen and by young professional men, drawn by social conscience and by what was for that generation the romance of 'the slums' and 'darkest London'. They specialised in clubs for men and boys. Alan Bartlett has shown how the missions in the strongly working-class south London borough of Bermondsey attracted large numbers of teenage boys through their boxing, football and cricket in the early 1900s. He gives the example of the Charterhouse Mission, housed in a large building with a church on the ground floor and space for the numerous boys' clubs on the upper floors. Members of the clubs were expected to attend church or join a Bible Class. For the many who were reluctant to attend a regular church service, the Bible Class offered a more attractive alternative, since the boys would be joining other boys of their own age and from a similar social class.[28]

However, the initiative to start a cricket or football club, and later clubs for many other sports, often came from young men who attended the church or belonged to one of the many subsidiary organisations which proliferated in later Victorian churches and chapels. Sometimes they had encouragement or assistance from a clergyman or a senior member of the congregation, but very often they seem to have acted on their own. Lupson's study of the origins of elite football clubs which started in a church or chapel offers many examples. Aston Villa (1874) was founded by members of the Bible Class at Aston Villa Wesleyan chapel in north Birmingham. They already had a cricket club and they decided that they also wanted a winter game. Initially they were not sure if they wanted to play with a round or an oval ball, and in their first game they played the first half with one kind of ball and the second half with the other. Everton (1878) began with a Methodist New Connexion Bible Class, though in this instance they had encouragement from the minister, who also played for the team. Birmingham City (1875) was founded by members of the Holy Trinity Cricket Club, which had been founded by members of the choir at that church. Southampton (1885) grew out of the St Mary's Young Men's Association, again with encouragement from the curate. Membership of the Association seems to have been mainly middle class, whereas the founders of Aston Villa were working class.[29] Churches and chapels in mid- and late Victorian England differed widely in their social constituency, but most sustained, as well as their more strictly, religious activities, a very active social life.

A commentator on Liverpool life in the later nineteenth century highlighted the crucial social role of churches and chapels, 'especially those Nonconformist ones where there is a deliberate effort to occupy the attendants so as to make them intimately acquainted'. He also pointed to the wide social functions of places of worship and the variety of motives for attendance at their services and participation in the associated organisations.[30] Choirs and Bible classes have already been mentioned. Their main purpose was to enhance the worship or improve the religious knowledge of younger churchgoers; but they also provided places where friendships were formed which readily, especially as interest in sport boomed from the 1870s onwards, led to the formation of a cricket or a football team. But going beyond the strictly 'religious', some churches and chapels, as early as the 1840s, were establishing Mutual Improvement Societies, where the young men would debate literature and politics or attend classes in history, geography and logic, as well as acquiring more practical skills, such as book-keeping.[31] These were evolving by the 1870s into Young Men's Associations, with an even broader programme, which soon included recreation, physical and mental. In the 1880s and 1890s, hundreds of Congregational churches formed guilds, some for 'Young People' and some for 'Young Men' or 'Young Women', which were aimed at those in their later teens and early twenties, and where it was taken for granted that the more strictly religious activities would be combined with the intellectual, the recreational and the social.[32]

The Young Men's Society at College Street Baptist church, Northampton, in the 1880s and 1890s is an example of the ways in which the programme could develop. It was founded in 1884 when the main emphasis was on the Bible class and devotional meeting, though there were also shorthand classes and 'mutual improvement' meetings. By 1886, when the Society had 139 members, there was a library with 450 volumes, chess and swimming clubs and an ambulance class. In 1888 there was also cricket and hockey, and in 1889 a cycling club. Such societies could develop a life of their own which potentially caused friction with more conservative members of the congregation, including some of those in positions of authority. The Young Men's Society at College Street had a long-running dispute with the Trustees because of the refusal of the latter to allow the school rooms to be used as a gym. The Trustees, while agreeing to the football club changing in the school rooms, refused permission for the storage of football equipment in the Sunday school kitchen. The young men, however, were able to hit back though the journal *Northamptonshire Nonconformist* which they produced over several years in the later 1880s and early 1890s, and which included a robust defence of their sporting programme. By the 1890s few would any longer object to sport being part of the programme, but there were concerns that it was beginning to occupy too large a part. In 1897 the president of the Bible class was complaining, 'in these days it seems that the stress of recreation on Saturday afternoon is so great that it needs some effort to attend a Bible Class on Sunday morning'. And in 1901 the minister expressed concern about the numerous organisations 'loosely identified with the church' which were good in themselves, but tend to become '*substitutes* for the church'.[33]

Charles Booth in describing the mainly middle-class Congregational and Presbyterian churches of north London, as well as many of the Baptist churches, wrote as follows:

> They use their churches without hesitation for any purpose which is not actually irreligious. Concerts, popular lectures, debates on social and political questions, all find a place . . . Young people are the life of these churches, just as of every individual family. They form the choir and organise concerts, devoting hard work to the necessary training. They are the members of the debating society, and they crowd to the lectures. Among themselves they get up minor clubs of all kinds. The pastor is ex officio at the head of everything, and perhaps once a year takes his place as president of the cricket club or choral union.[34]

The kind of place Booth had in mind was Park Chapel in Crouch End. While critics of church-based sport claimed that 'amusements' were replacing 'the preaching of the gospel', churches like Park Chapel seem to have combined a full sporting programme with support for missionary activity both at home and abroad. In 1896 it had about 1,000 members and ran two local missions. The annual report highlighted the work of the many overseas missionaries associated with the church. Their social union had a programme of debates and concerts. The Corbin Institute rented grounds for football, cricket and tennis and there was also a bicycle club and a swimming club. They had a library and a Bible class, and rooms for chess, draughts and bagatelle. The tennis club 'was a great success, being helped by the membership of many young ladies'. Their Blenheim Road Mission had a an 'exceedingly popular' gymnastics club for older boys.[35]

II

Clergymen and other religious workers who promoted sport were not simply trying to increase their congregations. Many of them could be termed evangelists for sport, and this is indeed a major point in Erdozain's critique. The error, he argues, lay not in the fact that church and chapel formed sports clubs, but in their claim that responsible Christians had *a mission* to promote sport. I will look at some of the forms that this fervent advocacy could take.

Some, perhaps stung by persisting claims that religion was effeminate, did so because sport was manly, and both church and society needed manly men. It is striking that clergymen and workers for the YMCA were still concerned to demonstrate their own manliness and that of Christianity more generally in the early twentieth century, by which time one might have assumed that 'muscular Christianity' was long-established and generally recognised.[36] A striking example of the promotion of sport as an aid to manliness was the Rev. G. Arbuthnot, a High Churchman who was Vicar of Arundel in the 1870s. He used his parish magazine to harangue his male parishioners about their lack of interest in manly exercise, and he made sure that the boys attending his schools got the message. In an article on 'Manliness' he wrote that

> Our late Vicar used to say that if ever the French landed at Littlehampton, he should put himself at the head of his schoolboys, and drive them back into the sea. We fear that if he had ever tried it, the poor old gentleman would have found himself left alone to do the fighting. Our opinion is formed from the sad want of manliness displayed by the majority of our boys – a deficiency which some of their parents we fear rather encourage. One won't play football, lest he be hurt; another can't run because he never tried to; and a third is even afraid to watch his more manly school fellows running and jumping. To try to exterminate these milksops, the Vicar has tried to encourage athletic sports at St Nicholas School, but we are sorry to say that the entries bear a miserable proportion to the numbers in the school.[37]

Some sporting clergy made even stronger claims for their favourite sport. In his famous book celebrating cricket as the national game, the Rev. James Pycroft, a Devon clergyman and former Cambridge Blue, had declared that 'The game of Cricket philosophically considered, is a standing panegyric on the English character.'[38] Moreover, Pycroft was one of the many people who believed that cricket contributed to social harmony. Social distinctions, he believed, were necessary and inevitable, but on the cricket field everyone was equal and men from different social classes could play in the same team. At the Church Congress in 1869 one of several speakers urging the clergy to be more active in promoting recreation was the Rev. William Glaister, a Nottinghamshire curate who claimed that 'the best Local Board of Health is a Cricket ground, and the best moral club a Cricket Club'. He concluded by 'pointing out to you how the salt of good manners, good morals, and every moral virtue is to be found in the cricket field, and gives a tone to every good cricketer'. And he asserted that Nottinghamshire was 'largely indebted for its high standard of morality to its numerous cricket clubs, and the great interest in cricket in that county by all classes'.[39] We can see here the claim that sport is a school for the formation of 'character', which was a constant refrain of educationalists in the later Victorian years, and which, even though the language may have changed, continues to be used by governments in the twenty-first century to justify their promotion of sport.[40]

By the 1890s it was no longer sufficient to refer to the 'manliness' of sports and other physical recreations. Women of the upper and upper middle classes had long been active in the hunting field and on the tennis court, and were now taking up hockey and cycling. Women from the lower middle and working classes were beginning to join them, at least in the latter two sports. In 1896 Mary Katherine Hughes, who was married to the Rev. Hugh Price Hughes, the country's most famous Wesleyan minister, wrote an article on 'Sports and Recreations', in a series of 'Letters to a Girl'. She argued that although the Puritans had done some great things, much of what they did was not helpful to present-day Christians. 'Recreation of some form or other is a law of our being ... To the healthy boy or girl, vigorous outdoor sports are, and ought to be a necessity.'[41]

Nor was it sufficient now merely to claim that sport was healthy. The promotion of sport had become a Christian duty. The case for sport was taken one stage further by an editorial in the *Sunday School Chronicle* in 1896 on 'The Saving of the Body'. The writer began by suggesting that 'The attempted divorce of body and souls has ever been the source of the keenest woes of mankind.' He accused the Catholic Church of downgrading the body: 'The lives of medieval saints abound in examples of extreme abstinence and bodily mortification.' But Jesus came to save the whole person. The practical message for Sunday School teachers was

> That in trying to accomplish the salvation of souls of our children, we should be careful not to treat as of little account the culture of the body. When the religion of the gymnasium and the cricket-field is duly recognised and inculcated, we may hope for better results than we at present attain ... Children should be taught that God has entrusted to them their bodies, and that He expects these bodies to be properly used and educated for His service ... Let children be told that their bodies are the most marvellous machines in the world and that their Maker requires them to be kept clear and bright by proper exercise. Above all, the fact that our bodies are temples of the Holy Ghost should be constantly emphasised. In thus seeking to save the body, it will be found that the salvation of the soul has also been accomplished.[42]

III

The sporting movement which had been growing fast in the later Victorian years received a further boost from the First World War. It was argued that the returning servicemen deserved better recreational facilities as a reward for their sacrifices. Even those who had previously resisted calls for institutes and recreational societies now felt unable to continue their opposition. Moreover, the nation's passion for sport was justified by the claim that it had contributed to the British victory. At Rose Hill Wesleyan church in Derby a recreation ground was purchased as a war memorial and in the pavilion a tablet was placed with the names of nineteen men associated with the church who had fallen. Reporting the opening ceremony in 1921, the local paper commented,

> Since the war there have been many and varied forms of war memorials, but, when Britain owed her victories on land and sea largely to the spirit of determination and grit inculcated on the playing field, what better form of memorial could there be than to lay out a recreation ground to the memory of those who gave their lives in the great war?

The five-acre field provided space for football, cricket and hockey, together with four tennis courts.[43]

At the peak of the boom in church-based sport, men and women, girls and boys, as well as playing purely for fun, were competing in Sunday school and Bible class leagues, and also in local leagues where they played against teams based on localities or places of work. Magazines from Birmingham churches in the 1920s and 1930s indicate something of the range of activity. At Stratford Road Baptist Church, where the minister conducting a mission was said to be opposed to old-style revivalism and was praised for his 'broad outlook, and virile and sportsmanlike attitude of mind', there was tennis and netball. At the conservative Evangelical St Christopher's, Springfield, there was tennis and cricket. Spring Hill Congregational church, while strongly objecting to the Parks Committee's decision to allow organised sport on Sundays, noted that 'We are not opposed to sport, we have Tennis, Cricket, and Football Clubs, &c', and their magazine also reported the activities of the Cycle Club and the Annual Display by the Girls' Gymnasium. Erdington Baptist church had bowling and tennis clubs, and in 1933 their magazine referred to the annual Football Service, 'which is always a big day'. The liberal Evangelical St John's, Sparkhill, had an athletic club whose programme included football, tennis, table tennis and billiards, and its daughter churches of St Bede's and St Edmunds also had a girls' gymnasium club and tennis clubs, where the lower subscriptions presumably reflected a more working-class membership. The Anglo-Catholic St Alban's had an athletic club, where the programme included football, cricket, tennis, netball, clock golf and bowls.[44]

The taken-for-granted relationship between church and sport was epitomised in the football Sundays or sportsmen's services which were first introduced in the 1890s, and were regular events in many churches and chapels from the 1920s to the 1970s, peaking in the 1930s.[45] A German visitor saw these as evidence that since the churches had now lost much of their influence with the upper classes and the intellectuals, they are 'compelled to meet the masses half-way'. This was not only 'opportunism' – it was also a recognition of the 'cultural value of sensible sport'. He had attended a 'football service' in a poor district of Islington where the preacher had claimed that if St Paul came to London, he would not miss the cup final. 'He maintained that Christ was the greatest of sportsmen, but that he was a victim of unfair play and was beaten by a "foul".' The author added that 'the clergy are tolerant of sportswomen too'. He noted that 'many parsons are skilled players of some kind of game, and the churches are willing organisers'. Bishop Winnington-Ingram of London was well known as a sports enthusiast, and he appeared here in a photograph, carrying a tennis racquet.[46]

Church-based sport soon spread from England to other English-speaking countries. Indeed William J. Baker argues that the Christian sporting movement began almost simultaneously in England and the USA. English writers such as Kingsley and Hughes certainly had an important influence across the Atlantic, but the American YMCAs, which erected their first gyms in 1869, were a few years ahead of their English counterparts in this.[47] Shirl Hoffman has found examples of church-based sports teams in the 1860s, but they became much more numerous from the 1880s and 1890s. Steven Stewart, who especially highlights the pioneering role of the YMCA and Boys' Brigade in Scotland, finds the first church swimming club in the 1880 with a more rapid growth of church sport, especially football, beginning in the 1890s.[48] Glasgow Celtic, though not based on a Catholic parish, was founded in 1887 by a Marist brother, partly to raise money for Catholic charities and partly to keep footballing youth within a Catholic environment.[49] In France the key decade was the 1890s, when, according to Michel Lagrée 'an irresistible movement, especially in favour of association football', swept across the Catholic youth clubs. To a much greater degree than in Britain or the United States, political influences played a big role in the development of French sport at this time. Like their Republican counterparts, sporting Catholics were strongly influenced by a spirit that was 'patriotic, even militarist', and they were equally concerned to win symbolic victories over the Republicans. The moment of triumph came in 1905 at the height of the church–state conflict, when Étoile des Deux Lacs, the football champions of the Catholic sporting federation, defeated the Republican champions, Gallia Club.[50]

Conclusion

The present-day promotion of sport by the Church of England appears to hark back to the 'Muscular Christianity' of the Victorian era. Indeed, since the 1970s, and more especially since the 1990s, just as older forms of church sport were in terminal decline, there has been a proliferation of newer Christian sporting organisations. But much has changed. For example, the pioneers of church-based sport in the 1850s, 1860s and 1870s frequently had a liberalising agenda: they were reacting against what they saw as the puritanical excesses of many Evangelicals in the early decades of the century. The leaders of church-based sport today are themselves mainly Evangelicals, albeit very different in important respects from their predecessors two centuries ago. At the local level, most of the newer clubs are attached to Evangelical churches, including some belonging to Pentecostal denominations which had no interest in sport in earlier times. Many are attached to congregations which grew out of the 1970s 'house church' movement. The social and political concerns, which were often explicit in the thinking of the nineteenth-century pioneers, are less apparent now. In the contemporary discourse the key word is 'mission', which potentially encompasses a very wide vision, often encapsulated in the 'life more abundant' or 'life in all its fullness' of which Jesus spoke, but which in practice foregrounds evangelism.

The 'muscular Christians' of the mid-Victorian years were of course responding to the demands of a specific social, political and religious context. Promotion of recreation was part of a wider mission to proclaim that Christianity was concerned with the 'whole man', 'body, mind and spirit'. Two other concerns were also prominent: a need to promote class reconciliation by responding to the grievances of the working class, of which the need of time and facilities for recreation was one; and the wish to refute claims that Christianity was 'effeminate'. Those 'muscular Christians' who were clergymen were also often reacting against the set-apartness of the clergyman – set apart not only because of the sacredness of his vocation, but also because of his avoidance of anything that might be deemed 'worldly' – as well often as his high social status. Such things as the use of sporting metaphors in sermons, or even joining the lads on the football pitch or in the boxing ring, could be a means of showing that he was an 'ordinary man' to whom other 'ordinary men' could relate.

Present-day advocates of church-based sport are responding to a radically different context. Most obviously the decline in churchgoing, gradual from the 1890s to the 1960s, has since then been much more rapid, and according to some surveys about half the English population claims no religion.[51] At the same time the place of sport in contemporary society, already considerable in the later nineteenth century, has grown very much further, aided especially by television. From the point of view of the Christian churches, a salient feature has been the collapse of the 'British Sunday' since the

1960s and even more since the 1990s. Professional sport on Sunday was rare before the 1960s, but now the scheduling of major events on that day is taken for granted, and in particular there is a full programme of Premier League football. No one will any longer go to church, as once they sometimes did, because of the lack of alternatives, and the numbers of those continuing with the religion they learnt from their parents is fast dwindling. So it is not surprising that Christians are looking for new ways of reaching those with no previous church connection, and not surprising that connecting with the world of sport seems to be one of the ways of doing this.

The Victorian pioneers of church-based sport were well aware of the difficulties they could face, whether from suspicious working-class teenagers or more puritanical fellow-Christians. At least nobody needs to be persuaded today of the value of 'the body'. The danger is more likely to be an exaggerated concern for the body.[52] Nonetheless the Victorians started with advantages that their modern counterparts will lack. In earlier times, and to some extent right up to the early 1960s, there was between the strongly committed churchgoers and those completely detached from the church, a large number of those who had a looser connection. In particular, most children attended a Sunday School, and though the majority dropped out around the age of twelve or thirteen, there was a connection which could be continued or revived through a church youth group or through other Christian youth organisations. Moreover, as suggested earlier, many churches and chapels had a very active social life which could draw in outsiders as well as the regular churchgoers. In the twenty-first century, this middle group has dwindled and most of its members belong to the older generation. The Church of England's Sport and Well-Being Project[53] is focused especially on children, the under 25s, those with disabilities (who are a major focus for the YMCA's sporting provision) and those who are 'Black, Asian and Minority Ethnic'. The project aims to attract people from these groups not only by forming new sports clubs and providing facilities, but also by forming links with local authorities and schools, and organising such things as after-school clubs and summer holiday camps. Those described as 'BAME' tend to be more religiously active than the population as a whole, though not necessarily as Anglicans. But Clive Field's research, based partly on census data, but more especially on polling, provides a vivid picture of the challenges the project will face in reaching children and the under 25s.[54] They already benefit from the availability of a range of leisure opportunities, not least on Sundays, far beyond anything that earlier generations could have imagined. They are also those most likely to appear in the census as having 'no religion'. Moreover, the polling suggests that a significant proportion have negative stereotypes of churches or even of 'religion'.

The connections between the history of sport and the history of religion remain largely unexplored. Few historians of sport are interested in religion – though there are some notable exceptions. Many historians of religion play or have played sport, but few regard it as an important field for research. There are some substantial studies of the relationship in the nineteenth century, but very few on the twentieth century – although Jack Williams's research, mainly on Lancashire, suggests that the involvement of churches in recreational sport peaked in the 1920s and 1930s and my own research suggests that it remained considerable in the twenty-five years after the Second World War. Work on religion and sport is especially scanty in at least two areas. One is Catholic sport. Plenty of work has been done on Catholic sport in other countries,[55] but very little in England. But maybe the biggest lack is of work on the role of religion in women's sport. For example, plenty has been written about sport in the YMCA but very little about the YWCA. Williams's research on Bolton in the interwar years suggests that while about half the football and cricket clubs in the town were based in a church, chapel or other religious organisation, well over half the clubs for hockey and rounders, the sports most widely played by women in the town, were church-based.[56]

In spite of the lack of contact between historians of religion and of sport, sport offers a vivid reflection of the changing relationships between 'church' and 'world' over the past two centuries. In the early nineteenth century Primitive Methodists not only abandoned sports which they had once enjoyed: they also attended sporting events in order to preach against them.[57] And while the Prims were especially proactive in their invasions of Satan's strongholds, Anglican Evangelicals and Calvinist Dissenters were equally insistent in urging their followers to avoid the risks of participating in frivolous and potentially sinful amusements.[58] In the early twentieth century sports clubs were attached to churches of most denominations. Their members were expected, or at least encouraged, to attend church services or Bible classes, but explicit evangelism was rare. In the early twenty-first century, Evangelicals are as positive about sport as their predecessors were negative, and Christians are urged to play sports, using this as an opportunity to form friendships with non-churchgoers and to talk to them about Jesus.[59]

Notes

1. 'Vatican creates new section "Church and Sports" on the occasion of Olympic games', Catholic News Agency, 2 August 2004, https://www.catholicnewsagency.com/news/1662/vatican-creates-new-section-church-and-sports-on-the-occasion-of-olympic-games.
2. 'Address of the Holy Father John Paul II to the Organizers and Participants in the 83rd Giro d'Italia Cycle Race', The Holy See, 12 May 2000, https://www.vatican.va/content/john-paul-ii/en/speeches/2000/apr-jun/documents/hf_jp-ii_spe_20000512_giro-italia.html; Kevin Lixey, 'The Vatican's Game Plan for Maximizing Sport's Educational Potential', in Nick J. Watson and Andrew Parker (eds), *Sports and Christianity* (New York: Routledge, 2013), pp. 250–68.

3. Miroslaw Ponczek and Adam Fryc, 'Catholic Popes and the Modern Sports Movement (from the Mid-Nineteenth Century to the Beginnings of the Third Millennium)', *Journal of Tourism, Recreation and Sports Management*, 1 (2013), pp. 11–20.
4. 'National Sport and Wellbeing project', The Church of England, accessed 4 March 2023, http://churchofengland.org/resources/national-sport-and-well being-project.
5. See Hugh McLeod, *Religion and the Rise of Sport in England* (Oxford: Oxford University Press, 2023). The timing of the decline is discussed on pp. 189–93.
6. Peter Lupson, *Thank God for Football!* (London: Azure, 2006).
7. Hugh Cunningham, *Leisure in the Industrial Revolution, 1789–1880* (London: Routledge, 1980), p. 181.
8. Peter Bailey, *Leisure and Class in Victorian England: Rational Recreation and the Contest for Control, 1830–85* (London: Routledge and Kegan Paul, 1978), pp. 92, 137.
9. Douglas Reid, 'Labour, Leisure and Politics in Birmingham, ca. 1800–1875' (PhD diss., University of Birmingham, 1985), pp. 132–5.
10. Jack Williams, 'Churches, Identities and Sport in the North, 1900–39', in Jeff Hill and Jack Williams (eds), *Sport and Identity in the North of England* (Keele: Keele University Press, 1996), pp. 113–36; Dennis O'Keefe, 'The Lord's Opening Partnership: Church and Cricket in Calderdale, 1860 to c. 1920', *Sport in Society*, 15 (2012), pp. 246–64.
11. Dominic Erdozain, *The Problem of Pleasure: Sport, Recreation and the Crisis of Victorian Religion* (Woodbridge: The Boydell Press, 2010).
12. Owen Chadwick, *The Founding of Cuddesdon* (Oxford: Oxford University Press, 1954), pp. 27–8, 104; J. C. Wigram, *A Charge Delivered at his Primary Visitation in November 1860* (London, 1860), pp. 22–3; Diana McClatchey, *Oxfordshire Clergy, 1777–1869* (Oxford: Clarendon Press, 1960), p. 230.
13. *Bell's Life in London*, 30 June 1844, 29 July 1855, 3 June 1865.
14. *Bell's Life in London*, 22 August 1858, 24 August 1856.
15. Bailey, *Leisure and Class*, pp. 80–123.
16. *Luton Times and Advertiser*, 26 June 1855; *Wakefield and West Riding Herald*, 29 June 1855; *Preston Chronicle*, 6 August 1859; *Bolton Chronicle*, 18 April 1863.
17. *Birmingham Journal*, 1 March 1856, 25 July 1857, 17 February 1858, 1 May 1859.
18. See Reid, 'Birmingham', pp. 102–8. The rationale for Miller's scheme was explained in a published sermon, John Cale Miller, *The Dying Judge's Charge Echoed from the Christian Pulpit, in a Plea for the Recreation of the Working Classes, as Essential to their Social and Religious Elevation* (London, 1854).
19. Bailey, *Leisure and Class*, pp. 42–50, 137.
20. *Bell's Life in London*, 25 June 1848.
21. *Official Report of the Church Congress*, 1866, pp. 38–54.
22. *Official Report of the Church Congress*, 1869, pp. 133, 144, 147–9.
23. *Official Report of the Church Congress*, 1874, pp. 422–3, 430–2; *Official Report of the Church Congress*, 1877, pp. 249–73, 366–406.
24. *Bristol Mercury*, 4 July 1857.
25. *Bradford Review*, 23 July 1859; *Huddersfield Chronicle*, 6 June 1857.

26. *Bolton Chronicle*, 3 July 1869; *Bolton Evening News*, 26 June 1878.
27. Church of the Messiah, Birmingham, Annual Reports 1879, 1881, 1888 (The Library of Birmingham, Local History Collection).
28. Alan Bartlett, 'The Churches in Bermondsey, 1880–1939' (PhD diss., University of Birmingham, 1987), pp. 162–3.
29. Lupson, *Thank God*, pp. 5–6, 122.
30. B. G. Orchard, *Liverpool's Legion of Honour* (Birkenhead, 1893), pp. 42–3.
31. Michael R. Watts, *The Dissenters*, 3 vols (Oxford: Clarendon Press, 1978–2005), vol. 3, pp. 174–5.
32. *The Independent*, 16 May 1889, 2 October 1891, 19 October 1893.
33. College Street Baptist Church, Northampton, Congregational Manuals 1884, 1886,1888, 1889, 1897, 1901; Minutes of Young Men's Society 1894–1901, 1 November 1897 and 6 December 1897 (Northamptonshire County Record Office); *Northamptonshire Nonconformist* (Northampton Local History Library). See also Hugh McLeod, '"Thews and Sinews": Nonconformity and Sport', in David Bebbington and Timothy Larsen (eds), *Christianity and Cultural Aspirations* (London: Sheffield Academic Press, 2003), pp. 28–30.
34. Charles Booth, *Life and Labour of the People in London*, 17 vols (London 1902–3), 3rd series, vol. 1, pp. 121–2.
35. Park Chapel, Crouch End, Year Book, 1896, 1898, 1899 (London Metropolitan Archives).
36. Bartlett, 'Bermondsey', p. 164; McLeod, *Rise of Sport*, p. 95.
37. *Arundel Parish Magazine*, May 1875 (West Sussex County Record Office).
38. James Pycroft, *The Cricket Field* (London, 1851), p. 23.
39. *Official Report of the Church Congress*, 1869, pp. 42–4.
40. See for example Malcolm Tozer, *The Ideal of Manliness: The Legacy of Thring's Uppingham* (Truro: Sunnyrest Books, 2015); Department for Media, Culture and Sport, *Game Plan*, with foreword by Tony Blair (London: Cabinet Office, 2002).
41. *Sunday School Chronicle*, 16 January 1896.
42. *Sunday School Chronicle*, 20 February 1896.
43. *Derby Daily Telegraph*, 4 July 1921.
44. Stratford Road Baptist Church *Magazine*, June 1923 and December 1923, August 1924; Spring Hill *Monthly Messenger*, June 1920, March 1923, May 1924; St Christopher's, Spring Hill, *Parish Magazine*, May 1924; Erdington Baptist Church, *Monthly News*, May and November 1933; St John's, Sparkhill, *Magazine*, October 1925, July 1926, September 1926 and October 1926; St Alban's, *Magazine*, February 1921, July 1924 and August 1924 (The Library of Birmingham, Local Studies Collection).
45. See McLeod, *Rise of Sport*, pp. 183–9.
46. Rudolf Kircher, *Fair Play: The Game of Merrie England*, trans. R. N. Bradley (London: W. Collins Sons and Co., 1928), pp. 41–2.
47. William J. Baker, *Playing with God: Religion and Modern Sport* (Cambridge, MA: Harvard University Press, 2007), pp. 34, 62–3.
48. Steven Jamieson Stewart, 'Physical Recreation and Muscular Christianity in Glaswegian Churches' (MRes thesis, University of Glasgow, 2021).
49. See Bill Murray, *The Old Firm: Sport, Sectarianism and Society in Scotland* (Edinburgh: John Donald, 1987).

50. Michel Lagrée, 'Sport et sociabilité catholique en France au début du XXe siècle', in P. Arnaud and J. Camy (eds), *La naissance du movement sportif associatif en France* (Lyon: Presses Universitaires de Lyon, 1986), pp. 327–35.
51. See the very extensive collection of statistics on contemporary belief and practice in Clive D. Field, *Counting Religion in Britain, 1970–2020: Secularization in Statistical Context* (Oxford: Oxford University Press, 2022).
52. See Jürgen Martschukat, *The Age of Fitness: How the Body Came to Symbolize Success and Achievement*, trans. Alex Skinner (Cambridge: Polity Press, 2021).
53. For discussion of the wider 'sports ministry' movement of which it is a part, see Andrew Parker, Rob French and Naomi Maturano, 'Exploring Sports Ministry in the UK: National Trends and Local Expressions', *Journal of Religion and Society*, 23 (2021), pp. 1–20.
54. Field, *Counting Religion*, pp. 68, 216–18.
55. For example, Laurence Munoz, *Une histoire du sport catholique: la Fédération sportive et culturelle de France, 1898–2000* (Paris: Harmattan, 2003); Juan Ramón Carbó (ed.), *Cuerpo y espíritu: Deporte y cristianismo en la historia* (Guadalupe, Spain: Universidad Católica San Antonio de Murcia, Servicio de Publicaciones, 2021); and numerous books and articles by Dries Vanysacker both on Catholicism and sport in Belgium and the Netherlands (in Dutch) and on the relationship between Catholicism and sport more generally (mainly in English).
56. Jack Williams, 'Churches, Sport and Identities in the North, 1900–1939', *Sport and Identity in the North of England*, p. 107.
57. Robert Colls, *This Sporting Life: Sport and Liberty in England, 1760–1960* (Oxford: Oxford University Press, 2020), pp. 150–1, 156.
58. McLeod, *Rise of Sport*, pp. 31–2.
59. Parker, French and Marturano, 'Sports Ministry', p. 10.

CHAPTER TEN

Henry Scott Holland and Social Christianity in the English *Fin de siècle*

Frances Knight

Henry Scott Holland (1847–1918) was a significant architect of social Christianity at the English *fin de siècle*.[1] His faith mobilised his critique of existing conditions in Britain, and further afield. Philanthropy would no longer suffice: what was needed was a Christianising of social structures, although he was vague about what this really meant. He immersed himself in numerous social and theological projects, including the Christian Social Union, the Oxford House settlement in Bethnal Green, and the Maurice Hostel in Hoxton. He was a prime mover in *Lux Mundi*, the theological bestseller of the 1890s, and for over twenty years he edited the monthly journal *Commonwealth*, with its subtitle '*a Social Magazine*'. Through his preaching, writing and general demeanour, he became a leading exponent of a style of faith that became characteristic of some quarters of the turn-of-the-century Church of England. He embodied a *fin de siècle* spirit that mingled optimism, and a belief in better things for the new century, with a pessimism that was deeply critical of the failings of the late Victorian world. Holland's theology drove him to take on ideas which Anglican clergy had often been wary of, and to extend and normalise the range of interests which it was usual, or indeed expected, for a clergyman to have. As a literary stylist he could be idiosyncratic, stretching grammatical conventions, and piling up images to evoke feeling and mood. He was nevertheless a successful popular communicator, mixing both ancient methods, such as preaching to large congregations, with those of the late nineteenth century, particularly regular journalism. He had a strong sense that the moment for action was at hand, and that if his generation of churchmen did not respond, the moment would be lost forever.[2] Today, Henry Scott Holland is mainly remembered as the author of the verses known as 'Death Is Nothing at All', lines which people seem to like or loathe in equal measure when they are used at funerals. But he was much more than a writer of sentimental or winsome verse.[3] This chapter focuses on the ways in which his social Christianity expressed itself in his long-standing concerns about the housing question. It argues that his views developed from a naïve youthful enthusiasm for slum missions, to support for the garden city movement, and then ripened into a radical urban theology.[4]

Holland as an Establishment Radical

Holland was born in 1847, and his early years were typical of the life of a young man in upper-class English society.[5] He was arty – fond of pre-Raphaelite painting, romantic poetry and music. By the time he arrived at Balliol College, Oxford in 1866, he was very interested in politics and economics, as well as theology. He was a friend of Gerard Manley Hopkins, and like others of his generation, he was much influenced by the idealist philosophy of Thomas Hill Green, who was his tutor.[6] Holland was elected to a post at Christ Church, Oxford immediately upon graduation and retained his connection there for the rest of his life. The Christ Church that Holland joined was an interesting environment for a young man who was temperamentally inclined to Anglo-Catholicism, but already developing radical sympathies. It still contained the very aged Dr Pusey, the veteran Tractarian who had held his chair of Hebrew since 1828, and Henry Liddon, Pusey's disciple and spokesman, who divided his time between the college and his canonry at St Paul's. In the 1870s, several generations of Anglo-Catholics were simultaneously in Oxford. Pusey, of course, was the first generation. Liddon, born in 1829, was of the second generation. Holland, and his slightly younger friend Charles Gore, who had been born in 1853, were the rising third generation, and it was Holland and Gore, together with their associates, who would push the movement in some new directions.

In the early 1870s, there was still an expectation that college fellows would get ordained, and Holland was ordained in 1872. His energetic campaigning spirit became rapidly apparent. He supported the foundation of two new Oxford colleges, St Stephen's House, an Anglo-Catholic theological hall for candidates preparing for overseas mission, and Lady Margaret Hall, for the education of women. He took an active interest in the Church beyond Oxford, founding the Christ Church Mission in Poplar (in east London), and supporting the Oxford Mission to Calcutta (founded in 1880) and the Church of England Purity Society (founded in 1883). Unmarried, inherently sociable and with an orientation towards community life, Holland proposed the foundation of a residential community in the East End of London, where Oxford graduates could settle for a couple of years before ordination. They would devote their time to learning about, and from, the life of the East End, whilst engaging in practical social and educational projects. Holland's 'settlement house' became the distinctively Anglo-Catholic enterprise known as Oxford House in Bethnal Green (opened in 1884, today it is a community development project and arts venue). Oxford House slightly predated Toynbee Hall, Samuel and Henrietta Barnett's more famous settlement in Whitechapel. It was the first of what would become a large number of settlements in deprived areas, initiated by universities and public schools.

Holland's appointment as a residentiary canon at St Paul's Cathedral in 1884 permitted him to immerse himself fully in London's religious life and social problems. It also gave him a strategic platform within English Christianity: the nave of St Paul's and the seating under the dome were often packed when he was preaching. With Gore, he began what was probably his most famous initiative, the Christian Social Union, an organisation devoted to studying social issues, and raising their profile within the church, in the expectation of action.[7] By the time it merged with the Industrial Christian Fellowship after the First World War, it had numerous local branches, and a mass membership of about six thousand men and women. It produced publications, most notably the *Commonwealth* monthly magazine, and various handbooks, and it sponsored events and conferences. Holland remained at St Paul's until he returned to Oxford in 1910 as Regius Professor of Divinity. There he promoted a radical plan to overhaul the teaching of theology. He wanted to see it taught with academic rigor, and adopting high philosophical and historical standards, rather than being driven by Anglican dogma. Even more controversially, he advocated the teaching of other religions besides Christianity in the theology faculty. Holland's scheme provoked considerable debate, much of it hostile, and it was rejected by Oxford's Convocation in April 1913.[8] The outbreak of the War vastly reduced the number of students and limited his scope for further action at the university. Immensely depressed by the War, Holland's health declined, and he died in 1918.

Holland as a Theologian of the *Fin de siècle*

The final years of the nineteenth century have often been seen as characterised by a queasy blend of optimism and pessimism, with people looking to the future in hope of a better time, whilst simultaneously desiring to cut their ties with the past.[9] I have discussed elsewhere some of Christianity's encounters with the mentality of the *fin de siècle* and it is noticeable, although not surprising, that at the points where they intersect, for Christians there is often a stronger strand of optimism than pessimism.[10] This is particularly true in the case of Henry Scott Holland, who, at least in his earlier years, appears to have excelled in optimism. 'I never met a more joyful person', wrote Henry Nevinson, as he recalled Holland the young don at Christ Church. 'He was born happy, just as he was born Christian, and he could not help it.'[11] Nevinson was one of Holland's many admirers – he emphasised his inspiring personality and extraordinary physical energy, but also considered that he could be irritating and twee in ways that no one else would have got away with. His close friend Mary Drew (Gladstone's daughter) was effusive, describing Holland as 'one of the most vivid and joyous figures in social life'.[12] She quotes another of Holland's friend, the Liberal politician and Christian activist G. W. E. Russell, as saying of Holland that 'He diffused joy by his own joy in living – he vanquished morbidity by his essential wholesomeness.'[13] In later life he suffered poor health, and also became more pessimistic. He failed to anticipate the coming of the Great

War, and when it started, he saw it as a sign of Christianity's failure.[14] He believed that war would have been impossible, if Christianity had had a meaningful influence on trade, industry, diplomacy and politics.[15]

Holland's theology was suffused with a type of incarnational Christianity that placed the needs of the world, rather than the expectations of the church, at the centre of the agenda. From that emerged his quest for social justice. Graham Neville observed that he referred every practical issue back to the doctrine of the incarnation, and his social and political policies followed.[16] The influence of F. D. Maurice had activated this shift in Holland, and although Maurice had died in 1872, he remained the presiding influence over many of the leading thinkers in both the Church of England and Nonconformity. Interwoven with this distinctively Maurician strand, there was the Anglo-Catholicism that Holland shared with many of his immediate circle in Oxford. *Lux Mundi*, with its telling subtitle *A Series of Studies in the Religion of the Incarnation*, was edited by Gore, but the plan originated with Holland, who wrote the first chapter. It became the manifesto for third-generation Anglo-Catholicism, as it attempted to bring together aspects of the Anglo-Catholic heritage with more contemporary approaches to reading the Bible, and some of the insights of Maurice. Gore in particular promoted respectful biblical criticism and kenotic Christology, the belief that during his life on earth, Jesus's knowledge was limited to that of a man of his day. The book celebrated, as part of the God-given universe, evolution, science, art and socialism. It was even positive about other faiths, a hint perhaps of the future direction of Holland's thoughts about the content of the theological curriculum. The book created a rift with Liddon, who was appalled that Pusey House, founded in memory of Pusey, and with Gore as its first principal, appeared to be turning into a centre for theological liberalism and social activism.[17] Liddon's concerns were amplified by the fact that Gore and Holland had formed the Christian Social Union (CSU) just a few months before the publication of *Lux Mundi*. The aim of the CSU, in the words of Holland, was 'to drag the social question into the Church', something which spoke directly to his Maurician instincts. Holland had to manage relations with Liddon delicately, because he encountered him not only at Christ Church, but also at St Paul's, where both men held canonries.

The extent of the intellectual shift between second- and third-generation Anglo-Catholics was reflected in Holland's memorial, composed after Liddon's death in 1890. Holland emphasised Liddon's positive qualities but was unflinching about his rigidity.

> His intellect, as such, would never stir. You could anticipate, exactly, the position from which he would start . . . Nothing occurred to colour or expand his intellectual fabric. To novel ideas – to the ideas that were still in growth, especially – he offered no welcome, so far as his own inner habit of mind was concerned.[18]

Holland diplomatically suggested that both men had arrived at the same goal – 'the doctrine of the Incarnation, as witnessed by Church and Scripture' but by different routes.[19] The routes were certainly very different. Rather than a simple reliance on the creeds, Holland acknowledged that he and his friends – the *Lux Mundi* group – had 'yielded to the sway of speculative floods, which had been set moving in German universities . . . Liddon has closed the doors instinctively'.[20] Thus Holland described the breach which occurred between the older and younger generations of late nineteenth-century Anglo-Catholic theologians. He made no direct allusion to the publication of *Lux Mundi*, which occurred ten months before Liddon's death, but the controversy would have been so well known, he did not need to. Holland claimed, rather disingenuously, to have been surprised that *Lux Mundi* created the reaction that it did. 'I never thought that we should induce anyone to read it outside the circle of our aunts and mothers, and a few patient-minded clergy. The old book itself looked conscious of its own dead weight: and never dreamt of this stormy and excited career.'[21] This breach with certain elements of his Anglo-Catholic past was significant. It propelled him forwards and freed him to take up new causes.

Holland as a Campaigner for Social Christianity

Holland's commitment to social Christianity inevitably took him in various directions. Through his connection with the Gladstones, the Russells, the Glynnes and the Lyttelltons, he had long been associated with the senior echelons of the Liberal Party, and he had been at Eton with the future Lord Rosebery. The Liberal Party's strong Nonconformist base, and predilections for non-denominational schooling and disestablishing churches (Ireland in 1870, and an ongoing campaign in Wales) meant that it was not the natural political home of Anglican clergy, although it had been easier while Gladstone, the pious Anglican high churchman, was still alive.[22] It became trickier during the Rosebery years, and even more so after Rosebery's resignation in 1896, which created a vacuum in leadership and policy. In January 1897, Holland organised a group of Liberal high churchmen, mainly senior clergy with a couple of laymen, to write to the Liberal whip Thomas Ellis. They seem to have been hoping to revive the fortunes of the Party by establish within it a caucus of senior Anglicans, who would press on social questions, and move the Party more in the direction of the Independent Labour Party, rather than defaulting to supporting 'the rich Liberal capitalist [who] is not necessarily more in sympathy with the workers than the rich Tory capitalist'. Holland and the other signatories made it clear that they were disenchanted with old-style Liberalism, which was out of touch with the social pressures on labour, and they hinted that unless the Liberal Party got a better grip on Labour questions, their sympathies were likely to shift to the ILP. 'It is a social policy that we want, and the leader who believes in it.' On the issue of disentangling the church from the state, they claimed they were 'quite willing to accept disestablishment when it is the nation's will', something that was more evident in Wales than in England. On education, they asked that church teaching should be provided for the children of churchmen, but after that, they welcomed the 'fullest popular representation on school boards of managers'.[23] In writing to Ellis, who was a Welsh Calvinistic Methodist, they were evidently trying to go some distance to accommodate Nonconformist sensibilities. They were also distancing themselves from Conservative Anglo-Catholics such as Athelstan Riley, who had roused Nonconformist ire on the London School Board.[24] It is not clear how Ellis replied.[25] Holland did not succeed in formalising a clerical pressure group within the Liberal party, although the CSU did work through three sympathetic MPs: the ageing radical Sir Charles Dilke, J. G. Talbot, brother of Holland's friend Edward Talbot, and the Scottish Harold (Jack) Tennant.[26] For a decade, the Liberals were out of power. When they won the election in 1906, Holland wrote a characteristically emotional *Commonwealth* editorial: 'We are all, I suppose, dazed and staggered. Such overwhelming moments carry with them such reproach. Why were we ever afraid? Why was there so little faith?'[27]

Holland edited the *Commonwealth* from its launch in 1896 until the time of his death, although he was assisted by Christopher Cheshire in the later years. The early issues bear the hallmarks of a *fin de siècle* journalistic enterprise. It was as if the team at the *Yellow Book*, which was the leading journal of *fin de siècle* aestheticism, had all been hired.[28] The first issue contained significant art coverage, poetry by the lesbian couple who wrote as Michael Field, a review of a book by the high priest of aestheticism Walter Pater, and contributions from Netta Syrett and Evelyn Sharp, who were *Yellow Book* regulars. Percy and Mabel Dearmer were the link between the *Yellow Book* and the *Commonwealth*. Percy Dearmer worked for the CSU and was one of the editorial team on the *Commonwealth* (together with James Adderley and G. Herbert Davis). His wife Mabel was a writer and artist who could draw in the style of Aubrey Beardsley. She was a contributor to the *Yellow Book* and provided artistic decorations to fill in odd gaps in the *Commonwealth*. The Dearmers had a circle of friends who overlapped the worlds of the late nineteenth-century aesthetic literary London scene and progressive Christianity,[29] and it was therefore unsurprising that several wrote for both publications.

Both journals appeared monthly, but the *Yellow Book* retailed at an eye-wateringly expensive five shillings, whilst the *Commonwealth* sold for just three pence. For this, the reader was given forty pages of content, and an art plate, typically of a Pre-Raphaelite work with socialist connotations, such as Ford Madox Brown's 'Jesus washing Peter's Feet'. The content was heavily left-leaning. Issue one included articles on 'The International Labour Congress', 'The ILP Conference', 'Labour Notes', 'A Living Wage', as well as articles on what we would now call the gender pay gap. There was also an introduction to biblical criticism, and an article by Charles Gore on prayer. Beatrice Webb was one of the better-known contributors. In typically optimistic fashion, Henry Scott Holland declared in his first editorial that the 'Commonwealth' – by which he meant a common life for all the citizens of one society – was about to triumph, as the old parties and political divisions were shifting and breaking apart. He warmed to this theme:

> Nationalise yourself, your interest, your sympathies, your joys. Socialise yourself, out of sheer and free goodwill for the Common Weal ... Everyone's sorrow is our sorrow, and all have a claim on our gladness ... Every act of man or woman in England to-day is a social fact ... the clothes we buy, the food we eat, the wages we give or take, our investments, our amusements; all this tells in ways beyond our ken, in directions beyond our control, on the lives and futures of our fellows.[30]

He promised his readers that the new magazine would cover everything: 'There is nothing that may not come within our cover. Not industry only, but art, joy, literature, games, music, woods, fields, hills, waters, songs, jokes, plays, beer, skittles ... We shall claim, for the cause of our common humanity, everything that is fairly and decently human.'[31] He promised that religion would also be discussed 'freely, gaily, instinctively, habitually, without effort and without apology'.[32]

By 1899, however, the tone of carefree, life-affirming gaiety promised in Holland's opening editorial had been tempered by the sombre character of much of the content. There was less focus on the arts and culture, and the art plate disappeared. More emphasis was being given to social questions, and the stark realities of the moral problem of urban poverty. A series on the realities of overcrowded London by the Christian social investigator George Haw ran from February until May of that year. Haw had been shocked by the housing crisis amongst skilled workmen who were willing to pay high rents, but for whom there was nothing available: 'A firm of house agents in the New Kent Road have lists of people waiting for houses four hundred deep' with prospective tenants bidding against each other to offer higher rents.[33] The result was gross overcrowding; Haw estimated that 900,000 people in London, the 'overcrowded fifth' lived more than two to a room, with less than 400 cubic feet of space for each person.[34]

None of this would have surprised Holland. As a young man, he had taken his joyful demeanour into his mission work in the East End of London, and his forays into Hoxton have attracted critical comment from some historians. Seth Koven saw them as evidence of the 'slumming' phenomenon, in which wealthy people sought excitement by mingling with the poor.[35] After spending time in Hoxton in 1873, Holland wrote to Edward Talbot, the warden of Keble College: 'It was intensely exciting and, we are inclined to say, very successful. The crowd gathered in a moment, a real live dirty crowd of roughs and streety women; they followed us – they sang a bit; they listened with extraordinary intentness, and solemnity. Only the little children attempted mockery.'[36] A more self-conscious person, or one who thought that his words might be quoted 150 years after the event, might have been more circumspect in revelling in the dirtiness of the people who had attended his mission service. But the twenty-six-year-old, writing in the first flush of his urban enthusiasm, had yet to appreciate the full implications of overcrowded and squalid living conditions.

A better understanding of the housing crisis developed during the 1880s. The Royal Commission on the Housing of the Working Classes reported in 1885. Various investigators, including Andrew Mearns, W. T. Stead, Richard Mudie-Smith, Charles Booth, William Booth and the journalists on the Nonconformist *British Weekly*, contributed to bringing attention to the situation in London, developing further the already well-established narrative of the 'unholy city'. What was newer was the acknowledgement that the environment itself was inherently corrupting, an insight which had consequences for the understanding of sin, which was traditionally accounted for as part of the human condition, and a consequence of the inherently fallen nature of man. 'Sin' in the late nineteenth century was in the process of redefinition. As Holland put it in a letter to his friend James Adderley, at around the time of the founding of the CSU, 'for the first time in all history, the poor old Church is trying to show the personal sin of corporate and social sinning'.[37]

The *Commonwealth* continued to devote considerable space to discussing housing problems.[38] It gave a warm welcome to the formation of the Garden City Association, in the Autumn of 1899. The Association was founded in order to promote the ideas of Ebenezer Howard, in his book *To-morrow: A Peaceful Path to Real Reform* which had been published in the previous year.[39] The *Commonwealth* reported that 'There is something fascinating about the proposal [Howard's plan for garden cities] and we shall not be surprised to find it taken up by many earnest minded people.'[40] By 1902, Holland had become a vice-president of the Garden City Association, together with Edward Talbot, who was now Bishop of Rochester, Bishops Winnington-Ingram of London, John Perceval of Hereford and several other Anglican clergy.[41] Percy Dearmer organised a CSU daytrip to George Cadbury's Bournville development near Birmingham, which whilst not a garden city, was described as 'The first instalment of Utopia, the first attempt in modern England to put Christianity into practice as the motive power of everyday-life.'[42] Howard's ideas were widely taken up, resulting in the foundation of Letchworth Garden City in 1904. Although Howard and many of his supporters were Congregationalists or had other Nonconformist sympathies, and the CSU restricted it membership to communicant Anglicans, CSU local groups lost no time in inviting Howard and other GCA lecturers to speak at their events.[43] In 1906 Holland and Dearmer ran a CSU Saturday outing to Letchworth, in which the morning was spent hearing about developments in the town, and the afternoon devoted to a 'conference on housing'. Holland presided, explaining that the purpose the Garden City was to combine the wholesome life of the countryside with the social life of the towns. The *Daily Mail* wrote up the event, reporting wryly that the 'bare-legged, sandalled children roaming around . . . and radiant sunshine made each £150 cottage and its garden an object more to be desired than the most "desirable mansion" in Mayfair'.[44] The CSU's support for the Garden City movement was finally cemented in 1917, when the *Commonwealth* moved its editorial and printing operations from London to Letchworth.

Holland's Urban Theology

It was characteristic of Christian housing reformers at the *fin de siècle* to talk about 'building the new Jerusalem' in ways which blended ideas from the Bible, Bunyan and Blake with plans for actually building new communities. Henry Scott Holland was particularly prone to this, and I have discussed elsewhere the ways in which he mixed a New Testament theology of civic interconnectedness with the rhetorical power of imagery derived from the Revelation of St John.[45] As he slipped between evocations of the 'Heavenly City', the 'City' and 'cities', it must have sometimes been difficult for audiences to catch whether he was using metaphors for the church (visible and invisible) or meaning actual cities.[46] One moment he was evoking 'Jerusalem on high' and the next suggesting that St Paul was a dedicated urban explorer. Paul had wanted to see Rome, Holland told an audience in North Wales. 'Today, he would have said, "I, the Apostle of the City of God, must, at all costs, see Paris, and London, and Manchester and New York."'[47]

It was significant that Holland chose to return to the city theme as the new century dawned. Writing his first *Commonwealth* editorial of the twentieth century had a particular resonance for someone shaped by the *fin de siècle* mentality in the ways that Holland was. He offered his readers a meditation on eschatological hope, with a dose of reproach about the actual situation that greeted Britons in January 1901:

> Always, we have hoped that, at last, the day has dawned, and earth would prove itself to be the very land which our Saviour trod and which he would make His own. Always we have in view the City to be built, not only that Heavenly Jerusalem, the mystic Bride, the Church of the Living God, but the earthly City that would bear its outer witness to the Spiritual Jerusalem, which is alone the mother of us . . . And is not this coming Century, slipping in upon us, clear and fresh and new, the one for which we have looked so long? . . . Its years are as yet undimmed and untainted. Its long happy days are waiting for us to begin . . . Shall we not, with might and main, set to work, and build Jerusalem in all this pleasant land?

Then he sounded the inevitable note of pessimism:

> Hopes have languished; ideals have lapsed. We thought of unbroken Peace, and we find ourselves girded about with wars and rumours of

war. We talked of Brotherhood: and we find ourselves at death-grip with those who, if any, should be our own brothers. We pictured a smiling land, in which a free people eat their bread in gladness and simpleness of heart, unalarmed and undivided: and we sadly look round London today.[48]

The 'earthly city' as the 'outer witness to the Spiritual Jerusalem' gets to the heart of what he was saying here. A Christian society required the cessation of the Boer War, social equality and practical attempts to deal with urban problems.

What else, besides F. D. Maurice and the temperamental habits instilled by the legacy of the Oxford Movement, had brought Holland to this point? Charles Gore, writing about his friend shortly after his death, explained that Holland's 'cosmic and humanitarian' Christ was derived directly from his appreciation of John's Gospel, the Apostle Paul and ancient Church Fathers, particularly Origen and Athanasius:

From this he argued that Christian doctrine, as an exposition of the particular life and person of Jesus of Nazareth should be found in congruity with the whole world movement towards truth and justice ... The Pauline conception of the risen and glorified Christ as the Head of the Body, the Church, arrested and held his mind. This essentially Catholic Church was to be for action in the world. Its function was gradually to gather into the redeemed humanity, and to consecrate into the one body, all that truly belongs to humanity, till 'the glory of honour' of all nations had been brought within the light of the Holy City.[49]

This was possibly a clearer explanation of the theology of Henry Scott Holland than anything that he wrote for himself. Holland was not a theologian in the systematic, philosophical or historical mode, nor was he a biblical scholar. His theological output was 'occasional' in the sense that he produced theological reflections for particular occasions and published them mainly as sermons and newspaper articles.[50] William Temple was unusual in claiming that 'behind all the fervour of feeling and the riot of words there was a massive and coherent philosophical theology'.[51] For most readers, however, Holland's style, though evocative, has also seemed somewhat opaque. His theology conveyed a mood, generated an idea or made a comment. This can be illustrated by a closer reading of his publication of 1911, *Our Neighbours*, which was unusual in being a book-length development of his social thought.

Our Neighbours was one of a number of 'handbooks' that the CSU produced, all of which were edited by Holland, on 'social questions from a Christian viewpoint'.[52] The book bears the hallmarks of his idiosyncratic style; he seemed to take particular delight in flashing and flaming imagery. Of Christ, he wrote, 'He flashed His Light upon this crowded earth; and in that one flash it was revealed to us that every man on earth was in a condition to become our neighbour.'[53] Ruskin and Carlyle, meanwhile, had 'flung the vivid lightning of their scorn into the night of our slum cities',[54] whilst the political economist Henry George had 'flared suddenly the flaming portent ... He flung out, in quivering rhetoric, with brilliant imaginative force, the criticism of our purse-proud prosperity which was waiting for full effective utterance.'[55] The language created an energising sense of an electrical storm breaking and bringing a change in the weather, after a spell of humid complacency.

Holland, in the *fin de siècle* mode of looking simultaneously backwards and forwards, mixed thoughts that seemed to come from different eras. Observations that still seem prescient mingled with assumptions that belong in the Victorian age. A central theme was the economic, and therefore the moral, interconnectedness of people who are unknown to each other. He used the example of a cargo of oranges from Barcelona, unloaded in London and sent across Britain, to illustrate the close links in the European supply chain.[56] All of the people involved with growing, distributing, selling and eating the oranges were actually neighbours, but global trade was now so complicated that they were not able to acknowledge themselves as such. People increasingly failed to see that 'Society was a vast act of co-operation, as much as of competition.'[57] For Holland, the old world of reciprocal relationships and neighbourly knowledge had completely broken down. In the old world, he asserted, 'The Cash-nexus was clothed in flesh and blood. Out of the higgling of the market we built up a real humane social structure.'[58] Now, although people remained economically bound together, they were strangers to each other. Just when business had brought them into contact, and they might be on the point of saying, '"Now you and we are comrades. Now we must share a common life. Now we must care for each other as neighbours" – lo! They are off, by train and tube and tram: they disappear no one knows where.'[59] Holland concluded:

> Our civilization, then, increases and intensifies our opportunity for communication: and yet more and more severs the ties that bind us to one another. It immeshes [*sic*] us in ever more and more complicated relationships: and then hides them from our eyes. It multiplies our neighbours infinitely: and yet allows us to live without ever coming across them, or knowing who they are ... We need never take our eyes off ourselves.[60]

Other themes in *Our Neighbours* have worn rather less well. Holland was never quite able to acknowledge the significance of the fact that a large proportion of the Christians in early twentieth-century Britain were not in fact members of the Church of England. The CSU limited full membership to communicant Anglicans. This, Holland insisted, was not because they wanted to exclude 'your excellent Nonconformist, but your fervid socialistic Nothingarian'.[61] Although he suggested that denominational cooperation was invaluable when contemplating public action, he argued, in ways which seemed somewhat tortuous, that it was the members of the national church who were required to assume particular responsibilities, for example feeding policy suggestions directly to the Home Office.[62] Equally, his descriptions of the thought processes of workingmen, and of the place of women, although fairly typical of the era in which they were written, have not stood the test of time.[63]

As noted earlier, Holland used 'city' language in ways that slid confusingly between theological categories and description of contemporary urban life. He described the revelatory moment when Christians appreciate that social problems cannot be ameliorated by voluntary efforts. 'There arises before us the vision of the City, the Municipality. Here is the organisation by which we are all linked up, by one life, in the common fellowship . . . The Town is the expression of our love for one another.'[64] A little later, he states that 'The City covers, at least, our immediate neighbourhood.'[65] Did this imply that, for rural dwellers, 'the City' as a 'spiritual Jerusalem' also meant the interconnected network of nearby cottages and farms? It is impossible to know.

After the realisation that voluntary efforts were no longer sufficient to solve social problems, Holland urged state intervention:

> We look to the Law of the State to carry out these moral obligations to our fellows which we once associated intimately with our voluntary and individual wills, but which have passed hopelessly beyond the utmost range of what we can achieve by any voluntary and individual efforts, however ready and however active. The State must take up our task of neighbourly responsibility, or it can never be taken up at all.[66]

This unflinching advocacy of state intervention, and the belief that the greater the regulation, the better the quality of life, roots the book in its early twentieth-century context. On the one hand, there was the relatively new realisation that only legislation could make a difference to issues such as the unregulated, casualised labour market. Holland declined to say whether he thought the state should own the means of production, but he did not rule it out.[67] State socialism was of course still only a theoretical possibility in 1911, and the Bolshevik revolution lay some years in the future. Holland's faith in state regulation made sense to him because he believed it could be underpinned by his incarnational vision. Politics and economics have – 'inevitably' – he said, 'to take into account the fact that the Divine Will can be believed to have become one with the flesh of man'.[68] The weakness of the argument was obvious, and when the First World War broke out, it became evident even to the perennially positive Holland that Christianity had simply not had the impact on politicians and economists that he had expected. *Our Neighbours* is interesting partly because it provides an insight into what churchmen thought was possible at the close of the Edwardian age, as they contemplated a world where 'We are all . . . made neighbours in the fraternity of the State.'⁶⁹ But what practical steps should be taken? This was never clear. As Paul Avis has pointed out, 'For Holland, for all his passion, socialism remained ethical, paternalistic, eschatological and ultimately quite unthreatening.'⁷⁰

For thirty-four years, St Paul's Cathedral gave Holland a platform for preaching to the City, and as Arthur Burns has noted, the opportunity to promote 'a distinctively Christian politics that would significantly influence the future direction of official church policy'.⁷¹ As we have seen, although some of his observations continue to be interesting and durable, Holland's optimism outran the realities of the early twentieth century, leaving him somewhat stranded. Nevertheless, in the years after his death his influence lived on. In 1920, his friends set up the Scott Holland Trust, with a remit for the delivery of lectures on the theme of 'the theology of the incarnation and its bearing on the social and economic life of man'. A succession of leading Christian thinkers continue to deliver the lectures at roughly triennial intervals, and a significant number have resulted in major publications. The Scott Holland Trust has therefore supported a century of creative thinking about Christian social theology, and related topics.⁷² Furthermore, Holland's insistence that churchmen should 'study the Urban problem' has been fully exploited. Urban theology emerged as a distinctive theological subdiscipline in the immediate post-Second World War period when E. R. (Ted) Wickham founded the Sheffield Industrial Mission and wrote extensively. It developed a higher profile in the decades which followed, with significant interventions in the wake of the publication of Harvey Cox's *The Secular City* in 1965. It received a further boost in the aftermath of the Archbishop of Canterbury's Commission on *Faith in the City* in 1985. This saw the set-up of an Urban Theology Group, and the publication of *God in the City* edited by Peter Sedgwick in 1995 and *Urban Theology: A Reader* edited by Michael Northcott in 1998. Some institutions began to make it their specialism. This was particularly true of the Urban Theology Unit (now the ecumenical Urban Theology Union), which was founded in inner city Sheffield in 1969, and the Lincoln Theological Institute, originally also founded in Sheffield in 1997, and now at the University of Manchester.⁷³ By the twenty-first century, 'urban theology' was seen as part of the bigger project of 'contextual theology'.

Urban theology has developed independently of Holland's influence, of course, but this chapter has shown that he anticipated some of the later developments in interesting ways. We have uncovered evidence of his particular interest in both garden cities and 'city' language, and we have seen that together with Gore, Holland was a very significant figure in injecting third-generation Anglo-Catholicism with an agenda for radical social thought. Among those in the next generation that he particularly influenced, there was his young colleague Percy Dearmer, the economic historian R. H. Tawney and William Temple. In 1907, Temple wrote to his mother that 'the thing that really lives with me is Scott Holland's extraordinary oration on the power of Christ to regenerate society here or anywhere else'.[74] It was a comment that suggests that Temple was responding to the same aspect of Holland's theology that Gore described in the passage cited earlier. Temple was, like Holland, a clergyman shaped in the heart of the Anglican establishment, with radical sympathies, and he appeared to be Holland's natural successor. Holland would certainly have approved of the Conference on Christian Politics, Economics and Citizenship (COPEC) over which Temple presided in 1924. As Adrian Hastings noted, the significance of COPEC was in weaning the Church of England off High Tory attitudes, and towards an acceptance of major social reform, and eventually, the welfare state.[75] Temple paid tribute to Holland in 1928, claiming that 'it is impossible to exaggerate the service rendered to the cause of Christian civilisation by his zeal, his width of sympathy, his glowing eloquence, his comprehensive philosophy'.[76] Temple's social radicalism was evidently fuelled by his memories of Holland. It was expressed further at the Malvern Conference in 1941, and in his book of 1942, *Christianity and Social Order*, which provided the Christian blueprint for Beveridge's welfare state, which was also something that Holland would have wholeheartedly endorsed. But the tone of *Christianity and Social Order* was altogether different from *Our Neighbours* in 1911. Holland's assumption of the right and duty of the Church of England to influence social policy no longer held true in 1942. Temple had to begin by challenging the belief that in politics 'the Church exercises little influence, and should exercise none', and he had to frame his argument in terms of defending the church from the charge of 'interference' in politics.[77] Holland would have probably found Temple's bleak realism on the curtailed role of Christian theology difficult to fathom; it was a powerful illustration of the ways in which mid-twentieth-century Britain was changing.

Notes

1. Earlier versions of this essay were delivered at Ripon College Cuddesdon, to commemorate the centenary of Holland's death in 2018, and at Clumber Park, for the Church Union annual lecture, in 2019. I am grateful for these invitations, and for the discussions which took place, and to Bill Jacob and the two anonymous reviewers for their comments on this article.
2. Writing to W. H. Ady in 1872, Holland stated, 'A new temper lies here – a new religious want; and the Church has done nothing yet to fit itself on to the new force. One feels so certain that if this generation of ours cannot manage it, it will never be done.' Stephen Paget, *Henry Scott Holland: Memoir and Letters* (London: John Murray, 1921), p. 61.
3. The lines were not intended to be read as a poem but were part of a sermon that Holland preached in 1910, during the lying-in-state of Edward VII. Their somewhat unsermonic nature reveals something of the quirky style of his preaching, which was frequently noted by contemporaries.

4. Holland receives frequent, but brief, mentions in many studies of the Church of England in the late nineteenth and early twentieth centuries, often appearing in a list with his notable Oxford contemporaries, such as Charles Gore, T. H. Green and G. M. Hopkins, but it is striking how little he has been studied in his own right. Several of his friends – Stephen Paget, Christopher Cheshire, Edward Lyttleton and G. W. E Russell – produced appreciative volumes in the years immediately after his death, and William Temple praised him regularly. He was 'rediscovered' in the early 1960s, in Michael Ramsey's *From Gore to Temple: The Development of Anglican Theology between 'Lux Mundi' and the Second World War* (London: Longmans, 1960) and in B. M. G. Reardon's *Henry Scott Holland: A Selection from His Writings* (London: Society for Promoting Christian Knowledge, 1962). Since then, there have been occasional more detailed discussions of aspects of his life and thought, including by Peter D'A. Jones, Graham Neville, Seth Koven, Daniel Inman, Paul Avis and Ralph Norman. See the notes elsewhere in this essay for full references to these works.
5. John H. Heidt, 'Henry Scott Holland', in *Oxford Dictionary of National Biography* online (article revised 2008).
6. Ralph Norman, 'The Law of Sacrifice: G. M. Hopkins, H. S. Holland and Oxford Anglicanism', *Religion and the Arts*, 22 (2018), pp. 405–28.
7. For an account of the Christian Social Union, see Peter d'A. Jones, *The Christian Socialist Revival 1877–1914* (Princeton, NJ: Princeton University Press, 1968), pp. 164–224.
8. Daniel Inman, *The Making of Modern English Theology: God and the Academy at Oxford 1833–1945* (Minneapolis: Fortress Press, 2014), pp. 202–17.
9. Much of the work on this subject has given greater weight to the pessimism than the optimism, although the tension between them is one of the characteristics of the *fin de siècle* frame of mind. The classic early study was Holbrook Jackson, *The Eighteen Nineties: A Review of Art and Ideas at the Close of the Nineteenth Century* (London: Grant Richards, 1913). Later general studies exploring mainly literary and cultural themes include Ian Fletcher (ed.), *Decadence and the 1890s* (London: Edward Arnold, 1979); Linda Dowling, *Language and Decadence in the Victorian Fin de Siècle* (Princeton, NJ: Princeton University Press, 1986); John Stokes, *In the Nineties* (Chicago: University of Chicago Press, 1989); John Stokes (ed.), *Fin de Siècle/Fin du Globe: Fears and Fantasies of the Late Nineteenth Century* (Basingstoke: Macmillan, 1992); Karl Beckson, *London in the 1890s: A Cultural History* (New York: W. W. Norton, 1992); Simon Houfe, *Fin de Siècle: The Illustrators of the Nineties* (London: Barrie and Jenkins, 1992); Elaine Showalter, *Daughters of Decadence: Women Writers of the Fin de Siècle* (New Brunswick: Rutgers University Press, 1993); Shearer West, *Fin de Siècle* (London: Bloomsbury, 1993); Sally Ledger and Scott McCracken, *Cultural Politics at the Fin de Siècle* (Cambridge: Cambridge University Press, 1995); Stephen Arata, *Fictions of Loss in the Victorian Fin de Siècle* (Cambridge: Cambridge University Press, 1996); Tracey Hill, *Decadence and Danger: Writing, History and the Fin de Siècle* (Bath: Sulis Press, 1997); Julie Lokis-Adkins, *Deadly Desires: A Psychoanalytic Study of Female Sexual Perversion and Widowhood in Fin de Siècle Women's Writing* (London: Karnac, 2013); Tim Youngs, *Beastly Journeys: Travel and Transformation at the Fin de Siècle* (Liverpool: Liverpool University Press, 2013).
10. Frances Knight, *Victorian Christianity at the Fin de Siècle: The Culture of English Religion in a Decadent Age* (London: I. B. Tauris, 2015).

11. Henry W. Nevinson, *Changes and Chances* (London: Nisbet and Co., 1923), p. 45.
12. Mary Drew, *Acton, Gladstone and Others* (London: Nisbet and Co., 1924), p. 65.
13. Drew, *Acton*, p. 56.
14. Paget, *Holland*, p. 207.
15. Holland's pessimism is seen in his wartime editorials for *The Commonwealth*, the first of which extended over eight pages in September 1914. See also F. A. Iremonger, *William Temple Archbishop of Canterbury: His Life and Letters* (Oxford: Oxford University Press, 1948), pp. 205–6.
16. Graham Neville, *Radical Churchman: Edward Lee Hicks and the New Liberalism* (Oxford: Clarendon Press, 1998), p. 155.
17. Inman, *Modern English Theology*, pp. 191–4.
18. Henry Scott Holland, 'Henry Parry Liddon', in *Personal Studies* (London: Wells Gardner, Darton, and Co., 1906), pp. 144–5.
19. Holland, 'Liddon', p. 150.
20. Holland, 'Liddon', pp. 149–50.
21. Paget, *Holland*, pp. 280–1.
22. Neville, *Radical Churchman*, pp. 200–1.
23. The letter was printed in full in the *Commonwealth*, February 1897, p. 58.
24. W. M. Jacob, *Religious Vitality in Victorian London* (Oxford: Oxford University Press, 2021), pp. 178–9.
25. Much of Ellis's correspondence is in the National Library of Wales, Aberystwyth, but neither the original of the letter, nor Ellis's reply, have been located.
26. Jones, *Christian Socialist Revival*, p. 185.
27. The *Commonwealth*, February 1906, cited by Neville, *Radical Churchman*, p. 155.
28. For the *Yellow Book*, see Knight, *Victorian Christianity*, pp. 46–51 and 223.
29. Knight, *Victorian Christianity*, pp. 215–30.
30. The *Commonwealth: A Social Magazine*, 1.1 (1896), p. 4.
31. The *Commonwealth*, 1.1, p. 5.
32. The *Commonwealth*, 1.1, p. 5.
33. The *Commonwealth*, 4.2 (1899), p. 36.
34. The *Commonwealth*, 4.3 (1899), p. 72. Four hundred cubic feet is 11.3 cubic metres.
35. Seth Koven, *Slumming: Sexual and Social Politics in Victorian London* (Princeton, NJ: Princeton University Press, 2004) pp. 252–4.
36. Paget, *Holland*, p. 69.
37. Paget, *Holland*, p. 169.
38. For example, Arnold D. Taylor, 'The Housing Problem in the Rural Districts', *Commonwealth*, 2.3 (1897); Arthur Sherwell, 'Life in West London: The Problem of Reform', 2.5 (1897) and continued over several issues; C. L. Marson, 'Our Unhappy Villages', 6.5 (1901) and C. F. G. Masterman, 'Homes for the People', 6.5 (1901).
39. For Ebenezer Howard, the Garden City Movement and the religious context of both, see Frances Knight, *Ebenezer Howard: Inventor of the Garden City* (Oxford: Oxford University Press, 2023).
40. John McNeill, writing in the *Commonwealth*, 4.11 (1899), p. 344.
41. Garden City Collection LBM3056.33.31. This document may be viewed online at http://www.gardencitycollection.com/object-lbm3056-33-31. The GCA

had around one hundred vice-presidents, many of whom were prominent Nonconformists, MPs and members of the London County Council, together with academics, scientists, artists and writers.
42. The *Commonwealth*, 7.9 (September 1902), pp. 245–6.
43. Howard spoke to the CSU in Berkhamsted in March 1902, and another GCA lecturer was invited to speak to the CSU in Exeter in 1904. *Bucks Herald*, 22 March 1902, and *Western Times*, 5 December 1904.
44. *Daily Mail*, 16 July 1906.
45. Frances Knight, 'The Victorian City and the Christian Imagination: From Gothic City to Garden City', *Urban History*, 48.1 (2021), pp. 37–53.
46. 'The City of God' was the title of a series of retreat addresses that Holland gave to clergy in the diocese of St Asaph in 1894. They were published as *God's City and the Coming of the Kingdom* (London: Longmans, Green, and Co., 1897).
47. Holland, *God's City*, p. 45.
48. The *Commonwealth*, 6.1 (1901), pp. 2–3.
49. Charles Gore, writing a chapter on the CSU, in Paget, *Holland*, pp. 244–5.
50. Holland began to publish volumes of sermons, many of which had been preached at St Paul's, on a regular basis from 1885. He also wrote a total of twenty-eight introductions to other people's books, which is measure of the esteem in which he was held. Paget, *Holland*, p. 329.
51. William Temple, *Christianity and the State* (London: Macmillan and Co., 1928), pp. vii–viii.
52. Jones, *Christian Socialist Revival*, p. 186.
53. Henry Scott Holland, *Our Neighbours: A Handbook for the C.S.U.* (London: A. R. Mowbray, 1911), p. 52.
54. Holland, *Neighbours*, p. 6
55. Holland, *Neighbours*, p. 6.
56. Holland, *Neighbours*, pp. 20–1.
57. Holland, *Neighbours*, p. 8.
58. Holland, *Neighbours*, p. 19.
59. Holland, *Neighbours*, p. 27.
60. Holland, *Neighbours*, pp. 28–9.
61. Jones, *Christian Socialist Revival*, p. 177; Paget, *Holland*, pp. 170–1. By a 'Nothingarian' he meant a socialist without religious belief.
62. Holland, *Neighbours*, pp. 61–2 and 72–3.
63. Holland, *Neighbours*, pp. 121–8 and 141–2.
64. Holland, *Neighbours*, pp. 74–5.
65. Holland, *Neighbours*, p. 78.
66. Holland, *Neighbours*, p. 86.
67. Holland, *Neighbours*, p. 86.
68. Holland, *Neighbours*, p. 144.
69. Holland, *Neighbours*, p. 107.
70. Paul Avis, 'Anglican Social Thought Encounters Modernity: Brooke Foss Westcott, Henry Scott Holland and Charles Gore', in Stephen Spencer (ed.), *Theology Reforming Society: Revisiting Anglican Social Theology* (London: SCM Press, 2017), p. 70.
71. Arthur Burns, 'From 1830 to the Present', in Derek Keene, Arthur Burns and Andrew Saint (eds), *St Paul's: The Cathedral Church of London 604–2004* (New Haven, CT: Yale University Press, 2004), p. 92.

72. Details of the original deed and a list of the lecturers, their topics and subsequent publications may be found on the website of the Scott Holland Trust. R. H. Tawney's *Religion and the Rise of Capitalism* arose from the first set of lectures, and other notable publications came from William Temple (1932), Maurice Reckitt (1947), V. A. Demant (1952), Michael Ramsay (1965), Alec Vidler (1969) Ronald Preston (1983), Ann Loades (1987), Alan Wilkinson (1998) and Rowan Williams (1998). The recent collection of essays edited by Stephen Spencer, *Theology Reforming Society: Revisiting Anglican Social Theology* (2017), is also the result of a conference convened to fulfil the terms of the Scott Holland bequest. Scott Holland Trust, http://www.scotthollandtrust.org.uk/, accessed 4 July 2022.
73. Urban Theology Union, https://utusheffield.org.uk/ and Lincoln Theological Institute, http://lincolntheologicalinstitute.com/, accessed 4 July 2022.
74. Iremonger, *Temple*, p. 125. See also Stephen Spencer, *Archbishop William Temple: A Study in Servant Leadership* (London: SCM Press, 2022), p. 21.
75. Adrian Hastings, *A History of English Christianity 1920–2000* (London: SCM Press, 2001), p. 179.
76. Temple, *Christianity and the State*, p. vii.
77. William Temple, *Christianity and Social Order* (London: Penguin Books, 1942), p. 10. Temple titled his first chapter 'What Right Has the Church to Interfere?' and the second 'How Should the Church Interfere?' His third chapter, 'Has the Church Claimed to Intervene before?', was a defence and explanation of ecclesiastical interventions in social questions from biblical times to 'Westcott, Gore and Scott Holland – whose names bring us down to living memory and contemporary problems' (p. 46).

CHAPTER ELEVEN

'Indignation would arise within you': Herman Bavinck on Racial Injustice in Europe and North America

James Eglinton

Recent years have seen a considerable increase in scholarly attention to the life and thought of Herman Bavinck (1854–1921), the great dogmatician of the neo-Calvinist movement that attempted to advance the historic Reformed tradition in a distinctly modern fashion in the late modern Netherlands. While this growth was initiated by the English translation of Bavinck's magnum opus, the four-volume *Reformed Dogmatics*, in the early twenty-first century, scholarship on Bavinck has also expanded in scope to appreciate the complexity and variegated directions found in his works. Although his most important work is widely held to be a magisterial effort in dogmatic theology, the same figure wrote significant works in psychology, pedagogy, literary criticism, biography and political theory, and also served as the leader of a political party, a parliamentarian, newspaper editor, prolific journalist and acclaimed travel writer.[1] In that light, this chapter concerns one important, although neglected, area of Bavinck's thought and work that emerged from his contributions as a travel writer – his contribution as a prominent early twentieth-century European critic of racial injustice in North America – and the role played by European experience in that criticism.

While I have previously explored aspects of his criticisms of racism in America in *Bavinck: A Critical Biography*, this chapter expands upon that work by setting it against a hitherto unexplored aspect of his race consciousness: namely, a formative (and troubling) rebuke in young adulthood through which he became aware of racial injustice faced by Jews in Germany in the 1880s, which precipitated a shift in Bavinck's attentiveness to the Jewish experience in the early twentieth-century Netherlands.[2] The starting point in that shift is chronicled in youthful letters between Bavinck and his lifelong friend Christiaan Snouck Hurgronje (1857–1936), alias Abd al-Ghāffar, a liberal theology student who later converted to Islam and rose to become perhaps his generation's most celebrated Orientalist.[3] By setting Bavinck's later views of race in America against the backdrop of an earlier experience of the plight of Jews in late nineteenth-century Germany, this chapter aims to break new ground in highlighting the international skein of factors that found expression in a distinctive attunement to experiences of ethnicity-based oppression (amongst other forms of discrimination) in Bavinck's mature theological writings. In that regard, Bavinck's contribution as a theological critic of racism is more complexly transatlantic than previous scholarship has suggested.

Revisiting Forgotten Critique

Herman Bavinck travelled to North America twice. His first trip, made in 1892, was occasioned by the Fifth General Council of the Alliance of Reformed Churches throughout the World Holding the Presbyterian System – an event to which Bavinck was sent as a Dutch emissary for his neo-Calvinist movement. Notably, his public lectures (and notes) from that trip espouse a philosophy of international travel that eschewed criticism of the foreign. The young Bavinck approached travel in a rigidly complementary frame of mind, for which reason his views on race in American society were muted indeed. His second journey across the Atlantic came in 1908, when he was invited to give the prestigious Stone Lectures at Princeton Theological Seminary. That journey was made in a different phase of life, and in an altogether different frame of mind. An older Bavinck had become openly and sharply critical of many aspects of American culture and Christianity – from the superficiality of its preaching, to the apparent religious neutrality of its public schools, to the deep sense of racialised hatred that he openly forecast might lead the American experiment to fail. In all of this, his critique of the American church – in his experience, a racially segregated community – was stinging.[4]

In more recent times, however, scholarly attention to the fruits of Bavinck's journey to Princeton has predominantly focused on the monograph that resulted from his lectures there: the apologetic work *Philosophy of Revelation* (first released in Dutch in 1908, followed by German and English versions in 1909, and more recently, in Chinese, Italian, Portuguese, and in a revised English-language edition).[5] In one notable contribution to that focus, Bratt's work on the context faced by Bavinck in that year has shed important light on the ways that political struggles on home turf (where he had experienced a bruising term as leader of the Anti-Revolutionary Party), as well as interaction with developments in late modern intellectual life more generally, provide a crucial layer of texture to our understanding of Bavinck's Princeton lectures.[6]

In that setting, however, one passing comment found in Bratt's description of the Bavinck revealed in those lectures merits careful reading, particularly in the exploration of the criticisms of American racism that would develop during that transatlantic experience. Commenting on the place of non-Christian religions (and thus, in Bavinck's mind, non-Western cultures) in the Stone Lectures, Bratt describes how Bavinck's addresses 'manifest a lingering Victorian, and therefore also imperial, confidence in the self-superiority of European to other civilizations'.[7] Elsewhere, I have argued that Bavinck's geopolitical imagination was undoubtedly a product of his colonial-era times.[8] The colonial tenor of a number of parliamentary speeches delivered by Bavinck in the 1910s certainly resonates with Bratt's view that the Stone Lectures pitted the notion of the 'civilised' European against the 'savage' other.[9] In that regard, Bratt's claim is not inaccurate.

However, his claim should also be read with care in order not to assume that the 'savage' non-Western world was the exclusive focus of Bavinck's 'civilised' European critique, that European civilisation was an oasis of contentment for Bavinck, or that European and American civilisations were one and the same to him.[10]

Indeed, while his Princeton audience might have been struck by particular criticisms of the pagan world, as has been noted, his European audiences in that year heard many public lectures on the evils of racialised hatred in American society. By 1908, Bavinck had become a diligent reader of a number of African American voices – amongst them, his contemporaries Booker T. Washington (1856–1915) and W. E. B. Du Bois (1868–1963) – and had become committed to the idea that oppressed voices should be heard on their own terms.[11] By this point in his life, that commitment was mirrored in his writings on theological ethics. In a booklet titled 'Christian Principles and Social Relationships' published in the same year, for example, Bavinck made the striking statement that 'Old Testament morality is written from the point of view of the oppressed.'[12] In making this claim, Bavinck drew (explicitly) on the work of Franz Brentano (1838–1917), an Austrian Catholic philosopher who married the Jewish woman Ida von Lieben (1852–94), and whose work was intertwined with the discrimination faced by Jews in Austria in the early twentieth century.[13] Evidently, the mature Bavinck moved somewhat fluidly between dogmatics, ethics and the realities of human experience (and that from the perspective of the oppressed), which he was ready to learn of from figures beyond his own Dutch Reformed confessional tradition: such was the case with figures as different as Brentano and Du Bois.

In particular, Bavinck's readiness to listen to the African American experience as told by African American voices stands out by its stark contrast to his neo-Calvinist colleague Abraham Kuyper (1837–1920), whose own American travel writings take more or less the opposite approach, namely, that of following a narrative of African American experience provided, almost entirely, by white Americans.[14] This chapter does not aim to compare Bavinck and Kuyper on this point – an effort that would necessitate the provision of a separate genealogy of Kuyper's own race consciousness and its place in his thought, which lies somewhat beyond the chapter's scope.[15] However, it does aim to demonstrate a number of connections in the development of Bavinck's approach that might provide an equivalent genealogy for Bavinck's approach. In turn, this might then foster a subsequent comparative account of this notable divergence between the neo-Calvinist movement's progenitors with regard to race. More immediately, though, it allows us to form a more fully orbed picture of the transnational factors that shaped Bavinck's eventual readiness to think theologically both from 'above' and 'below'.

Jews in Germany and the Netherlands in the 1880s

In comparison to his mature writings, Bavinck's ability to move fluidly between theological reasoning and human experience (and in particular, experiences of oppression) appears to have been notably underdeveloped in sources from his young adulthood. In the summer of 1880, his years as a student at Leiden University (1874–1880) were drawing to a close. That year, both Bavinck (then aged 26) and Snouck Hurgronje (then aged 23) defended their doctoral dissertations in Leiden – Bavinck on the ethics of the Swiss Reformer Ulrich Zwingli (1484–1531), and Snouck Hurgronje on the Hajj pilgrimage in Islam.[16]

In keeping with the academic conventions of their time, both students appended a series of short theses (*stellingen*) to their dissertations. To be defended orally, these theses provided doctoral candidates with an opportunity to demonstrate competence in areas often tangentially related to their dissertation topics.[17] In Bavinck's case, these theses (no examples of which were believed extant until discovered by John Bolt in the neo-Calvinist philosopher Herman Dooyeweerd's copy of Bavinck's dissertation) offer a window into the cut-and-thrust nature of his scholarly sparring with Snouck Hurgronje across Christian and Muslim lines in their student years: 'The Mohammedan religion', a provocative young Bavinck was prepared to argue, 'is of very limited ethical value.'[18] (It is also worth noting that in 1880, Bavinck had not likely met a Muslim in person.)

In that setting, such a bald assertion would not have come as a surprise to Snouck Hurgronje. In a letter dated to 18 May 1880, Bavinck had already consulted with him on possible *stellingen*, and had asked his friend to provide 'a couple of suitable Orientalist theses, one or two'.[19] Whether the young Bavinck was socially confident in performing this kind of abstract, combative inter-religious critique is difficult to ascertain. For unknown reasons, his doctoral defence – ordinarily a public affair – took place behind closed doors (albeit attended by Snouck Hurgronje), although to a good outcome: however he justified his critique of Islamic ethics, he passed *cum laude*.[20]

Snouck Hurgronje's defence came later that year, on 24 November 1880, by which time the new Doctor Bavinck had left Leiden for his parental home in Kampen, where his father, Rev. Jan Bavinck (1826–1909), was pastor of the town's Christian Reformed congregation. For that reason, Bavinck did not attend his friend's defence in person, although Snouck Hurgronje sent him a print copy, with additional theses included, in advance of the (also atypically private) ceremony.

On the day of Snouck Hurgronje's defence, Bavinck wrote to him, taking issue with thesis XXII, which reads, 'Anti-Judaic writings like *Der Talmudjude* by Prof. Rohling of Münster bear witness to the pettiness of their authors, rather than to the corruption of the Jews in Germany.'[21] Bavinck wrote,

> I received your dissertation in good order last Friday and have already looked into bits and pieces. Thank you for sending it. It looks particularly superb; an agreement of form and content. Amongst the propositions . . . only the twenty-second, to be blunt, I would have rather left out, not because your judgment on that (to me unknown) work by Rohling shall be wrong, but because I had wanted you not to give the appearance of being a defender of the Jews as though you saw no difference in *principle* between a modern Christian and an erudite Jew.[22]

The polemical theologian criticised by Snouck Hurgronje, the German Roman Catholic August Rohling (1839–1931) – of whose work Bavinck openly professed his ignorance – had published an earlier antisemitic work, *Der Talmudjude: Zur Beherzigung für Juden und Christen aller Stände*, which claimed Jews considered Christians as no better than animals, and that the Talmud sanctioned the murder of Christians by Jews.[23] Following its publication, Rohling offered to give 1,000 gulden to anyone who could find a flaw in his presentation of the Talmud, and became embroiled in legal battles with two prominent Viennese rabbis – Adolf Jellinek (1821–93) and Moritz Güdemann (1835–98) – who published refutations of his work.[24] That Bavinck knew nothing of Rohling is perhaps unsurprising: beyond regular criticism in the Dutch Jewish *Israelitische nieuwsbode* newspaper, which Bavinck is not likely to have read, he received scant attention in the Netherlands in the 1870s. His only appearance in Kuyper's *Heraut* – a neo-Calvinist newspaper that Bavinck certainly did read – came in 1879, in reference to Rohling's notorious anti-Protestant polemics.[25] In that regard, Snouck Hurgronje was somewhat atypical as a Dutch scholar who had taken notice of Rohling's antisemitism.

At his private Leiden doctoral defence, Snouck Hurgronje's voice of criticism towards Rohling had joined those of his public critics Jellinke and Güdemann. To the young Bavinck, skilled at abstract interfaith shadowboxing, and otherwise unaware of Rohling's work (or, at that time, of the theologically orthodox scholars in Germany who rejected Rohling's work, including Franz Delitzsch and Hermann Strack, or the German social context in which such inflammatory lies were spreading),[26] his friend's twenty-second thesis was troubling, in so far as Bavinck thought it risked relativising Judaism's theological differences with Christianity. In Bavinck's view, Snouck Hurgronje had prioritised criticism of Rohling (whose work Bavinck had only identified as supporting Christianity over Judaism) over the assertion of a principal difference between the religious beliefs of Jews and Christians. It is in this sense that Bavinck was squeamish about the impression that his friend was a 'defender of the Jews'. To the twenty-six-year-old Bavinck, the key priority in such a debate was the meticulous comparison of truth claims more or less in abstraction: although the young Bavinck saw theology as a real-world concern, at that point in his life, to talk about Christianity vis-à-vis Judaism (or Islam) was necessarily to talk, more or less exclusively, about 'difference *in principle*'.

It is worth noting, of course, that thus far in life, his own immediate experience of Christian–Jewish relations had been one of peaceful co-existence in the proactively pluralistic social environment that was post-1848 liberalised Dutch culture – a century in which the Dutch Jewish population had flourished in many regards.[27] (Earlier still, in its pre-liberalised phase, Dutch Jews had held full and equal citizenship since the Emancipation Decree of 1796, as part of a longer-term Dutch effort to cast Dutch Jewish identity in a national, rather than international, mould.)[28] Between 1869 and 1889, the Dutch Jewish population grew more rapidly than the non-Jewish Dutch population.[29] During these relatively prosperous years for Dutch Jewry, the nation's most prestigious university, Leiden, attended in that period by a young Herman Bavinck, was led by its first Jewish rector, Joel Emanuel Goudsmit (1813–82). By the time Bavinck wrote to Snouck Hurgronje in 1880, he was living in Kampen, a town that had been home to a settled Jewish community since the 1660s. In the 1880s, it was also normal for members of Kampen's Jewish community to attend public theological exams and debates held by the town's Christian Reformed theological seminary.[30] In that setting, theological antithesis with Jewish neighbours presented few challenges for civic neighbourliness.

In such a context, it seems the young Bavinck had not yet been prompted to think more deeply about *difference in experience* alongside *difference in principle*. That prompt came, however, in Snouck Hurgronje's reply to his critique. At this point, Snouck Hurgronje had already moved from Leiden to Strasbourg, at that time a German city, to pursue further studies under the famous Orientalist Theodor Nöldeke (1836–1930). There, he had come face to face with the simmering antisemitism that would soon give rise to the horrors that marked the twentieth century. It was a world from which both Bavinck and Snouck Hurgronje seem to have been sheltered in the Netherlands. In response to Bavinck's concern that his friend had become a 'defender of the Jews', Snouck Hurgronje wrote,

> You did not appreciate that I took on the task of protecting the Jews against the unfair, unseemly and not infrequently dishonest, but almost always untrue acts of accusation that people especially in Germany now fabricate against them . . . If I understand your way of seeing the relationship between a modern Christian and a Jew, you prioritise the distinction between them, at its core, in abstraction, and you wanted to see me stick to that abstraction, yes, even that I would make a pronouncement on it, when actually, there was not the least

reason for this. I was opposing, sincerely, the German (political as well as religious) movement against the Jewish *race*.³¹

From this letter, of course, it should not be assumed that Rohling was representative of all German Christian theologians. As has been noted, the likes of Delitzsch and Strack had also mounted opposition to his antisemitic writings. Although Bavinck would later go on to cite both extensively in his (as yet unwritten) *Reformed Dogamtics*, at this point their absence from Snouck Hurgronje's presentation of the situation in Germany only serves to highlight the young Bavinck's general lack of awareness of cultural developments across the border.

Further in the same letter, Snouck Hurgronje tried to enlighten that dim view by setting out a definition of Jewish identity as ineradicable on account of ethnicity, and as conceivable in a way entirely distinct from an individual's theological beliefs. In short, Snouck Hurgronje chastised Bavinck for the conceptual abstraction by which he had overlooked the reality that the experiences of Jewishness and Christianity are fundamentally different in this regard. Bavinck had been challenged to factor lived experience (through 'social economics or politics') into his theological reasoning. Snouck Hurgronje wrote,

> From this, you can rightly draw the conclusion that for me, the question 'modern Christian or Jew[?]' does not exist, there is no correlation to be understood [between them]; the first is someone, from whatever background, who holds to certain notions with regard to religion – the second is someone from a particular ethnic group, whether he be wholly, or not, or in no sense, removed from national preconceptions and religious concepts. I consider the question as one of social economy or, if you wish, of politics, and thus I refer to all German opponents of the Jews. Moreover, as regards that book, I am convinced that if you were to read it, indignation would rise up within you. Rohling preaches, sometimes almost explicitly, just as all the opponents of the Jews known to me do more or less covertly, the rising up of the common people against the Jews.³²

In essence, the issue of race was putting lives at grave risk, for which reason Snouck Hurgronje rebuked Bavinck for dealing with the question of 'Christianity or Judaism?' as a task to be met first with abstract apologetic precision, when in fact, anthropological concerns raised what he deemed to be the more immediate need. In effect, Bavinck was told that his theologising needed to be accompanied by a more pointed degree of realism precisely because the Jewish experience in Germany was unlike the Jewish experience on the Dutch side of the border, and was unlike the Christian experience in general.

Charting Change in Bavinck

To what extent can a change in Bavinck's handling of theology in relation to the experience of ethnically grounded oppression be charted in the years following Snouck Hurgronje's rebuke? In Bavinck's writings in the early 1880s, 'the Jews' typically denoted a historically distant theological alternative to Christianity rooted in New Testament references to Jews as a generic group. This can be seen, for example, in various texts published in that decade. In 'The Kingdom of God, The Highest Good', Bavinck writes of 'the Jews' in either abstract historical or eschatological senses.[33] In 'The Catholicity of Christianity and the Church', other than a brief mention of the place of Jews in fifteenth-century Catholic theology, his own handling of Jews is in strictly historical terms with regard to the New Testament.[34] In his early monograph on the theology of the ethical theologian Daniël Chantepie de la Saussaye (1818–74) – a book ostensibly written to provide a public clarification of the works of a theologian misunderstood in Bavinck's own circles – there is sparse mention of Jews beyond a general observation that Chantepie de la Saussaye held to a (seemingly moderately Kantian) view of Jews in the ancient world as having lost a sense of true freedom under the weight of religious authority, and that he regarded Christ has having united Jews and Gentiles into a single people.[35] In one text written in 1881, Bavinck dealt with Dutch Jews in his own day as contemporary but nonetheless hypothetical sparring partners on the issue of proper Sabbath observance.[36] This seems to be the general tenor of his writings on Jews and Judaism throughout that decade.

By 1894, however, this emphasis seems to have changed: in that year, writing on the future of Calvinism in the Netherlands, we find Bavinck supplementing the history of religious persecution faced by his own Christian Secessionist movement (a form of discrimination rooted in assent to politically unfavoured doctrines, rather than ethnicity) with an acknowledgment of the historic persecution of Jews at an earlier stage in Dutch history.[37] This awareness of the unequal experience of Dutch Jewry continued in 1902, in his anti-Nietzschean work on Christian ethics, *Current-Day Morality*, in which Bavinck both explicitly identified 'Jesus, Peter, Paul, and Mary' as 'Jews', and openly doubted that the legal equality of Jews in the Netherlands was respected across Dutch society: 'And the Jews, although emancipated in theory, are looked down on in many circles.'[38] Keenly aware of the sudden posthumous popularity of the atheist philosopher Friedrich Nietzsche (1844–1900) amongst his compatriots, Bavinck seems to have drawn a connection between their newfound affinity for Nietzsche's philosophy (which Bavinck characterised as both anti-Jewish and anti-Christian) with likely negative effects on Dutch Jews.[39] As has been noted, in 1908 – the year of his transatlantic racial awakening – Bavinck cited Franz Brentano (whose proximity to anti-Jewish discrimination in Austria was mentioned earlier in this chapter) in arguing that, 'Old Testament morality is written from the point of view of the oppressed.'[40]

It is important to recognise, of course, that this growing readiness to theologise in the light of the experience of oppression did not supplant Bavinck's practice of theologising in the light of scripture: in 1914, at the outbreak of the First World War, for example, he published 'The Problem of War', in which he engaged both in New Testament exegesis (arguing that Christ unites Jew and Gentile spiritually) and in a geopolitical argument critiquing Russia for its posture towards Russian Jewry.[41] This element of geopolitical critique continued throughout the remainder of Bavinck's life. In 1920, a year before his death, for example, he wrote against anti-Jewish riots in Eastern Europe, in *Christianity, War, and the Bond of Nations*.[42] By that point, he had become a markedly different figure to the twenty-six-year-old who criticised his student friend for being a 'defender of the Jews'. (Importantly, the 'critical friendship' shared by Bavinck and Snouck Hurgronje also continued throughout Bavinck's life. The last letter written by Snouck Hurgronje was received shortly before Bavinck's eventual passing.)

Conclusion: Mapping Out the Mature Bavinck

Returning to the starting focus on 1908, as the year in which Bavinck made the aforementioned (and memorable) admission regarding Old Testament ethics and the experience of the oppressed, and in which Bavinck positioned himself as a prominent Dutch theological critic of America's deep problems with race, this chapter has set out to demonstrate that his close and critical intellectual friendship with Christaan Snouck Hurgronje – a figure who could scarcely have been more unlike Bavinck in social, familial and religious terms – seems to have exerted a slow, but powerful, influence on Bavinck's eventual awareness of the importance of human experience (and in this instance, of the experience of discrimination on the grounds of race). This is seen in his thought regarding the African American experience, and the Jewish experience in Germany and the Netherlands, in the early twentieth century. Chronologically, it seems that his awareness of the latter gave rise to his sensitivity towards the former: the bluntness of Snouck Hurgronje's challenge on Rohling showed Bavinck something that he could not unsee.

The genealogy of this development adds an important layer to our understanding of the distinction between Bavinck's 'early' and 'mature' phases.[43] Perhaps most closely within scholarly appreciation of the distinctives of his 'mature' development, the argument that this phase was marked by an increasing capacity to hold doctrine and experience in closer proximity serves as a complement to Pass's insight that the 'mature' Bavinck sought a more nuanced view of non-Christian religions, and to my own argument elsewhere that in those years, Bavinck also emerged as an early exponent (again, contra Nietzsche) of what is now known as disability theology – a locus of discrimination that Bavinck also approached in relation to the experiences of the disabled on both sides of the Atlantic.[44] In each of these, a greater willingness to listen to the voices of human experience is palpable. Similarly evident is the impression that many things, in many places, caused indignation to arise within the mature Herman Bavinck.

Notes

1. Herman Bavinck, *Reformed Dogmatics*, ed. John Bolt, trans. John Vriend, 4 vols (Grand Rapids, MI: Baker Academic, 2003–8). Recent monographs focused on aspects of Bavinck's dogmatic work include: Cory C. Brock, *Orthodox yet Modern: Herman Bavinck's Use of Friedrich Schleiermacher* (Bellingham: Lexham, 2020); Nathaniel Gray Sutanto, *God and Knowledge: Herman Bavinck's Theological Epistemology* (London: Bloomsbury/T. & T. Clark, 2020); Bruce Pass, *The Heart of Dogmatics: Christology and Christocentrism in Herman Bavinck* (Göttingen: Vandenhoek and Ruprecht, 2020); Ximian Xu, *Theology and the Science of God: Herman Bavinck's Wetenschappelijke Theology for the Modern World* (Göttingen: Vandenhoek and Ruprecht, 2022). See, for example, James Eglinton, *Bavinck: A Critical Biography* (Grand Rapids, MI: Baker Academic, 2020), p. xv. Bavinck's account of a journey to North America in 1892 would later win the Dutch Royal Library Prize for Outstanding Travel Writing in 2010. See Herman Bavinck, 'My Journey to America', trans. James Eglinton, *Dutch Crossing*, 41.2 (2017), pp. 180–93.
2. Eglinton, *Bavinck: A Critical Biography*, pp. 247–9.
3. For a recent popular biography of Snouck Hurgronje, see Philip Dröge, *Pelgrim: leven en reizen van Christiaan Snouck Hurgronje* (Amsterdam: Spectrum, 2017). For a recent scholarly biography, see Wim van den Doel, *Snouck: het volkomen geleerdenleven van Christiaan Snouck Hurgronje* (Amsterdam: Prometheus, 2021). The correspondence shared by Bavinck and Snouck Hurgronje was published as *Een Leidse vriendschap: Herman Bavinck en Christiaan Snouck Hurgronje over christendom, islam en westerse beschaving* (Hilversum: Uitgeverij Verloren, 2021).
4. Eglinton, *Bavinck: A Critical Biography*, p. 248.
5. Herman Bavinck, *Wijsbegeerte der openbaring: Stone-lezingen voor het jaar 1908, gehouden te Princeton N.J.* (Kampen: J. H. Kok, 1908); *Philosophie der Offenbarung: Vorlesungen (Stone Lectures) für das Jahr 1908 gehalten in Princeton N.J. von Herman Bavinck, o. Professor der Theologie in Amsterdam*, trans. Hermann Cuntz (Heidelberg: Carl Winter's Universitätsbuchhandlung, 1909); *The Philosophy of Revelation: The Stone Lectures for 1908–1909, Princeton Theological Seminary* (New York: Longmans Green, 1909); *Filosofia della rivelazione*, trans. Ruffa Giorgio (Caltanissetta: Alfa & Omega, 2004); 启示的哲学 [Qǐshì de zhéxué], trans. Zhao Gang (四川人民出版社 [Chengdu City, China: Sichuan People's Publishing House], 2014); *A Filosofia da Revelação*, trans. Fabrício Tavares de Moraes (Brasília: Editora Monergismo, 2016); *The Philosophy of Revelation. A New Annotated Edition*, ed. Cory C. Brock and Nathaniel Gray Sutanto (Peabody, MA: Hendrickson Publishers, 2018). For examples of recent interaction with *Philosophy of Revelation*, see James D. Bratt, 'The Context of Herman Bavinck's Stone Lectures: Culture

and Politics in 1908', *The Bavinck Review*, 1 (2010), pp. 4–24; George Harinck, 'Was Bavinck in Need of a Philosophy of Revelation?', in John Bowlin (ed.), *The Kuyper Center Review. Volume Two: Revelation and Common Grace* (Grand Rapids, MI: Eerdmans, 2011), pp. 27–42; Nathan Daniel Shannon, 'Ontology and Revelation in Bavinck's Stone Lectures', *Scottish Journal of Theology*, 73.2 (2020), pp. 112–25.
6. Eglinton, *Bavinck: A Critical Biography*, p. 235.
7. Bratt, 'The Context of Herman Bavinck's Stone Lectures', p. 21.
8. See, for example, Eglinton, *Bavinck: A Critical Biography*, p. 268; James Eglinton, 'Planting Tulips in the Rainforest: Herman and Johan Herman Bavinck on Christianity in East and West', *Journal of Biblical and Theological Studies*, 6.2 (2021), pp. 277–92.
9. Bratt, 'The Context of Herman Bavinck's Stone Lectures', p. 21, n. 22; Eglinton, *Bavinck: A Critical Biography*, p. 268.
10. For more recent scholarship on Bavinck's feelings of *Weltschmerz* in Europe, see Eglinton, *Bavinck: A Critical Biography*, pp. 152, 188.
11. For the extensive, unpublished, handwritten manuscripts detailing Bavinck's research on the African American experience, see folder 66, Herman Bavinck Archive, Historisch Documentatiecentrum voor het Nederlands Protestantism 1800-heden, Vrije Universiteit Amsterdam.
12. Herman Bavinck, 'Christian Principles and Social Relationships', in John Bolt (ed.), Harry Boonstra and Gerrit Sheeres (trans.), *Essays on Science, Religion, and Society* (Grand Rapids, MI: Baker Academic, 2008), p. 126.
13. Steven Beller, *Vienna and the Jews: A Cultural History* (Cambridge: Cambridge University Press, 1989), p. 15.
14. Abraham Kuyper, *Varia Americana* (Amsterdam: Höveker and Wormser, 1898). See James Eglinton, 'Varia Americana and Race: Kuyper as Antagonist and Protagonist', *Journal of Reformed Theology*, 11.1–2 (2017), pp. 65–80.
15. See, for example, Ad de Bruijne, 'Abraham Kuyper's Surprising Love of the Jews', *Journal of Reformed Theology*, 11.1–2 (2017), pp. 24–46.
16. Herman Bavinck, *De ethiek van Ulrich Zwingli* (Kampen: Ph. Zalsman, 1880); Christiaan Snouck Hurgronje, *Het Mekkaansche feest* (Leiden: Brill, 1880).
17. In the Dutch universities, this aspect of the doctoral defence was compulsory until the 1980s. See Frans van Steijn, 'Het Rectoren College 1955-Heden', in L. J. Dorsman and P. J. Knegtmans (eds), *Universiteit en identiteit: Over samenwerking, concurrentie en taakverdeling tussen de Nederlandse universiteiten* (Hilversum: Verloren, 2017), p. 101.
18. Harinck and de Bruijn, *Een Leidse vriendschap*, p. 68, n. 2.
19. Harinck and de Bruijn, *Een Leidse vriendschap*, p. 68.
20. Harinck and de Bruijn, *Een Leidse vriendschap*, p. 70, n. 1.
21. Snouck Hurgronje, *Het Mekkaansche feest*, p. 199.
22. Harinck and de Bruijn, *Een Leidse vriendschap*, pp. 74–5.
23. August Rohling, *Der Talmudjude: Zur Beherzigung für Juden und Christen aller Stände* (Münster: Adolph Russell's Verlag, 1871).
24. Scott Spector, *Violent Sensations: Sex, Crime, and Utopia in Vienna and Berlin, 1860–1914* (Chicago: University of Chicago Press, 2016), p. 223; Jacob Katz, *From Prejudice to Destruction: Anti-Semitism: 1700–1933* (Cambridge, MA: Harvard University Press, 1980), pp. 285–6.
25. 'Leo XIII en het protestantisme', *De Heraut*, 21 December 1879, p. 3.

26. Alan Levenson, 'Missionary Protestants as Defenders and Detractors of Judaism: Franz Delitzsch and Hermann Strack', *The Jewish Quarterly Review*, 92.3–4 (2002), pp. 383–420; Barnet Peretz Hartston, *Sensationalizing the Jewish Question Anti-Semitic Trials and the Press in the Early German Empire* (Leiden: Brill, 2005), pp. 164, 212 and 216; Franz Delitzsch, *Rohling's Talmudjude beleuchtet* (Leipzig: Dörffling und Franke, 1881).
27. See, for example, Yosef Kaplan (ed.), *The Dutch Intersection: The Jews and the Netherlands in Modern History* (Leiden: Brill, 2008).
28. Bart Wallet, 'Dutch National Identity and Jewish International Solidarity: An Impossible Combination? Dutch Jewry and the Significance of the Damascus Affair (1840)', in Kaplan (ed.), *The Dutch Intersection*, p. 319.
29. J. C. H. Blom, 'Dutch Jews, the Jewish Dutch, and the Jews in the Netherlands, 1870–1940', in Hans Blom, David J. Wertheim, Hetty Berg and Bart Wallet (eds), *Reappraising the History of Jews in the Netherlands* (New York: Oxford University Press, 2017), pp. 215–24.
30. George Harinck and Wim Berkelaar, *Domineesfabriek: Geschiedenis van de Theologische Universiteit Kampen* (Amsterdam: Prometheus, 2018), p. 43.
31. Harinck and de Bruijn, *Een Leidse vriendschap*, p. 78.
32. Harinck and de Bruijn, *Een Leidse vriendschap*, p. 79.
33. Herman Bavinck, 'Het Rijk Gods, het hoogste goed', in *De vrije kerk*, 7.8 (August 1881), pp. 190–1 and 358; 'The Kingdom of God, the Highest Good', *The Bavinck Review*, 2 (2011), pp. 138–9 and 169.
34. Herman Bavinck, *De Katholiciteit van Christendom en Kerk* (Kampen: G. Ph. Zalsman, 1888), pp. 11–12 and 25; Herman Bavinck, 'The Catholicity of Christianity and the Church', *Calvin Theological Journal*, 27 (1992), pp. 226 and 233.
35. Herman Bavinck, *De theologie van Prof. Dr. Daniel Chantepie de la Saussaye* (Leiden: Donner, 1884), pp. 11–12.
36. Herman Bavinck, 'Het geweten', *De vrije kerk*, 7.1–2 (1881), p. 51.
37. Herman Bavinck, 'The Future of Calvinism', *Presbyterian and Reformed Review*, 5.17 (1894), p. 10.
38. Herman Bavinck, *Hedendaagsche moraal* (Kampen: J. H. Kok, 1902), pp. 15 and 44–5.
39. Eglinton, *Bavinck: A Critical Biography*, pp. 219–54; Bavinck, *Hedendaagsche moraal*, pp. 44–5.
40. Herman Bavinck, 'Christian Principles and Social Relationships', in John Bolt (ed.), Harry Boonstra and Gerrit Sheeres (trans.), *Essays on Science, Religion, and Society* (Grand Rapids, MI: Baker Academic, 2008), p. 126.
41. Herman Bavinck, 'Het probleem van den oorlog', *Stemmen des tijds*, 4 (1914), pp. 6 and 20.
42. Herman Bavinck, *Christendom, Oorlog, Volkenbond* (Utrecht: Ruys, 1920), p. 43.
43. See, for example, Bruce Pass, 'Introduction', in Herman Bavinck, *On Theology: Herman Bavinck's Academic Orations* (Leiden: Brill, 2020), p. 7; Eglinton, 'Planting Tulips in the Rainforest', pp. 277–9; Eglinton, *Bavinck: A Critical Biography*, p. 236.
44. See, for example, Pass, 'Introduction', p. 7, n. 24. Interestingly, in relation to this, Joshua Ralston has argued that Snouck Hurgronje's influence can also be seen in Bavinck's knowledge and view of Islam. See Joshua Ralston, 'Islam as Christian Trope: The Place and Function of Islam in Reformed

Dogmatic Theology', *The Muslim World*, 107.4 (2017), pp. 754–76. See, for example, James Eglinton, 'Dominion and Vulnerability: Herman Bavinck and Posthumanism in the Shadow of Friedrich Nietzsche', in Calum MacKellar and Trevor Starmers (eds), *The Ethics of Generating Posthumans: Philosophical and Theological Reflections on Bringing New Persons into Existence* (London: Bloomsbury, 2021), pp. 98–101.

CHAPTER TWELVE

'Woodbine Willie' and the Quest for a Social Christianity after the First World War

Timothy Larsen

Geoffrey Anketell Studdert Kennedy (1883–1929) was the Anglican priest who gained the greatest fame for his service as a military chaplain during the First World War. In 1918, he published *Rough Rhymes of a Padre* under his *nom de guerre*, 'Woodbine Willie', and he has also been known by that alternative name ever since. While there is no need to adjudicate these kind of exact rankings, Studdert Kennedy has received his fair share of claims to being at or near the top in various categories. His first biography asserted in 1962 that he was 'the most celebrated army padre of all time'.[1] Stuart Bell has recently judged that he was 'almost certainly the most widely known British chaplain of the First World War'.[2] Claude M. Blagden, who was bishop of Peterborough during his final years, recollected that in the 1920s Studdert Kennedy had been 'the best-known clergyman in the Church of England'.[3] A 2013 biography is yet more sweeping: 'Given his combination of a public speaker who drew in the crowds and an author whose books were constantly reprinted, he was unmatched not only by any other clerical figure but also by any political one in the 1920s.'[4] Because he is in the Church of England calendar, Studdert Kennedy has also been identified as a modern Anglican 'saint'.[5]

Studdert Kennedy has continued to receive a lively amount of attention in the twenty-first century, including two academic biographies, an anthology and a collection of essays inspired by his life and convictions.[6] Three of those four books have the word 'war' in their title, and it is certainly the case that interest in Studdert Kennedy has been focused primarily on his military service and his writings, thoughts and sayings about war and peace.[7] The telos of this chapter is on Studdert Kennedy as an advocate for social Christianity. This aspect of his witness has received less attention for several reasons. Most obviously, it is less dramatic than being a padre under fire on the Western Front. Secondly, Studdert Kennedy was only able to focus his ministry on social Christianity for a decade before he died unexpectedly at the age of forty-five, and therefore his contribution can be overlooked as a short one during a stretch of years which is often not considered a significant era in histories of Christian socialism. Finally, the 1920s were not a time when a clear and precise message could be given on the question of the church's response to social issues, but rather a period in which advocates were often uncertain about what sound economic policy was and anxious about excesses and errors in opposite-facing directions.

Nevertheless, Studdert Kennedy was a leading champion of social Christianity in the decade after the war. This was attested to by his contemporaries who were fellow labourers in the cause.[8] James Granville Adderley (1861–1942) is identified as a 'Church of England clergyman and Christian socialist'.[9] In 1890, Adderley joined one of the movement's earliest organisations, the Guild of St Matthew, and he became a member of the Christian Socialist League in 1908. In between, he helped to found the Christian Social Union. Adderley had worked closely with B. F. Westcott, Charles Gore and Henry Scott Holland. In 1924, he wrote a series of articles for the Industrial Christian Fellowship's magazine, the *Torch*. Its running title was 'The Man and His Message'. Each month, an article profiled a leading figure, moving chronologically from the 1840s to the 1920s. The series culminated thus:

> But being restricted for the moment to twelve articles, I am obliged to end my course with Mr. Studdert Kennedy. He could not be left out if the course was to be continued up to date. He represents the climax of the old movement and the beginning of a new one.[10]

It was natural to puff Studdert Kennedy in the *Torch* as he was the chief spokesman for the Industrial Christian Fellowship, but Adderley was sincere in both seeing the ICF as the new hope for the movement and Woodbine Willie as a major leader. In *Commonwealth: A Christian Social Magazine*, Adderley had observed, 'The I.C.F. has been fortunate in getting the most popular preacher of the day to be its mouthpiece.'[11] A leading figure in the history of the movement was William Temple. Studdert Kennedy and Temple were contemporaries. Here is Temple's testimony regarding him: 'Soon after the end of the war men knew that there was among us again a prophet of social righteousness in the true succession of Henry Scott Holland.'[12] P. T. R. Kirk, the General Director of the ICF, floated the possibility of his being buried in Westminster Abbey. The Dean squashed that idea emphatically: 'What! Studdert Kennedy? He was a Socialist!'[13] Any account of Anglican social Christianity in the first half of the twentieth century needs to reckon with the witness of Studdert Kennedy.

In an important article on Scottish Presbyterian churches and the First World War, Stewart J. Brown argued that there had been a strong social gospel movement in these denominations in the early years of the twentieth century, but this witness lost some of its credibility because during the Great War these churches forfeited 'their independent prophetic voice'.[14] Studdert Kennedy also dramatically failed to maintain an independent prophetic voice during the war, yet he nevertheless managed to channel the fame and goodwill he accrued during that conflict to enable him to gain a hearing for social Christianity in the 1920s. The war made him. He was still only an unpublished, unknown curate well into 1914. He first became a vicar in June 1914. The new vicar of St Paul's, Worcester, fervently encouraged the men in his congregation to enlist. He was a hit with the soldiers stationed at the nearby military base when he preached at their church parades. Studdert Kennedy himself volunteered to serve as a military chaplain, arriving in France in December 1915. As many other padres also did, he distributed cigarettes to the men. The brand to hand was Woodbine and he cultivated the persona of 'Woodbine Willie', the common soldier's friend. In August 1917, Studdert Kennedy was awarded the Military Cross for showing 'the greatest courage and disregard for his own safety in attending to the wounded under heavy fire'.[15] A little over a year later, he was gassed. His periods of service when he was assigned to the front, however, were few and relatively brief.

Instead, he was kept busy behind the lines giving addresses to as many soldiers as possible. Bishop Gwynne, Deputy Chaplain-General, told him that this was a more strategic deployment of him because he had been 'given by the Almighty the gift of the gab'.[16] In this capacity, Studdert Kennedy was assigned to be a speaker for the National Mission of Repentance and Hope, a major effort by the Church of England for a spiritual push that was held in the autumn 1916 and into 1917 – with events both on the home front and for the soldiers.[17] He was a notable success, winning over the men. He grabbed their attention by using slang and swear words in a most unclergyman-like manner. He could tell a good story. He made them laugh.

Studdert Kennedy confessed to another chaplain, F. B. Macnutt, that he wrote poetry, and Macnutt encouraged him to write a poem that would convey the message of the National Mission. He wrote 'Sinner and Saint: A Sermon in a Billet'. It was what Studdert Kennedy called a 'dialect' poem, imitating the speech of an ordinary, working-class soldier. It was a sensation. Macnutt used it as well and soldiers rushed up to ask for a copy. Eventually, Studdert Kennedy had enough such poems for a book, *Rough Rhymes of a Padre* (1918), which was enormously popular both with the soldiers and with civilians. Meanwhile, Macnutt was also getting together a collection of essays by Anglican padres on their responses to issues raised by the war, *The Church in the Furnace* (1917). Studdert Kennedy's chapter was 'The Religious Difficulties of the Private Soldier'. It too found its audience. Studdert Kennedy reworked it for a popular audience and included it in his *Rough Talks by a Padre* (1918). Its new title was 'Why Aren't All the Best Chaps Christians?' and it was also distributed separately as a pamphlet – one with enough enduring appeal that an edition was published in 1938.[18]

The visceral thrill of Woodbine Willie's poems, prose and talks was the unflinching way that he would say aloud what people were thinking – and in their own habitual way of expressing themselves – no matter that some might find this unbecoming in a priest or a pulpit. Here is a section of a poem which gives a soldier's musings on the church's teaching about the afterlife:

There's 'eaven and 'ell, They say so, – Well
I dunnow what they mean. But it's touch and go,
And I may soon know,
It's funny there's nothin' between.[19]

This was a technique for gaining the attention of those who usually tuned out parsons and for making people think about what was really true, but at times it seems like it was almost a compulsion. He could not help but hear in his head all the complaints and retorts, and he wanted his listeners or readers to know that he knew what they were thinking. Sometimes audience members could not discern the difference between what Studdert Kennedy believed and what was just him airing the views of others. Even when he was expressing his own view, he inclined towards doing so in a way intended to shock. Here is his way of correcting a view of God in which the deity is an all-powerful, passionless being watching the war in regal repose: 'It is the Almighty God we are fighting; He is the soul of Prussianism. I want to kill Him . . . I want to kill the Almighty God and tear Him from His throne.'[20] A review of Studdert Kennedy's *Food for the Fed-Up* (1921) observed, 'In this book there is also displayed another of the author's special gifts – that of saying what the average man is thinking, but either cannot or dare not say.'[21] The down side of this is that he was not a systematic or even consistent thinker. He is easy to catch in contradictions and sometimes descended into incoherence. Yet it might have been the one thing needful: it is difficult to overstate how exciting and reassuring many people found it to encounter a clergyman who demonstratively could see reality from their perspective.

It is a truism that as the First World War continued on, disillusionment set in. Studdert Kennedy – always quick to give voice to what people think – fully shared the view that the initial, blithe assumption that good would come out of the war was just cant and nonsense. War only produced evil.[22] The war was meaningless. This realisation created a desire in some people to dedicate themselves to doing something 'after the war' which retrospectively could give some meaning to the enormous sacrifices and losses – one could then point to that work and say that at least the war prompted people to undertake these needed changes. It is striking how many people during the war were preoccupied with thinking about what must be done 'after the war'.

Indeed, that was really the theme of *The Church in the Furnace*, which was trying to set out an agenda for 'the problems that confront the Church and Nation in the days of reconstruction which lie ahead'.[23] Macnutt became General Editor of a series of books and pamphlets published by the SPCK under the general title, 'After-the-War Literature'. Already in 1918, Studdert Kennedy was warning his readers that grave challenges lay ahead *après la guerre*: 'Our task when the war is over looks immense and terrible. Poverty at home, and fear abroad. Problems everywhere.'[24] In the dedication of his book, *Democracy and the Dog Collar* (1921), he made it clear that just as his ministry was focused on the fighting men during the war so it would now be focused on the labouring men: 'To the Working Men of Britain who were her soldiers once this book is dedicated with affection and respect.'[25]

As part of the National Mission, the archbishop of Canterbury had created five commissions to recommend how to respond to pressing issues. The Fifth Report was *Christianity and Industrial Problems* (1918). The Bishop of Winchester, Edward Talbot, had chaired this commission and when the report was reprinted in 1927 he recalled its impetus: 'It sprang out of the War.'[26] Talbot explained that the commission had decided that it would err on the side of being accused of meddling in practical matters where priests do not belong rather than to gravitate towards the side of affirming principles so abstract as to incline towards the platitudinous. The demand that generated the most attention was for 'a full living wage'.[27] And *Christianity and Industrial Problems* was concrete enough to secure foes. The Bishop of Hereford (soon to be translated to Durham) denounced it as 'a Socialist tract'.[28] Others would have found that description a commendation. The Church Socialist League adopted the Fifth Report as a platform to stand on. Those who have written on the Christian Socialist movement have often singled this report out as an unusually good document worthy of enduring praise.

John Oliver enthused, '*Christianity and Industrial Problems*, can without exaggeration be described as one of the finest and most important expressions of Christian opinion on social and industrial affairs ever produced by the Church of England.'[29] Moreover, the Fifth Report gained widespread support in the church. It was even given a quasi-official endorsement by being accepted by a committee of the Lambeth Conference of 1920.[30] For the purpose at hand, it became entwined with Studdert Kennedy's work after the war because *Christianity and Industrial Problems* was accepted as a basis for thought and action by the Industrial Christian Fellowship. The 1927 reprint was a ICF study guide edition.[31]

Since the days of the original Anglican Christian Socialists in the 1840s, various organisations had sprung up to advance their cause. By the far the largest was the Christian Social Union, founded in 1889. All other organisations counted their members in the hundreds whereas the CSU numbered its in the thousands. Westcott was a key supporter, as were Gore and Scott Holland. Its members and perspectives gained significant influence in the church, notably at the Lambeth Conference of 1908. Indeed, the Fifth Report itself had been fundamentally shaped by CSU views. Nevertheless, as the twentieth century progressed, there was a widespread suspicion that the CSU had had its day.[32] When Scott Holland died in 1918 it was apparent that it was time for an already moribund CSU to pass away as well.

There were a range of reasons for the growing dissatisfaction with the CSU. Some of them were choices which others would see as strengths: that it was an avowedly Anglican organisation, or one so dominated by Anglo-Catholics. Another was its rather vague, big-tent approach to questions of political and economic philosophy and policy. Certainly, a portion of the CSU was keen to be part of an organisation that would unequivocally avow socialism, and perhaps even align itself with the Labour Party. There was also a sense that the CSU was just a talking shop. It was mocked for its academic agenda: 'Here's a social evil; let's read a paper on it.'[33] Relatedly, it was dismissed as a body that discussed the problems affecting the lower classes but which did not draw in any working-class people in order to understand their perspectives and to work in solidarity with them.

The Navvy Mission Society was founded in 1877 as an evangelical effort to minister to a marginalised segment of the population. (Navvies were manual labourers who moved around the country to work on large works projects. Because this itinerant existence often meant that they did not have strong ties to communities, they were considered in need of spiritual care.) In 1919, it was transformed into the Industrial Christian Fellowship which, in 1920, had the CSU merge into it.[34] The ICF was remarkably successful at gaining support. It was ecclesiastically broader than the CSU, even including non-Anglicans, and it drew more widely from the breadth of the church, not least because of the Navvy Mission's evangelical ethos. It also drew support from across the political parties. Good at drawing in eminent figures, the ICF was the kind of organisation which could put on a special event and recruit the Archbishop of Canterbury to be the speaker. Although it continued a lot of the vagueness regarding specific political and economic policies that had frustrated some in the CSU, it nevertheless also did well at winning the support of Anglican socialists. This might have been due to its commitment to the Fifth Report. One difference from the CSU was that the ICF did a better job of drawing in some people from the working classes and being in contact with those communities. The Navvy Mission side gave that aspiration a head start. The ICF hired working men as paid agents. The ICF's magazine, the *Torch*, boasted that it 'circulates in the heart of industry'.[35] Adderley explained that the mission of the CSU had been to convert the leadership of the church to social Christianity, but 'Studdert Kennedy and the I.C.F. are now trying to convert the masses themselves'.[36]

The ICF was particularly attractive to clergymen who had served as padres during the war.[37] In fact, P. T. R. Kirk, its General Director, was a former padre. Kirk and others quickly decided that they wanted Studdert Kennedy to be the ICF's voice. He initially turned them down because the details of how his family would live could not be worked out. He finally accepted their offer in March 1921 and was appointed as the ICF's 'Messenger'. (Because the ICF referred to its missions as 'crusades', he was also called a 'Crusader'.)[38] It was natural that Studdert Kennedy would end up in some such position. He loved public speaking and could win over a crowd, but his way of doing so depended to a marked degree on the element of surprise (using salty language, lounging around causally rather than standing behind the pulpit and so on) and therefore he really belonged on the road rather than ministering to the same congregation. The Church of England, however, was not structured to provide itinerant positions and therefore an organisation such as the ICF was the way forward. The Archbishop of Canterbury saw the point and appointed Studdert Kennedy to St Edmund's, Lombard Street, London, a church without a vicarage that was stranded in a commercial district and therefore was considered a sinecure.

The F. D. Maurice cohort of the 1840s adopted the title 'Christian Socialists'.[39] In 1850, J. M. Ludlow founded the *Christian Socialist* journal. Others who heartily agreed with the aims of the movement, however, sometimes shied away from the label 'socialism'. What did it mean? Studdert Kennedy once observed, 'Righteousness is a word that has been much misunderstood, because it means so much . . . In common with words like Christianity, Socialism, Liberty, it is so difficult to define.'[40] Recurringly, champions of social Christianity used the word 'socialism' to describe their movement, but were careful to define it in capacious ways. Maurice asserted that 'Anyone who recognizes the principle of cooperation as a stronger and truer principle than that of competition, has a right to the honour or disgrace of being called a Socialist.'[41] In 1890, Gore insisted that he was using the term in a wide sense: 'Socialism is the opposite of Individualism.'[42] The Fifth Report honoured the original 'Christian Socialists' while also clarifying, 'The name did not imply any collectivist economic theory.'[43] And in 1922 Gore explained in an edited volume that all the contributors were 'Socialists in the general sense'.[44] After the war, this question of the general or specific sense had become more acute. Some Anglicans were chafing to break free from the vagueness and caution exemplified by the CSU. Early in the century, Temple had taken the bold step of joining the Labour Party. (This was deemed such an inappropriate thing for a clergyman to do that when Temple was elevated to the episcopate in 1921 he felt he needed to withdraw from the party.) Coming off the bench rather than on it – but likewise conceding that these two identities were not readily compatible – in 1919 Gore gave as one of his reasons for resigning as Bishop of Oxford, 'I'd like to join the Labour Party.'[45] Occasionally the more advanced souls would organise a little society of their own. The Church Socialist League, founded in 1906, stood for ending capitalism. When instead it was the CSL that ended (in 1923), its diehards regrouped to form the Society of Socialist Christians.[46] Conrad Noel, the 'Red Vicar' of Thaxted, pushed socialism in the direction of communism.[47] His organisation, founded in 1918, was the Catholic Crusade. These were all much smaller organisations than the ICF.

The Messenger was delighted that Charles Raven had showcased a noble Anglican tradition of Christian socialism.[48] Studdert Kennedy enthused that Maurice was 'the greatest churchman of the last century' and acquiesced in referring to him and his co-labourers as Christian socialists.[49] Nevertheless, he was emphatically on the side that wished to avoid using the word 'socialist' to describe his own identity. He strove to keep the ICF clear of that association:

> Not a single one of the activities of the I.C.F. has fallen under the control of Socialists. If any of them did I would sever my connexion with the Society immediately. I am not a Socialist and spend a considerable amount of my time exposing popular Socialist clap-trap, which is a curse to sane thinking, as popular Tory clap-trap is on the other side.[50]

Studdert Kennedy's mind made a strong association between socialism and unbelief. When young, he felt the challenge of the thought of Robert Blatchford, who was both a socialist and an atheist. In 1911, his critique of H. G. Wells was that 'he suffers as all Socialistic writers suffer' by failing to take sin into account.[51] Studdert Kennedy insisted that 'Scientific Socialism' was incompatible with Christianity.[52] He would sometimes refer to this unabsorbable version as 'Marxian Socialism'. Studdert Kennedy was always trying to warn workers away from Marx: 'He was not really a prophet, he was only a disease.'[53] This view was expressed in his article, 'Moses versus Marx'.[54] And One greater than Moses has come: 'Christ and Karl Marx are as fire and water, and cannot mix.'[55] Studdert Kennedy put the matter bluntly: 'There is not, and there cannot be, any truce between Marxian Communism and Christianity. They are both religions. Let us be quite clear about that. Karl Marx as an economist is dead, but as a founder of a religion he still lives, and his religion is enmity against God.'[56] Moreover, the word landed differently in the wake of the Russian Revolution. Already in 1919, Studdert Kennedy was warning that it was a cautionary tale: 'The most awful results can be seen in Russia.'[57] He read Anton Karlgren's *Bolshevist Russia* (1927): 'It is a tragic tale he has to tell. It is a book to make you weep.'[58] Studdert Kennedy retorted to working-class calls for the abolition of private property with the *reductio ad absurdum* that it is better for a person to have his or her own toothbrush.[59]

The lesson of Communist Russia for the working classes was the same lesson they had all just learned in the war: that good cannot be brought about by violence. This was a major burden of Studdert Kennedy's postwar message. He was seeking to convince the working classes that he and the church were with them in their efforts to increase their quality of life. Having won their ear, however, he warned that 'class war' was not the way to achieve these aspirations.

Unsurprisingly, he believed that a revolution would be a disaster; but he also thought that oppositional thinking in which the workers needed to overcome the capitalists and tactics such as strikes were 'class war'. Studdert Kennedy saw a direct connection to the lesson he had learned in the trenches:

> The very first thing that any true friend of Labour has got to make quite clear to the workers to-day is that there is just as little to be got out of industrial war in the long run as there is out of international war ... If we have learned anything from the past five years of hell, it surely ought to be that war never gets anything or anywhere.[60]

An adversarial stance towards capitalists was actually keeping the working classes from prosperity: 'We must increase production. What stands in the way? The old enemy – War. War between employers and employed. Let us get that fixed. Our great enemy, greater than Prussia ever was, is the Class War.'[61]

What was the path forward then? Studdert Kennedy decided that it was not his role to lead when it came to specific policies for tackling economic and industrial issues. During the war he reassured the Tommies he was on their side by letting them know that he was 'a strong Trades Unionist'; and he always emphasised that he stood with the Labour movement.[62] Still: 'I am not a member of the Labour Party, nor do I propose to become one, but for that very reason I feel the less inclined to confuse the movement with the party. They are two entirely different things.'[63] When the Labour Party for the first time became the official opposition, over 600 clergymen signed a memorial offering their 'sincere congratulations', which was presented to the Labour leader, Ramsay MacDonald. The *Church Times* reported, 'The list of signatures to the memorial is remarkable alike for the names it contains and for those it does not. Mr. Studdert-Kennedy and the Rev. P. T. R. Kirk, director of the Industrial Christian Fellowship, are not among them.'[64] Studdert Kennedy begrudgingly recognised that workers were sometimes forced into a situation that made striking appropriate, but his natural instinct was to think that a strike would be wrong. In the hysteria of the war, he went so far as to pronounce that strikers, because they were undermining the war effort, were traitors who 'ought to be shot'.[65] At a 1921 meeting of the ICF Council, Studdert Kennedy moved a resolution asserting that arbitration was the way to settle a dispute and therefore strikes should only be undertaken as a 'last resort'. Gore, however, proposed an amendment which affirmed that another legitimate reason to strike was to rally the spirits of down-beaten workers.[66] Unlike some priests committed to social Christianity, Studdert Kennedy was less inclined to be in public solitary with concrete working-class efforts at the polling station and picket line.

Nevertheless, Studdert Kennedy was an emphatic champion of social Christianity, that is, an insistence that addressing social problems such as poverty, unemployment and bad housing was an essential part of the gospel:

> What is sometimes called the social message of the Church, is not one department of its Gospel, and its individual message another; they are one. Either is nothing without the other ... The cry that is often

raised, that we are going to secularise religion, and take the clergy away from their 'purely spiritual' work, is the cry of the man who dare not face the Cross.[67]

That, however, was a message that a certain kind of otherworldly churchgoer needed to hear. Studdert Kennedy's main mission was to speak to disaffected churchgoers or non-churchgoers who knew that social problems needed to be tackled but who assumed the Church was not an ally. Thus Studdert Kennedy's main proclamations of social Christianity happened when he was addressing a thoroughly Christian audience. In 1925, the Bishop of London asked him to write a Lenten book. Studdert Kennedy used it to explain to believers that they could not separate the spiritual from the social gospel:

> If you feel no longing to right wrongs, to war against injustice and cruelty, to defy tyrannies, to abolish ugliness and dirt, look out! You are standing on a rotten piece of ground; it will give way beneath you when the hour comes, and you will go down. No rites, no ceremonies, no soft music and stately ritual will avail to save you . . . We are often told that the Church has nothing to do with social questions; that there is no social Gospel; and that we should stick to our real business of saving individual souls . . . but the souls we have to save are incarnate not disembodied souls, and there are conditions of life which are soul-destroying, not merely because they are painful, but because they are essentially degrading, inhuman, and wrong.[68]

A striking case is Studdert Kennedy's address to the Anglo-Catholic Congress of 1923. Speakers were assigned major doctrines and Christian practices as their subject. There were addresses on the incarnation, faith and baptism, the atonement, sacramental confession, the Holy Spirit and evangelisation. Studdert Kennedy's subject was 'Salvation' and it is fascinating that his sense of how to handle such a topic was to offer a manifesto for social Christianity:

> If we are to succeed in the re-evangelisation of England and of the world, we must definitely recognise that what is often called the social message of Jesus Christ is an essential part of the Gospel. It is not an addendum to it, it is not something which follows conversion; it is that to which men need to be converted . . . The social life must be brought right into the heart of our devotion . . . We must destroy within ourselves our present feeling that we descend to a lower level when we leave the song of the angels and the archangels and begin to study economic conditions, questions of wages, hours and housing.[69]

There was a reason why even a forthright socialist such as Temple heralded Studdert Kennedy as a prophet of social righteousness. Indeed, if the presentation so far has left the impression that Studdert Kennedy took a rather detached approach to the social issues of his day, that was not the impression he made upon his contemporaries. His genius was for painting in vivid language social conditions which any decent society should find intolerable. He would evoke what was real – and the closer you were to the bottom of the heap, the more you knew whereof he spoke – in portraits of 'consumptive children in Camberwell dying with rotten teeth'.[70] He would take the time to make his hearers feel what it must be like to be a day labourer at the docks who needs to feed his family, but who has gotten a little too old to be picked readily by the owners and more often than not goes home without having found work. People felt seen. As one man exclaimed after hearing Studdert Kennedy speak, 'That chap *must* have been on the dole or he could never talk like that.'[71] He also gave voice to people's outrage. His response to the slum housing that people were forced to live in was: 'My parish ought to be blown up.'[72] Nor was he aloof from all organisation. He led a protest march of 800 unemployed people.[73] Studdert Kennedy was also an active participant in the socialist-inflected Conference on Christian Politics, Economics and Citizenship (COPEC) in 1924, which was an effort to find a way forward on specific social issues.[74] But his main contribution was providing the fire, motivation and inspiration for others to engage in specific reforms. An influential pioneer of housing reform in his post-war era was Father Basil Jellicoe, the founder of the St Pancras Housing Association. He made a direct, significant difference in tackling slums. From first to finish Jellicoe insisted that Studdert Kennedy was his 'hero' and his 'liveliest inspiration'.[75]

And when it came to personal sacrifice, Studdert Kennedy was genuine. He has been compared to St Francis of Assisi and the resemblance when it comes to their attitudes towards possessions is stronger than one might imagine. Before the war, Studdert Kennedy had been a slum priest. Stories abound of his reckless habit of giving away whatever he had to whomever he met who was in need. He gave away almost all of his clothes and just wore a cassock all the time to disguise this fact. Marriage changed him in this regard all too little (there was a reason why St Francis stayed single). Studdert Kennedy married Emily Catlow in April 1914. Having hitherto been a curate, he received three offers for a permanent position. He informed Emily that his plan was to accept the one with 'the smallest income and the poorest people', vicar of St Paul's, Worcester, 'if you think you can manage it'.[76] Indicative of their life together was the day that Emily came home to find Geoffrey transporting their bed to the house of a poor invalid he had visited who did not look comfortable. Though his *Rough Rhymes of a Padre* was a runaway success, its author had predetermined that he would give all the profits to a charity.

Temple revealed that this was not the only time Studdert Kennedy gave away all he earned from a book.[77] He made a £200 contribution to the Miners' Distress Fund. He once spoke in a prison and promised everyone there that he would do what he could to help them when they got out: there was a steady stream of ex-convicts coming his way for years thereafter. The ICF was an advocacy group, but he would treat it as a relief agency and tell any down-and-out whom he met that if they would just go to its offices he was sure that someone there would find a way to help them. None of this was *merely* theatrical (and St Francis too could be theatrical): it was the overflow of a generous-hearted man who loathed to see suffering and deprivation in others and was willing to incur or risk it in himself to attempt to alleviate some of it.

While scholars have generally approached Studdert Kennedy in a spirit of admiration, those who have not have often been particularly concerned with issues of social reform. His nephew, Gerald Studdert-Kennedy, was irritated by the vagueness of the ICF platform and of his uncle and hints that they can be seen as obstructing real reform by pretending to be engaging in it.[78] A somewhat similar line has recently been taken by Mark Dorsett.[79] Studdert Kennedy was aware of this charge. In a revealing article, he reflected upon Luke 12:13–14, 'And one of the company said unto Him, Master, speak to my brother, that he divide the inheritance with me. And he said unto him, Man, who made me a judge or a divider over you?':

> ... it looks as if He had simply avoided an awkward question. It's all right talking beautiful generalities, but it's always when you get down to a particular case that the rub comes ... Ought not Christ to have been willing to apply His general principles to this particular case?[80]

Of course, the Messenger believed that his Master had done right. Moreover, Studdert Kennedy's critics have not appreciated the degree to which his approach has been vindicated. Wisdom is proved right by her children. People might wish that he had joined the Labour Party as Temple had done, but they ignore the fact that Temple felt a need to resign when he became a bishop. Arguably, Studdert Kennedy's place in the church was as a kind of missionary bishop to the working classes and therefore he was making the same calculation.

Studdert Kennedy had the insight to know what he did not know. He really did read up on and study the social issues of his day and he could grasp that there were no easy or obvious solutions to some of the most vexing ones. The 'practical' solutions being championed by some of the more ardent Christian socialists were often not solutions at all, but unworkable schemes. Despite his populism, Studdert Kennedy insisted that economic policy should be guided by experts:

> I am not a skilled economist. I do not fully understand money, neither do you. I don't know much about money, but I know enough to be quite sure that if you suppose you understand it, or could understand it, without a great deal of special training, you are – well, in plain terms, you are an ass.[81]

A lot of Christian socialists were making asses of themselves. John Oliver, in his study of Anglican social Christianity in the interwar period, laments the fact that so many of its leading voices championed 'Social Credit', a system that 'was based on a number of serious economic fallacies':

> It was a serious misfortune of the Christian social movement in the Church of England that many of its most active and influential members ... were persuaded to advocate this fallacious panacea, rather than the economic measures which Keynes as his associates were propounding from 1923 onwards.[82]

Not only did Studdert Kennedy avoid the trap of social credit claptrap, he grasped that Keynes was on to something:

> It might be justifiable to run railways at a loss, but it would only be justifiable provided you ran other things at a greater gain ... It is absolutely essential that we get clear in our minds that the accumulation of capital wealth, whoever holds it and whoever manages it, is a vital necessity. Mr. Keynes puts his finger on the pulse of that question ... .[83]

Studdert Kennedy was all for the principle that a worker should be paid a living wage, but he could also see through the facile and false assumption of some Christian socialists that the employers only needed to curb their greed and all would be well. He understood that in the post-war era industries were sometimes getting undercut by competitors abroad who paid their workers still less and that created a problem which could not be solved by attacking the owners of British firms. In his manifesto for social Christianity, Studdert Kennedy insisted that the 'revivalist' and the 'reformer' were both essential ministries that needed each other.[84] The truth about Studdert Kennedy is not that he was a vague and ineffectual social reformer, but rather that he was that most welcome kind of revivalist, one who grasps that the gospel is wider than simply the matter of individual salvation, that the kingdom of God includes social as well as spiritual welfare.

Studdert Kennedy's real ministry was that of a Christian apologist, commending the faith to the doubting and the disillusioned. *Rough Talks by a Padre* was his attempt to answer the objections to Christianity brought into sharp relief by the war. Every chapter points people to the Carpenter of Nazareth. Sometimes this is in the register of an evangelical altar call: 'Christ says to you to-night. Come back to the sacred service which has held the church together down the years.'[85] *The Hardest Part* was another effort at reconciling war-torn souls to their God. *Food for the Fed-Up* (1921) was an attempt to get modern doubters to affirm the Apostles' Creed.[86] *The Wicket Gate* commended the Lord's Prayer. To each their gifts. Studdert Kennedy was a passionate champion of the social gospel who pursued a ministry of reconciliation between the church and the working classes and between modern people and the God of the gospel. He represents one dedicated, prominent, eye-catching form which a commitment to social Christianity took after the war.

Notes

1. William Purcell, *Woodbine Willie: An Anglican Incident. Being Some Account of the Life and Times of Geoffrey Anketell Studdert Kennedy: Poet, Prophet, Seeker after Truth, 1883–1929* (London: Hodder & Stoughton, 1962), p. 98.
2. Stuart Bell, 'The Theology of "Woodbine Willie" in Context', in Michael Snape and Edward Madigan (eds), *The Clergy in Khaki: New Perspectives on British Army Chaplaincy in the First World War* (Farnham, Surrey: Ashgate, 2013), p. 95.
3. Claude M. Blagden, *Well Remembered* (London: Hodder and Stoughton 1953), p. 170.
4. Bob Holman, *Woodbine Willie: An Unsung Hero of World War One* (Oxford: Lion Hudson, 2013), p. 168.
5. Michael W. Brierley, 'Ripon Hall, Henry Major and the Shaping of English Liberal Theology', in Mark D. Chapman (ed.), *Ambassadors of Christ: Commemorating 150 Years of Theological Education in Cuddesdon 1854–2004* (Aldershot: Ashgate, 2004), pp. 89–155 (here p. 90); Michael Grundy, *A Fiery Glow in the Darkness: Woodbine Willie, Padre and Poet* (Worcester: Osborne Books 1997), p. 7.
6. Linda Parker, *A Seeker after Truths: The Life and Times of G. A. Studdert Kennedy ('Woodbine Willie') 1883–1929* (Solihull: Helion and Company, 2017); Dayne Edward Nix, *Moral Injury and a First World War Chaplain: The Life of G. A. Studdert Kennedy* (Lanham: Lexington, 2021); Kerry Walters (ed.), *After War, Is Faith Possible? The Life and Message of Geoffrey 'Woodbine Willie' Studdert Kennedy* (Eugene, OR: Cascade, 2008); Michael W. Brierley and Georgina A. Byrne (eds), *Life after Tragedy: Essays on Faith and the First World War Evoked by Geoffrey Studdert Kennedy* (Eugene, OR: Cascade, 2017). See also, Timothy Larsen, 'The Myth of Woodbine Willie: Reconsidering the Ministry and Theology of G. A. Studdert Kennedy', *Anglican and Episcopal History*, 92, 4 (December 2023), pp. 543–80.
7. For a recent chapter on Studdert Kennedy in a volume with war in its title, see Stuart Bell, 'From Collusion to Condemnation: The Evolving Voice of "Woodbine Willie"', in Angela K. Smith and Krista Cowman (eds), *Landscapes and Voices of the Great War* (London: Routledge, 2017), pp. 151–72.
8. Maurice B. Reckitt, *Maurice to Temple: A Century of the Social Movement in the Church of England* (London: Faber and Faber, 1947), p. 164.
9. N. C. Masterman, 'James Granville Adderley (1861–1942)', *Oxford Dictionary of National Biography*, accessed online at oxforddnb.com (published in 2004).
10. James Adderley, 'The Man and His Message: XII – Studdert Kennedy', *Torch* (December 1924), pp. 180–1.
11. Donald O. Wagner, *The Church of England and Social Reform since 1854* (New York: Columbia University Press, 1930), p. 307.
12. William Temple, 'The Man and His Message', in J. K. Mozley (ed.), *G. A. Studdert Kennedy by His Friends* (London: Hodder and Stoughton, 1930), p. 209.
13. Purcell, *Woodbine Willie*, p. 176.
14. Stewart J. Brown, '"A Solemn Purification by Fire": Responses to the Great War in the Scottish Presbyterian Churches, 1914–19', *Journal of Ecclesiastical History*, 45.1 (1994), p. 82.

15. *Edinburgh Gazette*, 20 August 1917, Supplement, p. 1678.
16. D. F. Carey, 'War Padre', in Mozley, *G. A. Studdert Kennedy by His Friends*, p. 131.
17. For this effort, see David M. Thompson, 'War, the Nation, and the Kingdom of God: The Origins of the National Mission of Repentance and Hope, 1915–16', in W. J. Sheils (ed.), *The Church and War* (Oxford: Basil Blackwell, 1983), pp. 337–50.
18. G. A. Studdert Kennedy, *Why Aren't All the Best Chaps Christians?* (London: Hodder and Stoughton, 1938).
19. 'Woodbine Willie', *Rough Rhymes of A Padre* (London: Hodder and Stoughton, n.d. [1918]), p. 29.
20. G. A. Studdert Kennedy, *The Hardest Part* (London: Hodder and Stoughton, n.d. [1918]), pp. 40–1.
21. A. C. Charles, 'Food for the Fed-Up', *Torch* (October 1921), p. 17.
22. G. A. Studdert Kennedy, *More Rough Rhymes of a Padre* (London: Hodder and Stoughton, n.d. [1918]), p. 80.
23. F. B. Macnutt (ed.), *The Church in the Furnace: Essays by Seventeen Temporary Church of England Chaplains on Active Service in France and Flanders* (London: Macmillan, 1918), p. xii. For military chaplains after the war, see Linda Parker, *Shellshocked Prophets: Former Army Chaplains in Inter-War Britain* (Solihull: Helion & Company, 2015).
24. Studdert Kennedy, *Rough Talks*, p. 199; Parker, *A Seeker after Truths*, p. 102.
25. G. A. Studdert Kennedy, *Democracy and the Dog Collar* (London: Hodder and Stoughton, 1921).
26. Edward S. Talbot, preface to *Christianity and Industrial Problems*, by Church of England National Mission of Repentance and Hope (London: Society for Promoting Christian Knowledge, 1927), p. vii.
27. Talbot, *Christianity and Industrial Problems*, p. 116.
28. H. Hensley Henson, 'The Church and Socialism', *Edinburgh Review*, 231.471 (January 1920), pp. 1–25 (here p. 6).
29. John Oliver, *The Church and Social Order: Social Thought in the Church of England, 1918–1939* (London: A. R. Mowbray and Co., 1968), p. 23.
30. Reckitt, *Maurice to Temple*, p. 163.
31. Talbot, *Christianity and Industrial Problems*, p. 219.
32. G. L. Prestige, *The Life of Charles Gore: A Great Englishman* (London: William Heinemann, 1935), p. 274.
33. Oliver, *The Church and Social Order*, p. 20.
34. The standard history of the ICF was written by Studdert Kennedy's nephew and it is a rather curious book as the author was not a Christian and could not grasp the point of many aspects of ministry: Gerald Studdert-Kennedy, *Dog-Collar Democracy: The Industrial Christian Fellowship, 1919–1929* (London: Macmillan, 1982).
35. See the journal's self-advertisement: *Torch* (May 1922), p. 19.
36. Adderley, 'The Man and His Message', p. 180.
37. Studdert-Kennedy, *Dog-Collar Democracy*, pp. 129–30.
38. Kirk's memorial tribute was titled, 'I.C.F. Crusader': Mozley, *G. A. Studdert Kennedy by His Friends*, p. 165.
39. Edward Norman, *The Victorian Christian Socialists* (Cambridge: Cambridge University Press, 1987).

40. G. A. Studdert Kennedy, *The New Man in Christ*, ed. W. Moore Ede (London: Hodder and Stoughton, 1932), p. 47.
41. Alan Wilkinson, *Christian Socialism: Scott Holland to Tony Blair* (London: SCM Press, 1998), p. 18.
42. Wilkinson, *Christian Socialism*, p. 55.
43. Talbot, *Christianity and Industrial Problems*, p. 17.
44. Oliver, *The Church and Social Order*, p. 122.
45. F. A. Iremonger, *William Temple, Archbishop of Canterbury* (London: Oxford University Press, 1948), p. 263.
46. Oliver, *The Church and Social Order*, p. 119.
47. Arthur Burns, 'Beyond the "Red Vicar": Community and Christian Socialism in Thaxted, Essex, 1910–84', *History Workshop Journal*, 75.1 (Spring 2013), pp. 101–24.
48. Charles E. Raven, *Christian Socialism, 1848–1854* (London: Macmillan, 1920).
49. Studdert Kennedy, *Democracy and the Dog Collar*, p. 23.
50. G. A. Studdert Kennedy, letter to the editor, *The Times*, 19 November 1926, p. 10.
51. J. K. Mozley, 'Home Life and Early Years of His Ministry', in Mozley, *G. A. Studdert Kennedy by His Friends*, p. 81.
52. G. A. Studdert Kennedy, *The Warrior, the Woman, and the Christ: A Study of the Leadership of Christ* (London: Hodder and Stoughton, 1928), pp. 122 and 254.
53. Studdert Kennedy, *Democracy and the Dog Collar*, pp. 59–60.
54. G. A. Studdert Kennedy, 'Moses versus Marx', *Torch* (August 1926), pp. 113–15.
55. G. A. Studdert Kennedy, *The Wicket Gate or Plain Bread* (London: Hodder and Stoughton, 1923), p. 125.
56. G. A. Studdert Kennedy, *The Law and the Gospel*, Crusade Leaflets No. 27 (London: Central Committee for Church Crusades, n.d.), p. 3.
57. G. A. Studdert Kennedy, *Lies!* (London: Hodder and Stoughton, 1919), p. 35.
58. G. A. Studdert Kennedy, 'Thank God for the Nobodies!', *Torch* (September 1927), p. 111.
59. Studdert Kennedy, *Democracy and the Dog Collar*, p. 106.
60. Studdert Kennedy, *Democracy and the Dog Collar*, p. 43.
61. Studdert Kennedy, *Lies!*, p. 50.
62. Studdert Kennedy, *Rough Talks*, p. 85.
63. Studdert Kennedy, *Democracy and the Dog Collar*, p. 7.
64. 'Church and Labour. Clerical Memorial to the Labour Party', *Church Times*, 16 March 1923, p. 297.
65. Studdert Kennedy, *Rough Talks*, p. 87.
66. Studdert-Kennedy, *Dog-Collar Democracy*, p. 96.
67. Studdert Kennedy, *The Wicket Gate*, pp. 209–11.
68. G. A. Studdert Kennedy, *The Word and the Work* (London: Longmans, Green, and Co., 1925), pp. 4–6.
69. G. A. Studdert-Kennedy, 'Salvation', in Francis Underhill and Charles Scott Gillett (eds), *Report of the Anglo-Catholic Congress* (London: The Society of Saints Peter and Paul, 1923), pp. 143–50 (here pp. 148–9). Parker does not discuss this source. Her excellent biography is much more focused on Studdert Kennedy's contributions to the peace movement in the 1920s: Parker, *A Seeker after Truths*.
70. Studdert Kennedy, *The Warrior*, p. 228.
71. Purcell, *Woodbine Willie*, p. 156.

72. Parker, *A Seeker after Truths*, p. 97.
73. Grundy, *A Fiery Glow in the Darkness*, p. 70.
74. Will Reason (ed.), *The Proceedings of C.O.P.E.C.* (London: Longmans, Green, and Co., 1924), p. 115.
75. Kenneth Ingram, *Basil Jellicoe* (London: Centenary Press, 1936), pp. 16 and 142.
76. Mozley, 'Home Life and Early Years', p. 88.
77. William Temple, 'The Man and His Message', in Mozley, *G. A. Studdert Kennedy by His Friends*, p. 206.
78. Studdert-Kennedy, *Dog-Collar Democracy*, p. 132; See also, Chris Bryant, *Possible Dreams: A Personal History of British Christian Socialists* (London: Hodder and Stoughton, 1996), p. 178.
79. Mark R. Dorsett, '"National Mission"? Geoffrey Studdert Kennedy, Edward Lee Hicks, R. H. Tawney, and the Social Witness of the Church of England', in Brierley and Byrne, *Life after Tragedy*, pp. 116–35.
80. G. A. Studdert Kennedy, 'Master Speak to My Brother', *Torch* (March 1926), pp. 33–5.
81. Studdert Kennedy, *Rough Talks*, p. 161.
82. Oliver, *The Church and Social Order*, pp. 123–4.
83. Studdert Kennedy, *Democracy and the Dog Collar*, p. 125.
84. Studdert-Kennedy, 'Salvation', p. 146.
85. Studdert Kennedy, *Rough Talks*, p. 143.
86. G. A. Studdert Kennedy, *Food for the Fed-Up* (London: Hodder and Stoughton, 1921).

CHAPTER THIRTEEN

Billy Graham, the All Scotland Crusade of 1955 and the Social Gospel

Kenneth S. Jeffrey

Billy Graham was the most popular and successful global Christian evangelist in the twentieth century. He led the All Scotland Crusade, a six-week evangelistic mission held at the Kelvin Hall in Glasgow, from 21 March to Saturday, 30 April 1955. It is estimated that 1.2 million people attended events organised by the Crusade and that 26,457 of them accepted Graham's invitation to be 'born again'. The aim of this chapter is to examine the constituent elements of Graham's sermons and critically explore the extent to which they discussed the social gospel. The primary sources that have been used include the evangelist's twenty-four sermons from the crusade, the Church of Scotland magazine *Life and Work*, minutes from the General Assembly of the Church of Scotland and several Scottish newspapers.[1] Secondary interlocutors include a range of Graham scholars and others who have written on this subject. Following a brief definition and history of the social gospel movement, this chapter will cover five themes. It will begin by reviewing the immediate historical context of Graham's visit to Scotland before going on to critically examine three essential elements of his gospel. The third section will consider the criticism the evangelist attracted from those who judged he did not preach a prophetic social gospel. Fourthly, an analysis of Graham's references towards social issues in his All Scotland Crusade sermons, and the support he received from Tom Allan, will be presented. Finally, a thesis will be offered that seeks to defend and explain Graham's approach towards the social gospel during the All Scotland Crusade in 1955 and his later ministry.

The social gospel movement, which appeared in America and Britain towards the end of the nineteenth century, had, according to Stanley, 'deep roots in evangelical tradition' that are found in the First Great Awakening and in 'the social witness of Charles Finney and Frances Willard in the nineteenth century'.[2] However, some scholars have suggested the particular origin of the social gospel is found during the Progressive Era of the late nineteenth and early twentieth centuries.[3] One of the most frequently cited definitions of the social gospel was composed in 1921 by Shailer Mathews, professor of New Testament interpretation at the University of Chicago Divinity School. He described this movement as 'the application of the teaching of Jesus and the total message of the Christian salvation to society, the economic life, and social institutions such as the state, the family, as well as to individuals'.[4] According to Mathews, the good news of the gospel offered redemption to individuals and to society, including its economic structures and civic institutions. During the first half of the twentieth century, as a result of the rising influence of fundamentalism upon Evangelicalism, the social gospel became associated with 'a doctrinally effete liberalism'.[5] Consequently, a 'damaging split [arose] between an understanding of mission as saving souls and a view of mission as social action'.[6] Nevertheless, after the Second World War, a series of articles and monographs appeared that sought to reclaim the social gospel for Evangelicals. Among them, Carl Henry regretted, in 1947, how 'evangelical Christianity has become increasingly inarticulate about the social reference of the Gospel'.[7] He went on to contend,

> No evangelicalism which ignores the totality of man's condition dares respond in the name of Christianity . . . [rather] evangelicalism must be armed to declare the implications of its proposed religious solution for the politico-economic and sociological context for modern life.'[8]

There was a growing recognition among post-war neo-Evangelicals, which Evans suggests included Graham, that the gospel had significant social implications that had to be rediscovered.[9] Interestingly, David King has acknowledged that while Graham embraced Henry's ideal, the evangelist's 'hope for larger social change rested in changing the hearts of individuals'.[10] The extent to which the evangelist from North Carolina embraced this vision of a gospel with a clear social conscience during the All Scotland Crusade in 1955 will be the subject of this chapter.

I

After the 1929 Union of the Church of Scotland and the United Free Church of Scotland, John White enthused the Kirk with Chalmers's old nineteenth-century vision of a godly commonwealth built upon strong parish ministries.[11] However, by the 1940s, this was replaced by a less conservative, more modern vision of mission that began to address the reality of the economic, social and political issues that affected people's daily working lives.[12] The 'Church, Community and State' ecumenical conference held in Oxford in 1937, which summoned the church to 'a more active role of the Churches in the struggle for social and economic justice', had a deep influence in Scotland.[13] This effect was perhaps most obviously revealed in the General Assembly's Commission for the Interpretation of God's Will in the Present Crisis, or the Baillie Commission as it became better known, that ran from 1940 to 1945. In a stinging criticism of the Church of Scotland, one report from the Commission railed, 'There can be no doubt that it is to the failure of Christians to realise and act upon these social implications of the Gospel that the present weakness of the spiritual life of our land must in no small part be attributed.'[14] The Kirk acknowledged how its unwillingness to embrace the social gospel helped explain the relative poverty of Scotland's spiritual life. Will Storrar has commented, 'the Baillie Commission saved the Church of Scotland from itself and for the Gospel'.[15] It provided the church with an opportunity to set itself free from an old, outdated approach to mission and to embrace a new method and mode of outreach that was contextualised for post-war Scotland. The Church of Scotland's *Into All the World* report, published in 1946, at the end of the Baillie Commission, recognised the significance of the moment and how circumstances had given the church an occasion to review its missiology in the light of the social changes that followed the Second World War. It realised how older methods of evangelism, including large crusades, had become outmoded, and that while 'the eternal gospel remains itself unchanged . . . it requires to be proclaimed in a new idiom, and presented in new ways and in fresh channels'.[16] In order to fulfil its vocation, the church needed to find more modern means of proclaiming the gospel that were socially relevant to the lived experiences of Scottish people.

This desire to find a new approach to mission in Scotland in the postwar years found expression in the Tell Scotland Movement that was led from 1953 to 1955 by Tom Allan. This ecumenical movement was supported by a coalition of Scotland's main churches including the Scottish Presbyterian, Episcopal, Baptist, Congregational and Methodist denominations. It sought to rediscover the apostolate of the laity, to empower ordinary people to become Christian witnesses and envision local churches to engage in local mission in order to evangelise Scotland.[17] *Life and Work* articles provide an insight into the kind of mission the movement sought to encourage among congregations. They betray an anxiety that the Kirk had become 'out of touch' with society and that a radical overhaul of local church life and work was long overdue to reach people beyond the walls of faith communities. A new pattern for congregational life and parish service was required to fulfil Allan's vision that the distance between the church and the everyday struggles of ordinary people be significantly reduced.[18] Meetings in people's homes, rather than in church buildings, and new types of parish evangelistic visitations were among the plans that were discussed and implemented.[19] In the meantime, congregational bible study groups and prayer meetings were established and local conferences were organised to generate interest in the movement.[20] New parish surveys were conducted to find out more about people living in local areas.[21] Training Schools were hosted to enthuse and educate local people.[22] In one piece, published in March 1954, an author said, 'We are expected by the Lord to be concerned about the people in physical need in our district.'[23] There was a broad recognition, demonstrated in the Tell Scotland movement, that mission in Scotland in the second half of the twentieth century would need to extend beyond public proclamations of the gospel at large crusades and would require congregations to become more actively engaged in local, social evangelism and outreach.

Accordingly, there was some disquiet expressed towards the visit of Billy Graham to lead the All Scotland Crusade in some of the national newspapers. There were concerns about the old-fashioned emphasis the evangelist placed upon personal salvation in his sermons. In an article entitled 'Conflicting views on Dr Billy Graham Visit' that appeared in the *Glasgow Herald* before the evangelist arrived in Scotland, a reporter wrote, 'it is objected that his evangelistic message is too limited, too narrow, too individualistic; that he has nothing to say about Christ as the Lord of history or about social and political issues'.[24] They continued to comment,

> In particular, the fear has been expressed that the mission of the Tell Scotland Movement which has been seeking to bring the Gospel to bear upon all the aspects of human life in modern society would be eclipsed by the Kelvin Hall campaign with its emphasis on personal decision and personal salvation.[25]

Concern was expressed that Graham's gospel and style of evangelism, with its explicit stress upon individual conversions, could replace the more holistic gospel that lay at the heart of the Tell Scotland Movement and articulated a greater interest in the social issues that were part of a modern society. Later, during the Crusade, the *Evening Times* featured an article by R. Iain Hutcheson on 15 April. He asked whether Graham's sermons held any relevance to the real issues that occupied the daily lived experiences of Glaswegians. 'People today are outwith the church', he explained, 'because they cannot see the relevance of the Gospel to the problems and difficulties they have to face day by day. They are not impressed', he continued, 'when kirk folk talk vaguely about Jesus Christ being the answer to all their problems. [Rather] They want to see Christians putting their beliefs into action, giving expression to their alleged concern for their neighbours.'[26] Implicit in these comments was the criticism that Graham's 'Jesus is the answer to your problems' gospel was too naïve and simple. The reputation of the evangelist's unwillingness to address wider, societal issues in his sermons, and his determination to preach entirely about individual salvation created a palpable atmosphere of apprehension in the press towards Graham's visit to Scotland.

Given this broad historical and religious context in Scotland, it is perhaps surprising that an invitation was extended from the Tell Scotland Movement to the Southern Baptist American evangelist to come and lead a crusade in Glasgow in 1955. It was, indeed, a highly contentious request. The motion, presented to the General Assembly of the Church of Scotland by the evangelical minister, Rev. James Philip from the Synod of Aberdeen, to extend an invitation to Graham faced two counter motions, the first of which was accepted and the second of which lost, before the Kirk was finally pleased to receive the deliverance, despite an impassioned appeal by George

Macleod.[27] The acceptance of the invitation, however, was reported in *Life and Work* in October 1954 in an article that said, 'He [Graham] felt that he could wholeheartedly participate in it [the Tell Scotland Movement], making his own contribution as an "awakener" and hastener of the essential Gospel message in the lives of the people.'[28] However, no particular details were provided that explained how this mass evangelism campaign would augment the local church mission initiatives or lay evangelism that had lain at the heart of the Tell Scotland Movement. In addition, *Life and Work* ran another article, in November 1954, that described quite forthrightly the differences in theology and doctrine that separated the American evangelist from the Church of Scotland. The piece simply said, 'We can't ignore our differences. We can't gloss over them.'[29] Rev. Prof. J. Pitt-Watson, who had been the moderator of the General Assembly of the Church of Scotland in 1953, confessed a 'sincere and conscientious division of opinion' remained within the Kirk over the invitation that had been extended to the evangelist from North Carolina.[30] More recently, Will Storrar has suggested the decision to invite the American to lead the All Scotland Crusade divided the supporters of the Tell Scotland Movement completely.[31] The proposal to bring Billy Graham to Glasgow in 1955 was fraught by disagreements.

II

There were three main constituent elements in the gospel Graham proclaimed in the Kelvin Hall: trouble; grace; and the altar call. In the first instance, he invariably spoke about sin, in people's lives and in the world, in order to create spiritual concern in the hearts and minds of his audience, and to reveal their need of a Saviour. The evangelist, in every sermon, spoke at length about personal sin and problems. During the first sermon of the All Scotland Crusade, on 22 March, he announced 'the Bible teaches that every one of us here tonight is sick' and told everyone they had a soul disease called sin.[32] Less than a week later, on 28 March, he told his audience, 'The Bible says that all of us are sinners. You're a sinner, I am a sinner. We were all born in sin, we're sinners by choice, we're sinners by practice.'[33] Sin, he continued, was breaking the Ten Commandments and was the fundamental cause of all the problems in people's lives, including domestic disputes, frustrations, evil desires and evil habits.[34] He went on to list various sins such as lying, gossiping, backbiting, anger, envy, greed, lust, and the greatest of all sins, pride.[35] The evangelist continued to explain that God hates sin, and that it makes him shudder with horror.[36] On the second evening of the Crusade, Graham addressed people's problems in their homes and at their places of work. He spoke about their lack of happiness, peace, security, joy and assurance.[37] He challenged them about their unfulfilled 'inmost longings and desires'.[38] He went on to explain how their difficulties and problems arose from their spiritual blindness.[39] Graham also empathised with people's tiredness, their frustrations and their boredom with the monotonies of life.[40] In all his sermons, Graham painted a bleak picture of the human lot. All people, he suggested, were sinners who were broken, lost and unhappy. Their lives were beset with difficulties and problems. There was no satisfaction, no joy or peace or assurance in the world.[41] The evangelist's message was in stark contrast to how Prime Minister Macmillan described life for Britons two years later in Bedford when he famously said, 'Let us be frank about it: most of our people have never had it so good.'[42] Billy Graham insisted upon the contrary, that life for everyone in Scotland was doom and gloom, and the reason for this was sin.

When Graham spoke about sin in the world, he employed the threat of international crisis to generate spiritual anxiety and persuade people to be converted.[43] It was the repeated practice of the evangelist to describe the dangers and perils that arose from critical situations on the world stage to create apprehension and uncertainty. Grant Wacker has observed how he 'invariably rehearsed a laundry list of statistics and anecdotes about the dire state of the world'.[44] Similarly, Thomas Long has commented how he began his sermons with 'a presentation of the present moment as one of extraordinary crisis'.[45] Meanwhile, Heather Murray Elkins has said, 'Graham intentionally created for his audiences a sense of being in real danger'.[46] He spoke about the Formosa situation during the Kelvin Hall meeting on 13 April and the response that America had made to the threatened invasion of Taiwan by China. He asked his audience, 'Does God matter when we find men on both sides of the Atlantic holding hydrogen bombs in their hands and waving those bombs over the world? Is God interested?'[47] The evangelist sought to excite unease by warning people of the risk of a third World War. Repeatedly and throughout the Scotland campaign, Graham described the trouble in the world represented by the risk of nuclear warfare and used this threat to arouse spiritual anxiety and create the desire for a new and a better life that he said was available to those who would be 'born again'.[48]

The second essential feature of Graham's gospel, presented in response to the sin found in people's lives and across the world, was the grace and love of God manifest in the life, death and resurrection of Jesus Christ. This grace, the evangelist declared, had the power to forgive those who repented of their sins, give them a new and a better life and transform the world. He inquired of his audience on the first night of the Crusade,

> Do you want to be whole? Do you want to be forgiven tonight, do you want to know that you are going to heaven, do you want to know that your past has been forgiven, do you want your life transformed tonight, do you want the joy and the thrill and the happiness that come in living for Christ . . . do you really want that kind of life?[49]

The repeated use of the pronouns 'you' and 'your', used ten times in this sixty-seven word statement, betray the emphasis Graham placed on the individual and how he presented the gospel primarily as a means of personal positive transformation and fulfilment. Following the example of Jonathan Edwards, Graham sought to awaken the affections of people and stimulate their desire for wholeness, forgiveness, eternal life, joy and happiness.[50] Graham proclaimed that giving their lives to Jesus would transform their worlds. 'He'll [Jesus] make it a thrill to wash dishes and scrub floors. He'll make factory work the greatest joy of your life. He'll change the whole business radically in your life', the evangelist promised.[51] Conversion, according to Graham, was the only way to a better, new, individual life. Jesus, he promised, would transform their lives and make them whole.

Jesus Christ, according to the evangelist, also provided hope for a world threatened by nuclear warfare. As the agent of creation and the sovereign Lord, the Son of God held all things together in the world and prevented the universe from being blown into a thousand pieces.[52] During his sermon at the Kelvin Hall on 25 March, he said,

> Did you know that this world would blow apart were it not for the cohesive power of Christ? And I am also convinced that when wicked and evil men seek to destroy civilisation by the horrible bombs they've built, the cohesive and restraining power of Christ will restrain them, so that we will not be destroyed as a human race ... It's a comforting thing to go to bed at night and to know that all these atoms that the scientists are splitting are held together by the Christ of this Bible.[53]

Jesus Christ, Graham believed, would protect the world from atomic bombs. He, the evangelist contended, was the only one who had the power to control the 'evil men' and their 'horrible bombs'. For the evangelist, only Jesus could prevent nuclear war and preserve world peace. He alone could provide personal assurance and global security.

The singular way to receive this peace and hope for individuals and the world, according to Graham, was by accepting his altar call invitation at the end of his sermon and being converted. This was the third element of Graham's gospel presentation. Night after night, the evangelist extended an appeal to his audience to stand up from their seats and walk quietly and reverently to the front of the platform from which he preached in the Kelvin Hall.[54] In so doing, Graham told the people they were making a life-changing decision. He invited them to say,

> I will follow, I will trust Him, [Jesus Christ] I want Him to touch my life. I want Him to forgive my sins, I commit myself to Him, I surrender my will to Him as Lord and Master and Saviour. And, from this moment on, I am going to serve Him and follow Him.[55]

A noticeable feature of this prayer are the seven statements that begin with the pronoun 'I'. This indicates the significance Graham attached to human agency in conversion. It was their decision and their choice to become a Christian. In a biting criticism, Uta Balbier has commented how, for Graham, 'Salvation was an individual transaction in which God was the producer, Graham was his salesman, and each audience member was a consumer.'[56] A further important aspect of the prayer is the seven references to 'Him', that is Jesus Christ, the object of each statement. Entering into a vital, living relationship with Jesus lay at the heart of the conversion experience Graham invited people to accept. They were asked to follow and trust him, and to surrender their will to him, to serve and follow him. It is noteworthy that the evangelist presented conversion in his altar call as an exclusive relationship between an individual and Jesus. Indeed, it is fascinating how Graham suggested, on occasions, that world peace rested upon the personal decision he asked men and women to make, to choose Jesus.[57] The manner of Graham's altar call, the third and final element of his crusade sermons, confirms how the gospel, according to the evangelist, was concerned fundamentally with personal salvation.

It is not inconsequential to note that seventeen of the twenty-four surviving sermons from the All Scotland Crusade were based on Bible passages that were concerned with encounters of individuals with Jesus. Each evening during the All Scotland Crusade, Graham preached to an audience of around 15,000 in the Kelvin Hall. At the last significant meeting of the campaign held at Hampden he addressed a crowd of 100,000. However, his sermons were always aimed at individuals. He was a 'one soul at a time' evangelist who preached tirelessly about people's personal need of salvation.[58] The conversion of individuals, Graham believed, lay at the heart of the economy of God's grace for the redemption of the world.

III

Graham's gospel was the focus of criticism before he arrived in Scotland.[59] American theologians, Paul Tillich and Reinhold Niebuhr, were among his harshest detractors across the Atlantic. Tillich judged his methods as 'primitive and superstitious', while Niebuhr castigated the evangelist's 'simplistic gospel and its shortcomings on social and moral responsibility'.[60] In Germany, where Graham led a crusade in Berlin in 1954, concern was expressed about the spotlight the evangelist shone on personal conversion, not to mention his theological simplicity.[61] The German Protestant theologian and rector of the University of Hamburg, Helmut Thielicke, further attacked Graham on account of his 'individual-centred doctrine of salvation'.[62] Others were concerned that the American offered an effortless path to salvation.[63] Meanwhile, Graham divided opinion and created conflict among the Methodists in Britain when he led the Harringay Crusade in London in 1954.[64] Both the secretary of the Methodist Youth Department, Rev. Bryan H. Reed, and the president of the Methodist Conference, Dr Donald Soper, found fault in 'Graham's fundamentalist approach and in particular his pronounced literalism', not to mention his 'rather outer-worldly gospel of personal salvation', which they believed belonged in the seventeenth century, and not in the twentieth century.[65] They were concerned that the evangelist's campaign would encourage an increase in the number of traditional, fundamentalist churches.[66] Graham divided opinion sharply in churches. His theology and practice of evangelism attracted significant criticism in Britain and Europe before he arrived at St Enoch's railway station in Glasgow on Saturday, 19 March 1955.

It was the evangelist's silence on social gospel issues that attracted the greatest criticism in Scotland, and not least from one of his chief antagonists George Macleod, leader of the Iona Community. Macleod and Tom Allan, leader of the Tell Scotland Movement, disagreed bitterly and fundamentally over Graham's visit to Scotland. Macleod's opposition to the evangelist was both theological and practical. He did not believe in mass evangelism or in professional evangelists, and argued that the American's crusade would distract the churches in Scotland from the work of the Tell Scotland Movement that was seeking to mobilise the laity and encourage local churches to engage in parish mission. He did not agree with Graham's use of altar calls and expected that many of the crusade's converts would become lapsed.[67] In addition, Macleod clashed over the evangelist's apparent obsession with an individual's relationship with Christ and his unwillingness to discuss the economic, political and social implications of the gospel.[68] The leader of the Iona Community believed in a Jesus Christ whose interest in the world reached beyond the individual soul. Macleod understood that Christian faith extended further than personal relationships with a Saviour, and it addressed issues such as nuclear warfare, poverty and racial discrimination to name but three. He also considered the local church to be the agent of change God would use to transform the world.[69] He summarised his opposition to the visit of Graham in the *British Weekly* in May 1954, when he said, 'If Billy Graham comes, I believe there will be a harvest of a sort and I am sure it will feel like summer for a while. What I am afraid of is that when the harvest is passed, and the summer is over we will still not be saved.'[70] Macleod's hostility towards Graham centred upon the different emphases each placed upon particular aspects of the gospel. The American evangelist believed that personal salvation sat at the heart of the good news, while the Scottish churchman maintained that God's purposes of redemption reached far and beyond the individual soul and extended to embrace wider social issues.[71]

Another outspoken critic of Graham was the deputy leader of the Iona community, Rev. T. Ralph Morton. Four years before the All Scotland Crusade, Morton's *The Household of Faith* was published in 1951. In this book, he sought to reflect upon the changing pattern of the church's life in Scotland in the post-war era, and examined the Iona community experiment.[72] Morton's purpose was to answer the question, 'How should Christians be trying to live in the world today?' In his response to this inquiry, he presented a holistic vision of Christian discipleship that was lived out in the realms of work and politics. As followers of Christ, Morton wanted believers to accept their calling to be salt and light in the world. He was also responsible for the booklet *Ecumenical Studies: Evangelism in Scotland* that was published by the Secretariat for Evangelism of the World Council of Churches in Geneva in 1954. This pamphlet examined the history of Scottish evangelism after the Second World War, and was reviewed in *Life and Work* in June 1955. In it, Morton sought to discover the attitudes of people outwith the church, including industrial workers, towards the Christian faith, to assess the effectiveness of traditional forms of evangelism and assess new experiments in evangelism.[73] He discovered there was a slight rise in the interest of people in religious matters, but that the efficacy of traditional forms of evangelism, such as large crusades, were considered to be weak. He advocated, therefore, a new understanding of lay-led, local church-based mission. Tellingly, in the conclusion of the pamphlet, Morton wrote,

> The problem of evangelism in Scotland is not the Gospel . . . [it] is that the mass of the people do not see any particular attraction in the life of the Church. They see in it a way of life that is respectable and worthy but irrelevant to their problems and their interests. Men dismiss the Church, but not Jesus. And in their failure to be allowed to see the body living out the love of Christ they are left with a sentimental picture of Jesus and a view of the world that has banished God.[74]

Morton espoused a gospel that was relevant to the problems and interests of ordinary Scottish working people. He advocated a gospel that addressed social issues directly.

Meanwhile, and perhaps most tellingly, in his conclusion to the pamphlet he wrote, 'the only effective way of getting in touch with men outside the Church has been the work of Church members themselves and not the work of professional evangelists'.[75] Hence, he called upon Christians across Scotland to receive their calling and vocation, however terrifying in its demands it would be, to become disciples of Jesus and evangelists.[76] Morton, on behalf of the Iona Community and others, presented an approach to evangelism that was diametrically opposed to that offered by the Billy Graham Evangelistic Association. The Scotsman believed old fashioned revivalist-styled, mass evangelism did not reach the unchurched and instead supported personal evangelism and local, parish missions.

Criticism of Graham, his theology and his methods, extended beyond Macleod and Morton and included several other Scottish voices too. Frank Bardgett has mentioned the opposition of Rev. James Currie, minister of Glasgow Pollok, who was a vocal critic of mass evangelism and the risk it carried of producing mass religious hysteria.[77] *Life and Work*, the Church of Scotland magazine, was largely supportive of Graham's visit and the All Scotland Crusade. Nevertheless, it published a letter in June 1955 from a self-confessed, left-wing Labour politician who asked,

> Doesn't he [Graham] know, I said to myself, that there must be spiritual warfare against the citadels of sin in human society ... as well as against the sin in the individual heart? Slaves were freed when Wilberforce attacked the institution of slavery – not when a sufficient number of slaveowners were converted and moved to give up their slaves. The great liberating movements of reform have come from the direct attack on social evils in the name of Jesus Christ as well as from the preaching of the Gospel of individual repentance.[78]

This local leader judged that Graham's obsession with personal salvation left him blind to the conversion that was also required of citadels and institutions of sin in society.

Furthermore, in response to the suggestion that *Life and Work* had been biased in favour of Graham and failed to reflect the sincerely critical attitude felt by many in Scotland towards the Crusade, two further letters appeared in the July 1955 edition of the magazine. The first author wrote,

> I would not wish to deny that there were some of the signs of the Spirit in the Crusade ... There is a real danger that this tremendous emphasis on individual salvation may blind many to the terrible dilemmas of living together as a Christian fellowship in a society which gives only limited recognition to the Christian Gospel in the ordering of its affairs.[79]

In the second letter, it was remarked,

> Some of us may have been sincerely afraid of the return of the kind of evangelicalism which seems to take no account of the way human sin entrenches and perpetuates itself in the structure of society ... [Graham appeared] to belittle the frontal attack on institutionalized sin.[80]

The common theme of these criticisms expressed against Graham in *Life and Work*, after the All Scotland Crusade had ended, is that he ignored institutional sin. He was so completely preoccupied by the conversion of individual souls that he disregarded the gospel's message towards social evils and injustices. This was the most significant charge opponents made against the American evangelist.

IV

There were, nonetheless, several rare occasions during the All Scotland Crusade when Graham addressed social issues in his sermons. On one occasion, he spoke about alcoholism and narcotic addiction, but only as it affected individual men and women.[81] Another time, he discussed 'domestic problems and immoral problems', but again only in so far as they affected individual people.[82] He mentioned racial prejudice briefly in one sermon, but only to make the point that Jesus was not bigoted.[83] Graham also spoke about poverty fleetingly, but only as it made buying clothes for children difficult for some people.[84] Nevertheless, and in response to a book written by a London journalist, J. F. Whaley, *Does God Matter?*, Graham asked his audience on 13 April, 'Is God relevant in the problems you face in the world, in the problems you face in your home, the problems you face in your factory, the problems you face in your own personal life?'[85] He went on,

> Is God interested in our social problems, the poverty, the illiteracy, the underfed . . . when one half of the world will go to bed hungry tonight? Is God interested? Is God interested in our racial problems? Is God interested in these things? There are racial problems in many parts of the world. Is God interested in our domestic problems?[86]

Graham presented these questions in an attempt to demonstrate the relevance of the gospel to the lived experiences of his audience, but it is noteworthy that this rhetoric was found in only one of his twenty-four sermons during the fourth week of the crusade. It was not a recurring theme in his preaching. Nevertheless, on the same evening, he continued to ask,

> Does God matter in our moral problems? . . . We have received more letters in the city of Glasgow on moral problems than any city I've ever been in. I am not saying that the moral problems are greater here than in other places; I am just saying that it is a very interesting fact that we're receiving scores of letters every day concerning moral problems, which indicate to me that the people of Glasgow are concerned about immorality in this city. That may be your problem.[87]

The evangelist was careful not to cause undue offence to his Glasgow audience. Nonetheless he raised the matter of 'moral problems' that had begun to affect modern societies as television shows disturbed domestic meal-times and celebrities supplanted family as significant influences on a younger generation.[88] Yet, in response to his 'Is God interested? Does God matter?' questions, the evangelist merely said, 'If you're ready to yield yourself to Jesus Christ, Jesus Christ can come into your heart and cleanse you of the past and give you victory in the future. If you're ready to pay the price of repentance and faith in Him.'[89] The evangelist's simple antidote to social, racial and moral problems was individual conversion and personal salvation. Graham believed this was how God wanted to transform lives and change the world.

During the last week of the crusade, Graham spoke about the social gospel directly on two occasions. In a sermon on 21 April, based on the Good Samaritan, Graham presented the question, 'Who is my neighbour?' and then answered, 'your neighbour is any man that has need.'[90] Then he went on to say,

We've heard a great deal about the social gospel. There is no such thing in Scripture as the social gospel. The Gospel is the Good News that Christ died for sinners, according to the Scriptures. But the Gospel does produce social results, and the Gospel does have social implications. And no man can be a Christian and not be conscious of the need of his fellow man . . . No person can be a Christian and not have compassion for those that are less fortunate and those that are in hospital. And pure religion and undefiled says something about caring for the widows, the orphans, and all of those in life that do not have the things that we have. The needs of India, the needs of Korea, the needs of the poverty-stricken areas of the world should ever be upon our souls. And we should do something about it, not just weep over it and talk about it and pray about it, but do something. Our faith means action, faith produces works. That's our responsibility, our neighbours as ourselves.[91]

Graham was unequivocal. He said there was no social gospel in the Bible. On the contrary, the gospel was solely concerned with the forgiveness of personal sin. Nevertheless, he was equally explicit when he spoke about the social implications of the gospel that included the active, compassionate care of Christians for the needs of others, including those who were hungry, poor and sick, at home and overseas. There were real consequences to becoming a Christian. One result, the evangelist remarked, was a new social conscience that would manifest itself in people's lives in practical acts of Christian service.

On one further, final occasion, on 23 April, Graham spoke again about the social gospel. In a sermon about Paul and Felix, Graham discussed repentance and giving up sins and surrendering one's will to Christ. He said,

You've got to surrender your will to Christ and then go back to your shop and live Christ; and go back to your factory and live Christ. The Bible doesn't have anything to say about a social gospel, but the Bible has plenty to say about the social results of the Gospel, and the social implications of the Gospel. And the Gospel, once received, is to go out and apply them in our daily lives . . . we are to love our neighbour as ourselves, we are to have compassion on the unfortunate round about us.[92]

Graham was again unambiguous. The Bible, he stated, had nothing to say about a social gospel. It simply did not, according to the evangelist, appear in the scriptures. However, he went on to describe the gospel consequences that followed conversion. There were, he said, social implications and results of believing in Jesus Christ. They included a new way of seeing the world and a new way of living within it. Surrendering one's life to Christ would result in a new life that involved loving neighbours and demonstrating compassion towards the unfortunate. We may speculate why Graham waited until the sixth and final week of the crusade before he directly addressed the matter of the social gospel. It is decidedly possible that he was responding directly to criticism he had received about how his sermons had ignored the broader consequences of being converted. Therefore, he took this opportunity, before he left Scotland, to explain and defend his position. He did not believe in a social gospel. He did not recognise this was biblical. Nonetheless, he believed in the personal social implications of becoming a Christian that involved a new life of love and service towards others in need in the world.

It is not insignificant that Tom Allan, leader of the Tell Scotland Movement, defended Graham's theology and practice of evangelism. He acknowledged there were significant differences of opinion among Scottish church leaders and 'much confusion in our thinking about the *aim* of evangelism'.[93] However, Allan defined evangelism, using a statement attributed to Archbishop Temple, the Archbishop of Canterbury from 1942 to 1944, who said, 'To evangelise is so to present Christ Jesus by the power of the Holy Spirit, that men will come to out their trust in God through Him, to accept Him as their Saviour and Lord, and serve Him as King in the fellowship of the Church.'[94] He further commented this was the explicit aim and purpose of the All Scotland Crusade led by Graham, and emphasised 'that the Christian experience in its essence is a personal experience, involving an articulate relationship between a man and God'.[95] Allan accepted that some people judged this definition of evangelism to be 'too narrow and limited . . . too individualistic'.[96] They believed it was 'silent on political and social issues, on the responsibility of the Church in society'.[97] The leader of the Tell Scotland Movement and the American evangelist were happy to accept this charge upon the basis that a clear distinction was recognised between the twofold commission God had given the church. Allan said the church was called to evangelise and to bear witness, and went on to say,

> It is my own growing conviction that if we would define more carefully the words 'evangelism' and 'witness', we would go far towards resolving the tension which exists in the Church today between those whose whole emphasis is on what has become known as the 'social gospel', and those who, with equal unbalance, are exclusively concerned with individual conversion.[98]

Greater attention and care, according to Allan, was needed to recognise and respect the differences that separated the two distinct divine callings upon the church. Nevertheless, the Scottish church leader remained unequivocal. 'There is no such thing as a "social" gospel. There is only the Gospel', he said.[99] Moreover, the ability of the church to witness and speak a prophetic word to the pressing social needs of the world depended, he maintained, upon the success of its evangelism and the conversion of people into a vital, personal relationship with Christ.[100] Accordingly, Tom

Allan offered unambiguous support to Graham and his presentation of the gospel in Scotland.

V

It is necessary, therefore, that the distinction Graham made between evangelism and witness is recognised. It is essential the American evangelist's support of these separate ministries of the church is acknowledged. It is also fundamental that his personal sense of vocation, as an evangelist, is respected. Graham was part of the post-war evangelical generation who, according to Stanley, had not been 'generally distinguished by their commitment to issues of economic or social justice'.[101] However, in the late 1960s they began to repossess the social gospel that had been lost from their tradition for the best part of seventy years.[102] This renaissance blossomed at the International Congress on World Evangelisation held in Lausanne in 1974. It became apparent in Switzerland that the 'geographical and cultural identity of evangelicalism' was beginning to change significantly.[103] The dominant control over the movement, long held by America and Britain, was challenged by new voices, including Padilla, Escobar, Costas and Gatu, from other parts of the world, and consequently the evangelical gospel was remoulded.[104] Although Lausanne did not achieve a settled position on the aims, content and nature of this gospel, it was clear that social action was being reclaimed by a significant number within the tradition.[105] Storrar contends the Lausanne Covenant demonstrated a reunion between evangelism and social concern in evangelical missiology.[106] However, Stanley has noted a 'more guarded attitude (among some American evangelicals) towards the broadening of the evangelical concept of mission which the Covenant undoubtedly represented'.[107] Moreover, he observed how Graham's enthusiasm for the Lausanne movement dissipated after the subsequent Mexico City meeting in 1975.[108]

However, fourteen months after the Swiss Congress, Graham wrote an article for the evangelical magazine *Christianity Today* entitled 'Our Mandate from Lausanne '74'. He applauded three major achievements of the conference. It provided 'a new look at world need ... a new look at world opportunity ... [and] a new look at Christian responsibility.'[109] Graham went on to say, 'Christian leaders have a clearer, more balanced perspective on evangelism and social responsibility.'[110] He presented nine opportunities and challenges that confronted evangelicals, and two concepts that had arisen from the congress. The second concept, he said, invited delegates 'to get involved in all the things that God wants done in our generation ... [in order to] promote a variety of good ends in a thoroughly evangelical way'.[111] Graham said he did not oppose this, but he commented,

> I believe that the many good ends sought by proponents of Concept Two should be carried out, but by evangelical organisations dedicated

clearly to those ends. Perhaps this could be done by the World Evangelical Fellowship, or by a new organisation created especially for those general social-political-ecclesiastical ends – which we all agree need attention.[112]

He carried on, 'What I counsel, therefore, is that we stick strictly to evangelism and missions, while at the same time encouraging others to do the other specialised work that God has commissioned the Church to do.'[113] This is a significant statement because it betrays the fact that, despite Lausanne, Graham continued to make a clear distinction between evangelism and witness. He believed he had been called to be an evangelist, and invite people into a personal, salvific relationship with Christ, while others were called to separate social gospel ministries.

The gospel according to Billy Graham, that he presented during the All Scotland Crusade in 1955 and throughout his life, proclaimed men and women were sinners, that forgiveness and the promise of a new, transformed life would be given to individuals by Jesus Christ upon their response to his altar call and the basis of their personal conversion. It further made known there were social implications for those who became Christians. They were expected, as individuals, to care for, love and serve those around them in need. According to Graham's theology, God would change the world, as one person at a time was born again and became a follower of Jesus. The answer to every public problem, not to mention the means of social and political reform, was to be found, the evangelist believed, in the conversion of individual men and women.[114] Graham, therefore, did not embrace the social gospel. He did not believe in it. He did not recognise its existence in the Bible. Hence, he failed to address directly the problem of sin as it existed more broadly and existentially within society. He did not speak about the need for economic structures or political institutions or social organisations to repent and be converted. The North Carolina evangelist was more 'concerned about the souls of men . . . [than the] the social and economic conditions that scar the soul'.[115] He preached about individual salvation, but not the redemption of wider societies. At the beginning of this chapter, the social gospel was defined by Mathews as 'the application of the teaching of Jesus and the total message of the Christian salvation to society, the economic life, and social institutions such as the state, the family, as well as to individuals'.[116] Upon this basis, it is judged that Billy Graham did not make the social gospel explicitly known in the Kelvin Hall campaign.

The aim of this chapter was to examine the constituent elements of Graham's sermons from the All Scotland Crusade of 1955 and critically explore the extent to which the evangelist proclaimed the social gospel. It started with a brief definition of the social gospel and traced the history of this movement within Evangelicalism. Then, five themes were discussed.

Billy Graham and the Social Gospel

The immediate historical context that surrounded Graham's visit to Scotland in 1955 was explored. It revealed how a new vision of evangelism and mission emerged within the Kirk following the Second World War that was sympathetic towards the social gospel movement. It also noticed the deep disagreements within the Church of Scotland that surrounded the invitation that was extended to Graham to lead the All Scotland Crusade. Next, the three constituent elements of Graham's gospel were examined. They included his understanding of sin and salvation, and the life-changing decision he invited people to make when they accepted his altar call invitation. Then, the criticism Graham received from international scholars, Macleod, Morton and others, towards his 'individual-centred doctrine of salvation' was reviewed.[117] There was a critical analysis of Graham's sermons that revealed his interpretation of the Bible's attitude towards social issues. Finally, the argument was presented that Graham did not preach the social gospel during the All Scotland Crusade in 1955.

Notes

1. Permission was granted to use quotations from Billy Graham's All Scotland Crusade sermons by the Billy Graham Literary Foundation who provided access to these sermons. Used by permission. All rights reserved.
2. Brian Stanley, *The Global Diffusion of Evangelicalism: The Age of Billy Graham and John Stott* (Downers Grove, IL: InterVarsity Press, 2013), p. 151; Christopher H. Evans, *The Social Gospel in American Religion: A History* (New York: New York University Press, 2017), p. 200.
3. Evans, *Social Gospel*, p. 2.
4. Ibid., p. 2.
5. Stanley, *Global Diffusion of Evangelicalism*, p. 151.
6. William Storrar, 'A Tale of Two Paradigms: Mission in Scotland from 1946', in David Searle (ed.), *Death or Glory: The Church's Mission in Scotland's Changing Society* (Edinburgh: Rutherford House, 2001), p. 56.
7. Carl Henry, *The Uneasy Conscience of Modern Fundamentalism* (Grand Rapids, MI: Eerdmans, 2003), pp. 13–14.
8. Evans, *Social Gospel*, p. 206.
9. Ibid.
10. David P. King, 'Preaching Good News to the Poor: Billy Graham and Evangelical Humanitarianism', in Andrew Finstuen, Anne Blue Wills and Grant Wacker (eds), *Billy Graham: American Pilgrim* (Oxford: Oxford University Press, 2017), p. 122.
11. Stewart J. Brown, 'The Social Ideal of the Church of Scotland during the 1930s', in A. R. Morton (ed.), *God's Will in a Time of Crisis: A Colloquium Celebrating the 50th Anniversary of the Baillie Commission* (Edinburgh: CTPI, 1994), p. 14.
12. Ibid., p. 26.
13. Ibid.
14. A. C. Cheyne, *The Transforming of the Kirk: Victorian Scotland's Religious Revolution* (Edinburgh: Saint Andrew Press, 1983), p. 192.

15. William Storrar, 'Liberating the Kirk: The Enduring Legacy of the Baillie Commission', in Morton (ed.), *God's Will in a Time of Crisis*, p. 60.
16. Alexander Forsyth, *Mission by the People: Re-discovering the Dynamic Missiology of Tom Allan and His Scottish Contemporaries* (Eugene, OR: Pickwick, 2017), p. 85.
17. Ibid., p. 2.
18. Ibid., p. 103.
19. *Life and Work*, April 1954, p. 93.
20. Ibid.
21. Ibid., p. 94.
22. *Life and Work*, June 1954, p. 149.
23. *Life and Work*, March 1954, p. 60.
24. 'Conflicting views on Dr Billy Graham visit', *Glasgow Herald*, 18 February 1955.
25. Ibid.
26. 'Is Billy Graham the answer?', *Evening Times*, 15 April 1955.
27. *The Principal Acts of the General Assembly of the Church of Scotland 1954 with the Minutes of the Proceedings* (Edinburgh: Morrison and Gibb, 1954), p. 533.
28. *Life and Work*, October 1954, p. 272.
29. *Life and Work*, November 1954, p. 281.
30. *Life and Work*, April 1955, p. 84.
31. Storrar, 'A Tale of Two Paradigms', p. 62.
32. Billy Graham, 'The Pool at Bethsaida' (John 5: 1–9), 22 March 1955, Glasgow, Scotland Crusade, p. 5.
33. Graham, 'The Ten Commandments' (Exodus 20), 28 March 1955, Glasgow, Scotland Crusade, p. 3.
34. Graham, 'The Pool at Bethsaida' (John 5: 1–9), 22 March 1955, Glasgow, Scotland Crusade, p. 6.
35. Ibid., p. 7.
36. Ibid.
37. Graham, 'The Moral Problem' (John 7:37–8:11), 23 March 1955, Glasgow, Scotland Crusade, p. 1.
38. Graham, 'Untitled' (John 11), 24 March 1955, Glasgow, Scotland Crusade, p. 9.
39. Ibid., p. 11.
40. Graham, 'The Woman at the Well' (John 4), 25 March 1955, Glasgow, Scotland Crusade, 4; Graham, 'The Ninth Commandment' (Exodus 20:16), 31 March 1955, Glasgow, Scotland Crusade, p. 3; Graham, 'Reconciliation' (Matthew 5:24), 4 April 1955, Glasgow, Scotland Crusade, p. 6.
41. Graham, 'The Ninth Commandment' (Exodus 20:16), 31 March 1955, Glasgow, Scotland Crusade, p. 3.
42. https://www.phrases.org.uk/meanings/youve-never-had-it-so-good.html, accessed 11 January 2023.
43. K. S. Jeffrey, 'The Threat of Crisis in the Sermons of Billy Graham during the All Scotland Crusade in 1955', *Scottish Church History*, 51.1 (2022), pp. 53–69.
44. Grant Wacker, 'Billy Graham's America', *Church History*, 78.3 (2009), pp. 489–511, pp. 502–3.
45. Thomas G. Long, 'Preaching the Good News', in Michel G. Long (ed.),

The Legacy of Billy Graham: Critical Reflections on America's Greatest Evangelist (Louisville, KY: Westminster John Knox Press, 2008), p. 6.
46. Heather Murray Elkins, 'The Tangible Evangelism of Billy Graham', in Long (ed.), *The Legacy of Billy Graham*, p. 22.
47. Graham, 'Untitled' (Matthew 6:33), 13 April 1955, Glasgow, Scotland Crusade, p. 2.
48. Jeffrey, 'The Threat of Crisis'.
49. Graham, 'The Pool at Bethsaida' (John 5:1–9), 22 March 1955, Glasgow, Scotland Crusade, p. 11.
50. Michael S. Hamilton, 'From Desire to Decision: The Evangelistic Preaching of Billy Graham', in Finsteun, Wills and Wacker (eds), *Billy Graham: American Pilgrim*, p. 45.
51. Graham, 'Joshua' (Joshua 24:15–16), 12 April 1955, Glasgow, Scotland Crusade, p. 7.
52. Graham, 'The ten commandments' (Exodus 20), 28 March 1955, Glasgow, Scotland Crusade, p. 5.
53. Graham, 'The woman at the well' (John 4), 25 March 1955, Glasgow, Scotland Crusade, p. 3.
54. Graham, 'The Pool at Bethsaida' (John 5:1–9), 22 March 1955, Glasgow, Scotland Crusade, p. 13.
55. Ibid., p. 13.
56. Uta A. Balbier, *Altar Call in Europe: Billy Graham, Mass Evangelism and the Cold-War West* (Oxford: Oxford University Press, 2022), p. 60.
57. Graham, 'The Coming Storm' (Luke 8:22–29), 2 April 1955, Glasgow, Scotland Crusade, p. 3.
58. Grant Wacker, *One Soul at a Time: The Story of Billy Graham* (Grand Rapids, MI: Eerdmans, 2019).
59. Balbier, *Altar Call in Europe*, p. 36.
60. Ibid., p. 36.
61. Ibid., p. 35.
62. Ibid., p. 36.
63. Ibid., p. 36.
64. Ibid., p. 33.
65. Ibid., p. 33.
66. Ibid., p. 34.
67. Frank Bardgett, *Scotland's Evangelist: DP Thomson* (East Kilbride: Thomson Litho, 2010), pp. 308–9.
68. Ibid., p. 309.
69. Ibid., p. 309.
70. G. F. Macleod, 'A General Assembly diary', *British Weekly*, 27 May 1954.
71. Ronald Ferguson, *George Macleod: Founder of the Iona Community* (London: Collins, 1990), pp. 270–5.
72. T. Ralph Morton, *The Household of Faith: An Essay on the Changing Pattern of the Church's Life* (Glasgow: The Iona Community, 1951); *Scottish Journal of Theology*, 6.2 (June 1953), pp. 217–18.
73. *Life and Work*, June 1955, p. 151.
74. *Ecumenical Studies: Evangelism in Scotland* (Geneva, 1954), pp. 51f.
75. Ibid., p. 51.
76. Ibid., pp. 51f.

77. Bardgett, *Scotland's Evangelist*, p. 310.
78. *Life and Work*, June 1955, p. 141.
79. *Life and Work*, July 1955, p. 165.
80. Ibid., p. 165.
81. Graham, 'Untitled' (John 11), 24 March 1955, Glasgow, Scotland Crusade, p. 12.
82. Ibid., p. 13.
83. Graham, 'The Woman at the Well' (John 4), 25 March 1955, Glasgow, Scotland Crusade, p. 2.
84. Ibid., p. 4.
85. Graham, 'Untitled' (Matthew 6:33), 13 April 1955, Glasgow, Scotland Crusade, p. 3.
86. Ibid., p. 3.
87. Ibid., p. 3.
88. Jennifer Buckett, 'Values and morals in American society: The 1950s versus today', http://stevenjthompson.com/varioustopics/culturaldecline/values_morals_in_american_society_1950s_vs_today.html#:~:text=teachers%20of%20morals%20and%20values%20in%20the%201950s.,society%20in%20comparison%20to%20those%20of%20the%201950s, accessed 12 January 2023.
89. Graham, 'Untitled' (Matthew 6:33), 13 April 1955, Glasgow, Scotland Crusade, p. 4.
90. Graham, 'The Rich Young Ruler' (Luke 10:17–25), 21 April 1955, Glasgow, Scotland Crusade, p. 5.
91. Ibid., p. 6.
92. Graham, 'Gallio, Felix, Agrippa' (Acts 18:17; 24: 25; 26:27–28), 23 April 1955, Glasgow, Scotland Crusade, p. 8.
93. Tom Allan (ed.), *Crusade in Scotland: Billy Graham* (London: Pickering and Inglis, 1955), p. 110.
94. https://bibleportal.com/bible-quote/evangelism-to-evangelize-is-so-to-present-jesus-christ-in-the-power-of-the-holy-spirit-that-men-shall-come-to, accessed 19 April 2023.
95. Allan, *Crusade in Scotland*, p. 110.
96. Ibid., p. 110.
97. Ibid., p. 110.
98. Ibid., p. 111.
99. Ibid., p. 111.
100. Ibid., p. 111.
101. Stanley, *Global Diffusion of Evangelicalism*, p. 151.
102. David Moberg, *The Great Reversal: Evangelism versus Social Concern* (London: Scripture Union, 1972); Stanley, *Global Diffusion of Evangelicalism*, p. 154.
103. Stanley, *Global Diffusion of Evangelicalism*, p. 179.
104. Ibid., pp. 164–9.
105. Ibid., p. 179.
106. Storrar, 'A Tale of Two Paradigms', pp. 58–9.
107. Stanley, *Global Diffusion of Evangelicalism*, p. 174.
108. Ibid., p. 177.
109. Billy Graham, 'Our Mandate from Lausanne '74: An Address to the Lausanne

Continuation Committee', *Christianity Today*, 4 July 1976, https://www.christianitytoday.com/ct/1975/july-4/our-mandate-from-lausanne-74-address-to-lausanne.html, accessed 19 January 2023.
110. Ibid.
111. Ibid.
112. Ibid.
113. Ibid.
114. Curtis J. Evans, 'A Politics of Conversion: Billy Graham's Political and Social Vision', in Finstuen, Wills and Wacker (eds), *Billy Graham: American Pilgrim*, p. 147.
115. Evans, *Social Gospel*, p. 1.
116. Evans, *Social Gospel*, p. 2.
117. Balbier, *Altar Call in Europe*, p. 36.

CHAPTER FOURTEEN

Social Christianity on the Mission Field: Shifting Patterns in British and American Protestant Globalism in the Nineteenth and Twentieth Centuries

Brian Stanley

International Christian philanthropy underwent major changes in purpose and emphasis between the second half of the nineteenth century and the later decades of the twentieth. The transformation affected both Catholic and Protestant Christianity in Europe and North America, but this essay will necessarily be more limited in scope. The first section of the essay will analyse the strategies employed by nineteenth-century British Protestant missions to plant sustainable churches in African and Caribbean contexts marked by the legacy or continuing presence of slavery or slave-trading. The second section will concentrate on the later years of the century, paying particular attention to China and India, where crises of endemic famine reordered missionary priorities and (in India) created new patterns of response to Christianity. The third and final section will suggest how patterns of missionary humanitarianism changed shape in the course of the twentieth century. It will adopt a broader geographical scope, noting the dominant role that the United States came to play in global Christian philanthropy, and paying particular attention to the impact of war in both Europe and Asia.

During the nineteenth century, Christians typically conceived of their God-given duty to the non-Western world primarily through the lens of the commission of Christ to bring the gospel of salvation to all nations. Through a host of voluntary agencies they pursued an extraordinarily ambitious agenda that embraced the regeneration and 'development' of non-Western societies, through conversion to Christianity and the dissemination of the supposed benefits of Western civilisation. Yet, by the close of the twentieth century, most of the Western mission agencies that had dominated Christian globalism in 1900 – and probably did so as late as 1945 – were a shadow of their former selves: some had disappeared entirely; others had reinvented themselves as transnational agencies for inter-church cooperation and international development; relatively few continued to make evangelisation prominent in their publicity and fundraising. It is true that in the course of the twentieth century, new mission agencies, conservative in theology, sprang up to continue the task of world evangelism, but what is striking is that today even these evangelical mission agencies increasingly frame their appeal to their supporting constituencies by giving emphasis to the transformation that Christianity can help to effect in impoverished societies, and correspondingly less emphasis to bringing a lost humanity to eternal salvation.

Christianity, Commerce and Civilisation in Africa and the West Indies in the Nineteenth Century

It would be tempting to characterise the change in overseas Christian philanthropy observable from the nineteenth to the twentieth centuries as a shift from conversion to development. That formulation, however, is much too stark, for it masks the extent to which mission agencies in the nineteenth century were committed to the promotion of social and economic transformation overseas. However, that commitment was shaped by the overriding priority of religious conversion, and the goal of the process was only rarely described as 'development'. More frequently, nineteenth-century Christian theorists viewed the promotion of indigenous social and economic advancement as an integral constituent of the process of 'civilisation'. Civilisation was not necessarily about conforming non-Western cultures to a European image – although among less discerning missionaries there was, sadly, a good deal of that. The most perceptive missionary strategists, such as Henry Venn in Britain or Rufus Anderson in the United States, believed that missions should encourage the social and economic conditions in which indigenous churches could flourish and grow, support themselves financially and produce their own educated leadership. In Britain, some of the most important influences shaping these ideas were Scottish, and can be traced to the distinctive amalgam that Scottish Protestants achieved between Enlightenment philosophy and evangelical theology.

The best-known expression of this ideology is the assertion of David Livingstone in his address to a packed Senate House in Cambridge on 5 December 1857 that 'Those two pioneers of civilization – Christianity and commerce – should ever be inseparable.'[1] Contrary to what is often supposed, Livingstone did not invent the coupling of the three 'C's', though he certainly popularised it. Neither were his words primarily intended to bestow divine approval on European colonial intervention in Africa. Rather, Livingstone was applying to the Zambesi region an antislavery recipe developed two decades previously by Thomas Fowell Buxton with regard to the Niger Expedition, his scheme for the elimination of the slave trade from West Africa. In a pamphlet published in 1840 Buxton expounded his belief that the only way to rid West Africa of the slave trade was to utilise her own 'vast, though as yet underdeveloped, resources'.

This would require bringing her population to arrive at the 'conviction (grounded on what their eyes see, and their hands handle) that the wealth readily to be obtained from peaceful industry exceeds the slender and precarious profits to be obtained from rapine'. The priority, therefore, was to convey 'Christianity, instruction, and the useful arts' to Africa's inhabitants.[2] Andrew Walls has suggested that Buxton's pamphlet could be termed 'the first serious essay in development theory'.[3] Buxton's remedy for the ills of West Africa drew on at least two separate sources of mission experience.

First, Buxton had developed a close working association and friendship with John Philip, a Scottish missionary of the London Missionary Society in the Cape Colony. Philip was the house guest of the Buxtons at their home at Northrepps Hall in Norfolk on two separate occasions, for a week in December 1826 and for twelve days in January 1837, which afforded him opportunity to engage in protracted conversation with Buxton on African affairs.[4] Philip was himself deeply indebted to the economic theory of the Scottish Enlightenment.[5] In *Researches in South Africa*, a two-volume work written at Buxton's encouragement and published in 1828,[6] Philip cited Adam Smith's *The Wealth of Nations* in support of his case that the solution to the virtual enslavement by white farmers of the Khoikhoi ('Hottentot') people of the Kat River region was to encourage the Khoikhoi to bring their labour and very limited resources of capital to a free market. In Smith's words, people had to be 'secure of enjoying the fruits of their industry' if they were to exert themselves to better their economic condition; they had to become small-scale independent producers.[7] He also cited the English economist Thomas Malthus, and made passing reference to Adam Ferguson and David Ricardo.[8] Nevertheless, Philip's debt to Enlightenment theorists should not be exaggerated. Despite the non-religious, quasi-ethnological nature of the book's title, the principal message of *Researches in Africa* was that it was the Christian gospel alone 'that elevates the savage in the scale of being'.[9] Civilisation had its place, above all as the necessary means towards the sustainability of an indigenous church, but for Philip, as for Buxton, and Livingstone after him, it possessed no power in and of itself to regenerate a lost humanity.[10]

The second source of mission experience that influenced Buxton's thinking was Jamaica in the aftermath of slave emancipation. From 1835, well before the termination of slave apprenticeship in 1838, the Baptist missionary James Phillippo, followed by other missionaries, began purchasing land (with the aid of wealthy English benefactors), in order to enable the apprentices, once released from their ties to the plantation owners, to become small-scale proprietors, growing subsistence crops, and some sugar for the export market. A series of free townships was created.[11] In the first four years of freedom the Baptist Western Union established no less than 3,300 freeholders on Jamaican soil.[12] A free and self-supporting Christian peasantry was to be the foundation of a new social order for Jamaica. Buxton believed that where Jamaica led, West Africa could follow.

However, the high hopes that British abolitionists held for Jamaica were soon to be dashed by the removal in 1846 of the duties that protected Jamaican sugar production, leading to a catastrophic economic collapse. Ironically, it was the advent of free trade that proved disastrous for the missionary vision of a free Christian peasantry in the Caribbean.

Despite such discouragement from Jamaica, Buxton's distinctively Christian concept of African development was adopted, not merely by David Livingstone, but also by Henry Venn, secretary of the Church Missionary Society (CMS) from 1841 to 1872. Venn was committed to a policy of 'development' in West Africa: if the African slave trade was to be eliminated, and if a self-supporting church was to be planted, then an African middle class had to be created through mission education and the encouragement of 'legitimate' trade in home-grown produce.[13] Venn's prescription for the economic advancement of the freed slave community of Freetown in Sierra Leone included the establishment of a savings bank, provident societies, model farms and the Fourah Bay Institution, which was to provide training in mechanical arts, agriculture and 'such other departments of knowledge as may contribute to . . . promoting the social improvement of their countrymen'.[14] From 1856, the CMS established a series of industrial institutions in its Yoruba Mission, to impart the skills necessary for cotton cultivation, which Venn had identified as the crop most likely to enable the emergence of a Christian middle class capable of supporting an indigenous African church.[15] The same ideal animated the new Niger Mission, inaugurated in 1864 under the leadership of the Sierra Leonean re-captive, Bishop Samuel Adjai Crowther. African Christian agency, comprising other re-captives, was to be the means of spreading both the gospel and free 'legitimate' trade on the Upper Niger.

The vision of a happy marriage between commerce and Christianity in West Africa lost much of its lustre after Venn's death in 1873. Some of the Sierra Leonean missionaries failed to live up to the exacting moral standards of the mission, and their willingness to engage in trade on their own account seemed to place in doubt their commitment to preaching the gospel.[16] During the 1880s a new generation of CMS missionaries arrived in the Niger Mission, men shaped by the rigorous holiness ideals of the Keswick Convention. They were sceptical of the worldliness implicit in the commerce and Christianity ideal, and impatient with the apparent inability of Bishop Crowther to discipline his wayward African Christian agents. Crowther died in 1891 a broken man, humiliated by his European missionary critics. Much has been written about the implications of this tragic episode in thwarting progress towards a truly indigenous African church, but what were its consequences for the Buxtonian ideal of Christian development – did it mark the end of that holistic philosophy of mission?[17]

Certainly one can find examples of Protestant missions after 1891 that continued to adhere to a broad ideal of the integration of evangelism and economic development. One striking case was that of the Livingstonia

Mission in what is now Malawi. Established in 1874 by a group of Glaswegian industrialists who were members – and among the most lavish funders – of the Free Church of Scotland created by the 1843 Disruption, Livingstonia, as its name suggests, sought to implement David Livingstone's vision of commerce and Christianity in the Lake Nyasa region. The domestic governance of the mission lay mainly in the hands of these wealthy laymen, at least three of whom were the original directors of the African Lakes Company, incorporated in 1878 with the aim of promoting legitimate trade and cash crop cultivation in the Zambesi region.[18] Specifically, the partnership between Livingstonia and the African Lakes Company was designed to wean the Yao people who inhabited the land to the south of Lake Malawi from their dependence on the coastal slave trade run from Zanzibar.

By 1881 it had become apparent that this strategy was not working; the Yao continued their involvement in the Muslim-controlled coastal trade. As a result, the Livingstonia Mission decided to relocate to a new site half-way up the shores of the lake at Bandawe. By 1910 the Nyasaland Missionary Conference had to confess that 'Among the Yao on the lake shore it is becoming the natural thing to be a Mohammedan.'[19] In the Nyasa region, as earlier in Jamaica and in the Niger Mission, commerce and Christianity proved less harmonious in practice than in theory. The Free Church missionaries who ran the Livingstonia Mission from its new base at Bandawe continued to instruct their Tonga pupils in such 'useful skills' as carpentry, brickmaking and printing, while mission-educated clerks and foremen played an increasingly central role in the labour economy of the region. But conversions to Christianity remained few until after the advent of a British protectorate between 1891 and 1894. What may have been more important in stimulating conversion was the arrival of a new generation of missionaries who, like Crowther's opponents on the Niger, were nurtured in the spiritual fervour of the Keswick Convention and the Evangelical movement affecting the British universities. The resulting revival that swept through the Livingstonia Mission in 1895 produced many more conversions than did the earlier strategy of proclaiming a gospel that combined spiritual and commercial regeneration.[20] Nevertheless, the Livingstonia missionaries continued to exhibit the distinctive emphases of the tradition of Thomas Chalmers – a dedicated focus on education, and a determination to encourage the social improvement of the individual through 'honest labour'.[21]

By the close of the nineteenth century the optimistic recipes for the regeneration of Africa prescribed by nineteenth-century Christian theorists were looking inadequate in the context of the rapid extension of both European commercial activity and colonial rule in the continent. More strident Christian voices began to demand a clearer demarcation between the aims of missions and the frequently destructive agendas of large trading companies and white settlers. In 1897 Joseph Booth, the maverick English

Baptist missionary to southern Africa, published a pamphlet, *Africa for the African*, which condemned the European scramble for African land as an act of plunder scarcely less heinous than the earlier exploitation of African labour by means of the slave trade.[22] It also posed the awkward question of why, 'if the missionaries be truly men of God ... do they not solemnly and sternly denounce the authors of the evil?'[23] Booth was a supporter of industrial missions, but no longer was this concept allied to the supposedly benevolent civilising designs of European governments. It is not accidental that Booth's teaching was a primary influence on his Yao cook and first convert, John Chilembwe, who in 1915 led an important, though short-lived, early anti-colonial rising against British rule.

Missionary Responses to Humanitarian Crises in China, India and the Congo in the Late Nineteenth Century

Antislavery was the principal driver of Western global humanitarianism for most of the nineteenth century. By 1888, when Brazil finally abolished slavery, the battle against slavery and the slave trade appeared to have been won, though in fact multiple forms of slavery continue to this day. For at least three decades from the late 1870s, a different focus dominated Western international philanthropy. Famine is a recurring phenomenon throughout history, but the period from 1876 to 1902 witnessed a series of catastrophic droughts and resulting famines that may have been unprecedented in geographical coverage, scale and impact. Worst affected were north China and north India, owing to the repeated failure of the monsoons, but famines also afflicted other parts of the world, such as Russia, Egypt and Brazil. Estimates of the aggregate death toll from famines in Asia during this period are staggering in their magnitude, ranging from 19.5 to 30 million in China alone, and from 12.2 to 29.3 million in India.[24]

The first wave of this series of drought-induced famines hit the five provinces of north China between 1876 and 1879, where between 9.5 and 13 million of a total population of some 108 million died. British and American missionaries were among the first-hand observers and reporters of the tragedy.[25] In response they were prominent in organising what may have been the first public famine relief appeal in history. With other members of the expatriate community in Shandong, missionaries formed a Famine Relief Committee in March 1877. This led in January 1878 to the establishment in Shanghai of a China Famine Relief Fund, with a London committee, presided over by the archbishop of Canterbury, following a month later. By September that year, when the subscription lists were closed, the London committee had raised over £32,000 (equivalent to over £4 million today), of which the missionary societies raised £16,000. It is significant that the largest portion of the missionary contribution came from James Hudson Taylor's China Inland Mission, a body normally associated with an emphasis on evangelism alone.[26]

As the first 'NGOs' working in non-European settings, mission agencies in China had pioneered a massive voluntary effort in international famine relief, and missionaries themselves had taken a leading role in distributing aid. However, the Welsh Baptist missionary Timothy Richard came to the conclusion that more than relief was required. His experience of the famine in the worst-affected province of Shanxi led him to advocate long-term structural reform as a solution to China's agricultural and economic problems. During the 1880s and 1890s Richard advocated programmes of state-led modernisation in China that bear comparison with the American social gospel of the same period, except that they were inspired by rural rather than urban crises.[27] Richard continued to believe that only Christianity could save the world, but his concept of salvation had now broadened. He wrote, 'The world all over is groaning under sufferings. The Christian religion alone attempts the salvation of the whole world. Asia, especially China, has millions dying of sheer starvation every year. Christians alone attempt to save these at present. Confucianism, Buddhism and Taoism have no practical scheme of deliverance.'[28]

Harrowing encounters with human suffering in the north China famine led Timothy Richard to question missionary approaches focused on the destiny of the individual soul and to formulate a social gospel addressed to the structural causes of disasters he believed to be not 'natural', but human and preventable. It is likely that some India missionaries reacted in the same way to the increasingly severe famines that afflicted India in the second half of the century, but what emerges more clearly from existing scholarship on the subject is the growing trend to reorientate Christian financial resources towards the care and elevation of the most marginal and vulnerable elements in society, especially orphans. Many of those orphaned by the Indian famines were taken into orphanages and given a Christian education. In some cases, missionaries encouraged the orphanages to become self-supporting through small-scale business enterprise. The American Presbyterian mission at Rakha in the United Provinces opened an orphanage in response to a famine in 1837–8, which set up carpet-weaving and tent-making industries, selling to the British army. After the Uprising of 1857, a joint-stock company was created, under the name of 'The Native Christian Orphanage Tent Factory Company'.[29] A later example of a development-type initiative, in this case pioneered by an indigenous Christian rather than by missionaries, was the cluster of institutions at Pune and Kedgaon in western India, which the high-caste woman convert, 'Pandita' Sarasvati Ramabai, established in response to the devastating famine of 1896–7. By the turn of the century Ramabai's Mukti Mission at Kedgaon housed some 2,000 children orphaned by the famines, who were instructed in a range of craft, technical and agricultural vocations, including printing, carpentry, tailoring, masonry and fruit farming.[30]

In a context where conversions of Hindus were scarce, the missions increasingly pinned their hopes for the future of the Indian church on children brought up in such Christian institutions. Although these hopes were frequently disappointed, the endemic crises of subsistence led missions to expand their social ministries to the marginal and vulnerable in Indian society, generating in response 'people movements' of collective conversion, bringing large numbers of depressed caste people (Dalits) into the churches. In the central Indian region of Chhattisgarh, one relatively small mission society, sent by the migrant German Protestant community in New Jersey, was feeding over 9,000 people a day in Chhattisgarh in 1896–7. An extensive conversion movement among the Satnamis of Chhattisgarh followed.[31] A social scientific survey of the people movements commissioned by the National Christian Council of India in 1928 reported that in every group of depressed caste Christians studied, the majority appeared to be chronically undernourished.[32] The depressed castes were increasingly responding to mission programmes of social relief and development by converting to Christianity. Gandhi's complaints in the 1930s that missions should cease proselytising the depressed castes and focus entirely on social ministries were, therefore, beside the point.[33] In India, to a greater extent than in China, styles of mission that embraced both short-term relief and longer-term social betterment proved to be the most productive in terms of indigenous response.

The great north Indian famine of 1896–7 did not merely reconfigure mission work in India itself; it also had an enduring impact on patterns of philanthropy in the West. This was notably the case in the United States, where reports of the Indian famine, as also of an earlier one in Russia in 1891–2, stimulated a remarkable convergence of missionary zeal and humanitarian compassion. The prime movers in the relief campaign were Louis Klopsch, evangelical proprietor of the New York-based *Christian Herald*, the largest-selling American religious newspaper, and his pastor at the 5,000-seater Brooklyn Tabernacle, Thomas De Witt Talmage. The *Christian Herald* also played an important part in orchestrating American aid on behalf of Armenian Christians in the Ottoman Empire during the massacres of 1894–5, but the American Christian response to the Indian crisis dwarfed both the earlier Russian and Armenian fundraising efforts. Between 1896 and 1910 Klopsch and Talmage used the paper to raise over a million dollars for Indian famine relief and the orphan fund that followed.[34] They made use of recent advances in printing technology to reproduce halftone photographs of starving children. Earlier abolitionist literature on both sides of the Atlantic had frequently included illustrations depicting the predicament of the slaves, but the tabloid pictorial journalism employed by the *Christian Herald* was without precedent in the history of philanthropy.[35]

Missionaries had taken occasional photographs of their work from the late 1850s, but it was the invention of the portable Kodak camera in 1888 that enabled the camera to become a regular item of missionary equipment. From the 1890s photographs began to feature regularly in missionary periodicals and, through the magic lantern, in slide shows in missionary meetings. Photographs had a unique capacity to bring home to domestic audiences the harrowing physical realities, not simply of famine, but also of European colonial brutality. In the Congo, missionaries began in the 1890s to take shocking photographs of victims of the rubber atrocities perpetrated by the agents of Leopold II's Congo Free State. From 1903–4 these photographs were published in the Christian press on both sides of the Atlantic, and included in magic lantern shows. It should be noted that Alice Harris, the most prolific photographer of the atrocities, and Dr Harry Guinness, the leading British missionary user of atrocity lantern slides, were both associated with the Congo Balolo Mission, a theologically conservative body that formed part of the cluster of faith mission enterprises founded by Guinness's father, Henry Grattan Guinness.[36] The Congo Reform Association whose agitation brought Leopold's Congo Free State to an end in 1906 owed much to the outpouring of evangelical moral indignation provoked by Harris and Guinness.

Graphic photographic images, whether of starving victims of famine in India, or of mutilated victims of the rubber atrocities in the Congo, thus played a pivotal role in arousing the Christian humanitarian conscience in the West. From this point on, visual images reproduced in newspapers and magazines, and later through films and television, became the most powerful driver of transnational Christian philanthropy. In the nature of the case, images direct attention to bodies, rather than souls. The implications for the funding of overseas missions, ultimately even of conservative ones, were immense.

The foregoing survey of nineteenth-century Western approaches to the regeneration of overseas societies suggests some general patterns. First, they remained overwhelmingly Christian in origin and purpose. Throughout the nineteenth century missionary societies were by far the largest agencies engaged in overseas philanthropy, and recipes for the economic sustainability of indigenous societies were written with the Christian community specifically in mind. Second, these agencies blended an ongoing commitment to religious conversion with a growing emphasis on a variety of programmes for short-term humanitarian 'relief' and/or longer-term 'civilisation', a term that embraced both social and economic development and processes of Christian education. Such coupling of spiritual and material regeneration was characteristic of the majority of Protestant missions, across the denominational and theological spectrum. Even conservative missions such as the China Inland Mission were prepared to play their part in caring for the victims of famine; in the case of the Red Rubber humanitarian campaign, the theologically conservative Congo Balolo Mission actually took the lead. Third, Christian programmes of social regeneration were usually directed at the non-Western world, and were premised on now discredited assumptions of the normativity of Western models of 'civilisation'. The goal of the process may have been the creation of self-sustaining Christian economies, but this teleological framework was typically distorted by culturally circumscribed notions of what a Christian society should look like. Fourth, by the end of the nineteenth century, Christian projects of international compassion were aided by the power of photographic images, and focused increasingly on the plight of children, and orphans in particular.

From Civilisation to Development in the Twentieth Century

The final part of this brief essay can only offer a summary overview of what happened to each of the four above-mentioned patterns in Western overseas philanthropy in the course of the twentieth century, but such an overview may be valuable as a pointer towards future research.

First, it is clear that after the First World War Christian mission agencies lost their near-monopoly of globally directed Western philanthropy, and were first rivalled and then increasingly supplanted by charitable organisations that pursued relief or development as ends in themselves, with no linkage to the encouragement of non-Western Christian communities. The earliest and most powerful of these secular philanthropic agencies was the Red Cross, founded in 1863 in response to the human suffering inflicted on Europe by the Crimean and Italian wars. Although Henri Dunant and the other Swiss founders of the Red Cross were profoundly influenced by the pietism of the Genevan *Réveil* of the early nineteenth century, the movement itself was established on a non-confessional basis.[37] The American Red Cross (ARC) collaborated with the *Christian Herald* in some of its early relief campaigns, but increasingly the ARC and the evangelical philanthropic efforts of Louis Klopsch followed divergent and rival pathways. By the end of the first decade of the twentieth century, it was apparent that the domination of American overseas relief campaigns by a single Christian newspaper was coming to a close. The ARC gained a crucial advantage in 1900 by securing congressional approval as 'the official voluntary relief organization of the United States'; additional competition came from newly established and extremely wealthy private foundations, such as the Rockefeller and Carnegie Foundations.[38]

Second, the previously close partnership between strategies for the birth or nurture of indigenous churches and wider programmes of social and economic development began to pull apart at the seams. In the United States especially, the broad Protestant constituency from which the *Christian Herald* had drawn its support was splintering. When applied to overseas fields, the social gospel implied an increasing emphasis on short-term humanitarian relief, which increasingly was channelled through secular agencies. However, it also implied a quite separate mission strategy, in which the mainline mission agencies focused on the longer-term goal of educating urban Christian elites for national and ecclesiastical leadership, notably in India, China and Japan. The older denominational missionary societies, to which social gospel enthusiasts gravitated, went into prolonged decline from the 1920s onwards. Most reached their peak in numbers of missionary personnel during that decade, and were hard hit by the crises that afflicted the global economy after 1929. The decline in missionary recruitment also reflected powerful currents of theological change in Western churches and the waning from 1920 of the Student Volunteer Movement in Anglo-American universities, which had previously supplied so much of the overseas missionary force.[39]

As recruitment to the older denominational missions declined, the younger conservative mission agencies, mostly known as 'faith missions', grew in popularity. They concentrated on the evangelisation of tribal peoples adhering to indigenous (then termed 'animistic') religions in Africa, Southeast Asia, Papua New Guinea and the interior of China and Latin America.[40] Conservatives, often known as fundamentalists by the 1920s, reasserted the primacy in mission strategy of preaching to the unevangelised in inland areas beyond the reach of previous Western contact, and grew more sceptical of the capacity of humanitarian benevolence to lead people to Christ.[41] As the twentieth century progressed, Christian overseas philanthropy thus became bifurcated by geography, institutional affiliation and theological orientation.

The third trend observable in twentieth-century overseas Christian philanthropy – a broadening of its geographical scope from the non-Western world to include Europe itself – in the nature of the case applies mainly, but not entirely, to North America. In contrast to the nineteenth century, American religious philanthropy, while continuing to give priority to large parts of the non-Western world, particularly the Orient, now began to pay rather more attention to the needs of supposedly Christian and 'civilised' Europe.

Latin America was not the only continent to be excluded from the agenda of the World Missionary Conference held in Edinburgh in 1910. Both North America itself and Europe, with the exception of that part of south-eastern Europe that lay within the boundaries of the Ottoman Empire, were similarly deemed to be part of the Christian rather than the non-Christian world.[42] The famine of 1891–2 had begun to attract the attention of the American Christian public to tsarist Russia; American Protestants typically conceptualised the relief that was given as an act of mercy on the part of the American Good Samaritan to a theologically estranged member of the Christian family – Orthodox Russia.[43] However, increasing numbers of the evangelical community on both sides of the Atlantic took the view that the Orthodox Church was spiritually apostate, and what Russia needed more than anything was preaching of the gospel. In Britain the pioneer of this approach was Granville Waldegrave, 3rd Baron Radstock, an Evangelical Anglican with close links to the Open Brethren. As early as the 1870s, Lord Radstock was active in encouraging movements of evangelical awakening among the Russian aristocracy.[44] After the Bolshevik Revolution of 1917, American

Methodists, Adventists, Baptists and Pentecostals, though differing in their estimation of the Bolsheviks, joined the campaign to save Russian souls, and witnessed rapid conversion growth. At the same time, more liberal Christians and secular humanitarians in the United States responded to the post-revolution civil war, and then to another severe Russian famine in 1921–2, by raising vast sums of aid to be distributed by the Friends' Service Committee or the American Relief Administration.[45] Awareness of the needs of continental Europe, and of Russia in particular, was beginning to polarise Christian philanthropy between conservative and liberal pathways of aid.

The impact of the Second World War accentuated this polarity still further, but it now became apparent in philanthropy targeted at Western as well as Eastern Europe, and was directed even to predominantly Protestant Germany. For mainline American Protestants and their British counterparts in the leadership of the historic churches, the crying need of post-war Europe, and devastated Germany in particular, was not evangelisation, but material relief and the longer-term economic development envisaged in the European Recovery Program (popularly known as the Marshall Plan) launched in 1948. Stewart Herman, pastor of the American church in Berlin, even called in December 1947 for the formulation of what he called 'a Marshall Plan for the Churches', which would combine spiritual and material aid in order to bolster Christian civilisation against the threat of Soviet communism.[46] Most pressing was the unprecedented scale of the crisis of human displacement: in the wake of the war between ten and fourteen million persons (Germans, Ukrainians and other nationalities) were displaced from their ordinary country of residence.[47] The enormity of the problem necessitated the creation of new international aid agencies. Some, such as Oxfam, established as the Oxford Committee for Famine Relief in 1942, and had substantial Christian influence, but were formally secular. Others were explicitly Christian. Lutheran World Relief began in 1945 as a response to the fact that an estimated 20 per cent of the world's Lutherans had been made homeless.[48] In 1946 American denominations represented in the National Council of Churches formed the Church World Service (CWS) with the aim of coordinating American Protestant responses to the refugee crisis in Europe. In 1947 the Church World Service, Lutheran World Relief and the National Catholic Welfare Program created a joint community hunger appeal, the Christian Rural Overseas Program (CROP), which organised 'Friendship Food Trains' and 'Friendship Food Ships' to transport staple foods for the hungry in Europe. Similarly in Britain, what is now Christian Aid originated in 1945 as 'The Christian Reconstruction in Europe Committee', a project of the British Council of Churches. At the global ecumenical level, the 'World Council of Churches in Process of Formation' established the Division of Inter-Church Aid and Service to Refugees in 1942. The age of the NGO had been inaugurated, and in 1946 the American government set up the Advisory Committee on Voluntary

Foreign Aid to exercise some control over this burgeoning voluntary internationalism.

Such relief efforts were characteristic of the 'mainline' or historic denominations, but neither North American nor British Evangelicals were indifferent to the magnitude of the post-war humanitarian problem. In the United States the National Association of Evangelicals, formed in 1942, established a 'War Relief Commission', which in 1945 sent its first consignment of clothing to Belgium to be distributed by the Belgian Gospel Mission, a mission that originated in an American campaign during the First World War to distribute evangelistic literature and humanitarian aid to Belgian troops.[49] As the geographical scope of the refugee problem and of Christian relief efforts broadened, the Commission was reconstituted in 1950 as an agency of global scope, 'World Relief'. The United Nations denominated 1959–60 as World Refugee Year, and in Britain the Evangelical Alliance opened a fund in 1959 to provide relief for refugees, giving it the unfortunate acronym of EAR Fund (Evangelical Alliance Refugee Fund). In 1967 the name was changed to the EA Relief Fund, which in turn provided the basis for the creation of Tearfund in 1968.[50]

Nonetheless, for many Anglophone Evangelicals, especially those in North America, the nature of the post-war crisis was more than merely humanitarian or economic. For them, the godless character of Nazism and the scandal of the Holocaust revealed the degeneracy of European Christendom. The emerging Cold War message that Germany, and Western civilisation as a whole, needed to be saved from the gathering threat of communism, thus merged with the priority of bringing evangelical revival and salvation to 'pagan' Europe. From 1947 American military bases in the allied zones of occupation – which would become 'West Germany' – became the nodes of a crusade to recall an apostate and shattered nation to its spiritual heritage as the birthplace of Protestantism. The pioneering agency was the Youth for Christ movement, whose bright and breezy evangelistic rallies for young people had become a feature of Chicago and a number of other American cities during the early 1940s. Youth for Christ was soon holding as many as 100 such rallies every weekend at military bases in the American zone. Furthermore, the campaigns soon extended their range from American servicemen to German youth.[51] Western Europe now became a significant theatre for American Evangelical missionary activity, and Protestant Germany became the hub of these efforts. The evangelist Billy Graham conducted five crusades in Germany between 1954 and 1970.[52]

While conservative American Christians focused their energies on world evangelism, the agencies established by the mainline churches in response to the refugee crisis in Europe became the instruments of a wider form of Christian internationalism committed to the economic development of poor nations outside Europe. Both the CWS and the CROP soon extended their ministry of compassion and relief to Asia, Africa and Latin America.[53]

Although the globalisation of humanitarian relief was not limited to the churches alone, Christians were at the forefront. At the second Assembly of the World Council of Churches (WCC) at Evanston, Illinois in 1954, the WCC Division of Inter-Church Aid and Service to Refugees followed the general philanthropic trend by having its geographical mandate extended from Europe to the whole globe. It was destined to grow into the largest department of the WCC. Moreover, its expanded geographical mandate encouraged a crucial shift in emphasis from inter-church aid to *diakonia* (service) to the world: the task of assisting the churches in their evangelistic mission could be left to the International Missionary Council, or, after its integration into the WCC in 1961, to the Department of World Mission and Evangelism of the WCC.[54]

For the Protestant mainline the new Christian globalism speedily relegated conventional missionary work to a secondary place. Events in Asia, the primary sphere of mainline American mission endeavours ever since 1910, accentuated the accumulating theological uncertainty about the nature of the apostolic commission into a more fundamental paralysis of missionary nerve among mainline Protestants in both North America and Europe.[55] The rapid expulsion of missionaries from communist China after China's entry into the Korean War in October 1950, with the accusations of being lackeys of imperialism ringing in their ears, provoked a period of profound and prolonged heart-searching about both the methods and the rationale of Western missions.[56] Most mainline denominational missions, already declining in their numbers since the late 1920s, now went into free fall. Only Evangelicals and fundamentalists continued without wavering in their commitment to the global task of religious conversion, and initially without paying much attention to the searching questions about the indigenisation and moral integrity of mission Christianity which the China experience had thrown up.

By the early 1950s the Marshall Plan was having its desired effect in rejuvenating the economy of West Germany. The focus of American philanthropy moved in response to other theatres in which the Cold War was being fought out. Chief among these was Korea. The Korean War was pivotal in the reorientation of evangelical global philanthropy. Bob Pierce, an energetic Youth for Christ evangelist, conducted two evangelistic tours of China in 1947–8, where he witnessed the advance of the communist armies and Mao Zedong's persecution of mission Christianity. His subsequent service in Korea during the Korean War led him in 1950 to collaborate with a Korean Presbyterian minister, Kyung-Chik Han, to found World Vision as an organisation dedicated to both evangelism and humanitarian relief, especially of orphans. Once again, the needs of orphaned Asian children played a pivotal role in redrawing patterns of Western Christian philanthropy. The power of images of suffering children was again crucial: Pierce was an enthusiast for the movie camera, and used it to great effect to produce films on China and Korea that conveyed to American evangelical audiences the message of the 'Red Plague' of communism, but also the desperate plight of children orphaned by the war.[57]

More than any other single organisation, World Vision was responsible for gradually convincing most American Evangelicals that short-term relief was a gospel imperative; some even became persuaded that longer-term development was one also. Tearfund in Britain played a similar role, but found the Evangelical constituency more consistently sympathetic to the integration of development projects within the sphere of Christian mission. Although a significant gap remained between Evangelical and 'mainline' global missiology, much of Western Protestantism by the end of the twentieth century had espoused a global philanthropic agenda that prioritised Christian versions of development. However, in contrast to the nineteenth-century programmes of Buxton and Venn, this agenda was not closely tied to recipes for the progress towards autonomy of indigenous churches. The 1974 Lausanne Congress on World Evangelization was a pivotal moment which enabled many, though by no means all, Evangelicals to espouse a theology of mission that gave an integral place to humanitarian efforts for justice and welfare.[58] In many non-Western contexts, governments tolerated only those mission agencies that were evidently committed to development work. Western governments and the World Bank became more willing to channel overseas aid through religious agencies. Evangelical church leaders in the Global South took note of the success of the mainline churches in securing grants, scholarships and other forms of overseas aid, and sought to join the club. Taken together, these various influences combined to narrow, though never wholly eliminate, the gap between 'conservative' church-centred mission and 'liberal' social and economic development that had opened up in the wake of the two World Wars.[59] Evangelical social Christianity had returned to the mission field, but it now exhibited features that Buxton or Venn might not have recognised.

Notes

1. William Monk (ed.), *Dr Livingstone's Cambridge Lectures*, 2nd edn (Cambridge, 1860), p. 165.
2. Thomas Fowell Buxton, *The Remedy: Being a Sequel to the African Slave Trade* (1840), new electronic edn in Cambridge Library Collection: Slavery and Abolition (Cambridge: Cambridge University Press, 2010), pp. 19–20, 61. DOI: https://doi.org/10.1017/CBO9780511783920. *The Remedy* was the sequel to a privately printed pamphlet: Thomas Fowell Buxton, *The African Slave Trade* (1839).
3. Andrew F. Walls, *The Missionary Movement from the West: A Biography from Birth to Old Age*, ed. Brian Stanley (Grand Rapids, MI: Eerdmans, 2023).
4. Tim Keegan, *Dr Philip's Empire: One Man's Struggle for Justice in Nineteenth-Century South Africa* (Cape Town: Zebra Press, 2016), pp. 110 and 215.

5. Andrew Ross, *John Philip (1775–1851): Missions, Race and Politics in South Africa* (Aberdeen: Aberdeen University Press, 1986), pp. 66, 81, 96 and 225.
6. Ibid., p. 105.
7. John Philip, *Researches in South Africa; Illustrating the Civil, Moral, and Religious Condition of the Native Tribes*, 2 vols (London, 1828), I, pp. 369–70, citing Adam Smith, *An Inquiry into the Nature and Causes of the Wealth of Nations* (1776), ed. Edwin Cannan (New York: Random House, 1937), p. 379.
8. Philip, *Researches in South Africa*, I, pp. 373, 378; Keegan, *Dr Philip's Empire*, p. 115.
9. Philip, *Researches in South Africa*, II, p. 359.
10. See my 'Christianity and Civilization in English Evangelical Mission Thought, 1792–1857', in Brian Stanley (ed.), *Christian Missions and the Enlightenment* (Grand Rapids, MI, and Richmond, Surrey: Eerdmans, 2001), pp. 169–97.
11. E. B. Underhill, *Life of James Mursell Phillippo, Missionary in Jamaica* (London, 1881), pp. 183–9; Catherine Hall, *Civilising Subjects: Metropole and Colony in the English Imagination, 1830–1867* (Cambridge: Polity, 2002), pp. 181–2.
12. William A. Green, *British Slave Emancipation: The Sugar Colonies and the Great Experiment 1830–1865* (Oxford: Clarendon Press, 1976), p. 171.
13. J. F. A. Ajayi, 'Henry Venn and the Policy of Development', *Journal of the Historical Society of Nigeria*, 1.4 (1959), pp. 331–42.
14. Jehu Hanciles, *Euthanasia of a Mission: African Church Autonomy in a Colonial Context* (Westport, CT: Praeger, 2002), p. 74.
15. M. A. C. Warren (ed.), *To Apply the Gospel: Selections from the Writings of Henry Venn* (Grand Rapids, MI: Eerdmans, 1971), pp. 190–4.
16. J. F. A. Ajayi, *Christian Missions in Nigeria 1841–1891: The Making of a New Elite* (London: Longmans, 1965), p. 245; see also C. Peter Williams, *The Ideal of the Self-Governing Church: A Study in Victorian Missionary Strategy* (Leiden: Brill, 1990), pp. 100 and 137.
17. The fullest analysis is by Williams, *The Ideal of the Self-Governing Church*, pp. 146–227.
18. John McCracken, *Politics and Christianity in Malawi 1875–1940: The Impact of the Livingstonia Mission in the Northern Province* (Cambridge: Cambridge University Press, 1977), pp. 30–2 and 44.
19. Ibid., pp. 55–6.
20. Ibid., pp. 121–3.
21. Ibid., pp. 179–80.
22. Joseph Booth, *Africa for the African* (1897), ed. Laura Perry (Zomba, Malawi: Kachere Series, 2007), pp. 10–11.
23. Ibid., p. 12.
24. Mike Davis, *Late Victorian Holocausts: El Niño Famines and the Making of the Third World* (London: Verso, 2001), p. 7.
25. Paul Richard Bohr, *Famine in China and the Missionary: Timothy Richard as Relief Administrator and Advocate of National Reform, 1876–1884* (Cambridge, MA: East Asian Research Center, Harvard University, distributed by Harvard University Press, 1972), p. xv; Kathryn Edgerton-Tarpley, *Tears from Iron: Cultural Responses to Famine in Nineteenth-Century China* (Berkeley, CA: University of California Press, 2008), p. 1.
26. Bohr, *Famine in China*, p. 95; Edgerton-Tarpley, *Tears from Iron*, p. 71.

27. Bohr, *Famine in China*, pp. 171–2.
28. Timothy Richard, 'Christian Missions in Asia' (n.d.), reprinted in *Conversion by the Million in China Being Biographies and Articles*, 2 vols (Shanghai: Christian Literature Society, 1907), I, p. 185.
29. Arun Jones, *Missionary Christianity and Local Religion: American Evangelicalism in North India, 1836–1870* (Waco, TX: Baylor University Press, 2017), pp. 241–3.
30. Robert Eric Frykenberg, *Christianity in India from Beginnings to the Present* (Oxford: Oxford University Press, 2008), pp. 400–3; Keith J. White, *Let the Earth Hear Her Voice: The Life and Work of Pandita Ramabai 1858–1922* (London: WTL Publications, 2022), pp. 492–3.
31. Chad M. Bauman, *Christian Identity and Dalit Religion in Hindu India, 1868–1947* (Grand Rapids, MI: Eerdmans, 2008), pp. 63–6.
32. J. Waskom Pickett, *Christian Mass Movements in India: A Study with Recommendations* (New York: The Abingdon Press, 1933), p. 123.
33. For Gandhi's anti-conversion campaign see Susan Billington Harper, *In the Shadow of the Mahatma: Bishop V. S. Azariah and the Travails of Christianity in British India* (Grand Rapids, MI: Eerdmans, 2000), pp. 306–38.
34. Heather D. Curtis, *Holy Humanitarians: American Evangelicals and Global Aid* (Cambridge, MA: Harvard University Press, 2018), pp. 123–5; Ian Tyrrell, *Reforming the World: The Creation of America's Moral Empire* (Princeton, NJ: Princeton University Press, 2010), p. 112.
35. Curtis, *Holy Humanitarians*, pp. 23, 29–30, 127 and 155–9; Heather D. Curtis, 'Picturing Pain: Evangelicals and the Politics of Pictorial Humanitarianism in an Imperial Age', in Heide Fehrenbach and Davide Rodogno (eds), *Humanitarian Photography: A History* (Cambridge: Cambridge University Press, 2014), pp. 22–46.
36. T. Jack Thompson, *Light on Darkness? Missionary Photography of Africa in the Nineteenth and Early Twentieth Centuries* (Grand Rapids, MI: Eerdmans, 2012), pp. 177–99 and 229–38; Kevin Grant, 'The Limits of Exposure: Atrocity Photographs in the Congo Reform Campaign', in Fehrenbach and Rodogno, *Humanitarian Photography*, pp. 64–88.
37. John F. Hutchinson, 'Rethinking the Origins of the Red Cross', *Bulletin of the History of Medicine*, 63.4 (1989), pp. 557–78, at p. 565; Caroline Moorehead, *Dunant's Dream: War, Switzerland, and the History of the Red Cross* (New York: Carroll and Graf, 1999), pp. 11–12 and 51.
38. Curtis, *Holy Humanitarians*, pp. 231–7, 248–50, 262 and 272.
39. Nathan D. Showalter, *The End of a Crusade: The Student Volunteer Movement and the First World War* (Lanham, MD: The Scarecrow Press, 1998).
40. Brian Stanley, 'Twentieth-Century World Christianity: A Perspective from the History of Missions', in Donald M. Lewis (ed.), *Christianity Reborn: The Global Expansion of Evangelicalism in the Twentieth Century* (Grand Rapids, MI: Eerdmans, 2004), pp. 74–5.
41. Curtis, *Holy Humanitarians*, pp. 263–7.
42. Brian Stanley, *The World Missionary Conference, Edinburgh 1910* (Grand Rapids, MI: Eerdmans, 2009), p. 50.
43. Curtis, *Holy Humanitarians*, pp. 27 and 34.
44. Harold H. Rowdon, 'Waldegrave, Granville Augustus William, Third Baron Radstock', *Oxford Dictionary of National Biography* (2004).

45. David S. Foglesong, *The American Mission and the 'Evil Empire': The Crusade for a 'Free Russia' since 1881* (Cambridge: Cambridge University Press, 2007), pp. 52–6 and 64–72.
46. James D. Strasburg, *God's Marshall Plan: American Protestants and the Struggle for the Soul of Europe* (New York: Oxford University Press, 2021), pp. 184–5.
47. Jan-Hinnerk Antons, 'Displaced Persons in Postwar Germany: Parallel Societies in a Hostile Environment', *Journal of Contemporary History*, 49.1 (2014), pp. 92–144, at p. 92. Originally a distinction was drawn between 'displaced persons' (those expelled from their homeland as a result of the Potsdam Agreement) and 'refugees' (those who fled East Germany of their own volition to escape communist rule), but subsequently the term 'refugee' became affixed to both categories; see James C. Enns, *Saving Germany: North American Protestants and Christian Mission to West Germany, 1945–1974* (Montreal: McGill–Queen's University Press, 2017), p. 241, n. 51.
48. Lutheran World Relief, https://lwr.org/about-lwr, accessed 8 March 2022.
49. *United Evangelical Action*, 6.3 (19 March 1945); Aaldert Prins, 'The History of the Belgian Gospel Mission from 1918 to 1962', https://www.academia.edu/1097 1154 (accessed 15 March 2022). I am grateful to Emily Banas, Buswell Library Archives and Special Collections, Wheaton College, for assistance with sources on the origins of the War Relief Commission of the National Association of Evangelicals.
50. Dena Freeman, *Tearfund and the Quest for Faith-Based Development* (London: Routledge, 2019), pp. 42–3.
51. Enns, *Saving Germany*, pp. 112, 114 and 116; Strasburg, *God's Marshall Plan*, pp. 172–83; see also Joel Carpenter, *Revive Us Again: The Reawakening of American Fundamentalism* (New York: Oxford University Press, 1997), pp. 166, 178–9, and 182; George M. Marsden, *Reforming Fundamentalism: Fuller Seminary and the New Evangelicalism* (Grand Rapids, MI: Eerdmans, 1987), pp. 60–3.
52. Enns, *Saving Germany*, p. 145; see also Uta A. Balbier, *Altar Call in Europe: Billy Graham, Mass Evangelism, and the Cold-War West* (New York: Oxford University Press, 2021).
53. Church World Service, https://cwsglobal.org/about/history/, accessed 9 March 2022.
54. Mark T. B. Laing, '"The Calling of the Church to Mission and to Unity": Bishop Lesslie Newbigin and the Integration of the International Missionary Council with the World Council of Churches' (PhD diss., University of Edinburgh, 2010), pp. 150–76.
55. Dana L. Robert, *Christian Mission: How Christianity Became a World Religion* (Oxford: Wiley-Blackwell, 2009), pp. 67–9 and 91.
56. George Hood, *Neither Bang nor Whimper: The End of a Missionary Era in China* (Singapore: Presbyterian Church in Singapore, in association with the Friends of the Church in China, Singapore, 1991).
57. David P. King, *God's Internationalists: World Vision and the Age of Evangelical Humanitarianism* (Philadelphia: University of Pennsylvania Press, 2019), pp. 35–6, 39, 41, 49–50 and 54; David R. Swartz, *Facing West: American Evangelicals in an Age of World Christianity* (New York: Oxford University Press, 2020), pp. 44–55.

58. Brian Stanley, '"Lausanne 1974": The Challenge from the Majority World to Northern-Hemisphere Evangelicalism', *Journal of Ecclesiastical History*, 64.3 (2013), pp. 533–51.
59. From a large literature on these trends, see especially King, *God's Internationalists*; Swartz, *Facing West*; Melani McAlister, *The Kingdom of God Has No Borders: A Global History of American Evangelicals* (New York: Oxford University Press, 2018); and Julie Hearn, 'The "Invisible NGO": US Evangelical Missions in Kenya', *Journal of Religion in Africa*, 32.1 (2002), pp. 32–60.

Bibliography of Stewart J. Brown
Professor Emeritus of Ecclesiastical History, University of Edinburgh

1978
'The Disruption and Urban Poverty: Thomas Chalmers and the West Port Operation in Edinburgh, 1844–47'. *Records of the Scottish Church History Society*, 20.1 (1978), pp. 65–89.

1981
Review of *Philanthropy in Victorian Scotland: Social Welfare and the Voluntary Principle*, by Olive Checkland, *History: Reviews of New Books*, 9.9 (August 1981), p. 216.

1982
Thomas Chalmers and the Godly Commonwealth in Scotland. Oxford: Oxford University Press, 1982. Awarded the Saltire Society of Scotland Prize in History. Reissued in 2006.
Review of *Court, Kirk, and Community: Scotland 1470–1625*, by Jenny Wormald, *History: Reviews of New Books*, 10.7 (May/June 1982), pp. 189–90.
Review of *Of Presbyters and Kings: Church and State in the Law of Scotland*, by Francis Lyall, *Church History*, 51.2 (June 1982), pp. 220–1.
Review of *Scottish County Government in the Eighteenth and Nineteenth Centuries*, by Ann E. Whetstone, *History: Reviews of New Books*, 10.9 (August 1982), pp. 227–8.
Review of *Government by Pen: Scotland under James VI and I*, by Maurice Lee, Jr., *Church History*, 51.3 (September 1982), pp. 349–50.
Review of *A Protestant in Purgatory: Richard Whately, Archbishop of Dublin*, by Donald Harmon Akenson, *History: Reviews of New Books*, 10.10 (September 1982), p. 268.

1983
Review of *Jacobite Estates of the Forty-Five*, by Annette M. Smith, *History: Reviews of New Books*, 11.5 (March 1983), p. 120.
Review of *Deer Forests, Landlords, and Crofters: The Western Highlands in Victorian and Edwardian Times*, by W. Orr, *History: Reviews of New Books*, 11.9 (August 1983), p. 203.

Review of *Enemies of God: The Witch-Hunt in Scotland*, by Christina Larner, *Church History*, 52.3 (September 1983), pp. 415–16.

1984

Review of *Church, Politics and Society: Scotland 1408–1929*, ed. by Norman MacDougall, *History: Reviews of New Books*, 12.7 (May/June 1984), p. 143.

Review of *Developments in the Roman Catholic Church in Scotland, 1789–1829*, by Christine Johnson, *Church History*, 53.3 (September 1984), pp. 403–4.

1985

'Thomas Chalmers'. In *Gestalten der Kirchengeschichte*, Vol. 9/1, edited by Martin Greschat, pp. 172–86. Stuttgart: Kohlhammer, 1985.

Review of *Industry and Ethos: Scotland 1832–1914*, by Sydney Checkland and Olive Checkland, *Albion: A Quarterly Journal Concerned with British Studies*, 17.1 (Spring 1985), pp. 124–6.

1986

Review of *The Scottish Enlightenment and the Militia Issue*, by John Robertson, *Albion: A Quarterly Journal Concerned with British Studies*, 18.4 (Winter 1986), pp. 718–19.

'Assimilation and Identity in Modern Scottish History', reviews of *Experience and Enlightenment: Socialization for Cultural Change in Eighteenth-Century Scotland*, by Charles Camic; *Scottish Urban History*, by George Gordon and Brian Dicks; *Perspectives of the Scottish City*, by George Gordon; *Church and University in the Scottish Enlightenment: The Moderate Literati of Edinburgh*, by Richard B. Sher; *Shetland Life and Trade, 1550–1914*, by Hance D. Smith; *Gaelic in Scotland, 1698–1981: The Geographical History of a Language*, by Charles W. J. Withers, *Journal of British Studies*, 25.1 (January 1986), pp. 119–29.

1987

Review of *The Scottish Enlightenment and Early Victorian English Society*, by Anand C. Chitnis, *Victorian Studies*, 30.4 (Summer 1987), pp. 522–3.

Reviews of *A Century of the Scottish People, 1830–1950*, by T. C. Smout; *A Political History of Scotland 1832–1924: Parties, Elections, and Issues*, by I. G. C. Hutchison; and *The Scots Abroad: Labour, Capital, Enterprise, 1750–1914*, by R. A. Cage, *Victorian Studies*, 31.1 (Autumn 1987), pp. 139–41.

1988

Review of *No Popery and Radicalism: Opposition to Roman Catholic Relief in Scotland, 1778–1782*, by Robert Kent Donovan, *Albion: A Quarterly Journal Concerned with British Studies*, 20.3 (Autumn 1988), pp. 531–2.

Review of *Passive Obedience and Prophetic Protest: Social Criticism in the Scottish Church 1830–1945*, by Donald C. Smith, *Church History*, 57.3 (September 1988), pp. 399–401.

1989

Review of *The Social History of Religion in Scotland since 1730*, by Callum G. Brown, *The American Historical Review*, 94.3 (June 1989), pp. 780–1.

Review of *Pigeon Holes of Memory: The Life and Times of Dr. John Mackenzie (1803–1886)*, by Christina Byam Shaw, *Albion: A Quarterly Journal Concerned with British Studies*, 21.4 (Winter 1989), pp. 690–1.

1990

'The Social Vision of Scottish Presbyterianism and the Union of 1929'. *Records of the Scottish Church History Society*, 24.1 (1990), pp. 77–96.

Review of *Defending and Declaring the Faith: Some Scottish Examples 1860–1920*, by Alan P. F. Sell, *Church History*, 59.4 (December 1990), p. 582.

1991

'Reform, Reconstruction, Reaction: The Social Vision of Scottish Presbyterianism, c. 1830–c. 1930'. *Scottish Journal of Theology*, 44 (1991), pp. 489–517. Inaugural Lecture as Professor of Ecclesiastical History.

'"Outside the Covenant": The Scottish Presbyterian Churches and the Irish Catholic Community in Scotland, 1922–1937'. *Innes Review*, 42.1 (Spring 1991), pp. 19–45.

'"A Victory for God": The Scottish Presbyterian Churches and the General Strike of 1926'. *Journal of Ecclesiastical History*, 42.4 (October 1991), pp. 596–617.

Review of *The Faith of the Scots*, by Gordon Donaldson, *Records of the Scottish Church History Society*, 24.2 (1991), pp. 253–4.

1992

'Norman MacLeod', 'Robert Rainy' and 'Revivals (British Isles)'. In *Encyclopedia of the Reformed Faith*, edited by Donald McKim. Louisville, KY: Westminster/John Knox Press and Edinburgh: Saint Andrew Press, 1992.

'"Echoes of Midlothian": Scottish Liberalism and the South African War, 1899–1902'. *Scottish Historical Review*, 71 (1992), pp. 156–83.

'Thomas Chalmers and the Communal Ideal in Victorian Scotland'. In *Victorian Values: Proceedings of the British Academy*, No. 78, edited by Thomas Christopher Smout, pp. 61–80. Oxford: Oxford University Press, 1992.

Review of *Evangelicalism in Modern Britain: A History from the 1730s to the 1980s*, by D. W. Bebbington, *The Scottish Historical Review*, 71.191/192, Parts 1 and 2 (April –October, 1992), pp. 246–8.

1993

'Church Accommodation Committee', 'Forward Movement, Scottish', 'French Revolution', 'Matthew Leishman', 'West Port Scheme (Edinburgh)' and 'John White'. In *Dictionary of Scottish Church History and Theology*, edited by Nigel M. de S. Cameron. Edinburgh: T. & T. Clark, 1993.

'Martyrdom in Early Victorian Scotland: Disruption Fathers and the Making of the Free Church'. In *Martyrs and Martyrologies: Studies in Church History*, Vol. 30, edited by Diana Wood, pp. 319–32. Oxford: Blackwell, 1993.

'The Ten Years' Conflict and the Disruption of 1843'. In *Scotland in the Age of the Disruption*, edited by Stewart J. Brown and Michael Fry, pp. 1–27. Edinburgh: Edinburgh University Press, 1993.

'The Campaign for the Christian Commonwealth in Scotland, 1919–1939'. In *Crown and Mitre: Religion and Society in Northern Europe since the Reformation*, edited by W. M. Jacob and Nigel Yates, pp. 203–21. Suffolk: Boydell, 1993.

Scotland in the Age of the Disruption, edited by Stewart J. Brown and Michael Fry. Edinburgh: Edinburgh University Press, 1993.

'Principal William Robertson (1721–1793) – A Bicentenary Commemoration'. *University of Edinburgh Journal*, 36.1 (June 1993), pp. 35–8.

Scottish Historical Review, edited by Stewart J. Brown and Alexander Grant. Vols 72–8 (1993–9).

Review of *The Invention of Scotland: The Stuart Myth and the Scottish Identity, 1638 to the Present*, by Murray G. H. Pittock, *Albion: A Quarterly Journal Concerned with British Studies*, 25.1 (Spring 1993), pp. 166–7.

1994

'"A Solemn Purification by Fire": Responses to the Great War in the Scottish Presbyterian Churches, 1914–19'. *Journal of Ecclesiastical History*, 45.1 (January 1994), pp. 1–23.

'The Social Ideal of the Church of Scotland in the 1930s'. In *God's Will in a Time of Crisis: A Colloquium Celebrating the 50th Anniversary of the Baillie Commission*, edited by Andrew R. Morton, pp. 14–31. Edinburgh: Centre for Theology and Public Issues, University of Edinburgh, 1994.

'Presbyterian Communities, Transatlantic Visions and the Ulster Revival of 1859'. In *The Culture and Cultures of Europe: The Irish Contribution*, edited by James P. Mackey, pp. 86–105. Belfast: Institute of Irish Studies, Queen's University of Belfast, 1994.

Review of *The Myth of the Empty Church*, by Robin Gill, *History*, 79.257 (October 1994), p. 519.

1995

'James Begg', 'Thomas Chalmers' and 'William Collins'. In *The Blackwell Dictionary of Evangelical Biography*, edited by Donald M. Lewis. Two vols. Oxford: Blackwell, 1995.

Review of *Traditions of Theology in Glasgow, 1450–1990*, by Ian Hazlett, *Records of the Scottish Church History Society*, 25.3 (1995), pp. 482–5.

1996

'The Disruption and the Dream: The Making of New College, 1843–1861'. In *From Disruption to Diversity: Edinburgh Divinity 1846–1996*, edited by David F. Wright and Gary D. Badcock, pp. 29–50. Edinburgh: T. & T. Clark, 1996.

'From Godly Commonwealth to Iona Community: Christian Visions of Scotland 1929–49'. In *Scotland to Slovenia: European Identities and Transcultural Communication: Proceedings of the Fourth International Scottish Studies Symposium*, edited by Horst W. Drescher and Susanne Hagemann, pp. 71–88. Frankfurt am Main: Peter Lang, 1996.

'An Eighteenth-Century Historian on the Amerindians: Culture, Colonialism and Christianity in William Robertson's *History of America*'. *Studies in World Christianity*, 2.2 (Autumn 1996), pp. 204–22.

Review of *Ireland and Scotland in the Age of Revolution: Planting the Green Bough*, by E. W. McFarland, *Albion: A Quarterly Journal Concerned with British Studies*, 28.3 (Autumn 1996), pp. 544–5.

1997

'Religion and the Rise of Liberalism: The First Disestablishment Campaign in Scotland, 1829–1843'. *Journal of Ecclesiastical History*, 48.4 (October 1997), pp. 682–704.

William Robertson and the Expansion of Empire, edited by Stewart J. Brown. Ideas in Context. Cambridge: Cambridge University Press, 1997. Paperback edition, 2008.

'William Robertson (1721–1793) and the Scottish Enlightenment'. In *William Robertson and the Expansion of Empire*, edited by Stewart J. Brown, pp. 7–35. Cambridge: Cambridge University Press, 1997.

Review of *Education and the Scottish People, 1750–1918*, by R. D. Anderson, *The American Historical Review*, 102.4 (October 1997), pp. 1169–70.

1998

'No More "Standing the Session": Gender and the End of Corporate Discipline in the Church of Scotland, c.1890–c.1930'. In *Gender and Christian Religion: Studies in Church History*, Vol. 34, edited by Robert N. Swanson, pp. 447–60. Oxford: Blackwell, 1998.

Review of *The Works of William Robertson*, by Richard B. Sher and William Robertson, *The Scottish Historical Review*, 77.203, Part 1 (April 1998), pp. 113–14.

Review of *Piety and Poverty: Working-Class Religion in Berlin, London and New York, 1870–1914*, by Hugh McLeod, *Labour History Review*, 63.2 (1998), pp. 206–7.

1999

'The Christian Socialist Movement in Scotland, c. 1850–1930'. *Political Theology: The Journal of the Christian Socialist Movement*, 1.1 (November 1999), pp. 59–84.

'Thomas Chalmers', 'Church of Scotland', 'John Erskine' and 'William Robertson'. In *Religion in Geschichte und Gegenwart*, 7 vols, edited by Hans Dieter Betz, Don S. Browning, Bernd Janowski and Eberhard Jungel. 4th edn. Tübingen: Mohr Siebeck, 1999–2004. English translation: *Religion Past and Present*. Leiden: Brill, 2007.

Review of *Religion and Society in Scotland since 1707*, by Callum G. Brown, *Records of the Scottish Church History Society*, 29 (1999), pp. 151–3.

2000

'Church–State Relations in Scotland after the Union'. In *The Challenge to Westminster: Sovereignty, Devolution and Independence*, edited by H. T. Dickinson and Michael Lynch, pp. 71–80. East Linton: Tuckwell Press, 2000.

'Gladstone, Chalmers and the Disruption of the Church of Scotland'. In *Gladstone Centenary Essays*, edited by David W. Bebbington and Roger Swift, pp. 10–28. Liverpool: Liverpool University Press, 2000.

Piety and Power in Ireland, 1760–1960, edited by Stewart J. Brown and David W. Miller. Belfast: Institute of Irish Studies, Queen's University of Belfast and Notre Dame, Indiana: University of Notre Dame Press, 2000.

'The New Reformation Movement in the Church of Ireland, 1801–1829'. In *Piety and Power in Ireland, 1760–1960*, edited by Stewart J. Brown and David W. Miller, pp. 180–208. Belfast: Institute of Irish Studies, Queen's University of Belfast and Notre Dame, Indiana: University of Notre Dame Press, 2000.

Scottish Christianity in the Modern World: Essays for A. C. Cheyne, edited by Stewart J. Brown and George McLeod Newlands. Edinburgh: T. & T. Clark, 2000.

'Presbyterians and Catholics in Twentieth-Century Scotland'. In *Scottish Christianity in the Modern World: Essays for A. C. Cheyne*, edited by Stewart J. Brown and George McLeod Newlands, pp. 255–81. Edinburgh: T. & T. Clark, 2000.

2001

'The End of the Old Established Church Ideal in Scotland, 1790–1850'. In *The Churches and Politics in Scotland under the Union Parliament*, edited by James Kirk, pp. 75–102. Edinburgh: Scottish Church History Society, 2001.

The National Churches of England, Ireland, and Scotland 1801–1846. Oxford: Oxford University Press, 2001.
'Thomas Chalmers', 'the Disruption' and 'John White'. In *Oxford Companion to Scottish History*, edited by Michael Lynch. Oxford: Oxford University Press, 2001.
'The Controversy over Dean Stanley's Lectures on the Scottish National Church, 1872'. *Records of the Scottish Church History Society*, 31 (2001), pp. 145–72. Presidential address.

2002

'Religion in Scotland'. In *Blackwell's Companion to Eighteenth-Century Britain*, edited by H. T. Dickinson, pp. 260–70. 2nd edn. Oxford: Blackwell, 2002.
'Thomas Chalmers'. In *The Dictionary of Nineteenth-Century British Philosophers*, edited by Alan P. F. Sell, Gavin Budge and W. J. Mander. 2 vols. Bristol: Thoemmes, 2002.

2003

'Reformed Churches, Presbyterian'. In *Encyclopedia of the Enlightenment*, edited by Alan Charles Kors. 4 vols. New York: Oxford University Press, 2003.
Review of *Lord Salisbury's World: Conservative Environments in Late-Victorian Britain*, by Michael Bentley, *Church History*, 72.3 (September 2003), pp. 675–6.

2004

'Thomas Chalmers'. In *The Encyclopedia of Protestantism*, edited by Hans Joachim Hillerbrand. 4 vols. London: Routledge, 2004.
'In Memoriam: Donald John Withrington'. *Records of the Scottish Church History Society*, 34.1 (2004), pp. 1–3.
'Robert Buchanan', 'John Caird', 'Thomas Chalmers', 'George Cook', 'Robert Gordon', 'Edward Irving', 'Andrew Mitchell Thomson', 'Robert Walker', 'Ralph Wardlaw', 'Sir Henry Moncreiff Wellwood', 'John White' and 'David Watson'. In *Oxford Dictionary of National Biography*, edited by H. C. G. Matthew and Brian Harrison. 60 vols. Oxford: Oxford University Press, 2004.
Review of *Particular Baptists in Victorian England*, by Geoffrey R. Breed, *Expository Times*, 115.12 (September 2004), pp. 426–7.

2005

'Brave New World? Norman Porteous and Scottish Presbyterianism in the Interwar Years'. *Theology in Scotland*, 12.1 (Spring 2005), pp. 21–36.
Review of *Faith and the Crisis of a Nation: Wales 1890–1914*, by R. Tudur Jones, translated by Sylvia Prys Jones, edited by Robert Pope, *Journal of Welsh Religious History*, new series, 5 (2005), pp. 102–4.

2006

'The National Churches and the Union in Nineteenth-Century Britain and Ireland'. In *Bonds of Union: Practices and Representations of Political Union in the United Kingdom (18th–20th Centuries)*, edited by Isabelle Bour and Antoine Mioche, pp. 57–78. Tours: Presses Universitaires Francois Rabelais, 2006.

Enlightenment, Reawakening and Revolution, 1660–1815, Vol. 7 of *The Cambridge History of Christianity*, edited by Stewart J. Brown and Timothy Tackett. Cambridge: Cambridge University Press, 2006. Chinese translation, 2012.

'Movements of Christian Awakening in Revolutionary Europe, 1790–1815'. In *Enlightenment, Reawakening and Revolution, 1660–1815*, Vol. 7 of *The Cambridge History of Christianity*, edited by Stewart J. Brown and Timothy Tackett, pp. 575–95. Cambridge: Cambridge University Press, 2006.

'The Martyr of Khartoum: General Gordon, the Mahdi and Christian Britain'. *Religious Writings and War: Les Discours Religieux et la Guerre*, edited by Gilles Teulié, pp. 247–71. Montpellier: Université Paul-Valéry – Montpellier III Press, 2006.

'In Memoriam: The Reverend Professor Emeritus A. C. Cheyne', *Records of the Scottish Church History Society*, 36.1 (2006), pp. 1–3.

2007

'Introduction'. In *Scottish Piety over Five Centuries – A Miscellany*, edited by A. C. Cheyne, pp. xiii–xix. Edinburgh: Dunedin Academic Press, 2007.

Review of *The Bible War in Ireland: The 'Second Reformation' and the Polarization of Protestant–Catholic Relations, 1800–1840*, by Irene Whelan, *The American Historical Review*, 112.1 (February 2007), pp. 280–1.

Review of *The Old Enemies: Catholic and Protestant in Nineteenth-Century English Culture*, by Michael Wheeler, *Expository Times*, 118.8 (May 2007), p. 402.

Review of *The Expansion of Evangelicalism: The Age of Wilberforce, More, Chalmers and Finney*, by John Wolffe, *Studies in World Christianity*, 13.3 (2007), pp. 296–7.

Review of *The Religious Condition of Ireland 1770–1850*, by Nigel Yates, *Journal of Religious History*, 31.4 (December 2007), pp. 505–6.

2008

'Church of Scotland' and 'Disruption in the Scottish Kirk'. In *Encyclopedia of the Modern World*, ed. Peter N. Stearns. 4 vols. New York: Oxford University Press, 2008.

'Religion and the European Enlightenment'. *Enlightenment and Secularisation: The Process of Modernisation in East and West*, edited by Zhao Lin and Deng Shoucheng, pp. 3–27. Wuhan, China: Wuhan University Press, 2008. Published in Mandarin.

Providence and Empire: Religion, Politics and Society in the United Kingdom, 1815–1914. Harlow: Longman/Pearson, 2008. Reissued, Abingdon:

Taylor & Francis/Routledge, 2015. Digital platform: *Routledge Historical Resources: 19th Century Empire*, 2021.
'In Memoriam: Professor Emeritus David F. Wright'. *Records of the Scottish Church History Society*, 38.1 (2008), pp. 1–3.
The Union of 1707: New Dimensions, edited by Stewart J. Brown and Christopher A. Whatley. Edinburgh: Edinburgh University Press, 2008.
'The Scottish Churches and the Union'. *Journal of the Society of Friends of Dunblane Cathedral*, 20.3 (2008), pp. 81–90.
Review of *Gilfillan of Dundee, 1813–1878: Interpreting Religion and Culture in Mid-Victorian Scotland*, by Aileen Black, *Church History*, 77.2 (June 2008), pp. 491–3.
Review of *An Educated Clergy. Scottish Theological Education and Training in the Kirk and Secession, 1560–1850*, by Jack C. Whytock, *The Journal of Ecclesiastical History*, 59.3 (July 2008), pp. 568–9.
Review of *The Age of Reason: From the Wars of Religion to the French Revolution 1570–1789*, by Meic Pearse, *Expository Times*, 119.10 (2008), pp. 495–6.

2009

'Preface'. In *Calvinism and the Peripheries: Religion and Civil Society in Europe*, edited by Ábrahám Kovács and Béla Levente Baráth, pp. xi–xiv. Budapest: L'Harmattan, 2009.
'The Enlightenment and the Reformed Societies of the Netherlands, Geneva and Scotland'. In *Calvinism and the Peripheries: Religion and Civil Society in Europe*, edited by Ábrahám Kovács and Béla Levente Baráth, pp. 25–44. Budapest: L'Harmattan, 2009.
'William Robertson, Early Orientalism, and the *Historical Disquisition on India* of 1791'. *Scottish Historical Review*, 88.2 (October, 2009), pp. 289–312.
'The Scoto-Catholic Movement in Presbyterian Worship c.1850–c.1920'. In *Worship and Liturgy in Context: Studies and Case Studies in Theology and Practice*, edited by Duncan B. Forrester and Doug Gay, pp. 152–63. London: SCM, 2009.
Review of *The History of the Free Church of Scotland's Mission to the Jews in Budapest and Its Impact on the Reformed Church of Hungary 1841–1914*, by Ábrahám Kovács, *Studies in World Christianity*, 15.2 (2009), pp. 196–7.

2010

'Religious Identity in a Century of Secularisation: The Edinburgh Churches since 1900'. *Book of the Old Edinburgh Club*, new series, 8 (2010), pp. 93–110.
'The Reform and Extension of Established Churches in the United Kingdom, c.1780–c.1870'. In *The Dynamics of Religious Reform in Church, State and Society in Northern Europe, 1780–1920: Political and Legal Perspectives*, edited by Keith Robbins, pp. 37–68. Leuven: Leuven University Press, 2010.

'Beliefs and Religion'. In *The History of Everyday Life in Scotland*, Vol. 3, edited by Trevor Griffiths and Graeme Morton, pp. 116–46. Edinburgh: Edinburgh University Press, 2010.

Review of *Converting Colonialism: Visions and Realities in Mission History, 1706–1914*, ed. Dana L. Robert, *Studies in World Christianity*, 16.1 (2010), pp. 103–4.

Review of *Empires of Religion*, edited by M. Carey Hilary, *Journal of Anglican Studies*, 8.2 (November 2010), pp. 251–2.

2011

'The Broad Church Movement, National Culture and the Established Churches of Great Britain, c.1850–c.1900'. In *Church and State in Old and New Worlds*, edited by Hilary M. Carey and John Gascoigne, pp. 99–128. Leiden: Brill, 2011.

'The Life and Preaching of F. W. Robertson', review of *Unutterable Love: The Passionate Life and Preaching of F. W. Robertson*, by Christina Beardsley, *Expository Times*, 122.6 (2011), pp. 298–9.

2012

'Religion and Society to c.1900'. In *The Oxford Handbook of Modern Scottish History*, edited by T. M. Devine and Jenny Wormald, pp. 78–98. Oxford: Oxford University Press, 2012. Paperback edition, 2014.

The Oxford Movement: Europe and the Wider World 1830–1930, edited by Stewart J. Brown and Peter Nockles. Cambridge: Cambridge University Press, 2012. Paperback edition, 2014.

'Scotland and the Oxford Movement'. In *The Oxford Movement: Europe and the Wider World 1830–1930*, edited by Stewart J. Brown and Peter Nockles, 56–77. Cambridge: Cambridge University Press, 2012.

Review of *Voices of Nonconformity: William Robertson Nicoll and the British Weekly*, by Keith A. Ives, *Journal of Scottish Historical Studies*, 32.2 (2012), pp. 213–15.

Review of *Enlightened Evangelicalism: The Life and Thought of John Erskine*, by Jonathan M. Yeager, *Church History*, 81.3 (September 2012), pp. 706–8.

2013

Religion, Identity and Conflict in Britain: From the Restoration to the Twentieth Century. Essays in Honour of Keith Robbins, edited by Stewart J. Brown, Frances Knight and John Morgan-Guy. Farnham: Ashgate, 2013.

'W. T. Stead, the "New Journalism" and the "Civic Church" in Late Victorian and Edwardian Britain'. In *Religion, Identity and Conflict in Britain: From the Restoration to the Twentieth Century. Essays in Honour of Keith Robbins*, edited by Stewart J. Brown, Frances Knight and John Morgan-Guy, pp. 213–32. Farnham: Ashgate, 2013.

'Chinese Influences on the European Enlightenment'. In *Selected Papers of the Beijing Forum 2012: The Harmony of Civilisations*, edited by Zhang

Zhifang, pp. 80–93. Beijing: Peking University Press, 2013. Also appeared in the *Papers of the Beijing Forum 2012: Faith and Society*. Beijing: Peking University Press, 2013, pp. 380–97.

2014

'William Reginald Ward (1925–2010)'. In *Biographical Memoirs of Fellows of the British Academy*, Vol. 13, pp. 438–62. London: British Academy, 2014.

'The Enlightenment and Public Faith'. In *Commitment, Belief, Knowledge: Celebratory Volume on the Occasion of the 475th Anniversary of the Debrecen Reformed Theological University*, edited by Károly Fekete and Zoltán Kustár, pp. 51–5. Debrecen: Debrecen Reformed Theological University, 2014.

'The Scottish and Irish Reformed Churches and the First World War'. In *Der Erste Weltkrieg in der reformierten Welt*, edited by Hans-Georg Ulrichs and Veronika Albrecht-Birkner, pp. 254–71. Neukirchen–Vluyn: Neukirchener Theologie, 2014.

'Churches and Communal Violence in the Late Nineteenth and Early Twentieth Centuries: A Comparison of Ireland and Scotland'. In *Irish Religious Conflict in Comparative Perspective: Catholics, Protestants and Muslims*, edited by John Wolff, pp. 107–28. Basingstoke: Palgrave Macmillan, 2014.

Review of *Excellent Dr Stanley: The Life of Dean Stanley of Westminster*, by John Witheridge, *Theology*, 117.3 (2014), p. 232.

Review of *Creating a Scottish Church: Catholicism, Gender and Ethnicity in Nineteenth-Century Scotland*, by S. Karly Kehoe, *Victorian Studies*, 56.2 (Winter 2014), pp. 321–2.

2015

'W. T. Stead and the Civic Church, 1886–1894: The Vision behind *If Christ Came to Chicago*'. *Journal of Ecclesiastical History*, 66.2 (April 2015), pp. 320–39.

Review of *The Fantasy of Reunion: Anglicans, Catholics, and Ecumenism, 1833–1882*, by Mark D. Chapman, *Theology*, 118.1 (2015), pp. 45–6.

Review of *Revolutionary Ideas: An Intellectual History of the French Revolution from the Rights of Man to Robespierre*, by Jonathan Israel, *Intellectual History Review*, 25.4 (2015), pp. 459–61.

2016

'Hugh Blair, the Sentiments and Preaching the Enlightenment in Scotland'. *Intellectual History Review*, 26.3 (September 2016), pp. 411–27. Special Issue: *Calvinism and the Enlightenment at Scotland and at Geneva in the Eighteenth Century*.

'"Where are our Dead?" Changing Views of Death and the Afterlife in Late Nineteenth and Early Twentieth-Century Scottish Presbyterianism'.

In *Death in Modern Scotland 1855–1955: Beliefs, Attitudes and Practices*, edited by Susan Buckham, Peter C. Jupp and Julie Rugg, pp. 267–86. Oxford: Peter Lang, 2016.

'The Reformed Churches and Awakening Movements in Revolutionary Europe, 1789–1830'. In *Reformed Churches Working in Unity and Diversity: Global Historical, Theological and Ethical Perspectives*, edited by Ábrahám Kovács, pp. 11–29. Budapest: L'Harmattan, 2016.

2017

'The Reformation Ideal of the Godly Commonwealth in Scotland: The Book of Discipline of 1560'. *Collegium Doctorum: Magyar Református Teológia*, 2 (2017), pp. 225–35.

'The Established Churches, Church Growth, and Secularization in Imperial Britain, c.1830–1930'. In *Comparative Secularization and Innovation in the North Atlantic World*, edited by David Hempton and Hugh McLeod, pp. 25–43. Oxford: Oxford University Press, 2017.

The Oxford Handbook of the Oxford Movement, edited by Stewart J. Brown, Peter Nockles and James Pereiro. Oxford: Oxford University Press, 2017.

'The Oxford Movement in Ireland, Wales and Scotland'. In *The Oxford Handbook of the Oxford Movement*, edited by Stewart J. Brown, Peter Nockles and James Pereiro, pp. 441–56. Oxford: Oxford University Press, 2017.

'Anglicanism and the British Empire, 1829–1910'. In *Partisan Anglicanism and Its Global Expansion, 1829–c.1914*, Vol. 3 of *The Oxford History of Anglicanism*, edited by Rowan Strong, pp. 45–68. Oxford: Oxford University Press, 2017.

Reviews of *Philanthropy and the Funding of the Church of England, 1856–1914*, by Sarah Flew and *Anglican Clergy in Australia, 1788–1850: Building a British World*, by Michael Gladwin, *Victorian Studies*, 59.2 (Winter 2017), pp. 325–8.

2018

'Providential Empire? The Established Church of England and the Nineteenth-Century British Empire in India'. In *The Church and Empire: Studies in Church History*, Vol. 54, edited by Stewart J. Brown, Charlotte Methuen and Andrew Spicer, pp. 225–59. Cambridge: Cambridge University Press, 2018. Ecclesiastical History Society Presidential Address.

'L'impérialisme britannique chrétien au dix-neuvième siècle: le cas de l'Église anglicane en Inde', trans. G. Vaughan. In *L'empire britannique, une communauté de destins?*, edited by Jean-François Dunyach and Alban Gautier, pp. 171–83. Rennes: Presses Universitaires de Rennes, 2018.

歐洲啟蒙運動：福音奮興運動與海外宣教 (The European Enlightenment, Christian awakenings and overseas missions), trans. Y. H. Sung.

Tainan, Taiwan: Tainan Theological College and Seminary Press, 2018. English version appeared as 'The European Enlightenment, Christian Awakenings and Overseas Missions: The Sinlau Lectures 2016'. *Theology and the Church*, 42.1 (January 2017), pp. 81–150.

'Dissent in Scotland, 1689–1828'. In *1689 to the Repeal of the Test and Corporation Acts*, Vol. 2 of the *Oxford History of the Protestant Dissenting Traditions*, edited by Andrew C. Thompson, pp. 139–59. Oxford: Oxford University Press, 2018.

Joint editor (with Charlotte Methuen and Andrew Spicer), *Studies in Church History 54: The Church and Empire*. Cambridge: Cambridge University Press, 2018. Sole author of Introduction, pp. 1–15.

Review of *A Singular Case: Debating China's Political Economy in the European Enlightenment*, by Ashley Eva Millar, *The English Historical Review*, 133.563 (August 2018), pp. 955–7.

'Reading Victorian Churches', review of *Unlocking the Church: The Lost Secrets of Victorian Sacred Space*, by William Whyte, *Expository Times*, 129.12 (2018), p. 583.

2019

'Moral Culture and Historical Progress in the Scottish Enlightenment'. *Modern Intellectual History*, 16.3 (November 2019), pp. 993–1005.

'Moderate Theology and Preaching in Enlightenment Scotland, c.1750–1800'. In *The Early Enlightenment to the Mid-Nineteenth Century*, Vol. 2 of the *Oxford History of Scottish Theology*, edited by Mark Elliott and David Fergusson, pp. 69–83. Oxford: Oxford University Press, 2019.

'After the Disruption: The Recovery of the National Church of Scotland, 1843–1874'. *Scottish Church History*, 48.2 (2019), pp. 103–25.

W. T. Stead: Nonconformist and Newspaper Prophet. Oxford: Oxford University Press, 2019.

2020

'China, Social Ethics and the European Enlightenment'. In *Ecumenism and Independency in World Christianity: Historical Studies in Honour of Brian Stanley*, edited by Alexander Chow and Emma Wild-Wood, pp. 243–61. Leiden: Brill, 2020.

2021

'Dissolving the "Sacred Union"? The Disestablishment of the Church in Ireland'. In *Religion in Britain, 1660–1900: A Festschrift for Peter Nockles*, edited by William Gibson and Geordan Hammond. *Bulletin of the John Rylands Library*, 97.1 (Spring 2021), pp. 145–60.

Review of *The Enlightenment That Failed: Ideas, Revolution, and Democratic Defeat, 1748–1830*, by Jonathan Israel, *Intellectual History Review*, 31.4 (2021), pp. 731–4.

Review of *Religion and Society at the Dawn of Modern Europe. Christianity Transformed, 1750–1850*, by Rudolf Schlögl, trans. by Helen Imhoff, *Church History and Religious Culture*, 101.4 (2021), pp. 632–4.

2022

'John Baillie', 'James Begg', 'Edward Caird', 'Robert Smith Candlish', 'Thomas Chalmers', 'Free Church of Scotland', 'William Cunningham', 'The Disruption', 'James Morison', 'Ten Years' Conflict', 'United Free Church of Scotland', 'United Presbyterian Church', 'United Secession Church', 'voluntaryism' and 'Wee Frees'. In *The Oxford Dictionary of the Christian Church*, edited by Andrew Louth. 4th edn. Oxford: Oxford University Press, 2022.

Review of *Scottish Presbyterian Worship. Proposals for Organic Change, 1843 to the Present Day*, by Bryan D. Spinks, *The Journal of Ecclesiastical History*, 73.3 (July 2022), pp. 677–8.

'Achievement and Heartbreak: An Eminent Victorian Archbishop', review of *In the Shadow of Death: A Life of Archibald Campbell Tait, Archbishop of Canterbury*, by John Witheridge, *Expository Times*, 133.12 (2022), pp. 555–6.

Forthcoming

'Churches, the State, and Politics – An Overview, 1800–1922'. In, *The Oxford Handbook of Religion in Modern Ireland*, edited by Gladys Ganiel and Andrew Holmes. Oxford: Oxford University Press.

Review of *Scottish Philosophy after the Enlightenment*, by Gordon Graham, *Scottish Church History*.

Review of *Prayer, Providence and Empire: Special Worship in the British World, 1783–1919*, by Joseph Hardwick, *English Historical Review*.

Review of *Crown, Mitre and People in the Nineteenth Century: The Church of England, Establishment and the State*, by G. R. Evans, *Journal of Church and State*.

Index

All Scotland Crusade, 217–33
Allan, Tom, 11, 217, 219, 225, 230–1
Alt, Heinrich, 69–71
atheism, 36–7, 42, 68, 77, 79, 138, 207; *see also* freethinkers
Africa, 239–43
America, 2, 4–11, 50–62, 133–7, 187–90, 195–6, 217, 231, 238, 244–52
American Christian Social Union, 4
American Civil War, 27, 50, 58–60
Anderson, Rufus, 239
Anglo-Catholicism, 9, 161, 170–4, 181, 209
Argyll, George Douglas Campbell, Duke of, 106, 108
Armley Gaol Visiting Committee, 28

Baillie Commission, 218–19
Baird, James/Baird Trust, 8, 11, 12, 85–95
Bands of Hope, 25–6, 30, 140
Baptist, 25, 136, 140, 143, 155, 157–8, 161, 219–20, 240, 243–4, 249
Baron d'Holbach, 36
Bavinck, Herman, 10, 12, 13, 187–96
Bible, 7, 23, 24, 30, 37, 39, 43, 53, 54, 61, 70, 75, 102, 103, 105, 119, 135, 137, 140–3, 156–8, 161, 165, 172, 177, 219, 221, 223, 224, 229, 232–3
Blackwell, Elizabeth, 116

Bolsheviks/Russian Revolution, 207, 248–9
Booth, Charles, 158, 176
Booth, Joseph, 242, 243
Boston, 134–6, 145
Bunsen, Karl Josias, 67–8
Bunting, Jabez, 19
Butler, Joseph, 42
Butler, Josephine, 115–17, 122
Buxton, Thomas Fowell, 4, 239–41, 252

Calvinism/Reformed theology, 37–8, 50, 52, 55, 57, 59, 61, 90, 92, 165, 174, 187–93
capitalism, 37, 66–7, 173, 206–8
Carey, George, Archbishop of Canterbury, 150
Carlile, Richard, 36
Carrubber's Close Mission, 134, 137–40
Chalmers, Thomas, xii, 1–6, 12–13, 35, 41, 44, 56–7, 61, 85, 87, 88, 91, 93, 95, 106, 242
charitable giving 20–1, 26–7, 68, 85–95, 126, 143–4, 243–5, 249–50
  impact of photography upon, 245–7
Chicago, 2, 5, 133–46, 250
Chicago Bible Institute, 141–3
China, 243–4, 251
China Inland Mission, 243, 246
Christian Social Union (United Kingdom), 169–72, 201, 204

Church of England, 9, 10, 28, 67, 72, 118, 152–5, 163–5, 169–3, 176, 179, 182, 200–6, 212, 248
Church of Scotland, 8, 35–42, 56, 85–95, 116, 138–9, 217–21, 226, 233
clergy, 5, 9, 38, 41, 74, 85, 89, 91, 125, 133, 141, 151–5, 159, 162, 169, 173, 209
Cold War, 222, 250–1
communism, 7, 58, 66–79, 142, 206–7, 249–52
Congo, the, 243, 246
Congregationalists, 42–3, 116, 135, 155–8, 161, 176, 219
Conservative and Unionist Party, 8, 28, 86
Contagious Diseases Acts, 117–18
Crowther, Samuel Adjai, Bishop, 241–2

Darby, John Nelson, 134
Davidson, Randall, Archbishop of Canterbury, 150
Dickens, Charles, 118
Discharged Prisoners' Aid Society, 28
Disruption of the Church of Scotland, 1, 39, 44, 85, 88, 124, 139, 242
divinity students/seminary students, 44, 54, 86, 94, 142, 171, 188, 192, 217
Dryer, Emma, 141
Du Bois, W. E. B., 10, 189
Dunant, Henri, 247

Edinburgh City Mission, 41
Edinburgh Zetetic Society, 36, 40–1
education
  in Magdalene asylums, 125–6
  of orphans, 244
  of slaves, 53–5
  of women, 170
  of working-class children, 24–6, 70, 88, 99–111
  theological, 140–5, 172, 181, 192
  see also Sunday schools, ragged schools, and divinity/seminary students
Ellis, Thomas, 173–4
emigration, 18, 50, 52, 249
Engels, Friedrich, 71–2, 79
England, 4–10, 17–30, 67, 72, 99–111, 118, 121, 150–65, 169–82, 200–13
Enlightenment, 36, 239, 240
Episcopalians (Scotland), 124–5, 219
Episcopalians (United States), 4, 53, 58, 136
Evangelical Alliance, 3, 44, 56, 250
evangelicalism, 3–11, 18, 28, 29, 37, 38, 44, 51, 56, 67, 85, 88–95, 100–1, 106, 110, 111, 133, 136–44, 152–4, 161–5, 205, 212, 217–20, 227, 231–3, 239, 242, 245–52
evangelism, 11, 24, 50–4, 57, 133, 136, 138, 141, 146, 150, 163, 165, 219–21, 225–6, 230–3, 239, 241, 243, 250–1
Exeter Hall, 100, 108

famine, 11, 18, 27, 238, 243–7, 249
Finney, Charles, 217
Free Church of Scotland, 41–3, 56, 87–8, 124, 126, 138–9, 242
freethinkers, 35–42, 45
French Revolution, 36, 53, 70
Fry, Elizabeth, 118, 125

Gall, James, 138–9
Gandhi, Mahatma, 245
Germany, 7, 13, 39, 66– 79, 141–2, 190– 3, 224, 249–51
Gifford, Lord, 92
Gillespie, William, 39–42

Glasgow Bible Training Institute, 143–5
Glasgow experiment, 2
Glasgow System, 117, 127
Glasgow United Evangelistic Association, 137, 143
Glasgow Zetetic Society, 36, 40, 42
Gore, Charles, 170–4, 178, 181–2, 201, 204, 206, 208
Graham, Billy, 10–12, 217–33
Guinness, Harry, 246
Guthrie, Thomas, 99–110

Harris, Alice, 246
Henry, Carl F. H., 218
Holland, Henry Scott, 5, 9, 169–82
Hopkins, Ellice, 115, 117, 122
Hughes, Hugh Price, 17, 29, 160, 162
Hurgronje, Christiaan Snouck, 10, 187, 190–5

India, 243–6
Industrial Christian Fellowship, 10, 171, 201–11
industrialisation, 1, 2, 7, 11, 18–19, 35, 44, 66, 87, 100, 136, 142, 204, 208, 226, 242
Inglis, John, 38, 40
Iona Community, 225–6
Ireland, 56, 116–18, 127

Jamaica, 240–1
Jews, 5, 18, 187–95
John Paul II, 150
Jones, Charles Colcock, 7, 53–60

Kennedy, Geoffrey Anketell Studdert, 10, 12, 200–12
Keswick Convention, 241–2
Kingsley, Charles, 5, 146, 162
Klopsch, Louis, 245, 247
Korea, 251–2
Kuyper, Abraham, 189, 191

Labour Party, 144, 205–11, 226
Lane, Libby, 150
Latin America, 248
Lausanne Congress on World Evangelisation, 11, 13, 231–2, 252
Leeds Ladies' Bible and Household Mission, 23
Leeds Methodist Sisterhood, 23
leisure, 152–5
Liberal Party, 25, 28, 87, 171–4
Liddon, Henry, 170–3
Livingstone, David, 239–42
Lücke, Friedrich, 72
Lux Mundi, 169, 172–3

Macdonald, Ramsay, 208
Macleod, George, 220, 225–6, 233
Macleod, Norman, 35, 39–45
Macmillan, Harold, Prime Minister, 222
Magdalene asylum, 8, 12, 115–27
Marshall Plan, 249, 251
Marx, Karl, 71–2, 79, 142, 207
Mathews, Shailer, 4, 217–18
Maurice, Frederick Denison, 3, 5, 172, 178, 206
Merkel, Angela, 69
Methodism, 6, 17–27, 30, 39, 53, 58, 72, 124, 136, 157, 165, 174, 219, 224, 249
  Forward Movement, 17, 23, 29
  Wesleyan Methodist Mission Society, 19
middle class, 9, 67, 69, 115, 139, 141, 153–8, 160, 241
missions/missionaries, 2, 5, 11–13, 17, 19, 21–6, 28–9, 41–3, 53–5, 58, 70–4, 85–6, 93–5, 110, 115–18, 124–5, 134, 137–41, 150, 156, 158–63, 169–70, 175–6, 181, 202–5, 211, 217–21, 225–6, 231–3, 238–52
women, 22–3, 74–8, 116
Montague, Charles, 107–8

Moody, Dwight L., 8–12, 133–46
Morton, Ralph, 225–6, 233
mothers' meetings, 23, 138, 140

Naismith, David, 74
neo-Calvinism, 10, 188–91, 194
Netherlands, the, 10, 13, 187–96
Nevinson, Henry, 171
New College, Edinburgh, 2, 139
Niebuhr, Reinhold, 224
Nietzsche, Friedrich, 194, 196
nonconformists, 9, 151–8, 173–6, 179

Owen, Robert, 37, 40, 42
Oxford Committee for Famine Relief (Oxfam), 249
Oxford House, 156, 170
Oxford Movement, 1, 178

Paine, Thomas, 36, 39, 41
paternalism, 1, 8, 11, 52–4, 60, 100
Philip, John, 240
Plymouth Brethren, 134
Presbyterians, 7, 40, 42, 50–62, 87–8, 124, 126, 136, 143–4, 158, 188, 201, 219, 244, 251
Princeton Theology Seminary, 54–5, 188–9
prostitution, 8, 115–27
Pusey, Edward Bouverie, 170, 172

ragged schools, 8, 12–13, 43, 99–111
Red Cross, 247
religious awakenings/revivals, 4, 7–12, 68–72, 78, 125, 133–7, 139, 143, 161, 212, 217, 221, 223, 226, 242, 248, 250
Richard, Timothy, 244
Robertson, James, 88
Roman Catholicism, 5, 39, 42–3, 118, 120–1, 124, 150, 153, 160, 162, 165, 189, 191, 238, 249

Russell, George William Erskine, 171
Russia, 195, 207, 245, 248–9

sacraments, 20, 53, 56, 58, 75, 91, 209
Sankey, Ira D., 136, 138
Scotland, 2, 6, 8, 11–13, 35–45, 56, 61, 85–95, 99–111, 115–27, 134, 137–40, 143–5, 162, 217–33, 242
Scottish Association for Opposing Prevalent Errors, 42–4
Settlement movement 156, 169–70
Shaftesbury, Lord Anthony Ashley-Cooper, Earl of, 12, 28, 67, 99–102, 105–11, 135
Sieveking, Amalie, 7, 13, 68–9, 74–9
slavery, 4, 7, 11–12, 50–62
    and spirituals 60–1
    see also education
Smiles, Samuel, 18, 108
Smith, Adam, 240
Smyth, Thomas, 7, 55–6, 59
social gospel, 1–6, 10–11, 17, 29–30, 116, 118, 121, 127, 133, 144, 201, 209, 212, 217–19, 225, 228–33, 244, 247
socialism, 1–4, 7, 10–11, 17, 37, 40, 44, 66–74, 77–9, 142, 145, 172, 180–1, 200, 205–7
Soper, Donald Oliver, Lord Soper, 17, 224
South Carolina, 54, 57
Sport, 137, 150–65
Spurgeon, Charles Haddon, 140–1
Stead, W. T., 2, 133, 176
Sunday schools, 21–5, 28–30, 134–5, 138, 141, 154–5, 160, 164

Taylor, James Hudson, 243
Tearfund, 250, 252
Tell Scotland Movement, 219–21, 225

Temple, William, Archbishop of Canterbury, 178, 181–2, 201, 206, 209–11, 230
theatre, 154–5
Thomson, Andrew (1779–1831), 38, 40, 61–2
Thornwell, James Henley, 7, 57–60
Tillich, Paul, 224
Toynbee Hall, 170
Tubman, Harriet, 61
Turner, Nat, 53–4, 58, 61

United Free Church of Scotland, 218
United Free Methodist Church, 24
University
  of Chicago, 217
  of Edinburgh, 138, 142
  of Glasgow, 91
  of Göttingen, 72
  of Hamburg, 224
  of Leiden, 10, 190
  of Manchester, 181
  of Oxford, 9, 170–1, 175
urbanisation, 1–8, 27, 30, 35, 41, 44, 66, 69, 71, 85, 87, 90, 93, 94, 100, 110, 133–5, 138–41, 169, 175–81, 247

Venn, Henry, 239, 241, 252
Vesey, Denmark, 53, 61
Victorian era, 2–3, 6, 8–9, 12, 18, 28–30, 88–90, 95, 100–1, 106, 144, 151–2, 156–7, 160–1, 163–4, 170, 179, 188
Voltaire, 36

Waldegrave, Granville, 248
Walls, Andrew, 240
Wardlaw, William, 116
Washington, Booker T., 10, 189
Watson, William, 100–2, 104
Wesley, John, 17, 72, 135
West Indies, 239–43
Wichern, Johann Hinrich, 7, 13, 68–74, 78–9
Williams, George, 135
working class, 7, 35, 43–4, 67, 72–3, 78, 95, 137, 145, 155, 157, 160, 163, 176, 205–8, 211–12
World Council of Churches, 251
World Missionary Conference, 248
World War One, 10, 161, 180, 201, 203, 247, 250
World War Two, 5, 151, 181, 233, 249

Yale University, 142
Young England, 1
Young Men's Christian Association (YMCA), 108, 134–7, 140, 143, 152, 159, 162, 164
Young Women's Christian Association (YWCA), 165
youth, 24–6, 43, 70, 72, 99–111, 138, 140, 153, 155, 160, 164, 210, 244–5
Youth for Christ, 250–1

EU representative:
Easy Access System Europe
Mustamäe tee 50, 10621 Tallinn, Estonia
Gpsr.requests@easproject.com

www.ingramcontent.com/pod-product-compliance
Lightning Source LLC
Chambersburg PA
CBHW050210240426
43671CB00013B/2276